THE VIBRATING UNIVERSE

The Vibrating Universe

N.C. Panda

MOTILAL BANARSIDASS PUBLISHERS
PRIVATE LIMITED • DELHI

Reprint: Delhi, 2002, 2008
First Edition: Delhi, 1995

ISBN: 978-81-208-1291-8

MOTILAL BANARSIDASS
41 U.A. Bungalow Road, Jawahar Nagar, Delhi 110 007
8 Mahalaxmi Chamber, 22 Bhulabhai Desai Road, Mumbai 400 026
236, 9th Main III Block, Jayanagar, Bangalore 560 011
203 Royapettah High Road, Mylapore, Chennai 600 004
Sanas Plaza, 1302 Baji Rao Road, Pune 411 002
8 Camac Street, Kolkata 700 017
Ashok Rajpath, Patna 800 004
Chowk, Varanasi 221 001

Printed in India
BY JAINENDRA PRAKASH JAIN AT SHRI JAINENDRA PRESS,
A-45 NARAINA, PHASE-I, NEW DELHI 110 028
AND PUBLISHED BY NARENDRA PRAKASH JAIN FOR
MOTILAL BANARSIDASS PUBLISHERS PRIVATE LIMITED,
BUNGALOW ROAD, DELHI 110 007

For my father,

Late Antaryami Panda

CONTENTS

PROLOGUE

THE ISSUE OF MONISM *versus* pluralism has been as old as mankind. The lay-man, without any sophistication in academicism, has a naive faith in pluralism. Each individual entity in nature is a reality for him. And this reality exists separately and independently with reference to the rest of nature, although different entities in nature may interact and co-ordinate among themselves.

Both monistic and pluralistic doctrines were accepted by different ancient Western philosophers. Parmenides and Spinoza represent substantival monism, i.e., the view that whatever exists is part of a single substance. Pluralism was accepted as truth in science from the beginning till the advent of the twentieth century. Both the macro- and the micro-worlds have innumerable units that were considered to be separate from one another. According to the pluralistic concept of classical science, the world consists of diverse entities that are substantially different. This idea of pluralism in science was reflected in philosophy. Although the rival schools of monism and pluralism existed in the domain of philosophy since the ancient time, pluralism became more acceptable to the modern philosopher. The twentieth century physicists have abandoned pluralism in favour of an attributive monism, i.e., the view that however many substances may exist, they are all of a single kind. In contrast, philosophy has lagged behind and has tenaciously adhered to pluralism even in the twentieth century. The famous philosopher Bertrand Russell was mostly a pluralist (he adhered for a time to a position he called neutral monism) although, towards the last part of his philosophic career, he expressed his willingness to accept the monism of modern science rather than the pluralism of older times. For Wittgenstein, philosophy is language analysis only with special reference to meaning in use. The logical positivists such as A.J.Ayer and the analytical philosophers avoid discussions on metaphysics which they strongly denounce. The issue of monism *versus* pluralism may not be entertained by them since they may think that such an issue is metaphysical. It is, however, not an issue of speculative metaphysics. All forms of matter and energy are substantially energy. This is not a speculation, but an empirical truth. All the four fundamental forces are different manifestations of a single one. When we trace back the history of the evolutionary Universe, we come to an initial state of a zero volume and an infinite density of the so-called singularity. We cannot conceive of even energy at this primordial state of the Universe. This was not matter; this was not energy; this could not be a force or interaction since there were neither matter particles nor energy particles to interact. But this could not be nothing. It was something and something of one unitary character.

The concept of monism in the Western philosophy has no parallel in the Indian thought. According to the different kinds of the Western monism, everything of the world is substantially one. If monism is atheistic, the *one substance* is the source of all diversifications. In case of theistic monism, God is different from the single material substance in the analogy of the potter and the clay. This is in reality a dualism rather than monism. But this has been classically known as monism. In the Indian system, the single primordial principle is Brahman (pure Consciousness) that is everything, to which nothing is second. The word "nondualism" (*advaita*) is preferred to "monism" to represent the corresponding Indian concept.

In the eighties of the twentieth century, the concept of the superstring has evolved in physics. This concept explains the diversity of the Universe in terms of the vibrations of the superstring. Accordingly, there are no molecules and atoms in reality, there are no protons, neutrons and electrons in reality; there are no real quarks, no real leptons; there are no real planets, no real stars and no real galaxies. The reality is the superstring; everything else is analogous to any one of the innumerable musical tones produced by the vibrations of the superstring.

In this book, an attempt has been made to critically review the different concepts of monism *versus* pluralism in philosophy and science and to synthesize a concept of nondualism compatible with the ancient philosophy of nondualistic Vedānta and nondualistic Śaivism and the modern scientific concepts of quantum physics, astrophysics, cosmology, relativity and superstring theory. This approach is non-materialistic. The nondual, unitary entity is Consciousness which is the source of the diversity of the Universe. Matter (matter and energy) is an evolutionary product of the Power (*Śakti*) of the primal Consciousness. The consciousness of the matter-evolute is a reflection of the primal Consciousness in the matter-evolute. The Power (*Śakti*) of the primal Being (Brahman or Consciousness) vibrates and so does the magical Universe appear. The appearance of the magic-show has a beginning, a sequence and an end. The cosmic phenomena repeat in cycles *ad infinitum*. The primary Being remains as such without undergoing any change whatsoever and without doing any function whatsoever. Its Power which is otherwise known as *Māyā* is deluding in nature; due to its concealing effect, B appears as non-B; it projects the world-image of diversity and impermanence. This projection of the world in appearance is brought about through the mechanism of the vibrations of the three strings (*guṇas*) of *Māyā* and the subsequent pulsation of the vitalizing principle (*prāṇa*) which is a second-generation product of *Māyā* (*āpaḥ* from *mūlaprakṛti* and *prāṇa* from *āpaḥ*). Is this *prāṇa* the superstring of modern physics? There cannot be any definite answer to this question at the present level of our knowledge.

In the traditional interpretation of the Advaita Vedānta, Brahman only is posited and the phenomenal world is negated. It is generally not appreciated that the world-negation has a meaning in consideration of the absolute and the empirical senses. When viewed in the absolute sense, the world is negated; but, in the empirical sense, the world is definitely posited. In contradistinction of this finer meaning, it is generally believed that the Advaita Vedānta altogether rejects the world. With such a wrong notion that has luxuriantly grown as weeds in the fields of philosophy, much emphasis has not been laid on the interpretation of the this-worldly phenomena.

Science which was purely empirical was one-hundred-per cent this-worldly. Only what was sense-perceptible was told by science, and on what was sense-imperceptible, although this-worldly, science remained silent. There was, however, a drastic change in the development of science in the twentieth century. The findings on quantum physics, superstrings, unified field and cosmology could not be explained purely on the basis of materialistic, mechanistic and empirical interpretations. Moreover, the necessity of recognizing Consciousness as the fundamental noumenal Being by the twentieth-century science was felt by some profound thinkers.

Two diverging streams, viz., Advaita Vedānta (along with Advaita Śaivism) and materialistic science have now a tendency to converge. The matter-rejecting nondualistic philosophy now explains the material phenomena in a more scientific way. The spirit-rejecting materialistic science is now bound to embrace spirituality in order to avoid its own created impasse and pierce the blind alley for finding a path which is more illuminated and smooth to walk. The difference between the this-worldly and the other-worldly phenomena has now disappeared. Can the two diverging streams converge, coalesce and fuse into a single one to flow as a great river to be merged into the sea?

The author has made all attempts to bring about the convergence, coalescence and fusion of the two diverging streams. The single river that has emerged as a resultant one reaches its goal without any checks, barriers and obstacles on the way. Is the convergence a forced one? Is it logical? Is it scientific? Is it purely speculative? Is it intrapolative and extrapolative rather than speculative? These questions are to be answered, not by the author but by the Expert Readers who are established elites in these specialized branches of human knowledge.

It is very often said that science is purely objective and free from bias and dogmas. It may be the "should" aspect of science. Is it also the "is" aspect of science? The answer of this question is both positive and negative. It depends upon the scientist who is not necessarily objective and who is not necessarily free from bias. For a person with already nested dogmas in his mind and with pores of the encircling membrane of the mind blocked and completely closed, he is difficult to be convinced, is convinced against his will. Hence goes the adage : A man convinced against his will is of the same opinion still. It is hoped that a reader who is a die-hard materialist will please examine the view-points given in this book with open mind.

It is irrational to explain away all physical cosmic phenomena by non-physical, spiritual agency. It is irrational to speculate explanations without any rational and empirical basis. But it is equally irrational to altogether reject spirituality if that becomes necessary to explain the findings of science in a more coherent and meaningful way.

The author's attempt will be successful if this book serves, as a stimulant and a catalyst, to stir the thought processes of intellectuals. It is not expected that such a book will be non-controversial. Any emerging thought appearing in the twilight zone cannot completely be non-controversial. Or, any new theory that tries to replace an established old one is bound to create much friction and face, not easily surmountable, resistance. This author rather invites controversy over the issue raised here; but he does expect constructive criticism and incisive analysis.

NRUSINGH CHARAN PANDA

ACKNOWLEDGEMENTS

My sincere thanks are due to M/s Motilal Banarsidass for their desire to reprint the book. The first edition of the book (1995) was published with the financial assistance from the Government of India, Department of Education, to whom I am indebted. In the publication of the first edition, Sri Kamakhya Prasad Singdeo, Ex-Minister, Government of India, and Sri Satyananda Mishra, I.A.S., Madhya Pradesh Cadre, helped me a lot purely in their personal capacity. I owe to them. I am grateful to Dr. Pramod Chandra Samal for the diagrams used in the book and to Sri Shiva Panigrahi for the cover-page art. I am glad to acknowledge the help of Dr. Bijoy Kumar Sahu for the first edition of the book and the current one also.

I gratefully acknowledge the permission of the following authors and publishers for quoting materials from their works:

Alfred A. Knopf, New York.

Monod, J., *Chance and Necessity,* 1971; Collins Fontana Books, Glasgow, 1974 (pp. 136-37; 167).

Bantam Books, New York.

Chopra, D., *Quantum Healing,* 1989 (p. 228).

Cambridge University Press, Cambridge, London.

1. Davies, P.C.W. and Brown, J., *Superstrings,* 1988 (p. 3).

2. Davies, P.C.W., *The Accidental Universe,* 1982 (pp. 1; 77; 110-11; 122).

3. Einstein, A. and Infeld, L., *The Evolution of Physics,* 1938 (foreword, p. xvii).

D. Van Nostrand, Princeton, New Jersey.

Capek, M., *The Philosophical Impact of Contemporary Physics,* 1961 (p. 319).

Harper Collins Publishers, New York; Penguin Books Ltd., London.

Heisenberg, W., *Physics and Philosophy,* 1989 (p. 69).

Mir Publishers, Moscow.

Podolny, R., *Something Called Nothing,* 1986 (pp. 37-38).

Oxford University Press, Oxford, London.

Pais, A., *Subtle is the Lord,* 1982 (pp. 440; 442; 443; 444; 465).

Random House UK Ltd., London; Flamingo (Fontana Paperbacks), London.

Capra, F., *Uncommon Wisdom,* 1989 (p. 111).

Routledge & Kegan Paul, London (through International Thomson Publishing Services Ltd., Hampshire, England).

George Allen & Unwin Ltd., London.

Russell, B., *A History of Western Philosophy,* 1975 (p. 550), Sheldon Press, Holy Trinity Church, The Society for Promoting Christian Knowledge, London.

Katz, S., *Mysticism and Philosophical Analysis,* 1978 (p. 96).

Thiel, R., *And There was Light,* 1958 (p. 345).

Transworld Publishers Ltd., London; Wildwood House, London.

Gribbin, J., *In Search of Schrödinger's Cat,* 1984 (p. 82).

While writing this book, I was mentally, *albeit* not physically, isolated from my family members due to my long hours of mental labour and meditative trance. Still they were glad to bear with me and did not deprive me of the warmth of their hearts. I take this opportunity of expressing my hearty thanks to Manorama (wife), Prakash, Bikash, and Bibhas (sons), Smita, Snigdha, and Arati (daughters-in-law), Shephali (daughter), Sudhir (son-in-law), Nivedita (Nita), Madhusmita (Mita), Lopamudra (Lopa), Arpita (Soma), Anvesha (Lisha)—grand-daughters, and Siddhartha (Munu, Munu-Raja)—grandson.

Agastya Bhavan NRUSINGH CHARAN PANDA
712 Shaheed Nagar
Khanduali Mandir Road
Bhubaneswar-751007 (India)

June 18, 1999

LIST OF ABBREVIATIONS

AB	Amṛtabindu
ABSS	Advaita-Brahmasiddhi of Sadānanda, Parimal Publications, Delhi, Ist ed., 1981.
AKV	Abhidharmakośavyākhyā
AU	Aitareya Upaniṣad
AV	Atharva Veda
BDPu	Brahmāṇḍa Purāṇa
BG	Bhagavadgītā
BGŚB	Bhagavadgītā Śāṅkara Bhāṣyam
Bhā	Bhāgavatam
BPu	Brahma Purāṇa
BS	Brahmasūtra
BSŚB	Brahmasūtra Śāṅkara Bhāṣyam
BU	Bṛhadāraṇyaka Upaniṣad
BUŚB	Bṛhadāraṇyaka Upaniṣad Śāṅkara Bhāṣyam
CU	Chāndogya Upaniṣad
CUŚB	Chāndogya Upaniṣad Śāṅkara Bhāṣyam
DBhā	Devī Bhāgavata
DPV	Dharmakirti's Pramāṇa Vārttika
GMK	Gauḍapāda's Māṇḍūkya Kārikā
GPu	Garuḍa Purāṇa
HV	Harivaṁśa
IU	Īśopaniṣad
IUŚB	Īśopaniṣad Śāṅkara Bhāṣyam
JU	Jābāla Upaniṣad
KLU	Kaivalyopaniṣad
KNU	Kena Upaniṣad

KNUŚB	Kena Upaniṣad Śāṅkara Bhāṣyam
KPS	Kundakunda's Pravacana-Sāra
KPu	Kūrma Purāṇa
KSBU	Kauṣītaki Brāhmaṇa Upaniṣad
KSU	Kauṣītaki Upaniṣad
KTU	Kaṭhopaniṣad
KTUŚB	Kaṭhopaniṣad Śāṅkara Bhāṣyam
LAS	Laṅkāvatāra-Sūtra
MaS	Mādhyamika-Śāstra
MAU	Māṇḍūkya Upaniṣad
MBh	Mahābhārata
MNU	Mahānārāyaṇa Upaniṣad
MPu	Matsya Purāṇa
MS	Manusmṛti
MSS	Mīmāṁsā-Sūtra
MTNU	Maitrāyaṇa Upaniṣad
MTU	Maitrī Upaniṣad
MTYU	Maitreyī Upaniṣad
MUU	Muṇḍaka Upaniṣad
MUUŚB	Muṇḍaka Upaniṣad Śāṅkara Bhāṣyam
NS	Nyāya-Sūtra
NVV	Nāgārjuna's Vigrahavyāvartani
PD	Pañcadaśī
PPu	Padma Purāṇa
PU	Praśna Upaniṣad
ṚV	Ṛgveda
ŚBrā	Śatapatha Brāhmaṇa
SD	Śāṅkhya-Darśana
SK	Śāṅkhya-Kārikā
ŚP	Śāntiparva
SPB	Sāṅkhya-Pravacana-Bhāṣyam
SPS	Sāṅkhya-Pravacana-Sūtra

ŚBrā	Śatapatha Brāhmaṇa
SD	Śāṅkhya-Darśana
SK	Śāṅkhya-Kārikā
ŚP	Śāntiparva
SPB	Sāṅkhya-Pravacana-Bhāṣyam
SPS	Sāṅkhya-Pravacana-Sūtra
ŚS	Śiva-Saṁhitā
SSM	Siddhasena's Sanmati
ŚSūV	Śivasūtram of Vasugupta
ŚU	Śvetaśvatara Upaniṣad
SUS	Sarvopaniṣatsāra
ŚUŚB	Śvetāśvatara Upaniṣad Śāṅkara Bhāṣyam
TĀR	Taittirīya Āraṇyaka
TBrā	Taittirīya Brāhmaṇa
TBU	Tejobindūpaniṣad
TS	Tattvārtha-Sūtra
TSUB	Umāsvāti's Bhāṣya of Tattvārtha-Sūtra
TTAS	Tattvārthādhigama-Sūtra
TU	Taittirīya Upaniṣad
TUŚB	Taittirīya Upaniṣad Śāṅkara Bhāṣyam
VāPu	Vāyu Purāṇa
VāS	Vājasaneyi Saṁhitā
VC	Vivekacūḍāmaṇi
VPDA	Vedānta-Paribhāṣā of Dharmarāja Adhvarīndra
VPu	Viṣṇu Purāṇa
VS	Vaiśeṣika-Sūtra
VSS	Vedāntasāra of Sadānanda
YB	Yoga-Bhāṣya
YS	Yoga-Sūtra of Patañjali
YV	Yajurveda

LIST OF FIGURES/ ILLUSTRATIONS

I

THE ONE *VERSUS* MANY IN THE VEDAS

In the long history of man (*Homo sapiens*) a basic question has persisted to be an unsolved puzzle "Is the universe monistic or pluralistic?" Whether man is primitive or civilized, illiterate or highly educated, he does perceive the pluralistic world, he appreciates the diversity in Nature, and thus gets a *prima facie* evidence of the existence of multiplicity among the *real* things of the world. He believes his sense-perceptions. He gets knowledge about the external world through his five sense-organs, viz., eyes, ears, nose, taste-buds in the mouth, and skin receptors. He relies on his sense-perceptions. And so is the world of plurality real for him.

Man saw the vast Earth and the infinite sky. He could not estimate the dimensions of the sky. He could not conceive of the boundaries of space. He could not make out the millions of galaxies. Even our own galaxy (the Milky Way) was unknown to him. But he could discern the Sun, the Moon, some planets of our solar system and the innumerable stars in the night sky. He observed diversity on the Earth. Mountains, rivers, seas and oceans, hills and valleys are numerous and scattered. The non-living objects on the Earth are too many. There are also diverse forms of life here. There are varieties of plants and animals. There are varieties of human beings. There are families, genera and species. In each species, there are many individuals. Man observed all this diversity in Nature. And so did he recognize pluralism in Nature.

With reference to the Vedic gods, controversy arises over the question of monotheism, polytheism, pantheism and henotheism or kathenotheism. There are thirty-three gods mentioned in the

Ṛg-Veda[1] and the Atharva-Veda[2]. Eleven of them are celestial, eleven are atmospheric and the rest eleven are terrestrial.[3] The celestial deities are Dyaus, the two Aśvins, Pūṣan, Viṣṇu and six of the Ādityas, viz., Sūrya, Savitā (or Bhaga), Mitra, Aryaman, Dakṣa and Aṁśa. The atmospheric deities are Indra, Varuṇa, Rudra, Maruts, Uṣas, Vāyu, Parjanya, Vivasvat, Yama, Prajāpati and Aditi. The terrestrial gods are Agni, Soma, Bṛhaspati, Apāṁ Napāt, Mātariśvan, Tvaṣṭā, and the goddesses Pṛthivī, Āpaḥ, Sarasvatī, Iḍā and Bhāratī.

Some scholars are of the opinion that the Vedic Aryans were Nature-worshippers. Powers of Nature were personified as Agni, Varuṇa, Vāyu, Indra, Uṣas, etc. Any natural power that is either benevolent or malevolent was worshipped. The "primitive mind" could imagine anthropomorphic forms of these deities. Any power of Nature, at which man expressed awe and wonder, by which he was immensely benefitted, by which his interests were adversely affected and by which he was fatally horrified, was made a deity (*deva* or *devī*). With a long list of thirty-three gods, the Vedic Aryans were considered to be undoubtedly polytheistic.

The *Puruṣa-Sūkta*[4] of the Ṛg-Veda gives an apparent impression that the Vedic Aryans were pantheistic. "Pantheism" is a Greek word (pan=all; theos=God), meaning "all in God". The world is a finite creation which is contained in the infinite being of God. The world is not everything of God. All the diverse units of the world are constituents or component parts of God Who is much larger than the total world. God is the total organism containing the lower organisms of the world as constituent parts. There was again the interpretation of the panpsychist-cum-pantheist. For him, God was the total Psychic Being whose constituents were the different units of the world. In this concept, every constituent entity was held to be sentient to some extent. Reality is organic and panpsychic. As an organism includes various organs, tissues in organs and multiple cells in each tissue, so does God include the world. The divine is not simply absolute but dipolar, having absolute and relative aspects.

In the opinion of Max Müller, the Vedic Aryans were henotheistic or kathenotheistic. They had a belief in individual gods alternately regarded as the highest. When the seer invokes a god, he ascribes all the attributes to him at that particular time. The god is eulogized at that moment as if he were the greatest and even the only god. But, in the very next stanza or hymn, this mighty god who monopolizes all the attributes in the previous stanza or hymn is described as dependent on others.

Henotheism is a Greek word formed by the fusion of two parts, *henos*, meaning "one" and *theos*, meaning "god". In this view, one supreme god is accepted, while not denying the existence of other gods. There are many Vedic hymns for the glorification of one supreme god. At the same time, there are also other hymns in the praise of other gods who are dependent on the supreme god.

It is not easy to get the real meaning of the Vedic language. It is still more difficult for persons with bias or prejudice or preconceived ideas to correctly interpret the Vedas. That has exactly happened with the scholars who have found polytheism, pantheism and henotheism in the Vedic texts.

That Reality is One and only One has been clearly given in the *Nāsadīya Sūkta*[5] of the Ṛg-Veda. Before the world of multiplicity was manifested, there had been one homogeneous, undifferentiated entity. An English rendering of the first five verses of this hymn is given below:

> Then (before the manifestation of the universe), there was neither non-existence (nothing) nor these manifested things; there was neither space nor the particles. By what was it pervaded? For whose contentment was it meant? What was this unfathomable profound *ambhaḥ* (cosmic waters)?
>
> There was neither mortality nor immortality, neither day nor night (there was no time). There was no differentiation. There was no *prāṇa*. It existed with its *Svadhā* (*Māyā* or *Prakṛti* or *Śakti*) as a single entity. Apart from this nondual one, there was nothing else whatsoever.
>
> In the beginning (before the manifestation), there was darkness, covered by darkness. The cosmic plasma (*salilaṁ, āpaḥ, ambhaḥ*) was an undifferentiated continuum. It originated from *Māyā* in a superheated condition (*tapasā*).
>
> In the beginning (before the manifestation), there was the Divine Desire (for a phenomenal universe), which was the first seed of the Cosmic Mind. The seers, seeking in their hearts, have discovered, by their wisdom, the bond that operates between the manifested universe and the unmanifested transcendental Being.

> The universe started in an explosive way and expanded below and above (in all directions) like a flash of the Sun's rays or lightning. Some of these were shedders of the seed and the others were strong and superb. The *Svadhā* (*Māyā* or *Prakṛti*) as the material cause of the phenomenal universe was inferior and the *Prayatiḥ* (the efficient cause—the Lord) was superior.

The next hymn of the Ṛg-Veda[6] gives a description of the oscillating universe. The manifestation and the dissolution of the universe are likened to a weaver's job. *Pumān* (the First Person, the Lord) spreads out (*tanute*) his web (the manifested universe); He rolls it up (*utkṛṇatti*). The threads are spread out on every side. The forward activity of the weaving is the *pravaya* and the backward activity is the *apavaya*. And so operate the *tasarāṇi* (shuttles of the weaver) alternately.

Thus the Vedic seer does recognize the transcendental Being which is one only. But, in his invocation, he praises and worships the functional God and not the transcendental Being. The phenomenal universe functions under the control of the One Lord Who is not different from the transcendental Being. The functional Lord is described in language by different names in accordance with the attributes and functions. And so is the apparent multiplicity of gods, the Vedic pseudo-pantheon.

The Ṛg-Veda[7] declares that Reality (the divine, well-winged *garutmat*) is One only, which is verbally expressed by the seers in diverse ways (*ekaṁ sadviprā bahudhā vadanti*). They call Him Indra (the resplendent), Mitra (the surveyor), Varuṇa (the venerable) and Agni (the adorable). They call the One by many names as they speak of the adorable (Agni) as Yama (ordainer) and *Mātariśvān* (cosmic breath). The wise seers verbally portray the well-winged Divine Being that exists as One only in many ways (*suparṇaṁ viprāḥ kavayo vacovirekaṁ santaṁ bahudhā kalpayanti*).[8] The Ṛg-Veda unambiguously declares monotheism in the following verse: "He is our father, generator and disposer. He knows all the worlds. He is one alone. All the names of all the gods refer to Him only. Other beings seek Him for information."[9]

The Vedic goddess Aditi may be taken as an example. She is a personification of Universal Nature. She is the source and substance of all things. The Ṛg-Veda describes : "Aditi is the sky;

Aditi is the intermediate firmament; Aditi is the mother, and the father and son; Aditi is all the gods, and the five tribes; Aditi is whatever has been born; Aditi is whatever shall be born."[10] This verse clearly shows that the Nature of plurality has an underlying unity which is termed Aditi. The eight Ādityas were born from her body.[11] They are her sons and still she has been described as the mother, the father, the sons, and the gods. Such statements cannot be explained rationally unless she is taken as the underlying unity in the multiplicity of Nature.

Another goddess, Diti, appears to be an antithesis, or a complement, to Aditi.[12] According to Sāyaṇa's interpretation, Aditi is the invisible whole of Nature and Diti comprises the separate creatures.

In Vedic cosmogony, Brahmā is the progenitor of the whole universe. He is the creator god. The *Taittirīya Brāhmaṇa*[13] describes Brahmā, the self-existent, the *sui causa* and the supreme austerity, as the son, the father and the mother. Here identity is established among the father, the mother and the son. Such a concept cannot be accepted as a valid one unless an underlying unitary principle beneath the apparently multitudinous surface is conceived of.

Deeper probe into the Vedic texts reveals that the different gods are not different from one another although they carry different names. Agni, Indra, Varuṇa, Viṣṇu, Mitra, Aryaman, Rudra, Tvaṣṭā, Pūṣan, Aṁśa, Bhaga, Hotṛ, Aditi, Sarasvatī, Bhāratī, Iḷā are different Vedic gods and goddesses. In spite of their apparent differences in identities, Agni is associated with them[14]; the same Agni is identified with gods such as Mitra, Varuṇa, Yama and Mātariśvān.[15] The Atharva-Veda[16] gives a description of Agni in the following way.

> Agni becomes Varuṇa in the evening and Mitra in the morning; becoming Savitā he moves through the air and becoming Indra he glows in the middle of the sky.

This hymn does bring about the identity of the Vedic gods. They are different in names, but one in reality. Agni becomes Varuṇa; he becomes Mitra; he also becomes Indra and Aryamā.[17] All the gods are comprehended in him. He encompasses all the gods as the felly rings the spokes.[18] This very simile has been given in another hymn of the Ṛg-Veda[19] when Agni is invoked.

> Through you, O Agni, Varuṇa enforces the laws, Mitra dispels darkness and Aryamā becomes bounteous. And thus all of them are universally comprehended in you in their functions. You encompass them all who are like spokes in a felly.

In a verse of the Ṛg-Veda,[20] Indra has been equated with Varuṇa and also with Tvaṣṭā. The Vedic seers refer to a single creator and sustainer by different names.[21] They undoubtedly use the names descriptively on the basis of the qualities and functions described. All the gods are essentially one, though manifested differently.[22]

While invoking Viśvakarman,[23] the Vedic seer has described him as the only Lord of the universe, as the creator, sustainer and controller. In the beginning, he was the agent of the manifestation of the cosmic waters (*āpaḥ*), which received the first or primeval germ, wherein all the bounties of Nature participate. The cosmic embryo is placed on the navel of that one who is never born and in whom all the beings abide. Viśvakarman, as depicted in the Vedas, is not only the Divine Architect, but also the Divine Controller and Sustainer. He is the One God.

In the *Hiraṇyagarbha Sūkta*[24] of the Ṛg-Veda, Prajāpati is invoked. This Prajāpati is *ka* as given in the *Śatapatha Brāhmaṇa.*[25] He is present from the very beginning. He is the sole Lord of all created beings. He upholds the earth and the heaven. He is the giver of physical and spiritual strength. All the enlightened beings obey his commands. He is the creator of all beings. He is the ruler of the whole universe. He supports all the worlds. He is the one who generated the vast and delightful cosmic waters (*āpaḥ*). He is the Lord of all. There is none other than he who has given existence to whatever has been manifested.

Prajāpati is generally regarded as the creator god. This function of creation has been described in the foregoing hymn of the Ṛg-Veda. But, here the functions of Prajāpati are not confined to creation only. He has been described as the single Lord who performs all functions such as creation, sustenance, supervision and control.

Brahmaṇaspati[26] is another Vedic god who has been described as the Lord of the universe. As a blacksmith causes his bellows to expand, so also does the Lord's desire cause manifestation of the primeval universe from the unmanifested existence. Subsequently space was formed and then other grosser things. Evolution of microparticles and particles proceeded. Dakṣa was generated from Aditi and *vice versa*. There was a rapid dynamic state of flux in the interconversion between space and particles, and matter-particles and energy-photons. These microparticles danced vigorously, randomly and chaotically. In this process of the dancing of the particles (*reṇu*), there were continual generations and annihilations. Afterwards the forces were differentiated, some particles were well-aligned and bonded, and this led further to nucleosynthesis.

Any casual reader of the Vedas considers Viśvakarman, Hiraṇyagarbha and Brahmaṇaspati as three different gods. But, in reality, all these three are identical. They are different like *aqua* and water. They are not identical like water, ice and steam, that are identical in molecular constitution, but dissimilar in state and properties. They are designated by different names depending upon the emphasis laid on the attributes and functions described in a particular hymn. Otherwise they are identical.

The Vedic seer is very emphatic about the unborn One which supports the multi-worlds. He raises the question, "What is that One Supreme Being, Who has upheld these six spheres in the form of the unborn ?"[27] In the *Vālakhiya*, it has been said: "There is one Agni kindled in many places; one mighty Sūrya who extends over all things; one Uṣas who illuminates this entire world; this One only has developed into the all." [28]

The problem of one-*versus*-many was aptly solved by the Vedic seers. The "many" refers to the phenomenal universe which is an empirical truth (*vyāvahārika satya*). The "One" refers to the non-dual Being that is the absolute truth (*pāramārthika satya*). The "One" is fundamental, immutable and timeless. The "many" appears at the beginning of time and dissolves at the end of time. This cycle repeats without beginning and end. Becoming is concerned with the "many". The One Being remains as Being without activity, origination and annihilation. The "One" is not perceptible to us through our senses. The "many" may be grasped by our senses directly or indirectly. And so the "One" is *asat* (non-existent) and the "many" *sat* (existent) for us.[29] Really speaking, the "non-existent" (unmanifested Being) is absolutely existent; and the "existent" (manifested universe) is empirically existent.

This explanation of *asat* and *sat* is in conformity with that given in the *Taittirīya Āraṇyaka*.[30] Prof. J. Muir's translation of the relevant portions of this *Āraṇyaka* is given here: "In the interval between the absorption of the previous, and the production of the subsequent creation, there was neither entity nor non-entity. The world at the time when, by possessing both 'name' and 'form', it is clearly manifested, is designated by the word 'entity', while a void which may be compared to such non-existing things as a "man's horns, etc. is called non-entity. Neither of these states existed; but there was a certain unapparent condition, which from the absence of distinctness, was not an entity, while from its being the instrument of the world's production, it was not a non-entity".

The *Puruṣa-Sūkta*[31] of the Ṛg-Veda describes the unity of the Godhead. The *Puruṣa* (the Lord) is One only. All this is verily the *Puruṣa*. Whatever of the past, the present and the future are merely the manifestations of the One *Puruṣa*. Thus, this hymn describes not only the unity of Godhead, but also the underlying unity of the diversity of the universe.

Similar to the concept of *Puruṣa*, the Atharva-Veda[32] presents the unitary principle of the Godhead and the universe with the concept of *Skambha*, considered as a vast embodied being co-extensive with the universe. The thirty-three Vedic gods are comprehended in him. They sprang from non-entity (unmanifested unitary existence), that is the highest member of *Skambha*, the fulcrum of the whole world in all its aspects. *Skambha* is the highest or greatest Brahman, who presides over the past, the future and the entire universe. It is identical with the self-existent (*svayambhū*[33]) Brahman that is the source of Prajāpati. This great imperishable Brahman is the one that was and is to be.[34] The *Śatapatha Brāhmaṇa*[35] contains a passage that later served as the seed material for the entire Vedānta philosophy. This passage contains, among other things, the following: "In the beginning Brahman was this (universe). .... It considered, 'How can I pervade all this world?' It then pervaded them with two things—form and name .... These are the two great manifestations of Brahman. .... Of these two, one is the greater, viz., form."

The *Taittirīya Brāhmaṇa*[36] says that Brahman is this entire universe. The same Brāhmaṇa[37] elsewhere contains the following passages: "Let us worship with an oblation that first-born god, by whom whatever exists in this universe is pervaded. That self-existent Brahma is the highest *tapas* (heat). He is son, father, mother. *Tapas* was produced as the first object." Brahman has been described as the single substance out of which everything of the entire universe is made. He is the forest. He is the tree of the forest. Out of that tree, the heaven and the earth have been fashioned.[38]

The words *Prajāpati* (Lord of creatures) and *Hiraṇyagarbha* (golden embryo) were used synonymously in the Vedas.[39] A verse of the *Vājasaneyi Saṁhitā*[40] is as follows: "Prajāpati moves within the embryo. Multiplicity is produced out of him, who does not become an offspring. The wise behold his womb. In him all the worlds stand". This very idea is given in the Atharva-Veda[41] in a slightly modified form. "Prajāpati moves within the embryo. Multiplicity is produced out of him who remains unseen. With his one-half he produced the whole universe. But what trace is there of his (other) half?" The *Vājasaneyi Saṁhitā*[42] says that nothing was born prior to him who pervades all worlds.

The *Śatapatha Brāhmaṇa*[43] contains a considerable number of passages on the subject of Prajāpati. In this Brāhmaṇa, Prajāpati is sometimes identified with the universe. It describes Prajāpati as the only one that existed in the beginning and as the only source out of which the universe of multifarious names and forms was evolved.

The Vedic seers poetically describe the single unitary Being as the substrate of the empirical multiple entities by different names according to the different attributes and functions under narration. *Prāṇa* may be taken as an example. In the Atharva-Veda,[44] a hymn has been dedicated to the deity *Prāṇa*. According to this hymn, the universe is subject to *Prāṇa* who is the Lord of all and on whom all is supported. He is the Lord of both the living and the non-living creations. He is *Virāj*; he is *Deṣṭā*. He is Sun and Moon. He is Prajāpati, Mātariśvan, Vāyu. The past, the future, everything is supported upon *Prāṇa*.

In the Atharva-Veda,[45] description of the *Ucchiṣṭa* (the remains of the sacrifice) has been given in a seemingly pantheistic language. The *Ucchiṣṭa* contains the name and the form, the world, Indra, Agni, the universe, heaven and the earth, all that exists, the waters, the sea, the moon and the wind. In it are both the existent and the non-existent. The *Ucchiṣṭa* is the sustainer of the universe and the father of the progenitor. The resounding waters, the thunder, the great *Śruti*, pebbles, sand, stones, plants, grass, clouds, lightnings and rain are embraced in the *Ucchiṣṭa*. Pantheism, in this description, is apparent, but not real. In a number of places in the Atharva-Veda, the oneness of the Supreme Being has been asserted. He who is the only Lord of the universe should be worshipped.[46] He is Rudra and Mahādeva; He is also *Aryaman* and Varuṇa.[47] He is Agni, the self-refulgent; He is Sūrya, the impeller and the Creator. He is verily *Mahāyama*, the great administrator and disciplinarian.[48] That the different names of all the Vedic gods refer to One Supreme Being only has been clearly given in the Yajur-Veda.[49] "Agni is that; the Sun is that; *Vāyu* and *Candramas* are that; *Śukra* or the Bright One is that; *āpaḥ* (the cosmic waters) is that; Prajāpati is that; that is Brahman". The Yajur-Veda[50] further reiterates that that is bodyless, woundless and sinewless.

The surface gives a variegated appearance, a mosaic scenario with different forms and colours; but beneath the surface is a homogeneous, undifferentiated, unbroken whole, one, non-dual, without a second. The underlying unitary Being cannot be perceived through any mediation. It is transcendental. It can be realized directly without any mediacy. All cognitions are possible due to It alone. It is the absolute Existence. It is Pure Consciousness. It is Bliss, devoid of joy and sorrow, agony and ecstasy. It is the substratum of the empirical universe of manifold appearances. It is the unfathomable, absolutely tranquil depth of the waters whose waves, ripples, surfs and bubbles constitute *saṁsāra* (the phenomenal universe). This is the quintessence of the Vedic metaphysics.

NOTES

1. ṚV, III. 6.9; VIII.28.1; 30.2; 35.3; 57.2; IX. 92.4.
2. AV, X. 7.13.
3. ṚV, I.139.11; AV, X. 9.12.
4. ṚV, X. 90.
5. ṚV, X. 129.
6. ṚV, X. 130.
7. ṚV, I. 164.46.
8. ṚV, X. 114.5.
9. ṚV, X. 82.3.
10. ṚV, I. 89.10.

11. ṚV, X. 72.8.
12. ṚV, V. 62.8.
13. TBrā, III. 12.3.1.
14. ṚV, II. 1.3-7 & 11; III.5.4; V.3.1; VII. 12.3; X.8.5.
15. ṚV, I. 164.46.
16. AV, XIII. 3.13.
17. ṚV, V.3. 1-2.
18. ṚV, V. 13.6.
19. ṚV, I. 141.9.
20. ṚV, IV. 42.3.
21. ṚV, IV. 53.2; V.82.7; VIII.87.2; IX.5.9; X.83.4; 170.4.
22. ṚV, III. 55.
23. ṚV, X. 81; 82; TBrā, II. 8.9.6.
24. AV, X. 121.
25. ŚBrā, IV. 22.5.
26. ṚV, X. 72.
27. ṚV, I. 164.6.
28. Vālakhiya, X. 2.
29. ṚV, X. 129.1.
30. TĀR, II. 8.9.3.
31. ṚV, X.90.
32. AV, X.7.
33. ŚBrā, X.6.5.9.
34. *Ibid.*, XIII. 7.1.1.
35. *Ibid.*, XI. 2.3.1.
36. TBrā, II. 8.8.9.
37. *Ibid.*, III.12.3.1.
38. *Ibid.*, II.8.9.6.
39. ṚV, V. 121.10; X.121.
40. VāS, XXXI. 19.
41. AV, X. 8.13.
42. VāS, XXXII.5.
43. ŚBrā, II. 2.4.1; VII.5.2.6; XI.5.8.1.
44. AV, XI.4.
45. AV, XI. 7.1.
46. AV, II.2.1-2.
47. AV, XIII. 4.4.
48. AV, XIII. 4.5.
49. YV, XXXII.1.
50. YV, XL.8.

II
VEDĀNTIC NON-DUALISM

THERE ARE DIFFERENT schools of Vedānta. Prominent among them are non-dualism (*advaitavāda*) of Śaṅkara, qualified non-dualism (*viśiṣṭādvaitavāda*) of Rāmānuja and dualism (*dvaitavāda*) of Madhva. The doctrine of non-dualism with reference to monism *versus* pluralism will be discussed in this chapter.

The quintessence of Advaita Vedānta may be given at the outset: Brahman alone is real. The world of plurality is illusory. The world-appearance is caused by the superimposition of nescience (*avidyā*) on Brahman. The individual soul (self or *jīva*) is the same as the Supreme Self or Brahman.

Before we proceed further, it may be appropriate to define the two words "reality" and "illusion". The Sanskrit equivalent of the word "reality" is *satya* (*as + kyap*). That which exists is *satya*. Three categories of existence (*trividhaṁ sattvam*[1]) are referred to in the Vedānta. For illustration, three types of statements may be cited here: (1) The blue sky exists, or darkness exists. (2) The earth exists. (3) Brahman exists. The first category mentioned here refers to *prātibhāsika sattā* (apparent existence). In this case, nothing really exists, but it appears to exist. The second category is concerned with *vyāvahārika sattā* (empirical existence). Things exist for all practical purposes. But, in reality, they do not exist as they appear to exist. They have a substratum, B, which is perceived as not-B, and this not-B is the thing empirically existent. The existence of Brahman, in category three, is absolute. It exists timelessly, without any change. Whatever is at present was in the past and will be in the future without undergoing any modification. It continues to be same during any time and also in the absence of time (before and after the world-period). It can never be contradicted by any means whatsoever (*bādhakajñānāntarābhāvāt*[2]). This B remains as B. It has absolute existence (*pāramārthika sattā*). When the Vedāntist says, "Brahman is real (*satya*)," he refers to this absolute existence.

A rope may be perceived as a snake. Nacre may be perceived as silver. A pillar may be perceived as a human being. These are examples of illusion. In all cases of illusion, a substance, S, is perceived as not-S. This not-S which is empirically perceived is non-existent as not-S, but is existent as S, although not perceived as S. In contrast to illusion, the phenomenon of hallucination is devoid of any substratum. One sees a tiger when there is no tiger to be seen and there is no other thing that may be mistaken as a tiger. The percipient has a mental impression of a tiger by virtue of his past experience. That mental impression is projected outside as a tiger that is perceived. One sees a ghost that does not exist. The percipient never perceived a ghost during his lifetime. But he has an image of a ghost through reading or hearing about ghosts. Such an imagined ghost has been imprinted in the mind of the percipient. This impression is projected out to be perceived as an externally existing ghost. Both these cases are examples of hallucination.

When Śaṅkara says that the world is an illusion, he means thereby that the world does not really exist as it appears and that Brahman is the substratum of the plurality of the world-appearances.

Brahman

Brahman is *satya*[3] (Reality). It alone exists. Nothing else exists. "Whatever exists is existent (*yadasti tat satyam*)." This is a tautology, an analytical statement. The root of the verb *asti* is *as* (which means "is"). The word *satya* (*as + kyap*) means "that which exists". Whatever is given in the subject is the same in the predicate. This statement is always true and cannot be contradicted in any condition. "Whatever is existent is Brahman (*yat satyaṁ tad brahma*)." "Brahman" is a name given to the ontologically existent Being. Question does not arise on the truth or falsity of this statement. It does not need any proof for its truth. Brahman is nameless (*anāmaka*[4]). We could have used any other name for it, and still our concept could have remained unaltered.

Whatever has been given in the foregoing paragraph regarding Brahman and existence may not be confused with the controversy on Anselm's ontological argument. His definition of God included existence and by the help of this definition he guaranteed the real existence of God. But verbal definitions don't create reality. Both Hume and Kant, in slightly different ways, argued against Anselm's deduction by saying that defining something is different from saying the thing exists. In their opinion, existence is not a property of something. When we say, "X exists", we claim thereby that the descriptions fit X in reality.

Anselm's ontological argument attributes necessary existence to God. From this necessary existence is improperly derived the real existence of God. There is utter confusion, however, in the "necessary" concept. A proposition of the sort "A = A" or "1 + 2 = 3" is necessary, since it is analytical (the latter being Kant's synthetic *a priori*). The proposition "not both p and not-p" is also necessary. "This coloured cloth is not colourless cloth" is necessary. This is, however, not the case with the proposition "God exists." Such a statement cannot be necessarily true. Similarly, a statement like "Whatever exists is Brahman" is different from "Brahman exists."

Only nihilism can discard the statement "Whatever exists is Brahman." The nihilist asserts, without any proof, of course, that there is not anything. He himself exists even if the whole universe other than himself is assumed to be non-existent. It is impossible for him to refute solipsism. If he accepts the existence of himself, he cannot successfully contradict non-dualism of Vedānta which equates "self" (*ātmā*) with "Self" or Brahman (*ātmā ca brahma*[5]). Of course, Advaita Vedānta does not support solipsism as such. But the nihilist has no valid argument in favour of nihilism. He may at least be a solipsist. Śaṅkara says that everyone must not accept the statement "I amn't" (*na nāhamastīti*[6]). This "I" is self-established (*svataḥsiddhaḥ*[7]). To none at all is the self altogether unknown.[8] This "I" is directly (*sākṣāt*) presented to everybody without any mediation (*aparokṣāt*),[9] this is the directly experienced self (*pratyagātman*);[10] this self (*ātmā*) which is present in everybody (*sarvāntaraḥ*[11]) is Brahman. This whole universe is rooted in that Self.[12] That root is existent and real. That is the Self (Brahman). That art thou.[13] Non-existent verily does one become if one knows Brahman as non-being; and existent does one become by knowing

Brahman as existent.[14]

That the world is not real, that it has empirical existence only, and that it is rooted in Brahman will be discussed at other places in this book. With both logical and empirical evidences, it can be proved that, from absolute point of view, the world is non-existent. If this is provisionally accepted at this point, and if the existence of Brahman is refuted, logical absurdity shall be the outcome. How can we conceive of the world as produced from nothing? The world is an effect and it must have a cause which must be regarded as existent.[15] We deny the snake which we erroneously perceive. We do that only after we cognize the rope on which the snake was superimposed. We deny the world which is unreal. While denying the world, we have to posit something else. If everything is denied, we end in nihilism.[16] In order to avoid it, something other than the world cannot be negated. That something is Brahman.

Advaita Vedānta rejects the idea of the origination of something from nothing.[17] Nor can something which already exists be reduced to nothing. The *Bhagavadgītā*[18] puts it in this way: No becoming of the non-existent and no annihilation of the existent are seen. This is the law of conservation of being (*sattā*). This law is not empirical, but is analytical. "Not p and not-p" is a necessary truth. "Nothing = something" and "something =nothing" are self-contradictory statements and hence cannot be true.

Following the foregoing arguments, one can very well appreciate that one (the nihilist) oneself becomes non-existent if one accepts Brahman as non-being. Advaita Vedānta takes a positive stand and declares that Being (Brahman) is the ultimate root of the whole universe. All in the universe are rooted in *sat* or Being that exists (*sanmūlāḥ*), abide in *sat* (*sadāyatanāḥ*) and supported by *sat* (*sat-pratiṣṭhāḥ*).[19]

Brahman is *Cit*[20] or Consciousness. It is *Jñāna*[21] (knowledge), *Prajñāna*,[22] *Prajñānaghana*,[23] *Vijñāna*,[24] *Vijñānaghana*,[25] all these terms being synonymous. The concept of consciousness, in this case, is unlike that used in psychology or epistemology of philosophy. Rāma (the name of a person) is conscious. Here "conscious" is a predicate of the subject. It is a functional property. It is a *guṇa* (quality) or *dharma* (property) of a *guṇin* (possessor of quality) or *dharmin* (possessor of property). When we say, "Brahman is *Cit*, *Vijñāna* or *Prajñāna*", we do not mean thereby that Brahman is an entity possessing knowledge or consciousness. The statement, "Brahman has consciousness" is not correct. It may be correctly stated as "Brahman is Consciousness."

Some critics hold that it is impossible for consciousness to be operative in the absence of an entity that is conscious. It may be mentioned here that Brahman is not a non-entity and that it is a positive entity. But this entity is not the possessor of consciousness; it itself is Consciousness. Consciousness and possessor of consciousness are concepts valid for biological individuals and even non-living individual entities. This concept is not applicable to Brahman that is not a *vastu*[26] (matter). Moreover, consciousness is never operative in Brahman. There is no moment when it is insentient and it does not change over from the state of insentience to that of sentience at any other moment. It never functions by virtue of being sentient. The Consciousness which is Brahman, being reflected on insentient matter, both living and non-living, imparts sentience to the latter.

The Naiyāyikas and the Vaiśeṣikas contend that *dharma* and *dharmins* are distinguishable. To cite an example, a jar is a *dharmin* (*dravya*) while its quality, e.g., hardness, is a *dharma*. In the Sāṅkhya system, there is no difference between *guṇa* (quality) and *guṇin* (the possessor of quality). The word *tattva* literally means thatness, i.e., the state of that (referring to a thing). In this sense, there is no difference between a *tattva* and a *guṇa*. Each of the twenty-five categories in the system is considered as a *tattva*, and not as a *tattvavat* (having *tattva*). When the three *guṇas*, viz., *sattva*, *rajas* and *tamas* are equipoised (in equilibrium, in *sāmyāvasthā*), they are collectively called *prakṛti*, which is itself a *tattva* (having no *tattva*). *Prakṛti* is the three *guṇas*, having no *guṇas*. In Buddhist philosophy, the existence of any *dharmin* (possessor of attributes, qualities or properties) is not recognized. The Buddhists speak of the *dharma* and not of the *dharmin*, which, at best, is equated with the *dharma*. The concept of the Vedāntist is not exactly what has been described here. According to Advaita Vedānta, at the empirical level, a manifested entity, by virtue of possessing attributes, is a *dharmin*, the attribute being the *dharma*. But, for the absolute (*pāramārthika*[27]) Being, devoid of all attributes (*sarvasaṁsāradharmavivarjitam*[28]), there is no relevance of both *dharmin* and *dharma*. The Being is Being. That's the identity statement. When the Vedāntist says, "Brahman is Consciousness", he states an identity proposition like "A is A" or "Consciousness is Consciousness."

How is the opponent wrong if he contends that Brahman is unconscious or insentient?

The non-eternality of the empirical world will be later discussed in the book. It may now be provisionally accepted that the world has a beginning and an end and that the world-cycles are endless.[29] The world does not appear from nothing. It is rooted in Brahman, figuratively taken as the cause[30] of the world. If Brahman is insentient, it cannot be the efficient cause of the world. It is necessary for the efficient cause to be sentient. Further, it is necessary for the efficient cause of the total universe to be omniscient.[31] Hence it would be illogical to ascribe insentience to Brahman. The Sāṅkhya philosopher theorizes that the insentient *pradhāna* is the cause of the world. Vedānta[32] refutes such a concept. Śaṅkara contends that the insentient *pradhāna* cannot have the potency of functioning as a witness (*na cācetanasya pradhānasya sākṣitvamasti*[33]).

After dissolution and before the next manifestation, Brahman alone exists. The cosmic egg appears, it explodes and expands and thus the universe starts functioning. Some persons say that the universe comes out of nothing. Vedānta refutes such a concept of nihilism. It further states that *abhidhyāna* (desire) is a prerequisite for the creation. A chair is made. Before the actual making of the chair, somebody (the carpenter or the person who placed order with the carpenter) desired to have a chair. God desired[34] to create the world. But, an insentient Being cannot desire. Thus it is concluded that Brahman is Consciousness.

For making a chair, consciousness of the carpenter is necessary. But this consciousness may be of a limited character. On the other hand, omniscience is necessary for creating the world. And hence Śaṅkara concludes that only the omniscient Brahman can be the cause of the universe.[35] In the construction of a building or a bridge, an engineer is necessary. He understands the blueprint and executes the construction work. The insentient building materials such as stones, bricks, sand, gravel, chips, cement and steel rods cannot automatically assemble themselves for the structure to be built. The builder must be conscious and intelligent to do the work. Hence Śaṅkara says: The omniscient Brahman must be the cause of the world, but not the insentient Nature or *pradhāna*.[36]

Whether somebody is an atheist or a theist, a scientist or a non-scientist, he observes the grand cosmic design. The universe has been well planned, intelligently and aesthetically designed. The whole blueprint has been drawn by a megacomputer. Who is the agent of this design (*racanā*)? Who is the designer? Who is the architect of this cosmic design? Insentient matter cannot design. And hence the *Brahma-Sūtra*[37] declares that God is the designer and the executor. While interpreting this design-aphorism Śaṅkara very strongly refutes the arguments of the Sāṅkhya philosophers who hold that the insentient *pradhāna* (primordial Nature) is the cause of the universe. As the brick or the mortar is not the architect of the building and an intelligent person is the architect, so does he infer that the insentient *pradhāna* is not the architect of the insentient Universe and that the Omniscient Lord (*Īśvara*) does this function.

It has already been said that the universe has been preplanned, intelligently designed and well-engineered. The One who intended this cosmic plan, designed it and engineered it is the *Īśvara* (God) aspect of Brahman. But, with these activities, the functioning of *Īśvara* is not over. He is the sustainer, the controller and the administrator of the universe. The universe has a ruler (*praśāsaka*[38]). He is *Īśvara*. The maintenance of the universe is not possible without the guidance of an intelligent transcendent ruler. Śaṅkara[39] adduces inferential evidences for the existence of such a ruler from the orderliness (*ṛta*[40]) of the world. He is the Inner-Controller (*antaryāmī*[41]). He is the Lord, the Supreme Controller[42] (*parameśvara, maheśvara*) of everything in the universe, micro and macro, movable and immovable, and living and non-living. Śaṅkara poses the question: "Is it possible for the insentient Nature (*pradhāna*) to excercise ruling (*praśāsana*) and controlling (*niyantraṇa*) power ?"[43] So he concludes that the Omniscient and Omnipotent Lord is the cause of the origination, the sustenance and the dissolution of the universe.[44] Thus the insentience of Brahman is inconceivable. It is necessarily to be inferred that Brahman is Consciousness.

Brahman is *ānanda* or Bliss.[45] When the word *ānanda* is used for human beings, it means "happiness", "joyfulness", ecstasy, opposite of sadness, grief, sorrowfulness (*viṣāda*) or agony. In its adjective form, it is used as a predicate. It is an attribute of somebody. When we say, "Brahman is *ānanda*", we don't use this term in an attributive or predicative manner. It is not correct to say, "Brahman has *ānanda*". "Brahman is *ānanda*" is an identity statement like "A is A". *Ānanda* is devoid of both joyfulness and sorrowfulness, free from both agony and ecstasy. The Absolute Being devoid of attributes and actions can neither be joyful nor sorrowful. *Ānanda* has no equivalent concept in Western philosophy and no equivalent word in many languages. We may commit conceptual and linguistic error if we don't try to find the meaning in the use of the word *ānanda* when applied to Brahman.

The *Brahma-Sūtra*[46] has eight aphorisms on *ānanda*. It says, "Brahman is *ānandamaya*".[47] Śaṅkara[48] contends that this "abundance of bliss" has been used for the Self (Brahman). The opponent pleads that the word "Blissful (*ānandamayaḥ*)" has been used instead of "Bliss (*ānanda*)". The suffix *mayaṭ* is used for modification (*vikāra*) as in "*mṛṇmaya*" (earth modified into a product). The *Brahma-Sūtra*[49] does not accept this idea. Śaṅkara[50] says that the suffix *maya* follows the prefixed word in the sense of abundance (*prācurya*). Such a grammatical use has been codified by the famous grammarian Pāṇini. Hence Śaṅkara concludes that *mayaṭ* has been used in the sense of plenitude or abundance and that *ānandamayaḥ* is not to be understood as "Blissful" in an attributive sense. He asserts that *ānanda* is not an attribute of Brahman and that it is identified with Brahman.

The *Māṇḍūkya Upaniṣad* and the *Taittirīya Upaniṣad*[51] have also used the word *ānandamaya* for Brahman. The *Taittirīya Upaniṣad* has made a graded evaluation of bliss.[52] The start is made from the human plane. The bliss in each subsequent plane is a hundredfold of the preceding one. The final plane of bliss which is the Bliss as Brahman is unsurpassable. The *Taittirīya Upaniṣad*[53] is unequivocal in giving the identity statement, "Brahman is *ānanda*".

Gauḍapāda[54] has identified *Prajñā* (Consciousness in the state of deep sleep) with *ānanda*. In the *Muṇḍaka Upaniṣad* and the *Praśna Upaniṣad*, Brahman has been described as *ānandarūpam*.[55] The identity of Brahman with *ānanda* has also been given in a number of other Upaniṣads.[56] All the Upaniṣadic seers have agreed that *ānanda* is not an attribute of Brahman, that it is not joyfulness or ecstasy, that it is a state free from joy and sorrow, and that Brahman and *ānanda* are equated.

Brahman is *ananta* (infinite). The *Taittirīya Upaniṣad* says: *satyaṁ jñānamanantaṁ brahma*[57] (Brahman is Existence, Knowledge and

Infinite). This word (*ananta*) has been used for Brahman in some other scriptures[58] also.

Here we may make an attempt to determine the contextual meaning of the word "infinite". If we continue to add one positive quantity to another positive quantity, we get an infinite series without an end. We may take the number 1 and go on adding 1 to it. Where do we end? We end *ad infinitum.* Actually it would be correct to say, "We never end". This mathematical concept has been applied to ontology and thereby we have committed conceptual error. The mathematics of infinity is tautological. When we go on adding one, we continue to think of the next number which may be named in any way. In the thought process of adding the number one, the mental postulation of the next number is implied. And this process is not to end anywhere. But, from this, it is wrong to deduce that some entity is infinite.

The etymological meaning of the word *ananta* is "that which has no end, no termination." Thus *ananta* does not mean "*asīma*, infinite"; it means "endless". But something cannot be endless unless it is beginningless (*anādi*). Śaṅkara says: "Whatever has a beginning is bound to be impermanent".[59] It has also been said that Brahman is *anādi.*[60] The simultaneous mention of *anādi* and *ananta* Brahman has been done in some scriptures.[61] We may analyze here two points: Firstly, an entity with a beginning has necessarily an end. In other words, that which is a product is bound to perish. Secondly, an entity without a beginning, i.e., one which is never a product, is bound to be endless. Here the word "end" is not to be confused with spatial or temporal end. If X does not continue to be X, but becomes Y or Y_1, Y_2 and Y_3, etc., we say, X ends, or X is terminated.

Something, X, begins. It means, X has started to become a product from some existing precursor. Energy is necessary to maintain X as X. A product is a packet of energy that is active and constantly changing. Motion or change is an invariable attribute of any product. With this attribute, each product is more or less destabilized. It has a tendency to regain stabilization. To achieve this goal, it undergoes a series of modifications towards lesser and lesser energy. Someones say it becomes stabilized with the least energy. As a matter of fact, it is completely stabilized with zero energy. When it attains zero energy, it ceases to be a product, but is not reduced to nothing; it dissolves in its original precursor.

In this long chain of events of a product, p_1 changes to p_2, p_2 to p_3, and so does the process continue through a series of changes. At each stage, one sub-product ends and another sub-product begins. No product is eternal. Śaṅkara means this when he says, "Whatever has a beginning must have an end."

Brahman has no initial cause and hence is *anādikāraṇa*.[62] It is uncreated.[63] It is not a product. It has no precedent state (*apūrvam*[64]). Any precursor does not change to be Brahman which is birthless (*aja*[65]). It itself does not change to anything else. It does not undergo modification (*avikāryam*[66]). It is not a precursor of any product; it has no subsequent state (*anaparam*[67]). Brahman, B, continues to remain as B, (B→B→B→B→ ......→B). It is Being only, without becoming. Wherever there is becoming, there is the question of cause (*kāraṇa*) and effect (*kārya*), time and space. Without becoming (*vikāra*), the Being (*sattā*) or Brahman is not only eternal (*nitya*[68]) but also timeless (*akāla*,[69] *sanātana*,[70] *śāśvata*[71]) and spaceless (*anākāśa*[72]). Without a precedent state and a subsequent state, it has no material cause and it itself is no material cause of anything.

Anything to be eternal and timeless, it must be attributeless, functionless,unchanging and unmoving. Exhibition or even latent possession of attributes such as form, colour, etc. involves expenditure of energy. In doing any work, energy must be expended. In undergoing modification, work is involved, and any work cannot be performed without expenditure of energy. Spatio-temporal motion is invariably accompanied by expenditure of energy. Any entity, with constant expenditure of its energy, will undergo decay and hence is finally to perish. Thus eternality and timelessness are not compatible with attributes, functions, modifications and motion.

Brahman is attributeless (*nirguṇa*[73]), functionless (*niṣkriya*[74]), unchanging (*kūṭastha*[75]), motionless (*acala*,[76] *niścala*,[77] *sthāṇu*,[78] *sthira*[79]), undecaying (*avyaya*,[80] *akṣaya*[81]) and imperishable (*akṣara*[82]). It is formless (*arūpa*,[83] *amūrta*,[84] *akāya*,[85] *nirākāra*[86]). Anything that has a structure, a shape and a size needs energy to maintain these characteristics. An entity cannot be eternal and timeless if it needs energy to maintain its micro or macro-structure, shape and size. What is unmodifiable, immovable, inactive and devoid of attributes is bound to be constant (*dhruva*[87]). A basic question is asked here: "What are the justifications for accepting the existence of an attributeless and actionless entity? Is a Being without becoming a valid concept?"

According to the Nyāya Vaiśeṣika school of Indian philosophy, what exists can be analyzed into three categories, viz., substance, quality and action (*artha iti dravyaguṇakarmasu*[88]). A substance is defined as that which possesses qualities and actions and is the substratum cause.[89] The substance is the substratum of change. It can exist by itself at the moment it is produced, without being joined by qualities and actions.[90]

The Buddhist philosophers do not recognize the existence of a non-functional being. Dharmakirti holds that being means becoming and that to be is to be capable of functioning in some way or the other.[91] He and his followers formulated a proof of their flux doctrine (*pratītyasamutpāda*). To be is to do something. Whatever exists has a causal potency. Whatever has a causal potency must not be non-functional. To have causal potency is the same as to be actually doing what is supposed to be done. Everything is in a perpetual flux. The Buddhist doctrine of flux rejects the notion of potentiality. It states that there is nothing which is non-functional and does not constantly change.

The Buddhists don't recognize anything like substance. This anti-substantialism finds its extreme expression in the doctrine of momentariness (*kṣaṇikavāda*) of the Sautrāntikas. The Buddhist non-soul doctrine (*anātmavāda*) is anti-eternalism and anti-substantialism. According to both these doctrines, there is only process, only flux; there is constant fluctuation without something being there to fluctuate; there is ever a dynamic state of flux without something being there to be fluxed. The Buddhists recognize transmigration without being there any transmigrating soul.

According to the Jaina philosophy, the fundamental characteristic of a substance is its existence,[92] and whatever exists undergoes changes through origin, decay and stability.[93] Kundakunda has defined a substance as that which undergoes the processes of origin, persistence and decay, without changing its "own-nature" (*svabhāva*) and which is endowed with qualities (*guṇa*) and accompanied by modifications (*paryāya*).[94] The own-nature of the substance is its existence (*sadbhāva*), which is always accompanied by qualities and modes and by origin, decay and continuity. This idea of "own-nature" in the early Indian philosophy was analogous to the notion of "essence" found in the Western philosophy. Like the Vaiśeṣikas, the Jainas accept the substance as the core of change or flux and the substratum of attributes. The Vaiśeṣikas differ from the Jainas in their non-acceptance of the "own-nature" of the substance as its existence. Siddhasena,[95] another expounder of Jaina ontology, has defined a substance as the combination of being (the existent) with becoming (origin, stability and decay). Reality is both being and becoming, permanence and change. Siddhasena asserts that there cannot be being without becoming and *vice versa*. Lord Mahāvīra acknowledged both permanence and change. Siddhasena says that there is no substance without modification, viz., origin, decay and continuance, which are the three constituents of a substance. He also says that there is no modification in the absence of an abiding something (a substance). A substance is the possessor of both qualities (*guṇa*) and modes (*paryāya*[96]). The qualities of a substance are its permanent attributes whereas its modes are temporary attributes which are subject to origin and decay.[97] Thus substance is regarded as both the core of change or flux and the substratum of attributes. It is being (*sat*) from the standpoint of its own-nature and becoming from another standpoint since there is no substance without the triple character of origin, decay and continuity.[98] The Jaina ontology does not distinguish being from becoming. The substance, in the Jaina analysis, is both being and becoming. Thus the Jainas make a grand compromise of flux and permanence.

Nāgārjuna, the Mādhyamika Buddhist philosopher, was a strong critique of the concepts of existence (*sadbhāva*) and own-nature (*svabhāva*) of the Jainas. He said: "If X exists, it exists always; if it does not exist at time t_1, it cannot exist at any time."[99] This view of Nāgārjuna avoided the extremes of eternalism and annihilationism by following the Middle Way. While rejecting the Jaina concepts of the existence and the own-nature of the substance, Nāgārjuna and his followers laid emphasis on their notion of dependent origination (*pratityasamutpāda*). All things (beings) dependently originate according to this concept. And hence they are bound to be empty of their own-nature (own-being).[100]

Aristotle and his followers were very much concerned with the idea of the substance as the logical subject. Such a notion was probably implied in the early Vaiśeṣika doctrine of the substance. Of course, the Vaiśeṣika school was never explicit on the connection between the concept of the logical subject and that of the substance. A new term, *dharmin* (property-possessor) was coined by the later Indian logicians including the Buddhists and the Naiyāyikas. This term (*dharmin*) is the nearest analogue for the "logical subject".

An entity that has properties is a *dharmin* and its properties are its *dharmas*. According to the Naiyāyikas and Vaiśeṣikas, earth, water, jars, chairs, stones, etc. are *dharmins*, while their qualities, e.g., softness, hardness, solid, liquid, etc. are *dharmas*. For the Buddhist philosopher, there is *dharma* only without any *dharmin*. To take an example, only the quality of tangibility such as hardness (*kāṭhinya*) and touch (*sparśa*) is regarded as existent *dharma*, without any such entity called *dharmin*. This Buddhist's *dharma* without any *dharmin* is analogous to the *tattva* of the Sāṅkhyas. In fact, *tattva* (literally meaning "thatness") is a *guṇa* (literally meaning "quality"). Each of the twenty-five categories of the Sāṅkhya system is itself a *tattva* which does not possess a *tattva* (not *tattvavat*). In the Sāṅkhya school of philosophy, there is no difference between a *guṇa* (quality) and a *guṇin* (quality-possessor).

Advaita Vedānta says that the Absolute Being (Brahman) is not a *dharmin*, is not a *guṇin*, and that still It is Existence (*satya*). Is this concept logically valid? Is there any logical error in the statement, "Attributeless X exists"? Is there any logical necessity in the statement, "Whatever exists is a *dharmin* (possessor of attributes)"? Let us analyze the concept of necessary truth. All analytical propositions are necessarily true. In such statements, the subject and the predicate are identical or they carry the same meaning. "A is A", being an identity statement, is analytical. It is a tautology. "Aqua is water" is also an analytical statement, both the subject and the predicate, carrying the same meaning and referring to the same substance. All such identity statements are bound to be true. If somebody says, "A is not-A", he is certainly wrong. The statement like "2 + 2=4" is also an analytical statement. What Kant called "synthetic *a priori*" is in reality analytical. If somebody says, "2 + 2=5", he is certainly wrong. "Not both p and not-p" is a necessary truth. If someone says, "Water is not water", he is certainly wrong, since he involves in self-contradiction. "Whatever exists is a *dharmin*" does not belong to the type, "A is A", "2 + 2 = 4" or "not both p and not-p". Hence there is no logical necessity for such a statement to be true. On the other hand, no logical fallacy is involved in the statement, "Attributeless X exists". Thus, the existence of an attributeless entity is not logically unacceptable.

The existence of something does not depend on our knowledge on it. The universe had existed billions of years before the appearance of man on the Earth. Gravity was operative and apples were falling prior to the discovery of the law of gravitation by Newton. The micro-organisms had existed before the microscope was discovered. The particles and micro-particles like the proton, the neutron, the electron, the neutrino, the quarks were discovered in the twentieth century only. But these micro-constituents of matter are as old as matter itself irrespective of man's knowledge about them. When we know an entity, it exists for us. Our knowledge may be right or wrong. Hence the existence of an entity, depending purely on our knowledge, may or may not be a fact. On the other hand, an entity may exist and we may not know it. Thus, the existence of an attributeless X cannot be disproved.

It has already been said that Brahman is Consciousness. This is exactly like "A is A", which is an identity statement. A statement like "Brahman is conscious" or "Brahman has consciousness" is not correct. A second statement "Brahman is Existence" is akin to the statement "Brahman is Consciousness". Advaita Vedānta does not give any importance to a statement like "Brahman exists", analogous to the statement "The cow exists". We define a cow. Through our sense-perceptibility, we observe a cow in conformity with our definition. And so do we confirm that the cow exists. Brahman is indefinable (*anirukta*[101]), subtle (*susūkṣma*[102]), unmanifested (*avyakta*[103]) and sense-imperceptible (*agrāhya, atīndriya*[104]). Hence it is impossible to verify the truth or the falsity of the statement "Brahman exists". Any proposition on Brahman cannot be a synthetic statement and must necessarily be an analytic statement. "Whatever exists is existent (*yadasti tat satyam*)". This is an analytic statement like "A is A". Such a statement is necessarily true. "Whatever is existent is Brahman (*yatsatyaṁ tadbrahma*)". The question of proving the truth or falsity of this statement does not arise since a name is given to whatever exists. Thus the proof of Brahman lies, not in sense-perception, but in language analysis (*brahma śabdapramāṇakam*).[105]

The statement "Whatever exists is Brahman" may be refuted by a nihilist who may assert that "Nothing exists". It is impossible on the part of the nihilist to prove what he asserts since he cannot deny his own existence.

Statements like "Brahman exists" and "Brahman does not exist", do not carry any meaning since Brahman is sense-imperceptible (*sarvakaraṇāviṣayatvāt*). The verb "exists" (*asti*) and its negative form "does not exist" (*nāsti*) are inapplicable to Brahman.[106]

Knowledge may be determinate (*savikalpaka*) or indeterminate (*nirvikalpaka*).[107] Brahman, being without any distinguishing feature, and having only one aspect, without two or opposite ones, is indeterminate.[108] Hence Śaṅkara says that Existence is Consciousness and *vice versa*.

Brahman is undifferentiated (*nirviśeṣa*[109]) and homogeneous. Any Reality, in the sense used in Advaita Vedānta, is bound to be undifferentiated. Products are born with differentiation. Expenditure of energy is involved with differentiation. Any entity that is beginningless, endless, eternal and timeless, unchanging, and imperishable cannot have differentiation. An entity, devoid of differentiation, is necessarily to ever continue as one only (*eka,*[110] *kevala*[111]) non-dual (*advaya,*[112] *advaita*[113]) and without a second (*advitīya*[114]). That One never becomes many. The One is eternally One in time; It is also the same One beyond time.

Reality (Brahman) that is ever undifferentiated is bound to be partless (*akala,*[115] *niṣkala*[116]). As the Upaniṣads say, it is *ekadhaiva*[117] or a single homogeneity. Śaṅkara has interpreted this *ekadhā eva* as *vijñānaghanaikarasa*[118] or homogeneous pure intelligence. Any entity that is undifferentiated is necessarily devoid of organs (*niravayava*[119]). For this reason, Brahman does not decay and remains as such.

The *Kaṭhopaniṣad* declares: "There is no diversity and multiplicity whatsoever (*neha nānāsti kiñcana*[120])". Where nothing else is seen, nothing else is heard, nothing else is recognized, there the only being is great and infinite (*Bhūmā*). This *Bhūmā* is immortal. On the other hand, the mortal world of plurality, of names and forms, empirically exists in a relative condition where multiplicity is seen, heard and recognized.[121] The *Bhūmā* exists alone without diversity and with none second to it. It is below and above; It is behind and in front; It is in the South and the North; It is in the East and the West. It is all this.[122] Similar is the language used in the *Muṇḍaka Upaniṣad*.[123] "In front is Brahman; behind is Brahman.

It is to the right and to the left. It spreads forth upwards and downwards. Brahman, indeed, is this universe." Śaṅkara[124] says that this pluralistic universe has no separate existence apart from the Person (Brahman). The seeming diversity is a homogeneous unit in reality. Brahman is above the sky, beneath the Earth and between these two. It is the past, the present and the future.[125] It is spread out through space, spread out through time. It is beyond space and time. Thus Brahman is all-pervasive (*sarvagata,*[126] *sarvavyāpī,*[127] *vibhu,*[128] *paribhu,*[129] *vyāptam,*[130] *tatam*[131]). In the Upaniṣadic language, It is *otaḥ protaḥ.*[132] It is all.[133]

Brahman is devoid of distinguishing characteristics (*aliṅga*[134]). It has no qualifying or quantifying mark. It is *alakṣaṇa*[135] (devoid of marks, symptoms). In the language of Śaṅkara, It is devoid of all empirical attributes (*sarvasaṁsāra-dharma-varjitaḥ*[136]) and devoid of all functions, changes and properties (*sarva-kārya-dharmātītaḥ*[137]). It does not attach itself to anything, it is unattached (*asaṅga*[138]). Being one alone, it is non-relational (*asambandha*[139]). It is without sound, without touch, without form, without taste, without odour, without decay, without beginning and without end.[140] Such an entity cannot be perceived through our senses. It is not an object[141] (*viṣaya*); It has no object; or in other words, It is objectless (*nirviṣaya*[142]). Being one alone without a second, it has no object to be perceived or to be acted upon. Neither is it a subject (*viṣayī*). It is self-contradictory to say that a non-functional entity is the doer of any action, the subject of any object and the enjoyer (*bhoktā*) of anything enjoyed (*bhogya*). It is devoid of the subject-object duality.[143]

Brahman is sense-imperceptible. Being devoid of form (*rūpa*), sound (*śabda*), odour (*gandha*), taste (*rasa*) and touch (*sparśa*), it cannot be perceived through the five receptor organs (*indriyas*), viz., the visual, the auditory, the olfactory, the gustatory and the tactile organs. Such an entity, unable to be grasped by the senses, is unthinkable (*acintya*[144]). No concept of Brahman can be formed in the mind.

No logic can be applicable to Brahman. That which is sense-imperceptible and unthinkable cannot be expressed by any language. We cannot use any synthetic proposition for Brahman. Where language is inapplicable, there logic has no relevance. Hence Brahman cannot be logically derived through the process of induction or deduction.[145]

According to Advaita Vedānta, Brahman is the knower and everything is known by it. It is impossible to know such a knower. The *Bṛhadāraṇyaka Upaniṣad* says: "For where there were duality, there one would smell another, see another, hear another, speak to another, think of another, understand another. Where, verily, everything has become the Self (absolute Brahman), whom and by what should one smell, whom and by what should one see, whom and by what should one hear, to whom and by what should one speak, on whom and by what should one think, whom and by what should one understand? By what, my dear, should one know the knower?"[146] The same idea is echoed in the same Upaniṣad elsewhere. "For where there were duality, there one would see the other, smell the other, taste the other, speak to the other, hear the other, think of the other, touch the other, know the other. But where everything has become the Self (absolute Brahman), whom and by what should one see, whom and by what should one smell, whom and by what should one taste, to whom and by what should one speak, whom and by what should one hear, of whom and by what should one think, whom and by what should one touch, whom and by what should one know? By what should one know him by whom all this is known? That self is "not this, not this". He is ungraspable for He cannot be grasped. He is indestructible for He cannot be destroyed. He is unattached for He does not attach Himself. He is unfettered, He does not suffer, He is uninjured. Indeed, by what would one know the knower?"[147]

Everything is known through Brahman. But it itself cannot be grasped by our senses. "You cannot see the seer of seeing; you cannot hear the hearer of hearing; you cannot think of the thinker of thinking; you cannot understand the understander of understanding."[148] The self inside, the inner controller (*antaryāmī*) is unperceived, but is the perceiver. "He is unseen but is the seer; he is unheard but is the hearer; he is unperceived but is the perceiver; he is not thought of but is the thinker. There is no other seer but he; there is no other hearer but he; there is no other perceiver but he; there is no other thinker but he."[149]

The omniscient Self knows everything; but we cannot know anything about it. "By the self alone, one perceives form (*rūpa*), taste (*rasa*), smell (*gandha*), sounds (*śabdān*), touches (*sparśān*) and coital pleasures (*maithunān*)."[150] While commenting on this, Śaṅkara says: "Everything indeed is cognized by the Self, but nothing remains to be unknown to Him who is omniscient."[151] The *Kena Upaniṣad* says: "Brahman is the ear of the ear, the mind of the mind, the speech of the speech, the *prāṇa* (viton) of the *prāṇa*, the eye of the eye."[152] "There the eye goes not, the speech goes not, nor the mind. We know not; we understand not. How can one teach this?"[153] "That which is not expressed through speech but that by which speech is expressed; that which is not thought of by the mind but that by which the mind thinks; that which is not seen by the eyes but that by which the eyes see; that which is not heard by the ears but that by which the ears hear; that which is not vitalized by the *prāṇa* (viton) but that by which the *prāṇa* is vitalized; that, verily, know thou, is Brahman and not what (people) here adore."[154] "The sun shines not there, nor the moon and stars. These lightnings shine not (there). Then where could this fire be? Everything shines by the reflection of the shining that. His shining illumines all this."[155] Thus the scriptures declare that our senses and mind function only through that and everything in the world is illumined by that. That being the fact, we cannot perceive that through our senses, cannot think of that through our mind and there is no way to throw light on that through which all illuminations are possible.

Brahman is without dimensions (*amātra*[156]), without space (*anākāśa*[157]), without time (*akāla*[158]), without inside (*anantara*[159]) and without outside (*abāhya*[160]). Such an entity is necessarily indeterminable (*aprameya*[161]). The question of measuring an entity that is spaceless, timeless, dimensionless and without inside and outside does not arise at all. Gauḍapāda[162] says that the *amātra* (without dimensions) Brahman is *anantamātra* (one with endless dimensions). The word *ananta* which is translated as "infinite" or "unlimited" has mathematical significance only, but no ontological significance. The universe (*jagat*) is a finite thing even though it is too vast. Anything that has a beginning and an end and anything that is a product is bound to be finite. The words "finite" and "infinite" are meaningless when applied to Brahman that is dimensionless and immeasurable. Any dimension can be measured and this measurement has an end. If something is without dimensions, it has to be endless (*ananta*).

Here a digression is necessary for a brief discussion on the epistemology of Vedānta in contrast to those of some other systems. How do we get knowledge about the external world? How do we get knowledge about Brahman? Before we discuss the second question, answer to the first question may be sought for.

That Śaṅkara is an illusionist is a popular notion. It is alleged that he does not recognize the existence of the world. Such an allegation is baseless. For him, Brahman is absolute truth (*pāramārthika satya*) and the world (*jagat*) is an empirical truth (*vyāvahārika satya*).

The *Brahma-Sūtra* asserts the existence of an external object-entity. It says: "There is no absence, because of perception" (*nābhāva upalabdheḥ*[163]). While interpreting this aphorism, Śaṅkara says that we cannot deny the existence of an external object which is actually perceived (*upalabhyate hi pratipratyaṁ bāhyo'rthaḥ.....na ca upalabhyamānasyaivābhāvo bhavitumarhati*[164]). He does not agree with the Buddhistic school of Vijñānavāda which reduces all things to mere ideas. However, he has not specified the exact mechanism of the perception of the external object-entity. The post-Śaṅkarite Advaita Vedāntists have described the mechanism of perception in the following manner. Brahman is pure Consciousness unmodifiable and self-manifest. It is not a knower, a doer and an enjoyer or a sufferer. The *jīva* (individual self) becomes a knower, a doer, an enjoyer or a sufferer due to the superimposition of egoism (*ahaṅkāra*)—a limiting adjunct (*upādhi*)—on it. The internal organ (*antaḥkaraṇa*), jointly comprising *buddhi* (*mahat* or intellect), *ahaṅkāra* and *manas* (mind), issues out through a sense-organ to an object and is modified into its form. The self (*jīva*) is reflected in the mental mode, erroneously identifies itself with the mode and apprehends an external object. This erroneous identification is possible due to superimposition.

In the Yoga system of Patañjali, perception is defined as that source-of-valid-ideas (which) arises as a modification of the inner-organ when the mind-stuff has been affected by some external thing through the channel of the sense-organs.[165] The modification of the mind or the mental mode (*citta-vṛtti*) itself cannot be the cognizer. The self (individual *jīva*) is the real cognizer. It is of the nature of intelligence. It illumines the *citta-vṛtti*. It is reflected in *buddhi*. This reflection is the cause of the *citta-vṛtti* becoming illumined. The *jīva* is falsely identified with its own reflection in *buddhi*. Thus, in the act of perception, the cognizer is the *jīva*, the instrument of cognition is the *antaḥkaraṇa* and the external object is the cognized entity. The Yoga system accepts the self-luminosity of the *puruṣa* (self).

According to Vedānta, the five sense-organs are insentient. They cannot cognize anything. Divested of the light of the self that is pure Consciousness, the different sense-organs are like wood or clods of earth (*svataḥ kāṣṭha-loṣṭa-samāni hi tāni caitanyātma-jyotiś-śūnyāni*[166]). On the other hand, Brahman is self-illuminated (*svayaṁjyotiḥ*[167]). It is illumined by Its own illumination (*svena bhāsā, svena jyotiṣā prasvapiti, atrāyaṁ puruṣaḥ svayaṁ-jyotir bhavati*[168]).

The Yogācāra Vijñānavāda of Buddhistic philosophy is a system of subjective idealism in contrast to the absolute idealism of Śaṅkara. There is no existence of the external world for the Vijñānavādin. But, in spite of the negation of the external world, the Vijñānavādin has a theory of perception. This theory is as follows: The apparent, external object is an unreal appearance (*saṁvṛta satya*). The only reality is a cognition (*citta*, synonymous with *manas* or mind, *vijñāna* or cognition, and *vijñapti* or apprehension). What is perceived as an external object is, in reality, a mere cognition. The cognition manifests itself. It is self-aware (*svasaṁvedya*). It does not need any other cognition to manifest itself. It appears, stays for a moment and disappears. Each momentary cognition is preceded and succeeded by other cognitions. These cognitions are related to one another, thus forming a stream of consciousness (*santāna*). Every individual is nothing but a stream of consciousness. The psychic continuum of a common individual is tainted with a mass of psychical dispositions (*vāsanā*) and interwoven with mental constructs (*kalpanā*). In the psychic continuum of an ordinary individual, there are two parallel streams of cognitions, not unrelated to each other, not different from the mind or cognition, and being nothing but cognitions. Out of the two series, the *ālayavijñāna* is a core of persisting stream of self-cognitions, characterized by ego-consciousness. The second series of object-cognitions is called *pravṛttivijñāna*. Consequent to the maturescence of psychical dispositions (*vāsanāparipāka*), object cognitions (*pravṛttivijñāna*) spring from self-cognitions (*ālayavijñāna*). Thus, the external objects that do not really exist are projected and presented by the mind. Such presentations do not owe to the external objects.

The *ālayavijñāna* is what is called *citta* (mind) by the Vijñānavādin. The manifold presentations (*pravṛttivijñāna*) are transformations of the *citta*. The internal mind or the stream of self-cognitions (*ālayavijñāna*) is transformed into manifold object-cognitions, thus subjective cognitions being transformed into objective presentations. Although object-cognitions appear to be distinct from self-cognitions, in reality, they are identical. With the destruction of the *avidyā* with psychical dispositions, there emerges a pure consciousness, completely devoid of egoism and free from subject-object distinction.

While refuting the claims of the Yogācāra Vijñānavādins on their doctrine of subjective idealism, Śaṅkara has interpreted the related aphorism[169] of the *Brahma-Sūtra* and has successfully adduced evidences in favour of the existence of an external world.

George Berkeley (1685-1753) was an Irish Bishop and philosopher who was a subjective idealist. He developed an idealist metaphysics, designed as a metaphysical defence of the Christian faith. For him, reality is made up of ideas, finite spirits and an infinite spirit. He identified being with perception ("to be is to be perceived", "*esse est percipi*"). He claimed that nothing material exists. He called his view "immaterialism". He identified the external world with our perceptions. He did not think of the existence of things outside human perceptions. Such a doctrine had to lead to solipsism.

David Hume (1711-76) was a British philosopher who developed the doctrine of sensationalism. He held that experience is composed of impressions and ideas, the latter being copies of impressions. Ideas can be traced to impressions, which, in turn, cannot be traced to their source. The common man assumes that impressions originate from an external world; but Hume asserts that we cannot know this from experience. In his opinion, we cannot demonstrate by any arguments that our perceptions are evoked by external objects. The scepticism of Hume led to agnosticism.

Immanuel Kant (1724-1804), the German philosopher, developed the doctrine of transcendental idealism. He pictured the world as divided into noumena (things-in-themselves) and phenomena. The noumenon exists objectively but cannot be known by us. The phenomena arise as a result of the ordering of the empirical materials by means of our subjective forms of time and space. To the raw data of sensation we contribute the forms of space and time. Kant holds that space is the form of the external sense, and time the form of the internal sense. Anything which is not in space and time is not experienced by us, and yet we never experience space or time. Hence space and time in which we order phenomena do not come from sensation but from ourselves. In the opinion of Kant, time and space, the laws of nature and causality do not reflect objective natural processes; these are subjective categories, which are *a priori*, innate in man. They precede our experience and play a decisive role in determining the picture of the world. We cannot go beyond our subjective experience, stresses Kant, because we immediately fall into antinomies and irresolvable contradictions.

Albert Einstein (1879-1955), the famous twentieth-century philosopher-scientist, criticized the subjective idealism of Berkeley for its reduction of the external world to perceptions. He held firmly to the idea that the world around man exists objectively, independent of his consciousness. He rejected the sensationalism of Hume.

In principle, the Yoga theory of knowledge and Śaṅkara's theory of knowledge would be acceptable to modern science. Śaṅkara has not subscribed to the view of the mind moving to the external object and taking the form of the latter. In the modern science of physiology, the first thing that happens in the process is the rise of a stimulus from the external object-entity. A few examples may be taken to illustrate the functions of the visual, auditory, olfactory, gustatory and tactile receptor organs.

For our cognition, a stimulus-generating substance, a stimulus-receptor, an impulse-transmission line, an impulse-receiving nucleus and a concept-forming agent are necessary. The lastly named factor, viz., a concept-forming agent, is not yet recognized by science. But a good deal of scientific knowledge is available with us regarding the functioning of the other factors.

The stimulus-generating substance may be in the body or outside it and it may be a chemical like the sugar (taste-stimulus-generating substance) or a volatile chemical in an odoriferous substance. It may be a physical agent like light to produce vision-stimulus or like sound-wave to produce auditory stimulus.

The stimulus-receptor is present in the sense-organ, viz., eye, ear, nose, mouth and skin. Once a stimulus is generated, it is transmitted through the fibres of a nerve in the form of an impulse which is electrical in nature. The impulse is received by some nuclei (nucleus is a group of nerve cells) in the brain. The brain has two cerebral hemispheres. Each hemisphere has four lobes, viz., the frontal lobe (for motor activity through the efferent nerve fibres), the parietal lobe (for receiving sensations through the afferent nerve fibres from all parts of the body), the temporal lobe (for receiving auditory impulse) and the occipital lobe (for receiving visual impulses). In addition, the olfactory bulb in the rhinencephalon receives the olfactory impulses. Corresponding to the five types of sense-organs, there are five loci in the brain to receive the external stimuli and interpret the message in the form of a cognition. In addition, there are collateral nerve-fibres that connect all cognitive areas in the brain for information and co-ordination.

One sees a red rose. The flower absorbs all the rays of light except the one corresponding to the red vision. There is nothing like red in the light. It is a narrow band of specific wavelengths of the electromagnetic wave. When light rays of certain wavelength fall on the retina of the eye, the cones, responsible for colour vision and located in the retina, respond to it. A nerve-impulse is generated and transmitted through the fibres of the optic nerve to the visual area of the occipital lobe of the cerebral cortex. There are specific cone areas in the retina for specific wavelengths of light. There are also specific nuclei in specific areas of the occipital lobe for specific wavelengths of light. Different nerve-fibres transmit impulses to different visual areas in the occipital lobe. One specific area is stimulated and thus we experience the red colour. We may see a black, a white, a yellow or a blue flower, if other specific areas of the occipital lobe receive the impulse which is electrical in nature. The colours are created in our brain. But there is no colour as such in the coloured flower.

One listens to the melodious tunes of the violin. The violin-string vibrates and consequently the air in contact vibrates with certain frequency and amplitude. The sound-wave reaches the external, middle and internal ears. There is an organ of Corti in the internal ear. This organ has a basilar membrane consisting of fibres. Different areas of the basilar membrane are specific to different frequencies of sound. A nerve-impulse is generated here. The impulse which is electrical in nature is transmitted through the fibres of the cochlear nerve which goes to the auditory area of the cerebral cortex in the temporal lobe. The auditory area has distinct sub-areas for specific frequencies of sound. Depending on the area stimulated, one experiences the sweet melodies of a music, or the frightening harshness of a thunder, or any other type of sound.

One smells the fragrance of sandal-paste. A volatile chemical emanates from the sandal-paste and reaches the internal nose. The olfactory glands present in the mucous membrane of the internal nose secrete mucus that dissolves the odoriferous chemical. The dissolved chemical stimulates the rèceptor cells, which are specific for specific types of odoriferous chemicals. A nerve-impulse is generated and transmitted through the olfactory nerve (the first cranial nerve) to reach the olfactory bulb of the rhinencephalon located in the anterior and ventral part of the cerebral hemispheres. Corresponding to specific odours, there are specific areas in the olfactory bulb. Analyzing the whole thing of olfacation, we come to know that the foul and nauseating smell of the faeces does not reside as such in the faeces itself and that the enchanting aroma of a sweet-smelling flower does not stay as such in the flower itself. The odour, pleasant or unpleasant, is created by our brain. In the object which is smelt, there are odoriferous chemicals which are responsible for generating an odour-stimulus in the internal nose.

The cane-sugar which is known as sucrose in chemistry is sweet to us. The quinine is bitter to us. The raw guava is astringent in taste. The tamarind is sour. Why is this difference in taste? Chemicals present in the thing that is eaten are responsible for generating stimuli in our taste-buds. There are different types of taste-buds in the mouth. The anterior two-thirds (the dorsal and lateral parts) of the tongue contain fungiform papillae. The posterior one-third of the tongue contains circumvallete papillae and foliate papillae. These are the taste-buds on the tongue. There are also taste-buds on the root of the soft palate. The taste-buds are specific for different types of taste. The specific chemical present in the thing that is eaten stimulates the specific taste-bud, and, as a result, an impulse is created. The nerve-impulse, thus created, is electrical in nature. The taste-impulse is transmitted to the brain through three different nerves. The facial nerve and the glossopharyngial nerve transmit the impulses from the anterior two-thirds and the posterior one-third of the tongue, respectively. The vagus nerve transmits the impulses from the root of the soft palate. These impulses reach the taste areas containing groups of nerve cells (nuclei) located in the parietal lobe of the two cerebral hemispheres. These cortical areas create the sensation of taste. Thus there is nothing like sweetness as such in the sugar. Both sugar and saccharin which are chemically unrelated generate stimuli in the taste-bud to create the sensation of sweetness in the cortex of the brain.

Different objects, by coming in contact with the skin, generate stimuli in the skin-receptors. There are different types of receptors in the skin. These are tactile receptors of different types for touch, heat receptor, cold receptor and pain receptor located in the microstructure of the skin. Nerve-impulses which are electrical in nature are generated and transmitted through different nerves to the central nervous system. The nerve that innervates the respective part of the skin carries the impulse to the brain either directly or through the spinal cord. With reference to the coital pleasure, the receptors (genital corpuscles) are present in the glans penis of the male; the free nerve-endings in the vestibule of the female genitalia function as receptors. All these sensations from the skin and the genitals are received by specific areas of the parietal lobe of the two cerebral hemispheres. These cortical areas create the tactile sensations, thermal sensations and the sensations of pleasure or pain. As such, there is really nothing like hotness in the boiling water, coldness in the ice and pleasure-sensation in a kiss. The external objects, by coming in contact with the skin, serve as sources of stimuli. The nerve-impulse which is electrical in nature has no intrinsic merit or demerit of pleasure and pain. The sensation which one experiences is created by some nerve cells in the cortex.

Science has not yet discovered what happens in the cerebral centres. How a concept is generated in the brain, what is the nature of a concept, what is the exact nature of experience, who is the experiencer or perceiver, all these questions have not been answered by science. The brain, the nerve-fibre in the brain, the nerve-cells in the brain, the neurons and the synapses are all matter, insentient matter. How is consciousness generated out of insentience? This is a basic question and a controversial issue. Is the brain equated with the mind? This is also a controversial issue. Advaita Vedānta differentiates the subtle body (*sūkṣma śarīra*) from the gross body (*sthūla śarīra*). The inner organ (*antaḥkaraṇa*), comprising *buddhi* or intellect, *manas* or mind and *ahaṁkāra* or ego, is the subtle body. This whole thing is one only with three functional variants. What is called *citta* in Pātañjala Yoga is the same as the inner organ, otherwise grossly termed as the mind in the Indian system. The mind is different from the brain which is part of the gross body. The brain is the instrument of the mind in man and animals with brains. In animals without brains, in animals without nervous system and in unicellular organisms like protozoa, bacteria and viruses, the non-neural body and the cellular protoplasm do function as the instrument of the mind. The brain-centres function in association with the mind that generates the concept. But, in Indian philosophy and psychology, the mind, being the principal component of the subtle body (*sūkṣma śarīra*), is material and insentient.[170] The mind itself is unconscious. The self which is pure Consciousness is reflected in the inner organ which is thus illumined.[171] The self erroneously identifies itself with its own reflection in the inner organ due to superimposition and so becomes the knower, the experiencer, the perceiver, the enjoyer and the sufferer. The apparent bondage of the self and the repeated rebirths are due to the impressions (*saṁskāra*) laid on the mind (*manas* or *antaḥkaraṇa*).[172] Through the functioning of the mind or the internal organ, the self behaves as if it is the doer or the enjoyer (*ātmanaḥ kartṛtvaṁ bhoktṛtvaṁ ca sati manasi nānyatheti*[173]).

Śaṅkara, the great Advaita-Vedāntin, states that the world we perceive exists, although not absolutely but empirically. We get knowledge on the external world through our five senses and our mind. But, is our knowledge true? Does our knowledge on the external world exactly correspond to what it really is? This question cannot be answered positively or negatively.

This finishes the discussion on our knowledge of the external world. The second question which has already been raised needs an answer. Can we cognize Brahman? Is It knowable or unknowable? Even if it is unknowable, is it realizable?

Brahman, being attributeless and functionless, cannot be grasped by our senses. It, being objectless (*aviṣaya*), is not related to anything (*sambandhāgrahaṇa*). Objects are known through the senses, but not Brahman (*svabhāvato viṣayaviṣayānīndriyāṇi, na brahmaviṣayāṇi*). Options depend on human intellection, whereas the valid knowledge of the true nature of a thing is not dependent on human intellection. It is dependent on the thing itself (*vikalpanāstu puruṣabuddhyapekṣāḥ; na vastuyāthātmyajñānaṁ puruṣabuddhyapekṣaṁ vastutantrameva tat).*[174]

Brahman is unknowable (*avijñeya*[175]). When Advaita Vedānta says, "Brahman is unknowable," it means thereby, "Brahman is sense-imperceptible". The same Vedānta recommends to know Brahman (*athāto brahma-jijñāsā;*[176] *āvṛttirasakṛdupadeśāt;*[177] *satyaṁ tveva vijijñāsitavyam;*[178] *tadanveṣṭavyaṁ, tad vāva vijijñāsitavyam;*[179] *so'nveṣṭavyaḥ sa vijijñāsitavyaḥ;*[180] *tameva dhīro vijñāya prajñāṁ kurvīta;*[181] *tameva viditvātimṛtyumeti*[182]). It is held by the Vedāntists that Brahman is unthinkable (*acintya*), because of the fact that it cannot be grasped by the senses.[183] But, at the same time, the scriptures declare, "Only by the mind is it to be perceived".[184] Brahman is to be realized intuitively and only by knowing Brahman everything is known. This idea has been expressed in the *Bṛahadāraṇyaka Upaniṣad* in a very forceful way. "Verily, O Maitreyi, it is the Self that should be seen, heard of, reflected on and meditated upon. Verily, by seeing, hearing, thinking and understanding the self, all this is known".[185] While interpreting the *Chāndogya Upaniṣad*[186] Śaṅkara gives a meaning to the word "*vijijñāsitavyam* (should be known)". He means "*sākṣātkaraṇīyam* (should be directly apprehended). Any object is known through the mediation of the senses. Brahman cannot be known through the senses and hence is unknowable (*avijñeya*). On the other hand, Brahman is knowable (*vijñeya*[187]) since no mediation is necessary for the realization (*svānubhava*) of Brahman. It is realized directly (*sākṣāt*), without any mediation (*aparokṣāt*[188]). It is the Self directly realized (*pratyagātman*[189]). One who has direct apprehension of Brahman identifies one's self (*jīva*) with the Self (Brahman). Then only does one understand the *mahāvākyas* (the great dicta) —"*ahaṁ brahmāsmi*"[190] (I am Brahman), "*prajñānaṁ brahma*"[191] (Consciousness is Brahman), "*ayamātmā brahma*"[192] (This self is Brahman), "*tattvamasi*"[193] (That thou art). He gets the experience that he is Brahman and utters inside, "*so'ham*" (He is I).

Some thinkers are opposed to the idea of getting knowledge directly, without the mediation of our senses. In this connection, the opinion of Katz may be quoted here:

> There are no pure (i.e., unmediated) experiences. Neither mystical experiences nor more ordinary forms of experience give any indication or any grounds for believing that they are

> unmediated. That is to say, all experience is processed through, organized by and makes it available to us in extremely complex epistemological ways. The notion of unmediated experience seems, if not self-contradictory, at best empty.[194]

There is utter confusion in the understanding of the meaning of "immediate knowledge", in its true perspective, by the philosophers who reject it. Śaṅkara's *sākṣātkaraṇa* (direct experience) or *aparokṣānubhūti* (immediate experience) refers to Brahman only, without any relevance to anything of the empirical world. He himself admits that the existence or non-existence of any empirical object can be known through sense-experience only, and that Brahman, being too subtle and sense-imperceptible, cannot be known through the senses. He further states that the question of the verification of the existence or the non-existence of Brahman is meaningless since Brahman is indefinable and sense-imperceptible. But, he argues, the empirical (*vyāvahārika*) world does not and cannot independently exist and its existence is illusory in the analogy of the appearance of a snake in the locus of a rope; and, if the empirical world is denied in the absolute sense, something else must be posited in order to avoid nihilism. The empirical existence is dependent upon the real existence (*pāramārthika satya*). If both the former and the latter are denied, we end in nothing (*śūnya* or nihil). And hence we have no alternative other than accepting an Absolute Being (*pāramārthika sattā*) which is Brahman.

Śaṅkara further asserts that everybody experiences *ahamasmi* (I am) and that nobody ever says *nāhamasmi* (I am not). The word 'self' has the same meaning as that of *ātmā* which is identical to the Self that is Brahman.

We acquire empirical knowledge about the external world through our senses only. But intuitional knowledge is not the same as empirical knowledge. The philosopher could think of the atom long before it was discovered in science. It was also not discovered in science by any method of direct perception. A fundamental scientist gets a flash of an idea; he makes a null hypothesis; by experimentation he tries to nullify the null hypothesis in order to prove his hypothesis. Hence, it is not a fact that the scientist does not make use of intuitional knowledge. It is also a fact that all scientific knowledge is not derived from experimentation; neither is the knowledge always confirmed by experimental verification. What a theoretical physicist claims to be true is based on mathematical deductions. If the rational knowledge explains some phenomena harmoniously, coherently and satisfactorily without self-contradiction and without contradiction of other proven knowledge, it is accepted as valid. Whether it is mathematics, philosophy, science, or any field of intellectuality, intuition plays a key role in the genesis of ideas. It is an oversimplification to say that *all* the knowledge of mankind is empirical only, acquired through sense-perceptions, and that intuition and rationality are totally non-functional in the genesis of knowledge.

The eighteenth-century Irish philosopher Bishop Berkeley analyzed "existence" in terms of two desiderata: (1) That which is perceived exists (*esse est percipi*). (2) That which perceives exists (*esse est percipere*). The former holds for physical objects that can only be known. The latter is true for human beings, spiritual things, such as angels, and God, collectively called by Berkeley as "spirits". A tree exists as long as a person perceives it. It still exists in the absence of a perceiving person or a finite mind since an infinite mind (God) perceives it. What we do perceive, (except, of course, our imaginations, dreams and hallucinations), said Berkeley, cannot be caused by our own minds, but are created by an infinite mind. He felt the necessity of the existence of an infinite mind to explain the existence of both of the perceived and the unperceived world.

Berkeley was a metaphysician. His metaphysics has little resemblance with that of Śaṅkara. The purpose of mentioning Berkeley's philosophy here is to emphasize his two concepts "to exist is to be perceived" (*esse est percipi*) or "to exist is to perceive" (*esse est percipere*). Both these concepts do not withstand analytical scrutiny.[195]

Immanuel Kant, in the eighteenth century, rejected metaphysics on the ground that one could not have knowledge beyond experience. He, however, said that we could know only the phenomena through our experiential knowledge and that the noumena (things-in-themselves) could not be known.

In the twentieth century, the Logical Positivists rejected metaphysics by their theory of meaning. In their opinion, a proposition is meaningful if and only if its truth or falsity is verifiable. Their

Principle of Verifiability declared all metaphysical statements as nonsense.

Wittgenstein combined many of the features of Kant and of the Verificationists in his approach to metaphysics. Kant recognized the limits of thought by approaching them through the medium of ideas and judgements, whereas Wittgenstein did it through words and sentences. Both of them insisted that valid statements could not be made beyond the area of experience. The early Wittgenstein, in his "picture theory" of meaning, dismissed metaphysics and, indeed, all philosophy, including his own, on the ground that it attempts the impossible task of saying what can only be shown; or, in other words, it tries to answer how a picture is related to what it pictures, or how language is related to the world. The "picture theory" of meaning, given in the *Tractatus* (1921), waned until Wittgenstein expressed his view of verificationism in his *Philosophical Remarks* of 1930. A sentence in this work purported to express: A proposition has a meaning only if a method of verifying the proposition is known. In other words, the meaning of a proposition is identified with its method of verification. Wittgenstein, in his later work of *Philosophical Investigations* of 1945-49, gave a theory which equated the meaning of a word with its use ("The meaning of a word is its use in the language" became the slogan). In spite of all these evolutionary changes in the philosophy of Wittgenstein, he did realize the existence of something that is inexpressible. It was his emphasis that it is impossible to express the inexpressible and that what can be shown cannot be said. Similarly, Kant did not deny the existence of the noumena, the things-in-themselves, which cannot be known but only thought of.

While prohibiting the use of language for the inexpressible, Wittgenstein has said: "What *can* be shown, *cannot* be said".[196] Śaṅkara's statement, "*tallakṣyate, na tūcyate*"[197] (That *can* be shown, but *cannot* be said), may be compared with what Wittgenstein has said.

The Upaniṣads have proscribed the use of language for Brahman. Even if one has direct apprehension of Brahman, one cannot describe it in any language. In this connection Śaṅkara[198] has said: All words used in a sentence are meant to convey sense to the listener by means of their link with notions of class (*jāti*), actions (*kriyā*), attributes (*guṇa*) and relations (*sambandha*). We describe genera like "cow", "horse", etc. We describe actions like "cooking", "reading", etc. We describe qualities like "white", "black", etc. We describe relations like "possessor of wealth", "possessor of cows", "inside", "outside", "below", "above", "with", "without", etc. Brahman has no genus, no attributes and no actions. Being one alone, it has no relations. All words would fail to describe the non-dual, objectless and self-existing Brahman. Hence says the *Taittirīya Upaniṣad*, "Whence words recoil (*yato vāco nivartante aprāpya manasā saha*[199])"

The seer vainly describes the indescribable Brahman in negative language. "Brahman is not gross, not subtle, not short, not long, not glowing hot, not greasy and smoothing, not shadow, not darkness, not air, not space, unattached, without taste, without smell, without eyes, without ears, without speech, without mind, without radiance, without *prāṇa* (vitalizing principle or viton), without a mouth, without dimensions, without inside and without outside."[200] It is a strong, natural urge of man to describe everything he can conceive of. The seer expresses the inexpressible in negative language and thereby he confesses that he cannot describe the indescribable. The seer of the *Muṇḍaka Upaniṣad*[201] also uses negative language in describing Brahman.

Contradictory language is also used for the description of the indescribable Brahman. "It is vast, subtler than the subtle, farther than the far and yet here near at hand".[202] "The unmoving Brahman is swifter than the mind. It outstrips those who run, although it itself stands still. It moves and moves not. It is far and near. It is inside and outside all this."[203] The *Bhagavadgītā* also echoes the same idea: "It is both outside and inside beings. It is what moves not and what moves. It is far off as well as near".[204] The *Kaṭhopaniṣad*[205] says: Brahman is smaller than the smallest and bigger than the biggest. While sitting, it moves far; while lying, it goes everywhere; it rejoices and rejoices not.[206] By these contradictory predicates, the Upaniṣadic seer conveys the idea of the impossibility of conceiving Brahman through empirical determinations and so Śaṅkara says that the *Ātman* is *viruddhadharmavān*[207] (with contradictory characteristics).

There is no way to describe Brahman in terms of other objects. The disciple repeatedly puts questions to his preceptor seer: "Is Brahman this" ("this" representing an object, X, Y, Z, etc.)? The preceptor repeatedly answers, "not this" (*neti*). [208] Such an answer is sometimes misunderstood as nihilistic. This is, however, a wrong interpretation. Vedānta recognizes the "full" (*pūrṇa*) and discards the "empty" or "void" (*śūnya*). The significance of the expression *neti* lies in "*pararūpapratiṣedha*"[209] (the negation of the form of the other object).

A conversation between a preceptor (Bādhva) and his disciple (Bāṣkali), narrated in the Vedic texts, may be cited here. Bāṣkali said, "O revered Sir, please teach me Brahman". Bādhva remained silent. The pupil repeated the question a second and a third time. Then the preceptor replied: "You do not comprehend, my dear. I have already spoken. This Self is Quiescence (*upaśānto' yamātmā*)".[210] Let us compare this with the last sentence given in the *Tractatus* by Wittgenstein, "What we cannot speak about we must pass over in silence".[211]

The non-dual (*advaita*[212]) Brahman is without parts (*akala*,[213] *niṣkala*,[214] *niravayava*[215]). It is unbroken (*akhaṇḍa*[216]). It is a whole (*kṛtsna*[217]) which is a continuum with homogeneity, without any heterogeneity at all. Anything that is to be divided and subdivided, to be transformed into products and to be differentiated must have a beginning and an end too. Such an entity cannot be eternal, since all these processes involve the expenditure of energy and the concomitant decay. Śaṅkara[218] puts forward arguments against the partial or the complete transformation of Brahman into the world.

That Brahman is non-dual and there is nothing second to it is the central theme of Advaita Vedānta. The topic of the differentiation of Brahman and its partial or complete transformation into the world is also outrightly rejected by this system of philosophy. At the same time, this system accepts the empirical existence of the world. How does it do it without the involvement of self-contradiction? Śaṅkara refutes the charge of self-contradiction by explaining the empirical existence of the world by the imagination of the multiple forms of the world through Nescience (*avidyākalpitarūpabhedābhyupagamāt*).[219] The world-appearance (*jagadavabhāsa*) is likened to the magic show performed by a magician whose own nature is not changed thereby, or alternately the dream appearances experienced by a person without any change of his own nature. And so does the *Brahma-Sūtra* say: **"Because the diverse kinds (appear) thus in the Self" (*ātmani caivaṁ vicitrāśca hi*[220]).** Thus, when considered in the absolute (*pāramārthika*) sense, there is Brahman alone and nothing else; and, when considered in the empirical sense, both non-duality and multiplicity are equally true (*ata ekatvaṁ nānātvaṁ cobhayamapi satyameva*[221]).

Brahman is the substratum (*adhiṣṭhāna* or *ādhāra*)[222] of the whole universe with its multiplicity. Like a multi-storeyed building standing on a rock-bottom, that functions as the foundation of the superstructure, Brahman is the foundation of the phenomenal universe. The fourth state of existence, viz., Turīya, unassociated with any limiting adjunct (*upādhi*), is the substratum of everything and all.[223] This foundation (*ādhāra*) is pure Consciousness (*Caitanya*). Brahman and the world-appearance are not interdependent. The world, for its existence, is wholly dependent on Brahman that is self-existent and self-sufficient, without dependence on the world or anything else.[224]

On the basis of the non-duality of Brahman, the world-appearance as magical or dream phenomena engendered due to Nescience (*avidyā*) and the dependence of the phenomenal world on Brahman alone, that itself is self-existent and self-sufficient, the Upaniṣadic seers, instead of negating the world, affirmatively declare as follows: "Self alone is all this (*ātmaivedaṁ sarvam*[225])"; "This all verily is Brahman (*sarvaṁ khalvidaṁ brahma*[226])"; "Brahman alone is this universe, the greatest (*brahmaivedaṁ viśvamidaṁ variṣṭham*[227])"; "This all is the Self (*idaṁ sarvaṁ yadayamātmā*[228]);" This is immortal, this is Brahman, this is all (*idamamṛtamidaṁ brahma idaṁ sarvam*[229])"; "All this pertains to the Self (*aitadātmyamidaṁ sarvam*[230])"

Māyā

Māyā is the power (*śakti*[231]) of Brahman. It is the self-power of the divine Being (*devātmaśakti*). As Brahman is beginningless, endless and eternal, so is *Māyā*, being the power of the former.[232] Although it is coeternal with Brahman, it is not an entity second to Brahman that is non-dual. It is not independent (*asvatantrā*[233]) of Brahman. It is dependent on God (*īśvarāśrayā, parameśvarāśrayā*[234]).

Māyā is the seed of the totality of the cosmic energy (*bījaśakti*[235]). All the matter of the universe, in whatever form, is merely energy packet. Hence, in the final analysis, all the matter including all the energy of the universe is differentiated (*vyākṛta*) energy, the seed of which is the undifferentiated power or *Māyā*. We do make use of energy. The whole universe cannot function in the absence of energy. We discover the laws of nature in connection with the working of energy. The complicated mathematical equations involving the functioning of energy can be precisely solved. Notwithstanding these positive, empirical aspects of energy, nothing can be said about its true nature. It may be defined like this; "Energy is that which has the ability to do work". The Sanskrit word *śakti*, being the equivalent of energy (*śak + ktin*), has been formed from the verb-root *śak* which means "to be able to work". Thus, whatever idea is contained in the word *śakti* is repeated in the definition. It is a redundant expression. We do not know anything about the "substance" of energy. It is that which has the ability to do work. But, what is that? What is its true nature? Science has not yet been able to answer this question. When this is the position in regard to energy, it is very natural to realize the still more elusive nature of the seed of energy (*bījaśakti*), i.e., *Māyā*, the power of Brahman.

A power is never an entity separate from the possessor of the power. The President of a country is a physical and biological entity; but his power is not so. We can locate the President; we cannot locate his power. The power of the President can be inferred from the results of his actions. In spite of relentless search for the physical detection of the power of the President in his residential and office buildings, in private and public places and in the personal garments and belongings of the President, we are doomed to fail to locate it. In spite of this, we come to know the power of the President when he declares a war, dissolves the Parliament and declares emergency. Similarly, we cannot physically detect *Māyā*; but we can infer its presence from the actions it does. And so says Vedānta: "*Māyā* can be inferred from the results of its actions" (*kāryānumeyā*[236]).

Much confusion has been created over the issue of the locus and the content of nescience (*avidyā*). The Vivaraṇa and the Bhāmatī are the two main post-Śaṅkara schools of Advaita. Padmapāda wrote *Pañcapādikā* which is a commentary on Śaṅkara's *Brahma-Sūtra-Bhāṣya*. Prakāśātman wrote *Vivaraṇa* which is an elucidation of *Pañcapādikā*. The Vivaraṇa school equates *avidyā* and *Māyā*. It is also of the view that the Self or pure Consciousness is the locus of *avidyā*. Vācaspati Miśra wrote a commentary on Śaṅkara's *Brahma-Sūtra-Bhāṣya* and titled it as

Bhāmatī after the name of his wife. According to this Bhāmatī school, nescience is of two kinds, viz., *mūlāvidyā* (root-nescience) and *tūlāvidyās*. The *mūlāvidyā* whose products are the universe and the *jīvas* (individual selves) is located in Brahman. The *tūlāvidyās* are many and they are the effects of *mūlāvidyā*. A *tūlāvidyā* is located in each *jīva*. Sureśvara, who was a disciple of Śaṅkara, has written about the locus of *avidyā* in the prelude to the third chapter of his book *Naiṣkarmya-siddhi*. In his opinion, Brahman, the pure Consciousness, is both the locus of nescience and its content as well. He is emphatic on the point that the not-Self cannot provide a location for nescience. The not-Self is a product of nescience, which precedes the former. Sureśvara argues that what exists already cannot be located in what issues from it. Sarvajñātman, who was a follower of Sureśvara, holds the view that Brahman is the locus as well as the object of *avidyā*. He further says that Brahman is both the *ādhāra* (locus of superimposition) and *adhiṣṭhāna* (substrate of superimposition) of *avidyā*. Here a question is raised by someone, "How can Brahman (pure Consciousness) be the locus and the content of nescience without being affected by the impurity of nescience?" This question cannot be solved but is to be dissolved. As a matter of fact, the whole issue of the locus and the content of nescience involves a pseudo-problem. It has already been explained that the power (*śakti*) of any possessor of power (*śaktimān*) does not reside anywhere. It is meaningless to ask the question, "Where is the locus of *Māyā*?" Brahman is spaceless (*anākāśa*). The undifferentiated, primeval *Māyā* is also spaceless. Space (*ākāśa*) is a product of *Māyā*. The concept of locus and space is inseparable. And hence we cannot ask any valid question regarding the locus of *Māyā*. Moreover, Brahman is not a *vastu* (object). An entity which is not an object cannot be the content of *Māyā*. When Śaṅkara says, "*Māyā* is *īśvarāśrayā* or *parameśvarāśrayā*", some scholars have interpreted it as "God serving as a locus for *Māyā*". Such an interpretation does not seem to be correct. The term *īśvarāśrayā* should mean "dependent on God" instead of "located in God".

Śaṅkara has used a number of terms as synonyms of *Māyā*. At various places, he has used words like *Māyā*,[237] *avidyā*,[238] *avyakta*,[239] *akṣara*,[240] *prakṛti*[241] and *mūlaprakṛti*[242] to refer to the same entity with different shades of meaning. The seminal power (*bījaśakti*) of *Īśvara* is *Māyā*. *Īśvara* is omniscient whereas *Māyā* is insentient (*avidyā* or *ajñāna*). The undifferentiated (*avyākṛtā*) *Māyā* is the *mūlaprakṛti* (*mūlaprakṛtiravikṛtiḥ*). It is subtle (*sūkṣma*) and hence sense-imperceptible. On account of its subtlety and sense-imperceptibility, it is named as *avyakta* (unmanifested). Along with *Īśvara*, *Māyā* is unborn, beginningless and endless. Thus it is *akṣara* (imperishable), although mutable (*vikārya*). The differentiated *Māyā* is called *prakṛti* (*prakṛtiśabdaśca vikāre dṛṣṭaḥ*[243]). The *mūlaprakṛti* (primeval nature) is the precursor of the manifested universe and it also is the receiver of the dissolved universe at the time of dissolution.[244] Before the manifestation of the universe, the *mūlaprakṛti* or *Māyā* remains in a quiescent, undifferentiated (*avyākṛta*) and unmanifested (*avyakta*) condition. In this state, its three constituents are in equilibrium or are equipoised (*sāmyāvasthā*[245]). Differentiation ensues with the disturbance of the equilibrium.

Māyā is otherwise known as *avidyā* or *ajñāna* which is often translated as nescience or ignorance. Clarification of this concept is necessary to dispel confusion. When we know something, we have knowledge (*jñāna*) about it. If we don't know anything about it, we have lack of knowledge (*ajñāna*) about it. *Avidyā* for *Māyā* is not used exactly in this sense. Brahman is Consciousness (*Cit* or *Jñāna*), whereas *Māyā* or *avidyā* is not-Consciousness (*acit* or *ajñāna*). Here we are talking about bipolarity. Reality is one only in the absolute (*pāramārthika*) sense, without any reference to bipolarity. But, for all empirical purposes, the bipolarity gains significance. One of the poles is *Cit* as pure Consciousness whereas the other pole is *acit*, Insentience or Nescience or *avidyālakṣanā*[246] in Śaṅkara's terminology. This *Māyā-śakti* is not an entity second to Brahman. As Vedānta asserts, it belongs to Brahman. *Māyā*, the material Nature (*mūlaprakṛti*), consisting of three strings, belongs to Viṣṇu (God).[247] This power of becoming (*prakṛti*) is Divine (*vaiṣṇavī*).[248] It belongs to Viṣṇu and functions as the womb or the cause of all beings (*mama prakṛtiḥ yoniḥ*).[249] *Māyā* belongs to the nature of Viṣṇu (*viṣṇoḥ svabhāvabhūtā*).[250] The whole universe is produced from this *prakṛti* of Viṣṇu.[251] His *prakṛti*, consisting of three strings, is of the nature of nescience (*avidyālakṣanā*).[252] *Māyā*, belonging to *Īśvara*, is the power of becoming (*prakṛti*), due to which all types of modifications take place (*vikārakāraṇaśaktiḥ*).[253] It is clearly mentioned that *Māyā* is God's *prakṛti* (*prakṛtiḥ bhagavataḥ triguṇātmikā māyā*),[254] and that it is His own (*svabhūtā*).[255] The *Māyā-śakti* is the power of the omniscient Lord (*sarvajña-syeśvarasyātmabhūtā māyāśaktiḥ*).[256] It is the self-power of the Divine (*devātmaśakti*), the power of the Great Self (*māyinaḥ paramātmanaḥ ātmabhūtā śaktiḥ*).[257] It is God's *Māyā* (*bhagavan-māyā*).[258] We cannot explain it away by saying that it is a negative entity. We cannot ignore it by thinking that it is nothing. Although Consciousness (*Cit*) or Brahman is the only absolute reality, *Māyā* or *avidyā* which is not-consciousness (*acit*) is a necessary pole of the bipolar existence so that the empirical world comes into being, maintains functioning and is finally dissolved. As Śaṅkara says, the object and the subject, the not-Self and the Self, the "you" and the "we" are by nature as contradictory as light and darkness.[259] But, in spite of this contradictoriness, Śaṅkara admits that *Māyā* is meaningful (*arthavatī*).[260]

Some Indian philosophical schools take *Māyā* positively and some others negatively. Vimuktātman, in his book *Iṣṭasiddhi*, has propounded the theory of *Māyā* by positive argument. He has stressed the positive rather than the negative nature of *avidyā*. On the other hand, those philosophers who consider *avidyā* (nescience) as lack of knowledge put emphasis on its negative nature. Is *Māyā* existent (*sat*)? Yes, it exists. But, unlike Brahman, it does not exist in the absolute sense. Its existence is dependent on Brahman. It exists as the power of *Īśvara* (God), but not as a separate (*pṛthak*), independent (*svatantra*) entity. As far as the existence of *Māyā* is concerned, it baffles human intellect and renders ordinary, logical language futile. It is expressed by apparently illogical language such as *sat* (existence) as well as *asat* (non-existence[261]), or not *sat*, not *asat* and not *sat* and *asat* (not existence-cum-non-existence).[262] Strictly speaking, it is indescribable or indeterminable (*anirvacanīyā*[263]). According to revealed knowledge (*śruti*), *Māyā* is unreal (*tuccha*); it is indescribable (*anirvacanīyā*) if tested through logical reasoning (*yukti*); but, empirically (*laukika*) speaking, it is real (*vāstavī*).[264]

Māyā which is not-Consciousness (*ajñāna*) is responsible for our false knowledge (*mithyā jñāna* [265]). As Śaṅkara says, the non-existent appears to us as the existent (*asadeva sadiva avabhāsate*) due to this *Māyā*. The field (*kṣetra*) which is the object (*viṣaya*) and the field-knower (*kṣetrajña*) which is the subject (*viṣayī*) are mutually superimposed, resulting in confounding the one with the other and also the attributes of the one with those of the other. This confusion is brought about due to the absence of discrimination of the real nature of the subject and the object. A rope is mistaken for a serpent and a mother-of-pearl for a piece of silver. This is *adhyāsa* or superimposition. Such knowledge we get is not true knowledge; it is *mithyā jñāna* (false knowledge). The world of multiplicity is attributed to the manifestation of this false knowledge.[266]

Māyā has projection power (*vikṣepa śakti*[267]) and veiling power (*āvaraṇa śakti*[268]). We observe X in the absence of anything or in the presence of non-X. The former is an example of hallucination; the latter is that of illusion. Both hallucination and illusion are due to the projection power of *Māyā*. We do not observe *sattā* (reality) as S, which is concealed or veiled by *Māyā*. Due to this veiling action, S is not observed as S. But S is projected as non-S which we perceive, imagine or speculate. Our vision is obscured or obliterated. As a result, we don't at all perceive *sattā* (reality), S; or we perceive S as not-S. *Māyā* deludes (*mohayati*[269]) our intellect and thereby blurs the clarity of our vision.

In the introduction to the *Brahma-Sūtra-Bhāṣya*, Śaṅkara has given a clear exposition of *adhyāsa* (superimposition). The insentient world of plurality is superimposed on the non-dual Brahman which is pure Consciousness. As a result, S is perceived as not-S, Self is perceived as not-Self (*atasmiṁstadbuddhiḥ*[270]). But how can light and darkness, which are opposite to each other, be equated? This is natural in the empirical use (*naisargiko 'yaṁ lokavyavahāraḥ*) to superimpose one substance (*dharmī*) on another and one's attributes (*dharma*) on another's due to lack of discrimination (*viveka*). Lack of true knowledge mixes up reality and unreality (*satyānṛte mithunīkṛtya*) and thereby the not-Self is superimposed on the Self and conversely the Self is superimposed on the not-Self. This is a usual thing with ordinary people to consider "I am this" (*ahamidam*) and "This is mine" (*mamedam*) to be true. Here "this" is the body. In the concept "I am this body", the body as such is superimposed on the Self, conceived as "I". In the concept "This body is I", a relationship with the Self is superimposed on the body. The attributes of the body are superimposed on the Self when someone says, "This is my body". Thus superimposition may be two-way. In essence, in superimposition, one thing appears as something else (*sarvathāpi tvanyasyānyadharmāvabhāsataṁ na vyabhicarati*). Thus, people experiene nacre (*śuktikā*) as silver (*rajata*), rope (*rajju*) as snake (*sarpa*) and one moon as two moons. Of course, one may argue that Brahman which is objectless and attributeless, being sense-imperceptible, is unknowable, that everybody superimposes something else on what is perceived by him in front, and that the question of superimposition of the not-Self on the unknowable Self does not arise. Śaṅkara holds that such an argument is not tenable. He contends that the Self is not absolutely beyond apprehension since it is apprehended as the content of the concept "I" and is an immediately perceived entity (*na tāvadayamekāntenāviṣayaḥ, asmatpratyayaviṣayatvāt, aparokṣatvācca pratyagātmaprasiddheḥ*). Neither is there any rule that something has to be superimposed on something else that is directly perceived through the senses. Thus, the superimposition of the not-Self on the Self, the two being opposite to each other, is not contradictory (*evamaviruddhaḥ pratyagātmanyapyanātmādhyāsaḥ*). This superimposition is *avidyā* (nescience). The experience of the thing-in-itself by the discriminatory knowledge separating the reality from the unreal superimposing object is *vidyā* or knowledge (*tadvivekena ca vastusvarūpāvadhāraṇaṁ vidyāmāhuḥ*). With this *vidyā*, the *bījaśakti* (seminal power) of *Māyā* is burnt (*vidyayā tasyā bījaśakterdāhāt*[271]). This being so, wherever there is a superimposition of one thing on another, that on which a thing is superimposed is not affected even in trace either by the merits or the demerits of the thing which is superimposed (*tatraivaṁ sati yatra yadadhyāsaḥ, tatkṛtena doṣeṇa guṇena vā'ṇumātreṇāpi sa na sambadhyate*).

Māyā is not only *īśvarāśrayā* (dependent on God), but also *īśvarādhīnā* (controlled by God). This is the major difference between the *pradhāna* or *prakṛti* of the Śāṅkhya and the *Māyā* of the Vedānta. The *prakṛti* of the Sāṅkhya is independent of the multiple *puruṣas* (selves) whereas the *Māyā* of the Vedānta is under the full control of the single *Puruṣa* who is *Īśvara* or God. God is likened to the magician and *Māyā* to the magic.[272] The magician is not affected by his magic. So is God who is not deluded by his *Māyā*.[273] Of course, *Māyā* affects everything else other than God.

It has already been said that Brahman is ever undifferentiated (*avyākṛta, nirviśeṣa*) and that Brahman and the power of Brahman (*Māyā*) are co-eternal, without a beginning and an end. *Māyā* (*mūlaprakṛti* or *avyakta* or *akṣara*) is also undifferentiated (*avyākṛtā*[274]). But, in the case of *Māyā*, the state of non-differentiation is not permanent. When its three constituents[275] (*guṇas*), viz., *sattva* (serenity), *rajas* (activity) and *tamas* (inertia), are in equipoise or equilibrium (*sāmyāvasthā*), there is no activity, no manifestation and no universe. This is the supine (*mahāśupti*)[276] condition of *Māyā*. When *Īśvara* (God) desires a universe to come into being and function, He disturbs the equilibrium of the three *guṇas*, with a preponderance of *rajas*. This is the beginning of manifestation, the initiation of cosmic changes. *Māyā* or *mūlaprakṛti*, differentiated into the cosmic products, is known as *prakṛti*. Thus the material cause (*upādāna kāraṇa*) of the universe is *Māyā*[277] which, being insentient, cannot be the agent of the cosmic activities. The efficient cause (*nimitta kāraṇa*) is *Īśvara*[278] who is omnipresent, omnipotent and omniscient and under whose control *Māyā* functions. For functioning as the efficient cause, *Īśvara* does not need any instruments unlike the common example of a potter, a weaver, a smith, etc.[279] *Māyā* is a great miraculous power[280] (*mahādbhutā, vicitraśakti, śaktirvividha*) which can create anything. It may be considered as both the material as well as the instrumental cause (*sahakārī kāraṇa*).[281]

Vedānta clearly asserts that *Māyā* or *mūlaprakṛti* is the precursor state (*prāgavasthā*)[282] of the universe. But, at the same time, it holds that the universe is not a modification (*pariṇāma*) of *Māyā* unlike the analogy of milk modified into milk products like curd, cheese, butter, etc.[283] *Māyā* is a wonderful power which can produce the pluralities of the world in a magical way. The world is not a really substantial entity. It appears in multiple forms by names and forms by the imagination of *Īśvara* through His wonderful power of *Māyā*.[284]

The cosmic egg that appears at the beginning of the creation is a manifested product of the unmanifest *Māyā*.[285] It does not emanate from Brahman or God. The divine power, *Māyā* is likened to a seed (*bīja*[286]) which is the preceding state of the entire universe (*jagataḥ prāgavasthā*). A big banyan tree is present in a tiny banyan seed in a potential state. And so is *Māyā* that serves as the seed of the entire universe.

The insentient *Māyā* cannot function in the analogy of a piece of log that itself does not become a chair. *Īśvara* who is omniscient acts as the efficient cause of the creation, sustenance and dissolution (*sṛṣṭi, sthiti, pralaya*) of the universe. But, without the power of *Māyā*, the functioning of *Īśvara* is not possible.[287] The *mūlaprakṛti* remains in a potential, quiescent state. The appearance of the cosmic egg is the initial process of the cosmic manifestation. This event marks the beginning of a great world period (*mahākalpa* or *para*). The first half of a *para* is the period during which the cosmic evolution takes place. It is the evolutionary phase of expansion. The second half of a *para* is the period of the cosmic involution which ends in the total dissolution of the entire universe in *Māyā*. This is the involutionary phase of contraction. As the *Bhagavadgītā* says, in one cosmic cycle, the Unmanifest (*avyakta*) becomes Manifest (*vyakta*) and finally the Manifest again becomes Unmanifest.[288] By this, one cosmic cycle is completed. But this is not the final story. The cosmic cycles are repeated *ad infinitum*.[289] These cycles operate without a beginning in the past and without an end in the future.

A question is sometimes asked: What is the role of Brahman in all the acts of the cosmic drama? The answer is a negative one. Brahman, being attributeless, actionless and changeless, does not play any role in the cosmic drama. Brahman, without attributes, functions and modifications, is eternal and timeless. The concept of a functioning Brahman is incompatible with its *sanātanatvam* (eternality and timelessness). With such a concept of Brahman, one is bound to say that Brahman is uncaused and that it is not the cause of anything and any action.[290] Of course, we come across Vedic and Vedāntic references that unambiguously mention that Brahman is the cause of the universe.[291] This is to be interpreted, however, figuratively and not literally. Advaita Vedānta holds that Brahman is the only non-dual one and there exists nothing second to it. *Māyā*, the power of Brahman, is not a second entity. *Īśvara* is Brahman with *Māyā* as the limiting adjunct (*māyopahitaṁ brahma*) and hence is not a second entity. When these points are considered, Brahman is to be accepted as the only cause of the world. Otherwise, Advaita Vedānta holds that *Īśvara* is the efficient cause, that *Māyā* is the material cause, and that Brahman is not the cause of the universe.

Advaita Vedānta has to incorporate the concept of *Māyā* in its system of philosophy. The world, which is undeniably an empirical entity, cannot originate from nothing.[292] Advaita Vedānta rejects the idea of the origination of something from nothing.[293] Simultaneously, Advaita Vedānta does not ascribe the origination of the universe to Brahman, since, in its view, Brahman is unmodifiable (*avikārya*) and existence only (*sanmātraṁ hi brahma*).[294] *Māyā*, the illimitable, wonderful power of Brahman, being indeterminable and indescribable, is the precedent state (*prāgavasthā*) of the universe, and it is also the final state of the dissolved universe.

Īśvara

It has already been said that Brahman is the only Reality, non-dual and without a second. This non-dual, absolute entity (*pāramārthika sattā*) is pure Consciousness, attributeless and actionless. Simultaneously, Advaita Vedānta recognizes the existence of the empirical universe and the individual selves (*jīvas*). The universe (*jagat ġam ¯kvip*) is ever in motion.[295] It is in physical motion from locus to locus or in the same locus and is mutable from state to state. It is intelligently designed (*racanā*). It functions in accordance with laws. Amid apparent chaos, the world functions as a cosmos. *Ṛta*[296] (orderliness) in the universe is observed and the apparent disorder also maintains a definite order. The different units and sub-units of the universe operate in harmony with one another and so is the universe called *saṁsāra* (*sam ¯sṛ ¯ghañ*). This well-designed, intelligently operated, harmonious and orderly universe is, however, insentient (*acetana, jaḍa*). The materialist has his own definition of consciousness. In his opinion, it is a property of matter in certain stage of the evolutionary process and is exhibited by human beings or, in a wider sense, by living beings (plants and animals). But, design, order, harmony and intelligent functioning of the universe are universal both in the non-living and the living world. The galaxies, stars and planets, the molecules, atoms and sub-atomic particles, the viruses, bacteria and plants, the amoeba, worms, insects, fishes, amphibia, birds, animals and men have been designed intelligently and do function intelligently. Man who is the most conscious of all the animals is unconscious of his own macro - and micro-anatomy, physiology, biophysics and biochemistry unless he is a doctor or a biologist who endeavours to know something but who does not know everything of the human system. But, surprisingly, irrespective of his knowledge or ignorance about his own body, there is ordinarily nothing wrong in his own embryological, anatomical, histological, physiological, biophysical and biochemical structurings and functionings. His own organs, tissues and cells function in coordination and with a purpose for the well-being and sustenance of the system as a whole, without depending on his consciousness and intellection. Moreover, life appeared on the earth at a much later stage, and the world, prior to the creation of life, evolved intelligently with a beautiful blueprint. From all such observations it is inferred that the world has a designer, an architect, an engineer, an executor, a ruler, a controller, who is one only and who is omnipresent, omniscient and omnipotent.

The world is a product like a pot, a jug, an armlet, a bracelet, a necklace, a ring, a chair, or a building. Every product is made of some material(s) such as earth, gold, wood, etc. The material of which a product is made is the material or substantial cause of the latter. An insentient (*jaḍa*) substance cannot design and engineer itself to be converted into a designed product.[297] For the intelligent designing and execution, a sentient agent is necessary. A potter, a goldsmith, a carpenter, or a mason is called the efficient or operative cause of the products enlisted here as examples. According to Advaita Vedānta, *Māyā*, the power of God, is the substantial cause (*upādāna kāraṇa*)[298] of the world, and God or *Īśvara* is its operative (efficient) cause (*nimitta kāraṇa*).[299] The operative cause must be sentient;[300] in addition, He must be omniscient (*sarvajña*).[301] Without omniscience and with sentience only, He cannot design, operate and control all. He must be omnipresent (*sarvagata*)[302] in order to perform His functions everywhere. Being present in one locality and absent elsewhere, He cannot discharge His functions simultaneously with reference to all. He must be omnipotent (*sarvaśakti*),[303] because, without this omnipotence, He cannot create, maintain and control all. In a number of places, it has been said in a figurative sense (but not in a literal sense) that Brahman desires and meditates to have a universe prior to a creative world-period. Since desiring or meditating is a mental function, and Brahman is non-functional, it is actually *Īśvara* who desires. Prior to the creation of the universe, *Īśvara* desired[304] to have it. Without a desire, there is neither the design nor the execution of the design. There is no need for *Īśvara* to desire since He is *āptakāma*[305] (One without unfulfilled desires). He has no want; He has no desire for the possession of anything; He does not need any pleasure; He has no pain and hence does not desire any relief of the pain. Without any relevance to any need, He desired to have the universe (*na prayojanavattvāt*).[306] He desired to create the universe as people engage themselves in sports (*lokavattu līlākaivalyam*).[307] His sportive activity of the creation is, however, not real in the absolute sense. It is a magical conjecture wrought through nescience.[308] *Īśvara* made a grand design (*racanā*)[309] of the cosmos. He made His own causal power operative and, as a result, His unmanifest power (*avyākṛtā* or *avyaktā māyā*) became manifest.[310] Without this *Māyā*, *Parameśvara* (God) would cease to be a creator.[311] He is in the full control[312] of His power (although all created entities are controlled[313] by *Māyā*), which is marvellous, magical and wonderful (*vicitraśakti*).[314] As a magician, who conjures magical performance, is not himself affected by his magic, so also is *Īśvara* who is not deluded[315] by His magic of *Māyā*. The creation is not real, but is magical. Since the universe is a magical creation and is usable as a sense-object, it is an empirical entity (*vyāvahārika sattā*), but not an absolute entity (*pāramārthika sattā*). However, anything that is an ęmpirical entity is not a non-entity, although, as an entity, it is fully dependent on the absolute entity. *Īśvara*, being omnipresent and all-pervading[316] (*sarvavyāpta, vibhu, paribhu*), enters[317] into all the entities that are magically created and thus becomes the indwelling spirit (*sarvāntara*)[318] of all the manifestations. He is the presiding Deity (*adhyakṣa*)[319] and witness (*sākṣī*)[320] of everything. He is the impeller (*pravartaka*), the inner controller (*antaryāmī*)[321] of everything. The whole universe functions under His sovereign rule (*praśāsana*).[322] He is the supreme Lord (*Īśvara, Parameśvara*)[323] of the totality of the manifestation of His *prakṛti* or *Māyā*. He is the supporter[324] (*bhartā, goptā*) of all.

Who is this *Īśvara*? Is He Brahman? Advaita Vedānta says that Brahman is the only Reality, one without a second. That being so, *Īśvara* cannot be a second Reality. Brahman and *Īśvara* may be taken to be identical. But, again, Advaita Vedānta asserts that Brahman is actionless and attributeless. The same Brahman that is actionless cannot be an agent, the operative cause of the universe. Brahman is without attributes; but *Īśvara* is with attributes (*saguṇa*)[325] by virtue of His possession of *mahāmāyā* (the great, wonderful power). Through the diverse powers of His *māyāśakti*, He creates all this diversity.[326] He does not have the tendency to work (*pravṛttirahita*), but He imparts the tendency to work to every created entity as a magnet does to the iron particles.[327] *Īśvara* is the impeller (*pravartaka*)[328] of created entities, although He Himself is bereft of *pravṛtti*. His presence in the *bhūta* (created thing) and His superintendence only (*darśanamātreṇa*) induces action in the *bhūta* and thus He becomes a *prerayitā*[329] (inducer of action) or *preritā*.[330] As the *Bṛhadāraṇyaka Upaniṣad* says, "He alone is the doer (*kartā*)[331]". It is necessary for any doer to possess attributes. It is God Himself, abiding in all living and non-living entities as their selves (*jīvātmans*), Who creates every effect through profound meditation.[332] Hence doubt arises in the oneness of Brahman without attributes and *Īśvara* with attributes. There are apparent references to two Brahmans,[333] one with limiting condition (*nāmarūpavikārabhedopādhiviśiṣṭam*) and another unconditioned (*sarvopādhivivarjitam*). There are also references to one higher (*para*) and another lower (*apara*) Brahman.[334] The higher Brahman is said to be attributeless (*nirguṇa*) and the lower Brahman with attributes (*saguṇa*). Some others say that attributes (*saguṇatā*) and attributelessness (*nirguṇatā*) are two aspects[335] of the same Brahman just like the two sides of one coin. If this concept is analyzed critically, its untenability will be established. The whole edifice of the non-dualism of Advaita Vedānta is collapsed if Brahman is taken as two entities or one entity with two aspects. It is logically unsound to hold the simile of the two faces of the one coin with reference to Brahman which is formless, undifferentiated and homogeneous. Brahman, being functionless, attributeless and non-relational, is indescribable, indefinable and inexpressible (*netyātmā*).[336] A statement such as "Brahman is *netyātmā* and with attributes" is self-contradictory and hence necessarily false. An entity may be *nirguṇa* in one condition (*avasthā*) and *saguṇa* in a different condition, without any involvement of self-contradiction. But the non-dual Brahman is unrelated to conditions (*avasthānapekṣa*). In consideration of all these arguments, Śaṅkara rejects the view of two Brahmans.[337] Of course, he refers to *Īśvara* or *Parameśvara* in many places in his commentaries. His concept of *Īśvara* is too subtle and needs a brief mention here.

Advaita Vedānta uses the word *upādhi*[338] (*upa samīpe sthitvā svīyaṁ rūpam anyatra ādadhāti iti upādhiḥ*—while remaining in the proximity, to take a form according to the other is *upādhi*) in a technical sense. It may be translated into English as "limiting adjunct". One common illustration may be given here for a proper comprehension of the term *upādhi*. Space (*ākāśa*), without interruption, may be termed the great space (*mahākāśa*). A pot placed in the great space contains a certain volume of space inside it. The space inside the pot (*ghaṭākāśa*) seems to be separated from the *mahākāśa*. If the pot is broken, the separateness of the *ghaṭākāśa* from the *mahākāśa* disappears. In this illustration, the pot is the limiting adjunct of the space. Brahman, seemingly associated with *Māyā* (the power of Brahman), is *Īśvara*.[339] *Māyā* is the limiting adjunct (*upādhi*) of *Īśvara*. The unconditioned (*upādhirahita*) Brahman is attributeless and functionless. The conditioned (*sopādhi*) Brahman or *Īśvara* has attributes and functions. When Śaṅkara refers to *Īśvara* or *Parameśvara*, he means thereby Brahman seemingly associated with *Māyā*. In an absolute sense, Brahman does not associate with anything including *Māyā*; but, in an empirical sense, It does associate with *Māyā*. All the cosmic processes involving emanation, sustenance and dissolution are empirical like a magical show in which the magician seems to be associated. So is *Īśvara* who is likened to the magician.

Advaita Vedānta has the doctrine of reflection (*ābhāsavāda* or *pratibimbavāda*).[340] Brahman reflected in *Māyā* is *Īśvara*. The same Brahman reflected in all products of *Māyā* is the Self of all (*sarvātmā*).[341] When It is reflected in a non-living entity, It is *bhūtātmā*.[342] When It is reflected in the *antaḥkaraṇa* (inner organ) of a living entity, It is *jīvātmā* or *jīva*.[343] As one Sun does not become many when reflected in many water-reservoirs, so is the one Self (*ātmā*) appearing to become many individual selves.[344] The reflection of the Sun in the vast ocean does not constitute a second Sun. And so is the reflection of Brahman in *Māyā*. *Īśvara* is not a lower Brahman; He is not a second Brahman; ontologically He is not a non-entity. He is the non-dual Brahman, not different from the unconditioned Being, although He is apparently conditioned by the limiting adjunct, *Māyā* (*māyopahitaṁ brahma*).

Brahman is the cause of the origin, sustenance and dissolution of the Universe. These three types of functions cannot be attributed to the non-functional, attributeless, unconditioned Brahman. It is *Īśvara* or the conditioned Brahman with attributes, Who is the Creator, Sustainer and Destroyer of the Universe.[345] Although *Īśvara* is one only, the non-dual one, He is named as Brahmā, Viṣṇu and Rudra or Maheśvara, depending on the attributes and functions.[346] *Īśvara*, with *rajas guṇa* (the quality of activity) and creative activity, is Brahmā; *Īśvara*, with *sattva guṇa* (the quality of serenity) and supporting activity, is Viṣṇu; and the same *Īśvara*, with *tamas guṇa* (the quality of inertia) and destructive activity, is Rudra or Maheśvara.

The Universe is an empirical entity. It has been created by *Īśvara* Who maintains it and Who will destroy it. *Īśvara* is the Lord and the Controller of the Universe. But, all the threefold functions, viz., origination, sustenance and dissolution, are fictionary; they are imaginations of *Īśvara* who projects through His marvellous power of *Māyā* or *Avidyā*.[347] This is a magical activity of creative projection, the sustenance of the projection and finally the withdrawal of the projection. Without the magician there is no magic. Without *Īśvara* there is no Universe. The whole empirical Universe is dependent upon Brahman; but the reverse is not true.[348] A show of magic is not possible without a magician whose existence is independent of the magical show. The subtle concept of *Īśvara*, as propounded in the Advaita Vedānta, is to be properly comprehended so that misunderstanding and confusion are dispelled.

Jīva

The self in each individual living being (including viruses, bacteria, worms, insects, animals and man) is called *jīva* or *jīvātmā*. The self in each individual non-living being such as atoms, molecules, stars, planets and satellites is called *bhūtātmā*. There is no entity, whether living or non-living, in which *Īśvara* is not present as the indwelling spirit.[349] No entity can function but for the presence of the indwelling spirit. Everything in the Universe is pervaded by Brahman. Each created entity (*bhūta*), whether non-living or living, acts as a limiting adjunct (*upādhi*). The consciousness in each limiting adjunct is a self—either *bhūtātmā* or *jīvātmā*. Thus Brahman is *sarvātmā*, the selves of all created entities.

Here a question arises: "How is the non-dualism of Advaita Vedānta reconciled with the existence of the multiple selves?" The answer is both simple and complicated. It is simple in the sense that Advaita Vedānta equates the multiple selves with Brahman.[350] If B = C, B = D, B = E and so on, C, D and E, etc., are not different from one another and all are indentical to B. There is nothing else other than B. That being so, the necessity of the nomenclature of C, D, E, etc., would not arise. But we have had these nomenclatures out of empirical necessity, due to diverse conditions to which the same one B is subjected. The unconditioned B is B alone. The conditioned B is C, D, E, F, G, H, etc. These conditions are not real. They are all empirical. And hence all the conditioned B's are empirical.

The conditions or limiting adjuncts (*upādhis*) are empirically true, but really false (*mithyā*).[351] They are magical entities conjured by *Īśvara* (God) through His power *Māyā*. Brahman is not truly conditioned by anything. But It is apparently conditioned by *Māyā* and the products of *Māyā*. Consciousness or Brahman conditioned by *Māyā* is *Īśvara*. The same Brahman conditioned by the products of *Māyā* is *bhūtātmā* or *jīvātmā*. When Brahman is apparently conditioned by a non-living entity, It is *bhūtātmā*; when It is apparently conditioned by a living entity, It is *jīvātmā* or *jīva*. The *sūkṣma śarīra* or *liṅga śarīra* (subtle body) or the *pañcakośa* (five sheaths) or the *antaḥkaraṇa* (inner instrument or inner organ) is the apparent limiting condition (*upādhi*)[352] of Brahman and, in that state, Brahman is known as *jīva*. There are innumerable *jīvas* as there are innumerable subtle bodies.[353] All the *jīvas*, that are only empirically true, are not really different from the one Brahman. As one sun or one moon, by being reflected in many water-reservoirs, are apparently perceived as many suns or many moons, so is one *Ātmā* or Brahman reflected in many subtle bodies.[354] As the great space (*mahākāśa*) apparently becomes many *ghaṭākāśas* (space limited within pots), and on the breakage of the pots, remains as the same *mahākāśa*, so is Consciousness or Brahman apparently conditioned,[355] or really unconditioned.[356] These *upādhis* or limiting conditions are superimpositions (*adhyāsa*) due to *avidyā* (nescience). On the removal of *avidyā* by the dawn of enlightenment (*vidyā* or *jñāna*), the identity of Brahman, *Īśvara* and *jīvas* is experienced.[357]

There are references in the Vedas and the Upaniṣads, apparently indicating the duality of *Īśvara* and the individual self (*jīva*).[358] "Two birds who are always united as companions cling to the same tree. Of these two, one (the *jīva*) eats the sweet fruit, and the other (*Īśvara*) looks on without eating". Śaṅkara interprets it in terms of non-dualism.[359] The individual self or *jīva* is an empirical entity. When considered from the empirical point of view as an embodied self, with the subtle body or the internal organ (*antaḥkaraṇa*) as a limiting condition (*upādhi*), the *jīva* is apparently separate from Brahman. Without the *upādhi*, the *jīva* is identical with Brahman. The *jīva*, by being deluded in ignorance (*avidyākalpita*), imagines himself as the enjoyer (*bhoktā*) of the empirical sense-objects (*bhogya*). This is an act of self-hypnotism only; otherwise the *jīva* is not really the enjoyer. It is a fact that the *jīva*, the *prakṛti* (the universe of names and forms) and *Īśvara* have been taken as the enjoyer (*bhoktā*), the enjoyable object (*bhogya*) and the impeller (*preritā*), respectively.[360] Śaṅkara says: "The *jīva*, *Īśvara* and *prakṛti* are the three forms of Brahman".[361] The *Brahma-Sūtra*[362] clearly states that *Īśvara* is different from the *jīva* and that the former is greater than the latter. The *jīva* falsely identifies itself with the limiting adjuncts imposed by name and form, conjured up by nescience, and imagines their attributes as its own. But the differences between *Īśvara* and the *jīva* remain as long as nescience (*avidyā*) operates; on enlightenment, nothing other than Brahman remains.[363] All dualistic dealings, brought about by unreal nescience, get sublated by right knowledge. There is no creation in that state. The mundane existence is an error arising from the non-recognition of the difference of the limiting adjunct (*upādhi*) constituted by the assemblage of body and senses which are a creation of name and form brought about by nescience. The empirical world which seems to be real does not exist in reality. The *Brahma-Sūtra* establishes identity of *Īśvara* and the *jīva* and ascribes the apparent differences to the limiting adjuncts conjured up by nescience. The *jīva* is an entity separate from *Īśvara* as long as it identifies itself with the gross and the subtle bodies which are non-Self. God is different from the *jīva* when the latter is imagined through ignorance (*avidyā*) as the embodied one, agent and experiencer. Brahman conditioned by the intellect is the *jīva*. With the sublating of the imagined conditions by true knowledge, the *jīva* is identified with Brahman.

Rebirth[364] of the *jīva* continues to take place and its transmigration is repeated unless and until the *jīva* renounces its clinging to the fruits of actions and attains liberation (*mokṣa*). The *jīva* imagines that it is the enjoyer (*bhoktā*) of pains and pleasures and the fruits of actions. It imagines to be related to the fruits of actions.[365] Once it stops imagining to be the enjoyer, experiencer and agent, it attains liberation and is no longer born. This is achieved by dispelling *avidyā* (ignorance) with *vidyā* (knowledge).[366]

Mind (*manas*)[367] which is the most important part of the inner instrument (*antaḥkaraṇa*) is the reservoir of all impressions (*karmāśaya*). All the impressions (*saṁskāras*) of lives are stored in the memory of the mind and the *jīva* is not the locus of the storage of these impressions.[368] In the Vedānta, the mind is material,[369] albeit subtle and imperceptible, and is not the soul (*jivātmā*). It is a product of *avidyā* (nescience). The transmigration of the *jīva* cannot be stopped as long as the mind is not completely erased and annihilated.[370]

The creation is unequal. Some *jīvas* suffer while some others enjoy. Some suffer more and some others less. The *Brahma-Sūtra*[371] says that God has nothing to do with this sort of inequality. The unequal creation is brought about in conformity with the virtues and vices of the individuals. Verily one becomes good by good action, bad by bad action.[372] One becomes according as one acts and behaves. The doer of good becomes good; the doer of evil becomes evil. One becomes virtuous by virtuous action and vicious by vicious action.[373]

It is argued[374] that, there being no reservoirs of *karma* prior to the creation, the inequalities of the individuals cannot be explained. The Vedāntin does not consider this as a defect since transmigration is beginningless.[375] In the great dissolution (*mahāpralaya*), all that has been created—the galaxies, stars and planets, the plants, animals, microorganisms and men and even the gods—are dissolved and merged into *Māyā* which is the power of Brahman. The *jīvas* potentially maintain their individualities even after they are dissolved into *Māyā*. What have been merged in *Māyā* again emerge in the next cycle of manifestation.[376] Creation is not accidental; its origin is not without any reference to cause and effect. The unmanifested potentiality becomes the manifested actuality. Without *karma* (reservoir of impressions originated by actions), there is no origin of the body and, without the body, neither is the origin of *karma*.[377] Cycles of creations and dissolutions were infinite in the past and will be infinite in the future since both Brahman and Its power are beginningless and endless.

With the death of the gross body (*sthūla śarīra*), the subtle body (*sūkṣma śarīra, antaḥkaraṇa*) does not perish. This subtle body functions as the limiting adjunct (*upādhi*) of the *jīva*.[378] The transmigration of the *jīva* continues until the subtle body is done away with by discriminatory knowledge and realization of Brahman.

The limiting adjuncts are many and so are the empirical *jīvas*. These *jīvas* have been empirically spoken of as parts (*aṁśa*) of *Parameśvara*.[379] But, in reality, this is not true. The *Bṛhadāraṇyaka Upaniṣad* categorically says that this self (*jīva*) is Brahman (*ayamātmā brahma*[380]). Brahman, being partless (*niravayava*) and undifferentiated (*nirviśeṣa*), is an unbroken whole and without parts. Śaṅkara strongly repudiates the concept of the difference of the *jīvas* from Brahman and establishes the identity. As long as the limiting adjuncts persist, the empirical difference of the *jīva* from Brahman cannot be denied. But the limiting adjuncts are products of imagination without being real. Knowledge (*vidyā*) dispels ignorance (*avidyā*) and thereby annihilates the limiting adjuncts. With the annihilation of the *upādhis*, the identity of Brahman and the *jīva* is re-established.[381]

In the opinion of the Vaiśeṣikas, the *jīva* is naturally insentient but becomes endowed with an adventitious sentience, as a result of the conjunction of the *jīva* and the mind. This position of the Vaiśeṣika is refuted by the Vedāntin for whom the *jīva* is the eternal cognizer.[382] Brahman is Consciousness and the *jīva*, being non-different from Brahman, is eternally conscious.

Jagat

Jagat (*gam kvip*) is a Sanskrit word, the English equivalent of which is "universe". This word is derived from the verb root *gam* which means "to go". Everything in the universe is in motion.[383] Every created entity is changeable or mutable. Although the mutability of the world is generally appreciated, the change that takes place every moment in every entity of matter and energy is not recognized by many persons. Our Sun may live for many billions of years. But it undergoes changes at every moment and does not remain the same for any two consecutive moments. If S stands for the Sun, t_1 for a particular time and t_2 ($t_1 + \delta t$) for the next consecutive time, S_1 at time t_1 does not remain as S_1 at time t_2. There are constant chemical changes inside the Sun and hence the intrinsic changes are continuous. There are also constant configurational changes with relation to the positions of galaxies, stars and planets and this involves extrinsic changes. So far as the molecular and atomic constitution of a person, X, is concerned, he does not remain the same in any two consecutive moments. The charcoal particle or the sand particle appears to be unmoving and unchanging. But the micro-particles inside it are ever in motion and ever mutable. Thus motion and mutability are necessary characteristics of all entities of the universe.

The universe is not independently existent. It depends upon Brahman for its existence. Brahman is the substratum (*adhiṣṭhāna*[384]) of the universe. We observe the waves, foams and surfs of the sea.

What we observe are phenomenally existent. But for the sea-water, the existence of the waves, foams and surfs would not be possible.[385] And so is the perishable (*kṣara*[386]) universe that phenomenally manifests on the surface of its substratum which is immutable, imperishable, beginningless, endless and absolute.

Śaṅkara's[387] description of the illusory and fugitive world bears some resemblance with Heisenberg's indeterminacy. The form of the world, as perceived and described, is uncertain. There is no way for us to be sure of anything of the world, which is like a dream, water of the mirage or a city in the sky. It cannot definitely be said how anything of the world starts, stays and finishes. We can observe the world sometimes as W and some other times as not-W, but we cannot get certainty about any of our observations.

Advaita Vedānta says that Brahman is real (*satya*) and the *jagat* (universe) is unreal (*mithyā*). This word *mithyā* has been used in Advaita Vedānta in a highly technical sense. It does not mean "false" or "non-existent". If something exists without any change, without past, present and future, and without depending upon anything else, it is real (*satya*). Such an absolute existence cannot be contradicted by any means, at any place and at any time.[388] On the other hand, the world which empirically exists, because of its relativity and conditionality, is ever mutable and ever uncertain. If it is W_1 at time t_1 it is W_2 at time t_2, and hence W_1 is contradicted at time t_2 and so is W_2 at time t_1. Moreover, our observations of the world as W_1, W_2, ... W_{n-1}, W_n, ... W_∞ cannot be said with certainty to correspond exactly with what W is. We cannot determine the noumenon from the phenomena. Such a flittering and glittering world, ever changing and ever uncertain, is *mithyā* (unreal).

It is a general misconception to hold that Advaita Vedānta is acosmic. In clear and unequivocal terms, Śaṅkara[389] has repudiated the claims of the Buddhist Vijñānavādins for whom the non-existent world is a subjective projection of the individual mind. The Vedāntin does posit an external world which is empirical (*vyāvahārika*) but not real in the absolute sense (*paramārthataḥ*).

There has also been confusion over the term "illusion". It is mixed up with the concept of hallucination. If A is perceived as B, C, D, E, etc., but not as A, it is a case of illusion. A rope is erroneously perceived as a snake. A nacre is mistaken as a piece of silver. A pillar is seen, by mistake, as a person. In each of the examples of illusion, there is some substratum. The rope, the nacre and the pillar are the substrata of the snake, the silver and the person, respectively. In the process of hallucination, on the other hand, there is the misperceived object without a substratum. One sees a snake when there is no rope nor snake. One's mind projects the image of a snake by recalling its memory, taking out the image out of the mind's storehouse of impressions and projecting the image on the screen of the external world. For the manifestation of such a hallucination, one must have previously experienced the vision of a snake. One sees a ghost when there is no ghost, there is nothing else to simulate a ghost, and one had not previously experienced the vision of a ghost. This is a second type of hallucination. In this case, the person has heard or read about ghosts, believed in them, made a mental picture of the ghost and stored the picture in the memory of his mind to be recalled on subsequent occasions. In a third type of hallucination, the mind makes a mosaic picture out of scissored cuttings of different stored impressions and projects the synthetic picture on the screen of the external world. Whatever may be the type of hallucination, the misperceived image has no substratum. Advaita Vedānta says that the absolute Brahman is the substratum of the phenomenal, empirical world which is an experiential illusion.

In the Vedas and the Upaniṣads, there are a number of references with categorical assertions on the identity of Brahman and the world. The *Puruṣa-Sūkta* of the Ṛg-Veda says: "Whatever is at present, was in the past and will be in the future is verily the Person.[390] The same thing is also given in the *Śvetāśvatara Upaniṣad.*[391] All this is verily Brahman.[392] All this is verily the Self.[393] The *Muṇḍaka Upaniṣad* says that *Puruṣa* (Brahman) is verily this world.[394] Śaṅkara interprets it by saying that the universe has no separate existence apart from the Person (Brahman).[395] The *Muṇḍaka Upaniṣad* further states: "Brahman, verily, is this immortal. Brahman is in front; Brahman is behind; (It is also) to the right and to the left. It spreads forth below and above. Brahman, indeed, is this universe. It is the greatest".[396]

The seers have contemplated a world-image (*viśvarūpa*) of Brahman. This world-image has been depicted in the *Puruṣa-Sūkta* of the Ṛg-Veda,[397] in the *Bhagavadgītā*[398] and some Upaniṣads.[399] It has been further said in the Vedas, in the Āraṇyaka and the Gītā that the whole universe constitutes a quarter or a minor fraction (*aṁśa*) of Brahman.[400]

All that has been said in the scriptures on the identity of Brahman and the universe may be construed in a figurative sense. Brahman is the only non-dual reality and there is no diversity whatsoever.[401] Hence Advaita Vedānta contends that there is nothing like a universe separate from Brahman. But, from this, one cannot infer that the insentient universe is identical with Brahman which is Consciousness and that the undifferentiated (*avyākṛta, nirviśeṣa*), homogeneous, unmodifiable (*avikriya*) and non-dual (*advaita*) Brahman can have parts unlike the multitudinous entities of the universe.

The doctrine of transformation (*pariṇāmavāda*) which is accepted in the Sāṅkhya philosophy is a prima facie concept in the Advaita Vedānta. According to this doctrine, Brahman or at least part of It has been converted into the universe. The Upaniṣads say: "That (the absolute Brahman) is full; this (the manifested universe) is full. Full came out of the full. After the emergence of the full from the full, (the latter) still remained as the full".[402] This is a clear statement which indicates the conversion of part of Brahman into the world. In the beginning (before the creation), there was Self (Brahman) alone.[403] There was nothing else other than the Self. It may be assumed that the world might have been created out of nothing or out of Brahman. Advaita Vedānta accepts *satkāryavāda* (creation of something out of something and not out of nothing) and rejects the idea of the creation of something out of nothing.[404] There are scriptural references which apparently show that this universe was, in the beginning, *asat* (non-existent[405]). But, this word *asat* has been used here in a special sense; it means "non-existent to the senses" since the primeval substance of the universe cannot be perceived by the senses. Here *asat* does not mean "nothing". This *asat* is a positive entity (*sat*) which is sense-imperceptible. What was there prior to the creation was neither *sat* nor *asat*, as declared in the *Nāsadīya-Sūkta* of the Ṛg-Veda.[406] It was not *sat* because it was unmanifested and sense-imperceptible. It was not *asat* because it was not nihil. In order to dispel the idea of *asat* being misconstrued as "nothing", the scriptures categorically state that this *asat* was *sat*.[407] Before the creation, it was unmanifested (*avyakta*) and sense-imperceptible and hence was *asat*. After the creation, it became manifested (*vyakta*) and could be directly or indirectly perceived by senses and hence is *sat*. As a matter of fact, it is logically impossible for nothing to be something and something to be nothing due to self-contradiction. Hence the *Bhagavadgītā*[408] declares the law of conservation of Being (*sattā*). Thus the concept of *ex-nihilo* creation is rejected. In such a situation, we have no alternative other than accepting Brahman as the source of the universe, since there was Brahman alone prior to the creation.

The scriptures declare that Brahman is the source (*yoni*) of the universe.[409] Everything of the universe has originated from Brahman, is being maintained by Brahman and, at the time of dissolution, will finally be merged into Brahman.[410] Brahman modified Itself, converted Itself into the world which is thus a modification or transformation of the former (*ātmakṛteḥ pariṇāmāt*).[411] As the *Taittirīya Upaniṣad* says, transformation of Brahman into the world was brought about by Brahman Itself (*tadātmānaṁ svayamakuruta*[412]). The *Muṇḍakopaniṣad*[413] says: "As from a blazing fire, sparks of like forms emanate by the thousands, so also, O dear, emanate many kinds of beings from the Immutable to which they return too". A number of scriptures[414] declare that Brahman is both the substantial (material or *upādāna*) and the operative (efficient or *nimitta*) cause of the world.

In the causal theory of Advaita Vedānta, the non-difference of the effect (*kārya*) from the cause (*kāraṇa*) is asserted.[415] It is held that the cause precedes the effect.[416] It is further held that nothing altogether new is produced out of the cause (material cause) and that what is potentially present in the cause is expressed in the effect. Thus the cause and the effect are identical in Advaita Vedānta. It has already been said that Brahman is the cause of the universe. It is inferred from this that Brahmạn and the universe are identical. Such an inference, however, is not valid as will be revealed from the succeeding paragraphs.

Questions arise here: Does the whole of Brahman change to become the world? Is part of Brahman converted to the world? Advaita Vedānta answers both these questions negatively. Brahman does not undergo any modification. The undifferentiated (*avyākṛta*) and immutable (*avikārya*) Brahman is partless (*niravayava, niṣkala*). A statement like "An undifferentiated and immutable Brahman is transformed into the world of pluralities" is self-contradictory and hence is not valid. Advaita Vedānta rejects the doctrine of transformation (*pariṇāmavāda*) in unequivocal terms.[417]

Śaṅkara[418] convincingly argues against the doctrine of transformation and rejects the idea that part or the whole of Brahman is transformed into the world. He asserts that the seed (*bīja*), root (*mūla*) or substratum (*adhiṣṭhāna*) of the cosmic modifications is Reality (*sat*) or Brahman.[419,420] Reality is subtle (*sūkṣma*) whereas the names and forms (*nāmarūpa*) of the manifold, mutable world are gross. The gross world is rooted in subtle Brahman, which is never modified into the world. Brahman, not being a product and not having a beginning, is not caused by anything else. It is causeless. Similarly, Brahman, being attributeless, actionless and immutable, is not a cause of anything else. Whatever has been said about Brahman as the material and efficient cause of the world is not literally correct, although it is meaningful if construed in a figurative sense.

According to one opinion, there is only one immutable Brahman and nothing else, and whatever is perceived in the empirical world is name and form (*nāmarūpa*[421]) only, without any reality in the so-called modifications. According to this interpretation, there is no change in the substance in the analogy of gold and the products of gold such as ring, necklace, armlet, etc. The unchanged substance changes forms and each form is known by a name. There is no substantial modification in gold which changes into different forms with different names. So is Brahman which, being Itself immutable, acquires forms and names of the worldly things.

The illustration given in the foregoing paragraph does not strictly hold good with reference to Brahman and the world. Gold and the ornaments made of gold have the same degree of reality or unreality as far as the substance is concerned. This is, however, not the case with Brahman and the world. Brahman is absolutely existent (*pāramārthika sattā*) whereas the universe is empirically existent (*vyāvahārika sattā*). The empirical world is a magical conjuration of *Īśvara* through His power (*māyāśakti*) that brings about the empirical modifications[422] and projects the variegated world-appearance.[423] That the world is not real, that it is the appearance of a magic show and that the conjurer is *Īśvara* whose magic power is *Māyā* is the established view of the Advaita Vedāntins.[424]

It is generally considered that the causal theory of Advaita Vedānta is *vivartavāda*. This is a doctrine which advocates that the world is only an appearance (*vivarta*) of Brahman and that all changes are not real but apparent. Śaṅkara has not used the word *vivarta* in his commentaries. The verbal form *vivartate* and the participle form *vivartamāna* have been used by him in a sense unlike the one attached to the word *vivarta*. The *vivartavāda* concept came into vogue in the post-Śaṅkara period. The empirical nature of the world, as given in the *Brahma-Sūtra*, the Upaniṣads and the *Bhagavadgītā* has been truly interpreted and depicted by Śaṅkara in his commentaries in a consistent and convincing manner.

Every magic play has its own rules and sequences. So is the world that has an efficient cause, a material cause, a sequence in creation, sustenance by laws and a sequence in dissolution. Anything that has empirical existence is not nothing. Hence these aspects of the empirical world will be briefly discussed in the following paragraphs.

The universe has not originated from the insentient *pradhāna* (primordial nature) or from atoms or from nothing or from some underworldly conditions. Nor can it originate spontaneously. Apart from the omniscient, omnipotent and omnipresent *Īśvara*, it can have no other source.[425] This statement of Śaṅkara and, at the same time, the unreality of the world, as interpreted by him, are to be coherently associated for a proper understanding of the cosmos.

Īśvara is the efficient cause[426] whereas *Māyā*, the power of *Īśvara*, is the material cause[427] of the world. *Māyā* is sheltered under *Īśvara* (*īśvarāśrayā*[428]) and under the full control of *Īśvara* (*īśvarādhīnā*[429]). No instrumental cause is necessary for *Īśvara* in conjuring the world and, for this purpose, *Māyā* may be considered as both the material and the instrumental cause.[430]

Māyā, the power of Brahman, is co-eternal with Brahman.[431] It has neither beginning nor end. Brahman falsely associates with Its own power, *Māyā*, which functions as a limiting adjunct (*upādhi*) and thus Brahman becomes *Īśvara*. Before the creation and after the dissolution of the world, *Māyā* remains in a quiescent, potential, undifferentiated and unmanifested (*avyākṛtā, avyaktā*[432]) state. It consists of three constituents[433] (*guṇa*) which are in equilibrium[434] in this state. When *Īśvara* desires[435] to create, He disturbs[436] this equilibrium and thereby the *rajas* (constituent of activity) constituent predominates over the *sattva* (constituent of serenity) and the *tamas* (constituent of inertia). Thus start the creative processes of differentiation.

The pre-creation state has been described in the Ṛg-Veda[437] and the *Viṣṇu-Purāṇa*[438] in a similar way. It was a state of neither existence nor non-existence. It was a positive entity of Consciousness; but nothing was manifested in this condition. This entity was alone; It was without *vāta* (*avāta*); otherwise speaking, it was functionless. It had its power (*svadhā, mūlaprakṛti* or *Māyā*). Except this One which was pure Existence and pure Consciousness, neither day nor night, neither particles nor field, neither sky nor earth, neither light nor darkness, neither life nor death was there. The subjectless, objectless, absolute Being desired (*kāmastadagre samavartatādhi*[439]) to create the universe, to be the only subject of multiple objects of cosmic becomings. The material cause of all the cosmic products was *tucchya*[440] (*Māyā* or *svadhā* or *mūlaprakṛti*). The first entity that was produced from *Māyā* was *āpaḥ*[441] (*apraketaṁ salilam* or undifferentiated waters). This *āpaḥ* is otherwise known as *kaḥ* or *nāra*.[442] The *kaḥ* appeared as a golden embryo (*hiraṇyagarbha*[443]). The Lord, who stayed inside the golden foetus, presided over it and controlled its functioning, was Prajāpati[444] or Brahmā who was the creative aspect of *Īśvara*, the only Lord of the universe. Brahmā is thus self-caused (*causa sui, svayambhū, ātmayoni*);[445] or otherwise speaking, *Īśvara* is the source of Brahmā (*brahma-yoni*[446]). Prajāpati was the bond (*sato bandhamasati niravindan*[447]) between the existent (the manifested) and the non-existent (the unmanifested).

The cosmic egg (*aṇḍa*) that was produced from *Māyā*[448] continued to remain in the oval form. After this quiescence, it exploded.[449] This was t_0 or the beginning of time with the explosion of the cosmic egg. Time is a non-entity, but a mental construct.[450] With becoming, occurrences of events and, especially, with sequential occurrences of two or more events, the concept of the relativity of time is born in the mind. The Upaniṣads say that the Self-caused Prajāpati who made the universe is the author of time (*kālakāra*[451]).

At the beginning of time when the cosmic egg exploded, *prāṇa* was produced from *āpaḥ*.[452] This *prāṇa* is an ever-active, vibrating and vitalizing principle which activates everything—living and non-living, movable and immovable. No activity is possible without this *prāṇic* principle.

Ākāśa[453] or space was born from *prāṇa* when the cosmic egg exploded. This *ākāśa*, being a product, is an entity unlike time which is a non-entity. It may be noted here that this emanated *ākāśa* is not the relative space of Einstein. There has been confusion in science and the Western philosophy over the concept of space and that of the three dimensions of space. The spatial dimensions (length, breadth, height or thickness) which are three in number are relative. This is, however, not true for space which is a positive entity and a source of all varieties of particles. The three space-dimensions and the one time-dimension are necessarily associated with any activity. The concept of an activity cannot be formed without the simultaneous concept of the four dimensions of space-time. This is what has been symbolically described by *arṇava* and *saṁvatsara* in the Ṛg-Veda,[454] the former symbolizing space and the latter, time.

The cosmic egg (*aṇḍa*) may be compared to the singularity of modern cosmology. With the explosion of the cosmic egg, space appeared and suddenly expanded to all directions. The explosion was too violent and the expansion was too sudden. The Ṛg-Veda describes the expansion as stretching out violently to all directions (*tiraścīno vitato raśmireṣāmadhaḥ svidāsīdupari svidāsīt*[455]).

An excessive quantity of heat was produced in the explosion of the cosmic egg (big bang). It was a superheated condition. The creation of multiple forms of energy and particles would have been impossible in the absence of the early superheated cosmic furnace. In this connection, the *Praśna Upaniṣad*[456] says: "Prajāpati produced much heat and thereby created pairs of *rayi* and *prāṇa*, from which He produced the world of multiplicity". The *Chāndogya Upaniṣad*[457] also says that, with the explosion of the cosmic egg, *rajata* (silver) and *suvarṇa* (gold) were produced. It is difficult to decipher this type of symbolic language (*rayi*, *prāṇa*, *rajata*, *suvarṇa*) and to ascertain their meanings in the light of modern science of cosmology. These word-pairs may mean matter (particles) and field, or matter and energy, or particles and forces.

The primordial furnace of the newly born universe has been compared to a sacrificial ritual (*yajña*). The *Bṛhadāranyaka Upaniṣad*[458] has used the word *aśva* (literally horse) in the sense of "energy". This word has been derived from the verb-root *aś* which means "to pervade", "to be able", "to eat". That which is able for doing a work is *aśva* (energy). The word *medha* which literally means "to kill" or "to sacrifice" has been used here with the meaning of annihilation. The Upaniṣad apparently describes an *aśvamedha yajña* (horse-sacrifice), but really gives a vivid picture of plasma-physics in the superheated condition of the early universe immediately after the big bang explosion.

The three entities, viz., *āpaḥ* (*kaḥ* or *arka* or *ambha*[459]), *prāṇa* and *ākāśa* (*kha* or space).[460] are non-different substantially.[461] but they differ from one another in their degree of subtlety. The subtlest entity among them is *āpaḥ*. *Prāṇa* is relatively less subtle than *āpaḥ* and *ākāśa* is less subtle than *prāṇa*, although both *prāṇa* and *ākāśa* are too subtle to be perceived by our senses. The *Chāndogya Upaniṣad* says: Prāṇa is full of *āpaḥ* (*āpomayaḥ prāṇaḥ*[462]). All these three are sequentially interconvertible; *āpaḥ* can be converted to *ākāśa* and *vice versa.*[463] There can be no direct conversion of *āpaḥ* to *ākāśa* and *vice versa*. *Āpaḥ* can be converted to *prāṇa* and then to *ākāśa*; and so is the back-conversion of *ākāśa* to *āpaḥ*. However, these conversions and reverse conversions do take place only in superheated[464] conditions in which input of energy is adequate.

There are some hymns in the Ṛg-Veda on *apāṁ napāt.*[465] The *āpaḥ* that has been referred to here has been adored as a god. Some verses of these hymns cannot be meaningfully interpreted without reference to the superheated plasma prevalent in the newly born universe immediately after the big bang explosion.

With reference to the early cosmogonical processes, the word *tapas*[466] has been used in the Vedāntic literature. Many commentators have translated this word as "austerity". "Brahman practised austerity and created the world." Such an interpretation is, however, not correct. The word *tapasyā* means "meditation with austerity", whereas the word *tapas* literally means "heat". The Upaniṣad says: "Brahman expands by heat" (*tapasā cīyate brahma*[467]). In the singular instrumental case, *tapas* has been changed to *tapasā* which means "by heat". Had it been *tapasyayā*, it would have meant "by austerity". When the seer says, *tapasā cīyate brahma*, he refers to the excessive heat production, the explosion of the cosmic egg and the subsequently expanding universe.

The Vedic seers were emphatic on the generation of products (*prajāḥ*) brought about by Prajāpati (Brahmā or the creative aspect of *Īśvara*) in the superheated condition immediately after the explosion of the cosmic egg. They describe this superheated state of cosmic plasma as *Aditi.*[468] *Prāṇa* vigorously vibrated (*kampanāt*[469]). Many types of micro-particles were formed in opposite pairs which have been termed by the Vedic seers as *Dakṣa.*[470] For a moment they lived in a violently dancing[471] condition. The next moment they were annihilated to give rise to other particles or energy. Light-particles (photons) were predominant at this early stage (*jyotirdarśanāt*[472]). There was a dynamic state of flux from particles to particles, particle-pairs to field and *vice versa*. The *Kaṭhopaniṣad*[473] says that Aditi is a product of *prāṇa* and the source of gods. There is a description of Aditi[474] in the Ṛg-Veda as the simultaneous progenitor and offspring. Aditi is the sky, Aditi the air, Aditi is mother, father and son. Aditi is all the gods and the five *bhūtas* (primary states of matter and energy). Aditi is whatever has been and will be born. The *Bṛhadāraṇyaka Upaniṣad*[475] says: Whatever particles of matter or energy are created by Aditi in the superheated cosmic plasma are immediately devoured by the same Aditi.

Space or *ākāśa* was a beehive of activity in the superheated condition.[476] It was producing particles that were again merged into it. This condition, however, changed due to the rapid expansion of *ākāśa* and subsequent cooling. Vedānta does not say that *ākāśa* expands into a void. It does not recognize anything like a void. It does recognize the full. When Vedānta says, "*Ākāśa* expands", it means thereby that the volume of *ākāśa* becomes greater and greater. *Ākāśa*, although vast, is limited in volume. Anything that is produced must have finite volume. *Ākāśa*, being a product,[477] is finite in volume which is the volume of the universe.

In the early stage of cooling, nucleogenesis took place; atoms and molecules were formed. Hydrogen became the principal element of the entire universe. The simplest and mostly prevalent hydrogen is an element with one proton in the nucleus and one electron in the orbit around the nucleus. The phenomena of a neutron splitting into a proton and an electron, with opposite charges, the capturing of the electron by the proton in an orbit around the latter and the circling of the electron around the proton have been beautifully depicted in a parable in the *Matsya Purāṇa*.[478] Brahmā (neutron) produced a daughter (electron) by splitting his own body (into proton and electron). The daughter was named Śatarūpā. Brahmā was attracted towards his own daughter; he embraced and kissed her. They copulated, remained in union and produced innumerable offspring. All matter is made of atoms and molecules of different elements all of which are made of proton(s) and electron(s). Many Indological scholars have condemned this so-called incest-story without understanding the implied meaning of the parable. It is wrong to speculate biological sex at this early stage of the development of the universe. It is further wrong to speculate anthropomorphism in the evolution of particles in the early stage of the universe. The big bang explosion was followed by particle evolution. It was followed by inorganic evolution, organic evolution and species evolution. The whole story of the different types of evolution relates to a period of fifteen billion (one billion = 10^9) years or more. There was no question of a man and a woman to copulate to produce the diverse elements and compounds. To summarize the whole story it may be said that *vāyu* (hydrogen in gaseous form) was produced from *ākāśa* (*ākāsād vāyuḥ*[479]).

The *vāyu* (hydrogen) was dispersed in space. At different loci in space, the *vāyu* was condensed by gravity. Each gaseous nucleus became a centre for further compression. This process of compression of the gas-ball resulted in increased production of heat (*vāyoragniḥ*[480]) that could liquefy the gas. This is the *āpaḥ*[481] or liquid of the Vedāntic scriptures (*agnerāpaḥ*[482]). This may not be confused with the *āpaḥ* (the cosmic plasma or waters) that originated from *Māyā*. There has been much confusion over the *pañcabhūtāni* (five prime states of matter-cum-energy). A *bhūta* (*bhū* + *kta*; that which has become) is not the element of chemistry. Anything that has been a product is a *bhūta*. It may exist in the state of a solid (*kṣiti* or *pṛthivī*), a liquid (*ap*), an energy (*teja*), a gas (*marut*) or space (*vyoma*). The word *āpaḥ* used with reference to any spherical body in space has a connotation of "a hot liquid ball rotating around its own axis". It may be noted here that the cosmogonic sequence, described with reference to the transformation of a gaseous ball to a molten ball and the subsequent steps, is not universal. The stars and most planets of most stars have not yet liquefied and solidified. Hydrogen gas, in gaseous form, is still the principal constituent of the majority of the stars. Hence the cosmogonic sequence from *āpaḥ* (liquid mass) onwards holds true for a planet like our Earth or other similar planets in other solar systems of our galaxy (Milky Way) or other galaxies.

In due course of time, heat was dissipated from the exterior part of our Earth. As a result, the periphery of the Earth was solidified, although its interior core still remains in molten condition. This process has been expressed by the Upaniṣads as "solid from liquid" (*adbhyaḥ pṛthivī*[483]).

The creation theory of Advaita Vedānta has had its special characteristics. First of all, it rejects any type of *de novo* creation (*creatio ex nihilo*[484]). Creation is really the manifestation of the unmanifest (*avyakta*[485]), a process of becoming grosser (*sthūla*) from the finer (*sūkṣma*).[486] It is an evolutionary process in which all the events of creation, instead of happening all of a sudden at a single moment, proceed gradually.[487] The Vedāntic scriptures do express the seminal evolutionary sequences in a nutshell.[488] Although the details are lacking, the principle[489] is unequivocally stated. The evolution in science is mechanical and based on chance-actions. Chance phenomena are not ignored in Vedāntic evolution. But what are called chances and random events are also law-based and mathematically precise. Vedāntic evolution is purposive and intelligence-regulated. *Īśvara* who is omniscient is the *adhyakṣa* (presiding Deity) of every entity of the universe. Everything in nature evolves only due to the presiding action of *Īśvara*.[490]

The evolution in science is linear, whereas it is helical in the Marxist concept. In the linear or the helical evolution, it is held that the universe is eternal, without a beginning and an end. Vedānta rejects the idea of an eternal universe. According to it, anything that is a product must have a beginning. The universe is a product and hence has a beginning. Secondly, anything that has a beginning must have an end.[491] No entity in the universe can maintain its form without expenditure of energy. No entity is without motion which needs expenditure of energy. All entities undergo modifications involving expenditure of energy. Matter and energy are in functional stages for which energy is to be expended. The universe is finite; although vast, it is not infinite. When it came into existence, it started with a zero energy-mass. The oppositely poised particles of energy and matter had a net value of zero. With constant expenditure and degradation of energy from the inception of the universe, it is expected that a time will come when the world cannot maintain itself and would cease to exist. There is perpetual transformation of different forms of matter and energy. But, in this process of transformation, some useful energy is converted to unutilizable energy. The latter goes on increasing with the arrow of time and the former continues to diminish in quantity. There is a final point when the whole universe cannot exist. Hence Śaṅkara concludes that the universe must have an end. Advaita Vedānta contends that the cosmic processes are cyclic. The world emanates from *Māyā*, undergoes a series of evolutionary processes, traverses back the pathway through involutionary processes, and finally dissolves in *Māyā*.[492] A crude example may be given here to stress the need of dissolution. In the operation a fridge, the gas absorbs the heat from inside the fridge and throws it outside. In the process, the gas must be compressed to the liquid state in order to repeat the cycle. Similar is the case with the universe, which is also an isolated system beyond which there is nothing, not even the so-called vacuum and the empty space. The unutilizable energy of the universe must be reconverted to the energy of Brahman (*māyāśakti*) for repeating the cycle.

The word *brahma-cakra*[493] (cycle of Brahmā) has been used in the Upaniṣads. The Ṛg-Veda[494] presents the concept of the cyclic universe. Hence the concept of the eternality of the universe with linear or helical pathway of evolution is not upheld in the Vedas and the Vedānta.

The concept of the oscillating universe is prevalent in science in the second half of the twentieth century. According to this concept, the universe begins with the singularity, expands and evolves, and then contracts back to the point of singularity. The world oscillates between the point of singularity and the maximum expanded volume through the explosive process of the big bang and the implosive process of the big crunch. The cosmological model of Advaita Vedānta is not the same as the oscillating universe. What is called the cyclic universe in Advaita Vedānta is not really cyclic also. Plane geometry with cycles is incapable to express the Vedāntic cosmological model. The "spider's universe"[495] is the terminology used to describe the cosmological model of Advaita Vedānta. *Māyā* is compared with the spider. The spider's net is thrown out from its own body; the net is again reabsorbed into it. Likewise the world is thrown out from *Māyā* in all directions in the phase of creation and reabsorbed into *Māyā* in the phase of dissolution. A knowledge of solid geometry is necessary to conceive of the geometric form of the model. The model is cyclic in the sense of the repetitions of two cycles or phases—one phase of emanation and a second phase of dissolution, one phase of appearance and expansion and a second phase of contraction and disappearance.

The cosmological model, as described in the foregoing paragraph, has another nomenclature in the Ṛg-Veda.[496] It is the weaver's model. The creation is likened to a weaver's job. The threads are spread out or extended on every side. The forward weaving is *pravaya*; the backward weaving is *apavaya*. The image of the forward and backward movements of the shuttles (*tasarāṇi*) of a weaver has been given. The creation phase is compared to the forward movement of the shuttles. The dissolution phase is like the backward movement of the shuttles.

Dissolution (*pralaya*) is also a gradual process. It is the reverse sequence of the creative processes.[497] The creative processes are events of becoming coarse and coarser whereas the dissolution processes are events of becoming fine and finer.[498]

There will be a time when the expanding universe stops further expansion and starts contracting itself. In the process of contraction, all solids are first liquefied. On further contraction of the liquid mass, too much heat is generated. As a result, the liquid mass is gasified. The process of contraction continues. Hydrogen, the simplest gas, disintegrates in the environment of excessive pressure. The sub-atomic particles also disintegrate, resulting in the conversion of all gaseous matter into space (*ākāśa*). The dissolution process is further accelerated. *Ākāśa* is converted to *prāṇa* which, in turn, is converted to *āpaḥ*. In the final stage of dissolution, *āpaḥ* is merged into *Māyā* or *avyakta*, the unmanifested **power of Brahman. The time of the final dissolution is the maximum** (t_m), beyond which there is no time. This sequence of dissolution, as has been described here, has been stated in a number of scriptures.[499] After the dissolution and before the next manifestation there is nothing else other than the non-dual Brahman with its own power. The world disappears, but is not reduced to nihil. It is merged into its original source from which it manifested.[500] *Paramātmā* (the Great Self) is the eater of all the movable and immovable, everything of the universe.[501] Similar idea has also been given in the Vedas[502] and the Upaniṣads.[503]

Vedānta consistently declares that the universe manifests from *avyakta* or *Māyā* and is finally dissolved in *Māyā*.[504] This process is repeated *ad infinitum*. It had no beginning in the past; it will have no end in the future. Vedānta further holds that both the phases of manifestation and dissolution are not mechanical; instead, these are guided and controlled by *Parameśvara* (God) whose power is *Māyā*.[505]

With reference to the duration of time for the manifestation and the dissolution of the universe, some scriptural evidences[506] are available. The *Viṣṇu Purāṇa* gives detailed information for making an estimate of the total life of the universe. A day (excluding the night) of Brahmā is known as a *kalpa*. According to one estimate, 5.13828 billion human years make one day of Brahmā, which comprises fourteen *manvantaras*.[507] According to a second estimate, 4.32 billion human years make one day of Brahmā.[508] The former estimate may be taken as an example to calculate the life of Brahmā. The duration of his night is the same as that of his day.[509] His year contains 360 days. He lives for one hundred years. His span of life is technically known as *para*,[510] which is 369.95616 trillion (one trillion = 10^{12}) human years, and his half-life (*parārdha*) contains 184.97808 trillion human years. According to the second estimate, a *para* contains 311.04 trillion human years. At the termination of a *kalpa*, during the night of Brahmā, the three worlds of *bhuḥ*, *bhuvaḥ* and *svaḥ* remain dissolved. This is called occasional dissolution (*naimittika pralaya*[511]). At the termination of a *para*, with the death of Brahmā, the total universe is dissolved in *Māyā*. This is the total or final dissolution (*prākṛta pralaya*). The phase of expansion of the universe lasts the first *parārdha*, from the beginning of time (t_o) to the mid-point of time ($t_{1/2}$). The phase of contraction of the universe lasts the second *parārdha*, from the mid-point of time ($t_{1/2}$) to the end or the maximum point of time (t_m).

In the cosmological model of Advaita Vedānta, the creation does not start from the singularity and again end in the singularity. The source of the empirical universe is *Māyā* which is also the final receiver. *Māyā*, the power of Brahman, is not an absolute entity, it itself being not existent, not non-existent and not existent and non-existent. And hence in the final analysis, the source and the goal of the empirical universe is Brahman which is Consciousness. In the evolution in science, consciousness is not primary, and it develops from matter as its property at some stage of evolution. What is said in science is accepted by Advaita Vedānta regarding the emergence of consciousness of beings.[512] On the other hand, Advaita Vedānta contends that there is nothing which is completely devoid of consciousness and that even the immovable beings are also conscious (*cetanāvantaḥ sthāvarāḥ*[513]). In the presence or in the absence of the universe, there is the absolute Consciousness which is primary and fundamental, and that is Brahman. Science has not yet been able to identify this fundamental Being. In this connection, the quotation of Fritjof Capra on the statement of Stanistav Grof may be cited here.

> This is a question which comes up again and again in psychedelic sessions at the transpersonal level, Grof explained, and there is a fundamental shift of perception. The question of conventional Western science—Where is the moment at which consciousness originates? When does matter become conscious of itself?—is turned upside down. The question now becomes: How does consciousness produce the illusion of matter? You see, consciousness is seen as something primordial, which cannot be explained on the basis of anything else; something that is just there and which, ultimately, is the only reality; something that is manifest in you and me, and in everything around us.[514]

Turīya

The *Māṇḍūkyopaniṣad* presents the quintessence of Advaita philosophy in which the concept of *Turīya* gains much importance. It says: Whatever was in the past, is at the present and will be in the future is Brahman. Whatever is beyond the three times is Brahman.[515] The *jīva* or the individual self is Brahman and it has four fourths (*ayamātmā brahma, so'yamātmā catuṣpād*[516]).

The first fourth of the self is Vaiśvānara which is active in the waking (*jāgarita*) state, cognitive outwardly (*bahiṣprajñaḥ*) and enjoying the gross (*sthūlabhuk*[517]). The second fourth is the *Taijasa* which is active in the dreaming state (*svapna*), cognitive inwardly (*antaḥprajñaḥ*) and enjoying the subtle.[518] The third fourth is the *Prājña* that is in the sphere of deep and dreamless sleep (*suṣupti*), in which there are no desires whatsoever. This *Prājña* is unified (*ekībhūtaḥ*); it is a cognition-mass (*prajñānaghana*); it consists of bliss (*ānandamaya*) and enjoys bliss (*ānandabhuk*[519]). It is the lord of all, the knower of all, the controller of all and the source of all; it is the origin and end of beings.[520]

The *Turīya* is the fourth state of the self. It is not inwardly cognitive, not outwardly cognitive, not both-wise cognitive, not a cognition-mass, not cognitive, not non-cognitive. It cannot be seen; it cannot be dealt with; it is ungraspable; it has no distinctive marks; it is unthinkable, indefinable. It is the essence of the consciousness of the oneness of the self (*ekātmapratyayasāram*). It is the state in which all phenomena cease (*prapañcopaśamam*). *Turīya* is quiescent (*śāntam*), blissful (*śivam*) and non-dual (*advaitam*). It this state, the *jīva* (individual self) is non-different from Brahman. The Upaniṣad states: He is the self. He is to be realized (*sa ātmā sa vijñeyaḥ*[521]).

Śaṅkara *versus* Gauḍapāda

Gauḍapāda was the grand-teacher of Śaṅkara. Both were non-dualistic Vedāntists. There are many things common in the systems of both these philosophers. Nevertheless, there are sharp differences also. What are the salient differences in the non-dualism of Śaṅkara and that of Gauḍapāda will be discussed here.

The non-dualism of Gauḍapāda has been very much influenced by the doctrine of Mahāyāna Buddhism. In shaping the main tenets of his non-dualism, he has borrowed some ideas from the Buddhist Yogācāras or the Vijñānavādins. Śaṅkara has also been charged by some as a crypto-Buddhist (*pracchanna bauddha*). Such a charge, however, has no solid foundation. He is a strong critic of Buddhist philosophy and has unequivocally rejected some of its basic concepts.

In book II of Gauḍapāda's Kārikā,[522] he tries to establish the unreality (*vaitathya*) of the external world, which is like a dream, an illusion or a city of *Gandharvas* (an imaginary city in the sky). The Vijñānavādins who are subjective idealists do not recognize the existence of the external world. They recognize the existence of cognitions (*vijñāna*) only. For them, the object of perception is nothing but a subjective cognition. They hold that the object (*viṣaya*) and its cognition (*jñāna*) are identical with each other, and further state that the external world is the creation or transformation of the mind. They account for the variety of perceptions (*pratyayavaicitrya*) by a recourse to the variety of subconscious impressions (*vāsanāvaicitrya*). As the seeds and sprouts are related to each other as causes and effects, so are perceptions and subconscious impressions (*vāsanā*) in the beginningless cycle of the *saṁsāra* (the cosmic existence). *Māyā* is Gauḍapāda's equivalent for the *vāsanā* of Maitreya, a prominent exponent of Vijñānavāda. For Gauḍapāda, the world which does not exist is a mere imagination (*kalpanā*) of the Self (*Ātman*) through its own *Māyā*.[523] Whatever is experienced in the dream is imagined in mind (*citta*). Those seen in wakefulness are also imagined in mind. The former are imagined inside; they are not fixed and hence vanish at once. The latter are imagined outside and are fixed. Our external world constitutes those that are imagined outside.[524] Gauḍapāda does not make any distinction between those imagined inside and those imagined outside.[525] In other words, he does not differentiate the dream experiences from the waking experiences and asserts the unreality of both these experiences alike.[526] Of course, he does recognize one single distinguishing characteristic; the waking perceptions are cognized with the sense-organs which are not necessary for the dream experiences.[527] In the series of imaginations, the first thing that is imagined by the Self is the *jīva* (individual self) and thereafter the other ideas (*bhāvas*), both external and internal.[528] It is to be noted here that the manifold worldly appearances are mere ideas for Gauḍapāda. In his opinion, whatever is seen in the waking state and the dream state is nothing but one's *citta* (mind).[529] All this is only *citta* (*cittamātram*). All what is experienced is visible to the mind only (*cittadṛśyam*) and what is visible to the mind is the mind. These ideas are prominent in the *Laṅkāvatāra-sūtra* and other sources of literature of the Yogācāras. Vijñānavāda exerted profound influence on Gauḍapāda who has described subjective idealism in his *Āgamaśāstra*. The subjective idealists of Buddhist philosophy use the term *ālayavijñāna* for the mind (*citta*). It is the stream of self-cognitions. It is transformed into manifold object-cognitions. These objective presentations (*pravṛttivijñāna*) owe their origin to the mind, and not to the external objects which do not exist. Thus subjective self-cognitions appear to be objective presentations which serve all empirical purposes. Object-cognitions appear to be distinct from self-cognitions, although, in reality, the former are identical with the latter. When *avidyā* (nescience) with *vāsanā* (psychical dispositions) is destroyed, consciousness, free from the duality of subject and object and devoid of egoism, becomes pure. This is the seminal concept of the subjective idealism of the

Yogācāras, who recognize cognition as the only ontological reality. Gauḍapāda has borrowed this concept from the Yogācāras. The external world does not exist for him. What we call the external world is simply the mental construct for Gauḍapāda. But he recognizes the unchanging, eternal (*nitya*) Brahman in contradistinction with the Vijñānavādin's everchanging cognitions (*vijñāna*) that are momentary (*kṣaṇika*) but that constitute a stream of consciousness (*santāna*) which is enduring (*dhruva*).

For Śaṅkara, the external world is not non-existent (*asat*) although it is not absolute (*paramārtha*). He urges that we cannot deny the existence of an external object which is actually perceived.[530] He is of the view that the existence of an object is independent of the act of perception. He admits the externality of the object to our perception on account of the very fact of perception.[531] Whether an object is possible or impossible is dependent only upon the operation or non-operation of the means of right knowledge.[532] What is clearly apprehended by all the means of right knowledge can never be considered to be impossible.[533]

The Vijñānavādin holds that an act of perception and an object of perception are identical with each other. He derives such an inference from the fact that we invariably apprehend an act of perception and an object of perception together. He asserts that nobody ever perceives an object of perception apart from the act of perception. Thus, in Vijñānavāda, the object is not distinct from its cognition. Śaṅkara refutes these arguments of the Vijñānavādin and contends that the act of perception and the object of perception are distinct from each other.[534] It is a fact that one can never perceive an object without the act of perception. But this inseparability is no proof of their identity. If X happens, Y happens and both of them happen together, their identity cannot be established from this mere concurrent happenings. The cognition is the means (*upāya*) and the object is the end (*upeya*). In the absence of an object there can never be a cognition which is the means of apprehending an object. Thus Śaṅkara refutes the notion of the Vijñānavādin that an object is identical with its cognition.

The Yogācāra argues that cognitions are perceived and hence they exist. The same argument is put forward by Śaṅkara to disprove the Yogācāra notion of the non-existence of the external world. The external objects are also perceived and hence Śaṅkara urges that their existence, independent of cognitions, is to be recognized.[535]

According to Vijñānavāda, cognitions are self-luminous or self-apprehending. Śaṅkara rejects such an idea and contends that cognitions are apprehended by the witness self (*sākṣin*) which is self-luminous. Cognitions are fleeting but the witness self is permanent. The witness self is the knowing subject; the cognitions are the known objects; and they are essentially different in nature. Śaṅkara attributes the variety of cognitions to the variety of objects. Although consciousness is common to different cognitions, the difference in the contents of cognitions is brought about by the differences inherent in the objects. The different objects qualify consciousness in different ways; but the consciousness which is common to all cognitions remains unaltered and permanent. Had there been no external objects, there would be no difference in the acts of cognition. Śaṅkara is emphatic on the point that consciousness and the external world can never be identified with each other. The Yogācāra does not recognize anything as a permanent entity. He regards the individual cognitions as discrete and momentary. They come into being in a moment; they pass away in the next moment. There is no individual continuity except one stream of consciousness (*santāna*). Śaṅkara urges that the Vijñānavādins must require one permanent, intelligent principle or the Self to witness the production and destruction of all these cognitions which are devoid of self-luminosity.[536]

In Vijñānavāda, the waking state and the dream state are equated. Gauḍapāda expounds the same idea in his *Āgamaśāstra*.[537] Śaṅkara does not agree with Gauḍapāda on this point.[538] He thinks that dream cognitions are essentially different from waking perceptions. Dream cognitions are contradicted by waking perceptions which are not contradicted by any empirical experience whatsoever. Besides, dream cognitions are of the nature of recollection whereas waking perceptions are perceptions of external objects. Recollection arises in the absence of an external object; for a perception to take place, the presence of an external object is necessary. Thus Śaṅkara is reluctant to explain the waking perceptions in the absence of external objects.

Thus, contrary to the popular misconception that Śaṅkara is an illusionist who advocates a type of acosmic Vedānta, his refutation of the subjective idealism of the Yogācāra system or the Vijñānavāda has been discussed here. Śaṅkara does posit the existence of the external world. Nevertheless, he is not a realist; without any doubt, he is known in the philosophical world as an idealist. But he is an absolute idealist instead of a subjective idealist. Brahman which is pure Consciousness is the absolute truth (*pāramārthika satya*) for him. But, being an absolutist and a non-dualist, he does recognize the manifold phenomena of the universe as a practical or empirical truth (*vyāvahārika satya*). The empirical truth, for Śaṅkara, is relative and dependent upon the absolute truth.

The practical truth in Śaṅkara's philosophy parallels the conventional truth (*saṁvṛti satya*) in Mahāyāna Buddhism. Gauḍapāda takes the help of this *saṁvṛti satya* to explain the manifold phenomena of the world. "Things (*dharmas*) which are said to be generated are not really born, but are empirically (*saṁvṛtyā*) born. Their generation is likened to *Māyā* (magical display), and that *Māyā*, too, does not exist".[539] Although Gauḍapāda is regarded as a non-dualistic Vedāntist, his use of the word *Māyā* has resemblance with Buddhist philosophy and has nothing common with the *Māyā* concept of Śaṅkara. Gauḍapāda says: "An illusive sprout germinates from an illusive seed. That sprout is neither eternal nor destructible. The same applies to all things".[540] According to Gauḍapāda, whatever empirically exists is imagined (*kalpita*[541]) only. It has no real existence in the absolute (*paramārtha*) sense. That which empirically exists is dependent (*paratantra*) for its existence or origination.

The theory of causation (*hetuphalabhāva*) is discarded by Gauḍapāda. He does not maintain the theory that the cause itself is the effect.[542] He does not find any reason for correlating cause and effect with certain order between them.[543] He asserts that nothing is produced either from itself or from anything other than itself.[544] The beginning of a cause cannot be proved; neither can be proved the beginning of an effect. As such does neither cause nor effect come into being.[545]

The stand taken by Śaṅkara on the theory of causation is, however, different from that of Gauḍapāda. To explain the existence and the functioning of the empirical world, Śaṅkara does recognize the empirical causes and effects. The distinction between the cause and the effect may be maintained as it is in common experience.[546] The foam, ripple, wave, bubble, etc. which are different modifications of the sea do not lose their individuality although all of them are non-different from the sea-water.

Śaṅkara says that the empirical distinction between the cause and the effect may be maintained for practical purposes (*vyavahārābhiprāyeṇa*) only. He further says that, in the absolute sense (*paramārthābhiprāyeṇa*), their non-difference (*tadananyatvam*) has to be recognized.[547] The elaboration of creation, etc. is made in order to declare the non-difference of the effect from the cause by means of examples of clay, etc.[548] Śaṅkara refutes the doctrine of difference in non-difference (*bhedābheda*). He does not find any difference between the cause and the effect, if considered in the absolute sense. The manifold world comprising space, etc. is the effect; its cause is the highest Brahman; in the absolute sense, the effect is non-different from that cause; apart from the cause, the effect cannot be an entity.[549]

In the opinion of Gauḍapāda, the embodied self (*jīva*) is an imagined one.[550] Śaṅkara holds that the embodied self is the Self (Brahman) with the body and the mind as the limiting adjunct. Without the embodied self, it is not possible to think of an empirical universe. If the existence of the embodied self is supplanted, the entire natural, empirical universe based on it is supplanted.[551] Śaṅkara proceeds with this line of thought a step ahead. The embodied self has no existence apart from Brahman, there being identity between the former and the latter. Thus, in the final analysis, the empirical universe has no existence apart from Brahman. Śaṅkara associates the empirical universe (*vyāvahārika jagat*) and its manifoldness (*nānātva*) with mistaken knowledge (*mithyājñāna*). On the dawn of true knowledge (*pāramārthika jñāna*), the manifoldness disappears and the principle of unity (*ekatva*) remains.

The doctrine of non-origination (*ajātivāda*) is an important aspect in the philosophy of Gauḍapāda. This has been borrowed by him from Buddhist philosophy. It has sometimes been a common misconception that Śaṅkara's Advaita Vedānta supports this doctrine of non-origination. It is, however, not true. Gauḍapāda's doctrine of non-origination is anti-Vedāntic and pro-Buddhist.

On this doctrine, Gauḍapāda says: "The existent is not born; whatever is non-existent is not born. For, disputing thus the adherents of non-two (*advaya*) proclaim the non-origination (*ajāti*)."[552] He further says: "Nothing is produced either from itself or from another; nor is anything born as existent, non-existent or both existent and non-existent".[553]

The Vedāntic theory is in favour of origination (*janmādyasya yataḥ*[554]). Gauḍapāda, being himself a Vedāntist, does not accept the concept of origination. He expresses his approval of the doctrine of non-origination of the *Advayavādins* or Buddhists. In this connection he says: "We applaud the non-origination being declared by them; we do not dispute; we listen to our non-dispute with them."[555]

Any school of Vedānta, including Śaṅkara's Advaita Vedānta, cannot accept the doctrine of non-origination. In Śaṅkara's system, nothing is born in the absolute sense. The non-dual Brahman ever remains as non-dual, without duality and multiplicity. But what is here said in the absolute sense is not the same in the empirical sense. There is an empirical world which is born, maintained and dissolved. At various places, Śaṅkara has given his clear opinion on the origin, sustenance and dissolution of the universe. In the empirical world causes are operative and effects are produced, the former preceding the latter.

Śaṅkara treats *Māyā* as an ontological principle. It is the power of Brahman, the material cause of the world and its final receptacle in which everything of the universe is dissolved. *Īśvara* functions as the Creator and the Controller of the universe through this power of *Māyā*. In Gauḍapāda's philosophy,[556] this word *Māyā* has been used a number of times. But its connotative meaning is different from what has been given in Śaṅkara's philosophy. Gauḍapāda's *Māyā* is a magical display, a deluding factor, but it is not an ontological principle. Gauḍapāda does not accept the existence of the universe; nothing is born nor destroyed in his system; there is no *Īśvara* for creating and controlling the universe; there are no causes and effects; hence his system does not need an ontological principle unlike the *Māyā* of Śaṅkara. Still the *Māyā* of Gauḍapāda is beginningless in the analogy of the *vāsanā* of the Bauddhas. The *jīva* (individual self) is deluded by *Māyā*. All the phenomena of the world and the world itself are imagined due to this deluding effect of *Māyā*. The mind vibrates and, as a result of this vibration, the concept of the duality of subject and object arises. The vibration of the mind is brought about by *Māyā*. Our experiences of duality of subject and object in both the dream and the waking conditions are born through this illusive power of *Māyā* which does not exist (*sā ca māyā na vidyate*[557]). It seems Brahman or *Ātman* is deluded by its own *Māyā*[558] and creates the manifold universe which is empirical but not real. In Śaṅkara's system, such a concept of Brahman or *Īśvara* being deluded by *Māyā* is not acceptable.

In Śaṅkara's *Advaita* (non-dualism), the *jīva* (individual self) is non-different from Brahman (Self). He compares Brahman with the great space (*mahākāśa*) and the *jīva* with the space in the pot (*ghaṭākāśa*). The gross and subtle bodies behave as limiting adjuncts (*upādhi*) in the analogy of the pots. On the destruction of the pots, the non-difference of Brahman and the *jīva* is restored. Similar idea regarding Brahman and the *jīva* has been expressed by Gauḍapāda.[559] But confusion has been confounded when Gauḍapāda says that the *jīva* is an imagined[560] one. Whatever we experience in the dream state and whatever we perceive in the waking state are all imagined. But, the *jīva* is imagined first prior to the imagination of all these things.[561] When Śaṅkara equates the *jīva* with Brahman, he cannot afford to assign such a fictional status to it.

The Buddhist philosophers use the three terms—*vijñāna*, *citta* and *manas*—interchangeably.[562] The Buddhist ideas have exerted profound influence on Gauḍapāda who has made a hybridization of the Vedāntic concept and the Buddhist concept of mind. As the Buddha says, all phenomena are *citta* (mind). Gauḍapāda has accepted this idea. Whatever one experiences in the dream state and whatever one perceives in wakefulness are nothing but one's *citta* or *manas* (mind).[563] The *citta* (*manas* or *vijñāna*) vibrates and this vibration (*spandana*) creates the concept of duality, the idea of subject (*grāhaka*) and object (*grāhya*[564]). The vibration is brought about by *Māyā*[565] and thus the manifold phenomena of the world (*prapañca*) is a magical display. In connection with the vibration of the *vijñāna* (mind), Gauḍapāda has compared it with the motion of a fire-brand (*alāta*).[566] When the mind moves, it appears as the perceiver (subject). These appearances are not produced from anything other than the *vijñāna*. When the mind is at rest, when it stops vibrating, the appearances are not in a place other than the *vijñāna*. With the vibration of mind, the appearances do not leave it to go out. With the quiescence of the mind, the appearances do not enter into it.

According to Gauḍapāda, the *antaścitta* (dream experiences) and the *bahiścitta* (waking perceptions) are imagined[567] by *Prabhu* (God). Thus, the appearances produced by the vibrating *vijñāna* or *citta* are not real and the *citta* itself is not real. The *citta* is not born and those made visible by the vibrating *citta* (*cittadṛśya*) are also not born.[568] The things are not produced from the mind, nor the mind from the things; neither the cause nor the effect has origination.[569] The mind is not an effect. It does not have any cause. It does not originate. Similarly, the appearances (things) are also not effects and they have no causes.[570]

In the Yogācāra or *Vijñānavāda*, nothing is real except the cognitions (*vijñāna*). The cognitions are momentary (*kṣaṇika*); they are not eternal (*nitya*); but the stream of consciousness (or cognitions) is enduring (*dhruva*). Being influenced by this idea of the Yogācāras, Gauḍapāda gives an ontological status to *citta* or *vijñāna*. The duality of the subject and the object is only the vibration of the *citta*. Without this vibration, the *citta* is objectless (*nirviṣaya*) and free from attachment (*asaṅga*).[571] Gauḍapāda declares that *aniṅgana* and *anābhāsa citta*, free from all types of distractions (*vikṣepa*), becomes Brahman.[572] Such a *vijñāna*, devoid of vibrations (*aspandamāna*), is *anābhāsa* (which does not produce appearances) and unborn (*aja*).[573]

Whatever duality is observed in both the movable and the immovable world is ascribed to the moving mind; once this mind (*manas*) is rendered non-mind (*amanībhāva*), the duality disappears.[574] The duality is appearance only, produced by the vibrations of the mind. With the cessation of the vibrations, all dualities disappear.[575] By specific methods of *yoga*, the mind can be restrained and rendered non-functional. For the indeterminate mind (*nirvikalpa manas*), there is no distinction of the subject and the object.[576]

But, what is this subject-less, object-less entity? Is it not the ontological Being? Can it be equated with the functionless, quiescent mind (*citta, manas, vijñāna*)?

Gauḍapāda undoubtedly is a non-dualist (*advaitaṁ paramārthataḥ*).[577] He mentions the non-dual Brahman in a number of places.[578] But it is a sheer confusion to equate Brahman with the non-functional, quiescent mind. Gauḍapāda has erred by mixing up *Vijñānavāda* and *Advaitavāda*. *Vijñāna* or the cognition of an individual being is not the same as the universal, pure Consciousness (*Cit*) which is Brahman. The stream of consciousness (*santāna*), if there is any, is not identical with the unchanging, eternal Consciousness (Brahman). In Advaita Vedānta, mind *albeit* subtle and imperceptible is material.[579] It is the principal component of the inner-organ (*antaḥkaraṇa*) or the subtle body (*sūkṣma śarīra*).[580] With the release of the *jīva*, with its re-identification with Brahman, as a consequence of the attainment of knowledge (*vidyā*) and the removal of nescience (*avidyā*), *manas* or mind is completely annihilated. Gauḍapāda has introduced confusion in his philosophy by equating the undisturbed *citta* with Brahman. He himself has stated that the *citta* is imagined. That being so, a fictional entity cannot be the unchanging, eternal, non-dual being.

NOTES

1. VPDA, Ch. II.
2. BSŚB, II. 1. 14; VPDA, Ch. IV.
3. TU, II. 1. 1; BU, V. 4. 1; V. 5. 1; MTU, VI. 3; VI. 8; VII. 7; CU, VI. 8. 7; VI. 9. 4; VI. 10. 3; VI. 11. 3; VI. 12. 3; VI. 13. 3; VI. 14. 3; VI. 15. 3; VI. 16. 3; VIII. 3. 4.
4. GMK, III. 36.
5. BSŚB, I .1. 1; II. 3. 17; BGŚB, II. 17; BU, IV. 4. 5; IV. 4. 25.
6. BSŚB, I. 1. 1.
7. BSŚB, II. 3. 7.
8. BGŚB, II. 18.
9. BSŚB, Intr.; BGŚB, II. 18; BU, III. 4. 1; III. 4. 2; III. 5. 1.
10. BSŚB, Intr. ; I. 1. 4.
11. BU, III. 4. 1; III. 4. 2; III. 5. 1; ŚU, III. 21; VI. 11; KTU, II. 2. 9-12; BSŚB, II. 2. 2.
12. KTU, II. 3. 1; BG, XV. 1-3.
13. CU, VI. 8. 7; VI. 9. 4; VI. 10. 3; VI. 11. 3; VI. 12. 3; VI. 13. 3; VI.14. 3; VI. 15. 3; VI. 16. 3.
14. TU, II. 6. 1.
15. KTU, II. 3. 12-13.
16. BSŚB, III. 2. 22; II. 1. 14; II. 3. 7; II. 3. 9; TUŚB, II. 6. 1.
17. BS, II. 2. 26.
18. BG, II. 16.
19. CU, VI. 8. 3-6; BSŚB, II. 3. 9; IUŚB, 4.
20. BS, III. 2. 16; BSŚB, I. 3. 19; III. 2. 16; III.2. 18; BUŚB, IV. 4. 18; ŚS, I. 1; ŚU, VI. 11; VI. 13.
21. TU, II. 1. 1.
22. AU, III. 3.
23. BU, IV. 5. 13; MAU, 5.
24. BSŚB, I. 1. 4; BU, III. 9. 28.

25. BU, II. 4. 12; BUŚB, IV. 4. 20.
26. GMK, IV. 45.
27. BSŚB, I. 1. 4; I. 3. 19; II. 1. 27; GMK, I. 17.
28. BUŚB, III. 7. 23.
29. ṚV, X. 190. 3; BS, I. 3. 30; II. 1. 36; BSŚB, I. 3. 30; II. 1. 36; BG, XV. 3; BGŚB, IX. 7-8; ŚU, I. 6; VI. 1; ŚUŚB, I. 4; VPu, I. 5. 59-61; Mbh-ŚP, 231. 48-9.
30. BS, I. 1. 2; I. 4. 23; BSŚB, I. 4. 23; II. 1. 14.
31. BSŚB, I. 1. 2; I. 1. 11; II. 1. 14; II. 2. 1; II. 2. 3; II. 2. 4.
32. BS, I. 1. 5.
33. BSŚB, I. 1. 5.
34. ṚV, X. 129. 4; BS, I. 1. 5; I. 1. 18; I. 4. 24; II. 3. 12; II. 3. 13; BSŚB, I. 4. 23; II. 1. 5; II. 3. 13; CU, VI. 2. 3-4; AU, I. 1. 1; PU, VI. 3; TU, II. 6. 1.
35. BSŚB, I. 1. 10.
36. BSŚB, I. 1. 11.
37. BS, II. 2. 1; BSŚB, II. 2. 1.
38. BS, I. 3. 10-11; I. 3. 43; BSŚB, I. 3. 11; II. 3. 23; BU, III. 7. 3-23; III. 8. 7-9; IV. 4. 22; MAU, 6; ŚU, II. 17; III. 1, 2, 4, 17, 18; VI. 12, 17; TU, II. 8. 1; KTU, II. 2. 12; BG, IV. 6; VIII. 9; X. 3.
39. BUŚB, III. 8. 9.
40. ṚV, X. 190. 1; MNU, I. 6; II. 6, 7; V. 5; VIII. 1; XII. 1.
41. BS, I. 2. 18; BSŚB, I. 2. 18; BU, III. 7. 3-23.
42. BSŚB, I. 3. 11; I. 3. 30; BG, X. 3.
43. BSŚB, I. 3. 11.
44. BS, I. 1. 2; I. 1. 4; I. 1. 10-11; I. 4. 23-28; BSŚB, I. 1. 2; I. 1. 4-5; I. 1. 10-11; I. 2. 2; I. 2. 9; I. 4. 23-28; II. 1. 14; II. 2. 1-2; BU, II. 5. 19; ŚU, VI. 9; ŚUŚB, I. 4; MAU, 6; TU, III. 1. 1; III. 2. 1; III. 3. 1; III. 4. 1; III. 5. 1; III. 6. 1; CU, III. 14. 1; CUŚB, III. 14. 1; BG, XIII. 16; BGŚB, VII. 6; XIII. 19.
45. BU, III. 9. 28; TU, II. 4. 1.
46. BS, I. 1. 12-19.
47. BS, I. 1. 12.
48. BSŚB, I. 1. 12.
49. BS, I. 1. 13.
50. BSŚB, I. 1. 13 (For the grammatical use of *mayaṭ*, see Pāṇini's *Aṣṭādhyāyī*, V. 4. 21).
51. MAU, 5; TU, II. 5. 1.
52. TU, II. 8. 1.
53. TU, II. 8. 1; II. 9. 1; III. 6. 1.
54. GMK, I. 4.
55. MUU, II. 2. 8; PU, II. 10.
56. MTU, VI. 13; VI. 23; VI. 27; KLU, 14; KSBU, III. 8 TBU, 8.
57. TU, II. 1. 1.
58. CU, I. 9. 2; BU, II. 4. 12; KTU, I. 3. 15; ŚU, I. 9; V. 1; V. 13; MTU, II. 4; VI. 17; VI. 28; VII. 4; JU, 2; BG, XI. 11; XI. 37; XI. 47.

59. TUŚB, Introduction (*na hi nityaṁ kiñcidārabhyate. loke yadārabdhaṁ tadanityam*).
60. KTU, I. 3. 15; ŚU, V. 13; BG, X. 3; XIII. 19; XIII. 31; BGŚB, XIII. 31.
61. MTU, I. 3. 15; ŚU, V. 13.
62. BGŚB, XIII. 31.
63. BS, II. 3. 9; ŚU, VI. 9.
64. BU, II. 5. 19; GMK, I. 26.
65. BU, IV. 4. 20; IV. 4. 22; IV. 4. 24-25; KTU, I. 2. 18; MUU, II. 1. 2; ŚU, II. 15; IV. 5; MTU, II. 4; VI. 17; VII. 1; GMK, I. 16; III. 1; III. 19; III. 26; III. 33; III. 36; III. 43; III. 47; IV. 11-13; IV. 38; IV. 57; IV. 80-81; IV. 93; BG, II. 21; IV. 6; VII. 25; X. 3; X. 12.
66. BSŚB, I. 1. 4; I. 2. 22; II. 1. 14; II. 1. 27; II. 3. 7; BUŚB, IV. 5. 14; BG, II. 25; BGŚB, II. 18; II. 20; II. 25.
67. BU, II. 5. 19; GMK, I. 26.
68. BSŚB, I. 1. 4; BU, IV. 4. 23; KTU, I. 2. 18; I. 3. 15; II. 2. 13; ŚU, I. 12; III. 21; IV. 21; VI. 2; VI. 17; MTU, VII. 8; MUU, I. 1. 6; III. 1. 5; KLU, 16; GMK, I. 3; III. 33; IV. 11; IV. 59; IV. 72; IV. 82; BG, II. 18; II. 21; II. 24; II. 26; II. 30; III. 15; III. 31; IX. 6; X. 9; XI. 52; XIII. 9; XVIII. 52; BGŚB, II. 18.
69. MTU, VI. 15; ŚU, VI. 5.
70. KTU, I. 3. 16; II. 2. 6; III. 3. 1; MTU, II. 4; VI. 28; KLU, 8; BG, II. 24; IV. 31; VII. 10; VIII. 20; XI. 18; XV. 7.
71. KTU, I. 2. 18; MTU, II. 4; VI. 28; BG, II. 20; X. 12; XI. 18; XVIII. 56.
72. BU, III. 8.8 (*anākāśam*); IV. 4. 20 (*para ākāśāt*).
73. ŚU, VI. 11; MTU, VI. 10; VII. 1; BG, XIII. 14; XIII. 31; BGŚB, II. 20; XIII. 12; XIII. 31.
74. BSŚB, I. 1. 4; ŚU, VI. 12; VI. 19; ŚUŚB, VI. 12; BGŚB, XIII. 12.
75. BSŚB, I. 1. 4; BG, XII. 3; XV. 16; BGŚB, XII. 3; XV. 16; SUS, 1 & 3.
76. MTU, II. 7; VI. 23; VI. 38; VII. 3; GMK, III. 37; BG, II. 24.
77. GMK, III. 22; III. 45; IV. 8; IV. 80; BG, II. 53.
78. BG, II. 24.
79. MTU, II. 4; II. 7; VI. 23; VI. 28; VII. 3.
80. KTU, I. 3. 15; ŚU, III. 12; VI. 10; MTU, VI. 18; MUU, I. 1. 6; III. 2. 7; GMK, I. 10-26; BG, II. 17; II. 21; IV. 1; IV. 13; VI. 24-25; VII. 13; IX. 18; XI. 4; XI. 18; XIII. 31; XIV, 5; XIV. 27; XV. 1; XV. 5; XV. 17; XVII. 20; XVIII. 56.
81. MTU, II. 4; VI. 28.
82. BU, III. 8. 8-11; V. 2. 1; V. 3. 1; V. 5. 1; V. 5. 3; KTU, I. 2. 16; I. 3. 2; ŚU, I. 7-8; I. 10, IV. 8; IV. 18; V. 1; MTU, VI. 2; VI. 4-5; VI. 23; VII. 6; VII. 11; MUU, I. 1. 5; I. 1. 7; I. 2. 13; II. 2. 2-3; PU, IV. 9-10; V. 5; CU, I. 1. 1; I. 1. 5-10; I. 2. 14; I. 3. 6-7; I. 4. 1; I. 4. 4-5; II. 10. 3-4; BG, VIII. 3. ; VIII. 11; VIII. 21; XI. 18; XI. 37; XII. 1; XII. 3.
83. BS, III. 2. 14; BSŚB, III. 2. 14; KTU, I. 3. 15; ŚU, III. 10; KLU, 6; GMK, III. 36.
84. BU, II. 3. 1; II. 3. 3; III. 3. 5; MTU, VI. 3; VII. 1-2; MUU, II. 1. 2; PU, I. 5; GMK, II. 23.

85. YV, XL. 8; IU. 8.
86. BSŚB, III. 2. 14.
87. BU, IV. 4. 20; KTU, I. 3. 15; MTU, VI. 38; VII. 3; BG, XII. 3.
88. VS, VIII. 2. 3.
89. VS, I. 1. 15.
90. VS, VII. 2. 26; IX. 1. 1; IX. 1. 3.
91. DPV, Ch. II, Verse 3.
92. TS, V. 29.
93. TS, V. 30.
94. KPS, Ch. II, Verses 3-4.
95. SS, Ch. I, Verses 11-12.
96. TS, V. 37.
97. TSUB, V. 40.
98. KPS, Ch. II, Verse 7.
99. MaS, Ch. VII, Verses 30-31.
100. NVV, Verse 22.
101. TUŚB, II. 6. 1.
102. KTU, I. 3. 12; MUU, I. 1. 6; III. 1. 7; MTU, II. 5; ŚU, IV. 14; V. 12; VI. 3; KLU, 16; GMK, II. 23; BG, XIII. 15; BGŚB, XIII. 15.
103. BG, II. 25; BGŚB, II. 25.
104. KTU, I. 3. 15; II. 3. 7; II. 3. 9; MTU, II. 5; II. 7; MUU, I. 1. 6; III. 1. 8; MAU, 7; BU, III. 4. 2; III. 7. 23; IV. 5. 15; BSŚB, I. 1. 2; II. 1. 27; BGŚB, II. 21; II. 25; XIII. 12.
105. BS, II. 1. 27; BSŚB, II. 1. 27.
106. BSŚB, I. 1. 2; BGŚB, XIII. 12.
107. VPDA, Ch. I.
108. BSŚB, III. 2. 21.
109. BS, II. 3. 7; BSŚB, II. 3. 7; III. 2.16-18; BUŚB, III. 8. 12; IV. 4. 20; BU, IV. 5. 13.
110. BU, I. 4. 11; I. 4. 17; I. 6. 3; CU, VI. 2. 1; MUU, I. 2. 5; II. 2. 5; AU, I. 1; TU, II. 8. 1; IU, 4; ŚU, I. 3; III. 1; III. 7; IV. 1; VI. 11; VI. 12; VI. 15; MTU, VI. 4; VI. 17; KLU, 6; GMK, I. 1; II. 5; III. 5.
111. ŚU, I. 11; IV. 18; VI. 11.
112. KLU, 19; GMK, II. 35; IV. 45; IV. 80.
113. MAU, 7; 12; GMK, I. 10; I. 16; I. 17; II. 18; II. 36; III. 18.
114. CU, VI. 2. 1-2; KLU, 23.
115. ŚU, VI. 5; MTU, VI. 15; PU, VI. 5.
116. ŚU, VI. 19; MUU, II. 2. 9; III. 1. 8; KLU, 23.
117. BU, IV. 4. 20.
118. BUŚB, IV. 4. 20.
119. BSŚB, I. 1. 4; BGŚB, II. 17; II. 20; II. 25; XIII. 31.
120. KTU, II. 1. 11; BU, IV. 4. 19.
121. CU, VII. 24. 1

122. CU, VII. 25. 1; TU, II. 1. 1.
123. MUU, II. 2. 12.
124. MUUŚB, II. 1. 10.
125. BU, III. 8. 7.
126. ŚU, III. 11; III. 21; MUU, I. 1. 6; BG, II. 24; III. 15; XIII. 32; BSŚB, III. 2. 19.
127. ŚU, VI. 11; BSŚB, I. 1. 4.
128. KTU, I. 2. 22; II. 1. 4; MTU, VI. 7; MUU, I. 1. 6; KLU, 6; ŚU, III. 21; IV. 4; GMK, I. 1; I. 10; BG, V. 15; X. 12.
129. IU, 8.
130. BGŚB, VIII. 22.
131. BG, II. 17; VIII. 22; IX. 4; XI. 38; BGŚB, VIII. 22.
132. BU, III. 8. 7; III. 8. 11; IUŚB, 4.
133. BU, II. 4. 6; II. 5. 1; BGŚB, II. 16.
134. KTU, II. 3. 8; MTU, VI. 31, VI. 35; VII. 2; ŚU, VI. 9.
135. MAU, 7.
136. KTUŚB, II. 3. 8.
137. BUŚB, III. 9. 26.
138. BU, III. 8. 8; III. 9. 26; IV. 2. 4; IV. 3. 15-16; IV. 4. 22; IV. 5. 15; GMK, IV. 72; IV. 96.
139. BSŚB, I. 1. 2; BGŚB, XIII. 12. 4; GMK, IV. 16.
140. KTU, I. 3. 15.
141. BSŚB, I. 1. 2; I. 1. 4; BGŚB, II. 25; XIII. 12.
142. MTU, VI. 34; GMK, IV. 72.
143. BSŚB, *Adhyāsa-bhāṣyam*, Introduction.
144. BGŚB, II. 25; XII. 3; MTNU, VI. 17; MAU, 7; MTU, V. 1; VI. 17; VI. 19; VII. 1; KLU, 6; GMK, IV. 41; IV. 52.
145. KTU, I. 2. 9; MTNU, VI. 17; MS, I. 5.
146. BU, II. 4. 14.
147. BU, IV. 5. 15.
148. BU, III. 4. 2.
149. BU, III. 7. 23.
150. KTU, II. 1. 3.
151. KTUŚB, II. 1. 3.
152. KNU, I. 2.
153. KNU, I. 3.
154. KNU, I. 5-9.
155. MUU, II. 2. 11; KTU, II. 2. 15; ŚU, VI. 14.
156. BU, III. 8. 8; MAU, 12; GMK, I. 23; I. 29.
157. BU, III. 8. 8; IV. 4. 20.
158. MTU, VI. 15.
159. BU, II. 5. 19; III. 8. 8; IV. 5. 13; GMK, I. 26.

160. BU, II. 5. 19; III. 8. 8; IV. 5. 13; GMK, I. 26.
161. BU, IV. 4. 20; MTU, V. I; VII. 1; BG, II. 18; XI. 17; XI. 42.
162. GMK, I. 29.
163. BS, II. 2. 28.
164. BSŚB, II. 2. 28.
165. YS, I. 7 (Transl. by J. H. Woods).
166. BUŚB, IV. 4. 18.
167. BSŚB, I. 1. 4; III. 2. 18; VC, 211.
168. BUŚB, IV. 3. 9.
169. BSŚB, II. 2. 28.
170. CUŚB, VI. 5. 1.
171. BU, IV. 4. 18; BUŚB, IV. 3. 10; CUŚB, VI. 11. 2 (*cetanāvantaḥ sthāvarāḥ*); KNU, I. 2; ŚU, VI. 14; KTU, II. 2. 15; MUU, II. 2. 11; BG, XV. 6.
172. MTU, VI. 34; BU, IV. 4. 6; BUŚB, IV. 4. 6; ABSS, Ch. IV, p. 295; VSS, 61-69; VPDA, Ch. I.
173. CUŚB, VII. 3. 1.
174. BSŚB, I. 1. 2.
175. MS, I. 5; BU, III. 4. 2; III. 7. 23; III. 8. 8; III. 8. 11; IV. 5. 15; MUU, I. 1. 6; ŚU, III. 19.
176. BS, I. 1. 1.
177. BS, IV. 1. 1.
178. CU, VII. 16. 1.
179. CU, VIII. 1. 1-2.
180. CU, VIII. 7. 1.
181. BU, IV. 4. 21.
182. ŚU, VI. 18.
183. BGŚB, II. 21. 5.
184. BU, IV. 4. 19-20; IV. 5. 6; KTU, II. 1. 11; II. 3. 9; MUU, III. 1. 9; BGŚB, II. 21. 5; ṚV, I. 61. 2; BSŚB, IV. 1. 1-2.
185. BU, II. 4. 5.
186. CUŚB, VIII. 1. 1.
187. BS, I. 1. 1; BSŚB, I. 1. 1; I. 1. 4; II. 1. 4; II. 2. 2; IV. 1. 1-3; BU, I. 4. 7; I. 4. 15; II. 4. 5; IV. 4. 21; IV. 5. 6; CU, VIII. 7. 1; MUU, II. 2. 9; TU, II. 1. 1; ŚU, I. 10; KNU, I. 4; BGŚB, XIII. 15.
188. BU, II. 4. 1; III. 4. 2; III. 5. 1; BSŚB, Intr.
189. BSŚB, Intr. ; I. 1. 4; KTU, II. 1. 1; SUS, 1 & 3.
190. BU, I. 4. 10.
191. AU, V. 3.
192. BU, II. 5. 19.
193. CU, VI. 8. 7; VI. 9. 4; VI. 10. 3; VI. 11. 3; VI. 12. 3; VI. 13. 3; VI. 14. 3; VI. 15. 3; VI. 16. 3.

194. S. Katz, *Mysticism and Philosophical Analysis*, Oxford University Press, New York, 1978, p. 96.
195. A. R. White, *Methods of Metaphysics*, Croom Helm, London, 1987.
196. L. Wittgenstein, 1977 (Ist German edn, 1921; Ist Engl. edn, 1922). *Tractatus Logico-Philosophicus*, 4.1212, p. 26. London: Routledge & Kegan Paul.
197. TUŚB, II. 6. 1.
198. BGŚB, XIII. 12. 4.
199. TU, II. 9. 1.
200. BU, III. 8. 8.
201. MUU, I. 1. 6.
202. MUU, III. 1. 7.
203. IU, 4; 5.
204. BG, XIII. 15.
205. KTU, I. 2. 20.
206. KTU, I. 2. 21.
207. KTUŚB, I. 2. 21.
208. BU, II. 3. 6; III. 9. 26; IV. 2. 4; IV. 4. 22; IV. 5. 15.
209. BSŚB, III. 2. 17.
210. BSŚB, III. 2. 17.
211. L. Wittgenstein, 1977 (Ist German edn, 1921; Ist English edn, 1922). *Tractatus Logico-Philosophicus*, 7, p. 74. London: Routledge & Kegan Paul.
212. BU, IV. 5. 15; CU, VI. 2. 1; BGŚB, XIII. 12.
213. ŚU, VI. 5; MTU, VI. 15.
214. ŚU, VI. 19; MUU, II. 2. 10; BGŚB, XIII. 12. 4.
215. BGŚB, II. 17; II. 20. 2; II. 25. 1; XIII. 31.
216. VC, 478; 494.
217. BS, II. 1. 26; BSŚB, II. 1. 26.
218. BSŚB, II. 1. 26-27.
219. BSŚB, II. 1. 27.
220. BS, II. 1. 28.
221. BSŚB, II. 1. 14.
222. CU, VI. 8. 7; CUŚB, VI. 2. 2; KTUŚB, II. 3. 12; IUŚB, 4; AU, III. 3; ŚU, IV. 11; GMK, IV. 45; BSŚB, II. 2. 3; BGŚB, X. 39; VC, 231; VPDA, Ch. VII.
223. VSS, 49.
224. TUŚB, II. 6. 1.
225. CU, VII. 25. 2.
226. CU, III. 14. 1.
227. MUU, II. 2. 12.
228. BU, II. 4. 6.
229. BU, II. 5. 1.

230. CU, VI. 8. 7.
231. BSŚB, I. 2. 22; II. 1. 14; II. 1. 24; ŚU, 1. 3; IV. 1; ŚUŚB, I. 3; BGŚB, XIII. 5; XIII. 19; XIV. 3; XV. 1; XV. 16; VC, 110.
232. BG, XIII. 19; BGŚB, XIII. 19; XV. 4; XV. 16; ŚU, IV. 5; GMK, I. 16; VC, 110.
233. BS, I. 4. 3; BSŚB, I. 4. 3; I. 4. 9; ŚUŚB, I. 3; ŚU, IV. 10; BGŚB, IV. 6.
234. BSŚB, I. 2. 22; I. 4. 3.
235. BSŚB, I. 4. 2-3.
236. VC, 110.
237. BSŚB, I. 4. 3; II. 1. 14; ŚU, IV. 10; KTUŚB, I. 3. 11; BGŚB, Intr.; IV. 6; VII. 14; VII. 25; IX. 10; XIII. 19; XIII. 29; XIV, 3; XV. 16; VC, 110.
238. BSŚB, I. 2. 22; I. 4. 3; III. 1. 14; KTUŚB, I. 3. 11; BGŚB, VIII. 20.
239. BSŚB, I. 2. 22; I. 4. 2-3; KTUŚB, I. 3. 11; BG, VIII. 18; VIII. 20; BGŚB, Intr.; XIII. 5; VC, 110.
240. BSŚB, I. 2. 22; I. 4. 3; MUU, II. 1. 2; BG, XV. 16; BGŚB, XV. 16.
241. BSŚB, I. 4. 2; II.1. 14; II. 3. 9; ŚUŚB, I. 9; ŚU, IV. 10; BG, IV. 6; IX. 7-8; XIII. 19; BGŚB, Intr.; IV. 6; VII. 6; IX. 7-8; IX. 10; XIII. 29; XIV. 3.
242. BSŚB, I. 4. 8; I. 4. 11; BGŚB, Intr.
243. BSŚB, I. 4. 2.
244. BSŚB, I. 4. 2; II. 1. 14; II. 3. 9; BGŚB, XIV. 3; IX. 7-8; XIII. 19; XIV. 3; IX. 10; XV. 16; DBhā, I. 2. 5.
245. BSŚB, I. 4. 8.
246. BGŚB, IX. 10.
247. BGŚB, Intr.
248. BGŚB, IV. 6.
249. BGŚB, VII. 6.
250. BGŚB, VII. 14.
251. BGŚB, IX. 7.
252. BGŚB, IX. 10.
253. BGŚB, XIII. 19.
254. BGŚB, XIII. 29.
255. BGŚB, XIV. 3.
256. BSŚB, II. 1. 14.
257. ŚUŚB, I. 3.
258. ŚUŚB, I. 9.
259. BSŚB, Intr. (*Adhyāsa-Bhāṣya*).
260. BSŚB, I. 4. 3; BGŚB, XIII. 19.
261. ŚUŚB, I. 9; Bhā, III. 5. 25; DBhā, I. 2. 5.
262. VC, 111.
263. ŚUŚB, I. 9; BSŚB, II. 1. 14; PD, VI. 130; VC, 111.
264. PD, VI. 130.
265. BGŚB, XIII. 26.

266. BSŚB, II. 1. 14.
267. VC, 113; 117; VSS, 51; 54.
268. VC, 115; VSS, 51-54; BGŚB, VII. 25; ŚU, VI. 10; ŚUŚB, VI. 10.
269. BGŚB, IV. 6; BG, VII. 25; BGŚB, VII. 25.
270. BSŚB, Intr.
271. BSŚB, I. 4. 3.
272. BGŚB XV. 4.
273. BSŚB, II. 1. 9.
274. BSŚB, I. 2. 22; I. 4. 9; BGŚB, XIII. 5; BU, I. 4. 7.
275. ŚU, IV. 5; BGŚB, Intr. ; IV. 5-6; VII. 13-14; IX. 7 & 10; XIII. 19 & 29; XIV. 3-4.
276. BSŚB, I. 4. 3.
277. BSŚB, I. 4. 2; I. 4. 9; BG, VIII. 18-19; BGŚB, VII. 6; IX. 7-8; XIII. 19-20; XIV. 3-4; XV. 16; Bhā, III. 5. 25.
278. BGŚB, VII. 6; IX. 7-8; XIII. 19-20; XIV. 3-4; XV. 16; Bhā, III. 5. 25.
279. BSŚB, II. 1. 24-25; ŚU, VI. 8.
280. BSŚB, II. 1. 24; II. 1. 30; II. 1. 33; ŚU, IV. 1; VI. 8.
281. BGŚB, XIII. 19.
282. BSŚB, I. 4. 2-3; I. 4. 9.
283. BSŚB, II. 1. 27.
284. BSŚB, II. 1. 14; II. 1. 27; BS, II. 1. 28; MUUŚB, II. 1. 3.
285. ṚV, X. 129. 3; YV, XXXI. 19; BGŚB, Intr. (*nārāyaṇaḥ paro'vyaktād aṇḍamavyaktasambhavam*); XIV. 3; MS, I. 12; CU, III. 19. 1; ŚU, III. 4.
286. BSŚB, I. 2. 22; I. 4. 2; I. 4. 3; II. 1. 14; BGŚB, XIV. 3; XV. 16.
287. BSŚB, I. 4. 3; BGŚB, VII. 6; XIII. 19.
288. BG, II. 28.
289. ṚV, X. 190. 3; BSŚB, II. 1. 36; BG, XV. 3.
290. BSŚB, I. 1. 4; I. 3. 1; II. 1. 1; II. 1. 26-27; II. 3. 9; BS, II. 3. 9; ŚUŚB, I. 3; ŚU, VI. 8; VI. 9.
291. BS, I. 1.2; I. 4. 24-27; II. 1. 16; BSŚB, I. 1. 11; I. 2. 9; I. 4. 15; I. 4. 23; I. 4. 27; II. 1. 14; II. 1. 16; II. 1. 30; II. 1. 37; TU, II. 7; MUU, I. 1. 6; III. 1. 3.
292. BS, II. 2. 28; II. 2. 30; CU, III. 19. 1; VI. 2. 1-2; VI. 8. 4-6; VI. 9. 2; VI. 10. 2; CUŚB, VI. 12. 2.
293. BS, II. 2. 26; BG, II. 16.
294. BSŚB, II. 3. 9.
295. IU, 1.
296. ṚV, X. 190. 1; MNU, I. 6; II. 6-7; V. 5; VIII. 1; XII. 1; TU, III. 10. 6.
297. BSŚB, II. 2. 1.
298. See ref. 277 of Ch. II.
299. See ref. 278. of Ch. II.
300. BSŚB, I. 1. 10; II. 2. 3; BUŚB, III. 8. 9.
301. BS, I. 1. 11; BSŚB, I. 1. 5; I. 1. 11; II. 1. 14; II. 1. 22; II. 2. 1-2; II. 2. 4; MUU, I.1. 9; MAU, 6; GMK, III. 36; III. 47; MTU, VII. 1; PU, IV. 10; VSS, 38.

302. See ref. 126-131 of Ch. II.
303. BSŚB, I. 1. 5; I. 1. 11; II. 1. 22; II. 1. 24; II. 2. 2; II. 2. 4.
304. See ref. 34 of Ch. II.
305. BSŚB, II. 1. 32-33; BU, IV. 3. 21; IV. 4. 6; ŚU, I. 11; MUU, III. 1. 6; GMK, I. 9.
306. BS, II. 1. 32.
307. BS, II. 1. 33; BSŚB, II. 1.33.
308. BSŚB, II. 1. 33.
309. BS, II. 2. 1; BSŚB, II. 2. 1.
310. BSŚB, I. 2. 22; II. 1. 14; BGŚB, IX. 10; XIII. 5; XIII. 19; XIII. 29.
311. BSŚB, I. 4. 3.
312. BGŚB, Intr.; IV. 6; IX. 8.
313. BGŚB, IV. 6; IX. 8.
314. BSŚB, II. 1. 24; II. 1. 30.
315. BSŚB, I. 1. 17; II. 1. 9; BGŚB, VII. 25.
316. ŚU, III. 21; VI. 11; IU, 8; KNU, II. 22; MTU, VI. 7; MUU, I. 16; GMK, I. 1; I. 10; AU, I. 3. 13; BG, II. 17; II. 24; V. 15; VIII. 22; IX. 4; X. 12.
317. BU, III. 7, 3-23; ŚU, II. 17; TU, II. 6. 1.
318. BU, III. 4.1-2; III. 5. 1; MTU, VII. 6.
319. ṚV, X. 129. 7; TBrā, II. 8. 9; ŚU, VI. 11; BG, IX. 10; BGŚB, IX. 10.
320. ŚU, VI. 11; BGŚB, IX. 10; VPDA, Ch. I.
321. BS, I. 2. 18; BSŚB, I. 2. 18; II. 2. 3; BU, III. 7. 3-23; MAU, 6; VSS, 38.
322. BS, I. 3. 11; BSŚB, I. 3. 11; BU, III. 8. 9; ŚU, III. 1-2; BG, VIII. 9; VSS, 38.
323. BS, I. 3. 43; BSŚB, I. 3. 11; BU, IV. 4. 22; KTU, II. 2. 12; MAU, 6; ŚU, I. 10; VI. 7; VI. 12; VI. 17; BG, X. 3; XIII. 22; BGŚB, Intr.; IV. 6; XIII. 19; VSS, 38.
324. BS, I. 3. 10; ŚU, III. 2; IV. 15; VI. 17; BG, XIII. 22.
325. BS, II. 1. 30; II. 1.37; II. 2. 2; BSŚB, I. 1. 11; II. 2. 2; II. 2. 4; III. 2. 22; CU, III. 14.2; III. 14. 4; VIII. 7. 1.
326. BS, II. 1. 28; BSŚB, II. 1. 28; BU, IV. 3. 10; ŚU, IV. 1.
327. BS, II. 2. 2; BSŚB, II. 2. 2.
328. BSŚB, II. 2. 2.
329. MUUŚB, III. 1. 1.
330. ŚU, I. 6; I. 12; ŚUŚB, I. 7.
331. BU, IV. 3. 10.
332. BSŚB, II. 3. 13.
333. BSŚB, I. 1. 11; III. 2. 22; BU, II. 3. 1; MTU, VI. 3.
334. PU, V. 2; BSŚB, I. 3. 13; IV. 3. 14.
335. BSŚB, I. 1. 11; I. 3. 13; III. 2. 21-2; IV. 3. 14.
336. BU, III. 9. 26; IV. 2. 4; IV. 4. 22; IV. 5. 15.
337. BS, III. 2. 18; BSŚB, I. 1. 11; III. 2. 18; BUŚB, III. 8. 12.
338. BSŚB, I. 1. 17; I. 2. 20; II. 1. 22; BGŚB, XV. 7.

339. BSŚB, I. 2. 22; III. 8. 12; MTYU, 61; VC, 243-4; VPDA, Ch. VII.
340. BS, II. 3. 50; III. 2. 18; BSŚB, II. 3. 50; III. 2. 18; III. 2. 21; BGŚB, XV. 7; ABSS, Ch. IV, p. 198; VPDA, Ch. VII; S. J. Woodroffe, *Śakti and Śākta*, Ganesh & Company, Madras, 8th ed., 1975, p. 198; SPS, II. 35.
341. BSŚB, IV. 3. 14; BU, III. 4. 1.
342. MTU, III. 2-3; III. 5; IV. 1-3; VI. 10; BSŚB, III. 2. 18; AB, 12.
343. ABSS, Ch. IV, pp. 202-3.
344. BSŚB, I. 1. 11.
345. BS, I. 1. 2; I. 1. 4; I. 4. 23-28; BSŚB, I. 1. 2; I. 1. 4-5; I. 1. 10-11; I. 2. 2; I. 2. 9; I. 4. 23-28; II. 1. 14; II. 2. 1; BU, II. 5. 19; ŚU, VI. 9; ŚUŚB, I. 4; MAU, 6; TU, III. 1. 1; CU, III. 14. 1; CUŚB, III. 14. 1; BGŚB, VII. 6; XIII. 16; XIII. 19.
346. MTU, VI. 8; VII. 7; ABSS, Ch. IV, pp. 200-1.
347. ṚV, VI. 47. 8; BU, II. 5. 19; BSŚB, I. 1. 17; I. 3. 19; II. 1. 21; ŚU, III. 1; BGŚB, XV.4.
348. BSŚB, II. 1. 9; III. 2. 21.
349. TU, II. 6. 1; ŚU, II. 17; BU, II. 5. 18; III. 7. 3-23; CU, VI. 3. 2; BSŚB, III. 2. 21.
350. BSŚB, I. 1. 1; I. 1. 11; II. 1. 21; II. 3. 17; III. 2. 20; BGŚB, II. 17; BU, I. 4. 10; II. 5.19; IV. 4. 5; IV. 4. 25; CU, VI. 8. 7; VI. 9. 4; VI. 10. 3; VI. 11. 3; VI. 12. 3; VI. 13. 3; VI. 14. 3; VI. 15. 3; VI. 16. 3.
351. BUŚB, III. 8. 12; BGŚB, XIII. 13.
352. ABSS, Ch. IV, pp. 202-3; p. 295; VSS, 61-2; 72; VPDA, Ch. I; Ch. VII; VC, 125, 154, 165, 167, 184, 207; MTYU, 61.
353. ABSS, Ch. IV, pp. 202-3.
354. BS, II. 3. 50; BSŚB, II. 3. 50; BGŚB, XV. 7; VPDA, Ch. VII.
355. GMK, III. 3-4; BGŚB, XV. 7.
356. BUŚB, III. 8. 12; BSŚB, I. 1. 11.
357. VC, 244.
358. ṚV, I. 164. 20; MUU, III. 1. 1; ŚU, IV. 6; KTU, I. 3. 1.
359. MUUŚB, III. 1. 1; BS, I. 1. 16-17; I. 2. 20; II. 1. 21; BSŚB, I. 1. 16-17; I. 2. 20; I. 3. 19; II. 1. 21.
360. ŚU, I. 12; BGŚB, XIII. 20-1.
361. ŚUŚB, I. 9.
362. BS, I. 1. 16-17; I. 2. 22; II. 1. 21-22.
363. BSŚB, II. 1. 22.
364. KTU, II. 2. 7; KTUŚB, II. 2. 7; BU, III. 2. 13; KṢU, III. 8; BGŚB, XV. 8.
365. BSŚB, II. 3. 17.
366. BSŚB, I. 3. 19; I. 4. 3; III. 2. 21.
367. BUŚB, IV. 4. 6.
368. VC, 169; 174; 179; 191; 211.
369. CUŚB, VI. 5. 1.
370. BU, IV. 4. 6.
371. BS, II. 1. 34.
372. BU, III. 2. 13.

373. BU, IV. 4. 5.
374. BS, II. 1. 35.
375. BS, II. 1. 36.
376. BS, I. 3. 30; BSŚB, I. 3. 30; VPu, I. 5. 59-61; MBh, ŚP, 231. 48-9; ṚV, X. 190. 3.
377. BSŚB, II. 1. 36.
378. BGŚB, XV. 8-9.
379. BS, II. 3. 43; BG, XV. 7.
380. BU, IV. 4. 5.
381. BSŚB, II. 3. 17.
382. BS, II. 3. 18.
383. IU, 1.
384. AU, III. 1. 3; CU, VI. 8. 4-7; KTU, II. 3. 1; BG, XV. 1-2; KTU, II. 3-12-13; VPDA, Ch. VII.
385. BSŚB, II. 1. 13.
386. BG, XV. 16.
387. BGŚB, XV. 3.
388. BSŚB, II. 1. 14.
389. BS, II. 2. 28; II. 2. 30; BSŚB, II. 2. 28; II. 2. 30.
390. ṚV, X. 90. 2.
391. ŚU, III. 15.
392. CU, III. 14. 1; MTU, IV. 6; BU, II. 5. 1.
393. BU, II. 4. 6; CU, VI. 8. 7; VII. 25. 2.
394. MUU, II. 1. 10.
395. MUUŚB, II. 1. 10.
396. MUU, II. 2. 12.
397. ṚV, X. 90.
398. BG, XI.
399. BU, III. 7. 1; MUU, II. 1. 4; ŚU, III. 14 & 16.
400. ṚV, X. 90. 3; TĀR, XXX. 12; BG, X. 42.
401. BU, IV. 4. 19.
402. BU, V. 1. 1; IU, Invocation.
403. AU, I. 1. 1; BU, I. 4. 10-11; I. 4. 17.
404. BS, II. 2. 26; BG, II. 16.
405. CU, III. 19. 1; TU, II. 7. 1.
406. ṚV, X. 129. 1.
407. CU, III. 19. 1; VI. 2. 1-2; TU, II. 6. 1.
408. BG, II. 16.
409. BS, I. 4. 27; BSŚB, I. 4. 27; II. 1. 14; MUU, I. 1. 6-7; III. 1. 3; ṚV, I. 104. 1.
410. BS, I. 1. 2; BSŚB, I. 1. 2; TU, III. 1. 1.
411. BS, I. 4. 26.
412. TU, II. 7. 1.

413. MUU, II. 1. 1.
414. BS, I. 4. 23; BSŚB, I. 1. 2; I. 1. 5; I. 2. 2; I. 2. 9; I. 4. 23-8; II. 2. 1; MUU, II. 1. 3.
415. BS & BSŚB, II. 1. 9; II. 1. 14-19; II. 3. 6; BGŚB, VIII. 22; BUŚB, I. 5. 14; I. 6. 1.
416. BS, II. 1. 16.
417. BS, II. 1. 26-7; BSŚB, II. 1. 26-7.
418. BSŚB, II. 1. 14.
419. CUŚB, VI. 12. 2.
420. CUŚB, VI. 4. 4.
421. BU, I. 4. 7; CU, VI. 1. 4-6.
422. BGŚB, XIII. 19.
423. BS, II. 1. 28; BSŚB, II. 1. 24; II. 1. 30; II. 1. 33; ŚU, IV. 1; III. 8.
424. BSŚB, II. 1. 1; II. 1. 14.
425. BSŚB, I. 1. 2.
426. BS, I. 1. 2; I. 1. 4; I. 4. 23-28; BSŚB, I. 1. 2; I. 1. 4-5; I. 1. 10-11; I. 2. 2; I. 2. 9; I. 4. 23-28; II. 1. 14; II. 2. 1-2; BGŚB, VII. 6; IX. 7-8; XIII. 19; XIV. 3; BU, II. 5. 19; MAU, 6; TU, III. 1. 1; CUŚB, III. 14. 1; ŚU, VI. 9; ŚUŚB, I. 4.
427. BSŚB, I. 4. 2-3; II. 1. 14; II. 1. 24-25; ŚUŚB, I. 3; BGŚB, VII. 6; VIII. 18-19; IX. 7-8; IX. 10; XIII. 19; XIV. 3; XV. 16.
428. BSŚB, I. 2. 22; I. 4. 3.
429. BS, I. 4. 3; BSŚB, I. 4. 3.
430. BS, II. 1. 24-25; BSŚB, II. 1. 24; BGŚB, XIII. 19.
431. BSŚB, I. 2. 22; II. 1. 9; BGŚB, XIII. 19; XV. 16; MUU, II. 1. 2; VC, 108.
432. BS, I. 4. 2; BSŚB, I. 2. 22; I. 4. 2-3; BG, VIII. 18; BGŚB, Intr. ; XIII. 5; KTU, II. 3. 7-8; BU, I. 4. 7; VC, 108.
433. ŚU, IV. 5; BGŚB, Intr. ; VII. 6; XIII. 19; XIV. 3; VC, 108.
434. SPS, I. 61; VPu, I. 2. 33-54.
435. ṚV, X.129. 4; BS, I. 1. 5; I. 1. 18; I. 4. 24; II. 3. 12-13; BSŚB, I. 4. 23; II. 1. 5; II. 3. 13; CU, VI. 2. 3; VI. 2. 4; TU, II. 6. 1; AU, I. 1. 1; PU, VI. 3.
436. Bhā, III. 20. 12.
437. ṚV, X. 129. 1-3.
438. VPu, I. 2. 23.
439. ṚV, X. 129. 4.
440. ṚV, X. 129.3.
441. ṚV, X. 129. 3; BU, V. 5. 1.
442. ṚV, X. 121. 1-9; X. 190. 1; BU, V. 5. 1; KTU, II. 1. 6; MS, I. 10.
443. ṚV, X. 121. 1; ŚU, IV. 12.
444. ṚV, X. 121. 10; YV, XXXI. 19; MUU, I. 1. 9; PU, I. 4.
445. BU, II. 6. 3; IV. 6. 3; VI. 5. 4; KTU, II. 1. 1; ŚU, VI. 16; ŚBrā, I. 9.3. 10; TBrā, III. 12. 3. 1.
446. MUU, III. 1. 3.
447. ṚV, X. 129. 4.

448. BGŚB, Intr. ; MS, I. 11-13; YV, XXXI. 19; ŚU, III. 4.
449. CU, III. 19. 1.
450. GMK, II. 14.
451. ŚU, VI. 16.
452. ṚV, X.121. 3; BS, I. 1. 23; BU, I. 4. 17; I. 5. 12-13; I. 5. 23; II. 3. 4-5; III. 9. 9; CU, I. 11. 15; III. 15. 4; III. 18. 4; V. 1. 1; V. 6. 3; VII. 26. 1; MUU, II. 1. 3; III. 1. 4; IV. 1. 3; PU, II. 6-7; II. 9; II. 13; GMK, I. 6.
453. KTU, II. 1. 7; PU, VI. 4; TU, II. 1. 1.
454. ṚV, X. 190. 1-2.
455. ṚV, X. 129. 5.
456. PU, I. 4.
457. CU, III. 19. 1.
458. BU, I. 2. 6-7.
459. BU, I. 2. 1-2.
460. PU, VI. 4.
461. CU, IV. 10. 4-5.
462. CU, VI. 6. 5; VI. 7. 1; VI. 7. 6.
463. BS, I. 1. 23; BU, I. 5. 13; MUU, II. 1. 3; PU, VI. 4; KLU, 15.
464. BU, I. 2. 6; KTU, II. 1. 6.
465. ṚV, II. 35; X. 30.
466. BS, II. 3. 10; BU, I. 2. 6; CU, VI. 2. 3; PU, I. 4.
467. MUU, I. 1. 8.
468. ṚV, I. 89. 10; I. 164. 33; X. 72. 4 & 6; KTU, II. 1. 7.
469. BS, I. 3. 39; KTU, II. 3. 2-3; GMK, IV. 47-49; 51-52; 72.
470. ṚV, I. 164. 33; X. 72. 4.
471. ṚV, X. 72. 6.
472. BS, I.1. 24; I. 3. 40.
473. KTU, II. 1. 7.
474. ṚV, I. 89. 10.
475. BU, I. 2. 5.
476. CU, I. 9. 1.
477. BS, I. 1. 22; II. 3. 1-2; TU, II. 1. 1.
478. MPu, I. 3-5.
479. BS, II. 3. 8; TU, II. 1. 1.
480. CU, VI. 2. 3; TU, II. 1. 1.
481. BS, II. 3. 11; CU, VI. 2. 3; TU, II. 1. 1.
482. TU, II. 1. 1.
483. BS, II. 3. 12; BSŚB, II. 3. 12; BU, I. 2. 2; CU, VI. 2. 4; TU, II. 1. 1.
484. BS, II. 2. 26; CU, VI. 8. 4-6; BG, II. 16.
485. BSŚB, I. 4. 2-3; KTU, I. 3. 11; ŚUŚB, VI. 10; BG, VIII. 18; VIII. 20.

486. CUŚB, VI. 12. 2.
487. BSŚB, II. 3. 6; MUUŚB, I. 1. 8 *(krameṇa, na yugapat.).*
488. CU, VI. 2. 3-4; MUU, II. 1. 3; PU, VI. 4; TU, II. 1. 1.
489. CU, VI. 3. 1; TU, III. 1. 1; III. 2. 1; III. 3. 1; III. 4. 1; III. 5. 1; III. 6. 1.
490. ṚV, X. 129. 7; BG, IX. 10.
491. TUŚB, Intr. *(na hi nityaṁ kiñcidārabhyate, loke yadārabdhaṁ tadanityam.).*
492. BG, IX. 7-8; DBhā, I. 2. 5.
493. ŚU, I. 6; VI. 1.
494. ṚV, X. 190. 3.
495. BU, II. 1. 20; MUU, I. 1. 7; ŚU, V. 3; VI. 10; ŚUŚB, VI. 10.
496. ṚV, X. 130.
497. BS, II. 3. 14; CUŚB, III. 14. 1.
498. BSŚB, II. 3. 14.
499. MBh, XII. 339. 29; VPu, VI. 4. 12-35; VPDA, Ch. VII.
500. BSŚB, I. 1. 2; I. 1. 4-5; I. 1. 11; I. 2. 2; I. 2. 9; I. 3. 30; II. 2. 1; II. 3. 14; TU, III. 1. 1; ŚUŚB, I. 3.
501. BS, I. 2. 9; BSŚB, I. 2. 9; BG, XIII. 16.
502. AV, XI. 7. 1.
503. KTU, I. 2. 25.
504. BG, VIII. 18-19; BGŚB, VIII. 18-19.
505. BSŚB, II. 3. 13; BG, IX. 7-8.
506. BG, VIII. 17; Bhā, XII. 4. 3-4; VPu, I. 3. 5; I. 3. 16; I. 3. 20-22; III. 2. 50; VI. 3. 10-12; VI. 4. 9.
507. VPu, I. 3. 16; I. 3. 20-22; III. 2. 50; VI. 3. 12.
508. VPu, VI. 3. 10-12.
509. VPu, VI. 4. 9.
510. VPu, I. 3. 5.
511. Bhā, XII. 4. 3-4.
512. TU, III. 2. 1; III. 3. 1; III. 4. 1; III. 5. 1; III. 6. 1.
513. CUŚB, VI. 11. 2.
514. S. Grof, Quoted by F. Capra, in "*Uncommon Wisdom*", Flamingo (Fontana Paperbacks), London, 1989, p. 111.
515. MAU, 1.
516. MAU, 2.
517. MAU, 3.
518. MAU, 4.
519. MAU, 5.
520. MAU, 6.
521. MAU, 7.
522. GMK, II. 31.
523. GMK, II. 12.

524. GMK, II.13.
525. GMK, II. 14.
526. GMK, II. 9-10.
527. GMK, II. 15.
528. GMK, II. 16.
529. GMK, IV. 63-66.
530. BSŚB, II. 2.28.
531. BSŚB, II. 2.28.
532. BSŚB, II. 2. 28.
533. BSŚB, II. 2. 28.
534. BSŚB, II. 2. 28.
535. BSŚB, II. 2. 28.
536. BSŚB, II. 2. 28.
537. GMK, III. 33-36.
538. BSŚB, II. 2. 29.
539. GMK, IV. 58.
540. GMK, IV. 59.
541. GMK, IV. 73.
542. GMK, IV. 11-13.
543. GMK, IV. 14-21.
544. GMK, IV. 22.
545. GMK, IV. 24.
546. BSŚB, II. 1. 13.
547. BSŚB, I. 4. 14.
548. BSŚB, II. 1. 14.
549. BSŚB, II. 1. 14.
550. GMK, II. 16-19.
551. BSŚB, II. 1. 14.
552. GMK, IV. 4.
553. GMK, IV. 22.
554. BS, I. 1. 2.
555. GMK, IV. 5.
556. GMK, I. 16; II. 19; II. 31; III. 19; III. 24; III. 27-29; IV. 58; IV. 61.
557. GMK, IV. 58.
558. GMK, II. 19.
559. GMK, III. 3-4; 7-8; 11.
560. GMK, II. 12; II. 17.
561. GMK, II. 16.
562. LAS, X. 459.
563. GMK, IV. 63-66.

564. GMK, III.29; IV. 47-48; IV. 61-62; IV. 72.
565. GMK, III. 29; IV. 61.
566. GMK, IV. 47-51.
567. GMK, II. 13-16.
568. GMK, IV. 28; IV. 46.
569. GMK, IV. 54.
570. GMK, IV. 76-77.
571. GMK, IV. 72.
572. GMK, III. 46.
573. GMK, IV. 48.
574. GMK, III. 31.
575. GMK, IV. 47; 48; 72.
576. GMK, III. 34.
577. GMK, I. 17; II. 36; III. 18.
578. GMK, I. 25-26; III. 33; 35; 46.
579. CUŚB, VI. 5. 1; MUU, II. 1. 3; Chennakesvan, S., *Concept of Mind in Indian Philosophy*, Motilal Banarsidass, Delhi, 1980, pp.44-45.
580. BU, IV. 4. 6; BUŚB, IV. 4. 6; ABSS, Ch. IV. , p. 295.

III

NON-DUALISM IN KĀSHMIRĪ ŚAIVA PHILOSOPHY

In the second chapter of this book, the salient features of the absolute idealism of Śaṅkara have been discussed. Kāshmirī Śaivism is another important school of monistic idealism or idealistic monism which also contains features of realistic idealism or concrete monism. The literature on Śaiva monism is vast. Important source books that have been referred to on this topic are: *Śiva Sūtra,*[1] *Pratyabhijñāhṛdayam,*[2] *Spanda-Kārikā,*[3] *Īśvara-Pratyabhijñāvimarśinī,*[4] *The Doctrine of Vibration,*[5] and *An Outline of History of Śaiva Philosophy.*[6]

The *Śaiva* philosophy of Kāshmir is the philosophy of the triad (*Trika*), viz., (1) Śiva, (2) *Śakti* and (3) *Nara* (the bound soul). According to another version, the *para* (the highest), the *parāpara* (identity in difference) and the *apara* (difference) constitute the *Trika*.

There are three categories of literature in the *Trika* system. These are : the *Āgama Śāstra*, the *Spanda Śāstra* and the *Pratyabhijñā Śāstra*. It is believed that the *Āgama Śāstra* was primarily a revelation. It was then handed over from the teacher to the pupil by tradition. Among the *Āgama Śāstras*, the *Śiva-Sūtras* are very important. These *sūtras* (aphorisms) were revealed to Vasugupta who lived either in the last part of the eighth century or the beginning of the ninth century A.D. Kṣemarāja's *Vimarśinī* is one among the many commentaries on the *Śiva-Sūtras*. The *Spanda Śāstra* is on the doctrine of vibration. It elaborates the system mainly from the point of view of *Śakti*. The principal *Spanda Śāstra* is the *Spanda-Sūtra* or *Spanda-Kārikā*, written by Vasugupta. There are several commentaries on this *Kārikā*. The *Spanda-Nirṇaya* of Kṣemarāja is one of them. The *Pratyabhijña Śāstra* contains the philosophy proper of the *Trika* system. Somānanda composed *Śivadṛṣṭi*. Utpala who was a disciple of Somānanda wrote *Īśvara-Pratyabhijñā* which is an important work on the monistic Śaiva philosophy. Several commentaries on this book are available. Abhinavagupta who lived in the tenth century A.D. wrote a commentary on it under the title *Pratyabhijñā-Vimarśinī*. He also wrote *Tantrāloka* in twelve volumes. Bhāskarakaṇṭha wrote a commentary (*Bhāskarī*) on *Īśvara-Pratyabhijñā*. Kṣemarāja who was a pupil of Abhinavagupta wrote *Pratyabhijñāhṛdayam* which is a digest of the *Pratyabhijñā Śāstra*.

The word *pratyabhijñā* means re-cognition. The individual self or the *jīva* is divine and not different from *Śiva*, the Supreme. In spite of this complete identity of the *Jīva* and *Śiva*, the former forgets his real nature, gets alienated and identifies him with his psychophysical mechanism. He thereby fails to recognize his own real nature. The *Pratyabhijñā* philosophy propounds the theory and practices by the knowledge and praxis of which the *jīva* recognizes himself as the *Śiva* (the Supreme Reality).

The philosophical background of the *Pratyabhijñā* system will be briefly discussed here.

Ultimate Reality

The ultimate reality is *Cit* or *Parāsaṁvit*. This is a word which is untranslatable. It is being translated here as "Consciousness" with a connotation different from the conventional one. A subject is conscious of an object. The "I" (*aham*) is conscious of "this" (*idam*). Where distinction exists between the subject and the object, "I" and "this", there is involved the duality. In Śaiva monism, there is no duality of subject and object in *Cit* or *Parāsaṁvit*. It is Consciousness without knower-known duality, subject-object relation. Thus it is non-relational. *Parāsaṁvit* is the immediacy of feeling in which exists the distinction of neither "I" nor "this".

Brahman in Advaita Vedānta is pure Consciousness (*jñāna* or knowledge) which is inactive (*niṣkriya*). The *Pratyabhijñā* philosophy also accepts *Parāsaṁvit* as *Prakāśa* (light or knowledge). But it is not knowledge alone. It is *prakāśavimarśamaya*, both knowledge and activity. As *Prakāśa, Paramaśiva* (the Supreme Reality) has knowership (*jñātṛtva*) and, as *Vimarśa*, He has doership (*kartṛtva*). In the *Trika* system, the Ultimate Reality is not inactive.

There is no contradiction in the *Śiva-Śakti* concept in the monistic Śaiva philosophy. The *Prakāśa-Vimarśa* concept is the same as the *Śiva-Śakti* one. It does not violate monism; it does not involve dualism. It is a bipolar concept in which the Ultimate Reality is a coalescence into undivided unity of *Prakāśa* and *Vimarśa*.

Prakāśa is the eternal light without which nothing can appear. It is the *Śiva* aspect of *Parāsaṁvit*. But mere *Prakāśa* cannot be the sole nature of Reality. It may be likened to the diamond that does not know itself as possessor of brightness. Reality knows itself by *Vimarśa* that is its second aspect. This self-knowledge, according to *Pratyabhijñā* philosophy, is an activity. Kṣemarāja says that *Vimarśa* is the non-relational immediate awareness of I.[7] He further says: "If (*Parāsaṁvit* were merely *Prakāśa*) devoid of *Vimarśa*, it would be powerless and inert".[8] The *Vimarśa* (I-consciousness) aspect of the Ultimate Reality is responsible for the manifestation, maintenance and reabsorption of the universe.

Cit (the Ultimate Reality) is conscious of itself as *Cidrūpiṇī Śakti*. This consciousness is *Vimarśa*. It is the mirror in which Siva realizes His own grandeur, power and beauty. It is the power of doership (*kartṛtva-śakti*) of Śiva. This *Vimarśa* is variously named as *Parāśakti, svātantrya, aiśvarya, kartṛtva, aphurattā, sāra, hṛdaya* and *spanda*.[9]

Pratyabhijñā non-dualism is at variance with that of Śaṅkara. According to Śaṅkara's Vedānta, Brahman is only *Prakāśa* (*jñāna* or knowledge) without any activity. The Ultimate Reality, being Pure Consciousness and inactive, has nothing to do with the creation, sustenance and dissolution. Śaṅkara had to explain the empirical world and he could not do it with his Brahman concept. And so was the necessity of a second concept—that of *Māyā*. The world is manifested from *Māyā* in which it finally dissolves. But, the *Māyā* of Śaṅkara is insentient (*jaḍa*). It cannot be the efficient cause; it cannot be the architect and the engineer; it cannot be the ruler and the Lord. An intelligent principle, an omniscient, omnipotent and omnipresent being is necessary for the creation, maintenance and dissolution of the world. Thus came the concept of *Īśvara* in Śaṅkara's Vedānta. Consciousness (Brahman) apparently limited in *Māyā* (*māyopahitaṁ caitanyam*) is the *Īśvara* of Advaita Vedānta. The Absolute Reality is Brahman which is attributeless (*nirguṇa*). *Īśvara* is Brahman with attributes (*saguṇa*). The lordship, omniscience, omnipotence and creating power of *Īśvara* are only through the medium of *Māyā* which is the limiting adjunct (*upādhi*) of the former.[10] The *Pratyabhijñā* philosopher asserts that the so-called non-dualism of Śaṅkara is reduced to dualism with two ontological beings, viz., Brahman and *Māyā*. In the philosophy of Śaiva monism, *Paramaśiva* (Ultimate Reality) is both *Prakāśa* (knowledge) and *Vimarśa* (activity) without any contamination of dualism.

In both Sāṅkhya and Advaita Vedānta, the *Puruṣa* or *Ātmā* (Brahman) is inactive. The *Pratyabhijñā* philosopher does not accept the meaning of activity as given in the Sāṅkhya or Advaita Vedānta philosophy. In his opinion, the word "activity" should not be used here in a crude sense. He, of course, agrees to the view that Brahman or *Paramaśiva* does not work like a potter, weaver or watch-maker. His *Vimarśa*, the very *icchā* (the will of the Divine), is spiritual energy of infinite force that has the potentiality to proliferate into any form and that actualizes the proliferation of forms from the subtlest to the grossest.

Paramaśiva has *svātantrya* or unimpeded sovereignty which expresses itself into *icchā* (will), This *icchā* immediately translates itself into knowledge (*jñāna*) and activity (*kriyā*).

It is the *svabhāva* or the very nature of *Paramaśiva* to manifest. According to the Śaiva monistic philosophy, there cannot be Divinity without creativity and activity. In this connection, Abhinavagupta says: "If the Ultimate Reality did not manifest in manifold variety, but remained in a single state, it would neither be the Lord with all-controlling power nor sentient being with omniscience, but it would be something like a pot".[11]

Advaita Vedānta of Śaṅkara associates knowledge (*jñātṛtva*), but not activity (*kartṛtva*) with Brahman. In contrast, *Pratyabhijñā* philosophy contends that both knowledge and activity are the very nature of *Paramaśiva*. He has infinite power (*śakti*), but the following five are considered as the main ones:

1. *Cit*. By this power of self-revelation, *Paramaśiva* shines by Himself. He is known as Śiva in this aspect.

2. *Ānanda*. This is absolute bliss which is otherwise called *Svātantrya* by which *Paramaśiva* is able to do anything without any

extraneous aid. The Supreme is known as *Śakti* in this aspect.

3. *Icchā*. This is the will of the Supreme to do anything. In this aspect, He is known as *Sadāśiva* or *Sādākhya*.

4. *Jñāna*. This is the power of knowing of the Supreme. He is known as *Īśvara* in this aspect.

5. *Kriyā*. This is the power of activity of the Supreme. By this power, He assumes any and every form. In this aspect, He is known as *Sadvidyā* or *Śuddhavidyā*.

Cit (Śiva) and *Ānanda* (*Śakti*) are the very nature (*svarūpa*) of *Paramaśiva*. He is never inactive. His activities are five-fold, viz., emanation or projection (*sṛṣṭi*), maintenance (*sthiti*), withdrawal (*saṁhāra*), concealment of the real nature (*vilaya*) and grace (*anugraha*). Thus He is called *pañcakṛtyakārī* (performer of the five-fold act). He is eternally active and His activity does not cease even when He assumes the form of an empirical ego (*jīva*). In the *Pratyabhijñā* system, the Supreme, if considered as divested of activities, is as good as unreal. In this connection, Maheśvarānanda expresses his view by saying: "*Parameśvara* (the Highest Lord) always performs the five-fold actions as His very nature. Without these activities, the Self (*Ātmā*), as defined in *Māyā*-Vedānta, etc., would be as good as unreal".[12]

It has already been said that *Paramaśiva* is both *Prakāśa* and *Vimarśa*. The "I" (subject) is the *Prakāśa* aspect; the "this" (object) is the *Vimarśa* aspect. Unlike in Advaita Vedānta, the "I" and "this", the subject and the object are in an undivided unity. The *Vimarśa* is the *Śakti* which has been called as the "Heart of the Supreme Lord" (*hṛdayaṁ parameśituḥ*) by Kṣemarāja in his *Parāprāveśikā*. In Advaita Vedānta, *Māyā* is the power (*śakti*) of Brahman. In *Pratyabhijñā, Vimarśa* or *Śakti* is one of the two aspects of *Paramaśiva* (the Supreme Self). As the Supreme Reality is Śiva, so also is It *Śakti*. The "I" is the Self and the "this" is the Self. This *Vimarśa* or *Śakti* is not contentless. "Like the great banyan tree potentially existing in the seed, the entire universe with all the movable and immovable beings lies as a potency in the heart of the Supreme".[13]

In Śaṅkara's Vedānta, Brahman is *kūṭastha* or ever changeless, and is not associated with the ever-changing world. In *Pratyabhijñā*, the Supreme Self (*Paramaśiva, Maheśvara, Cit, Parāsaṁvit*) is the changeless principle of all changes. Whatever changes are brought about in the universe are done through the agency of *Vimarśa* or *Citi*. "The divine power is known as *Citi* whose essence is self-consciousness. It is also known as *Parā Vāk*. It is in itself ever present. It is *Svātantrya* (Absolute Sovereignty), the main power of the Supreme Self".[14] "This *Citi* is the inner, creative flash which, though in itself unchanging, is the source of all apparent changes. It is the absolute being. It is beyond the determinations of space and time. In essence, it is the very heart of the Divine Being (*Parameṣṭhī*)".[15]

Svātantryavāda or the doctrine of the Absolute Sovereignty and Freedom of the Divine will to express itself in any way it likes has been given by Abhinavagupta in the following words: "Therefore the Lord, *Paramaśiva* who is Consciousness of the nature of *Prakāśa* and *Vimarśa*, who appears as subject from Rudra down to the immobile entities, who appears as object like blue, pleasure, etc., seemingly separate but really inseparable, expresses through the glorious might of *Svātantrya* (Free Will) which is not different from *Saṁvit* (Universal Consciousness) and which does not conceal by any means the real nature of the Supreme. This is the exposition of *Svātantryavāda*".[16]

The non-dualism of Śaṅkara accepts *Māyā* as an ontological principle. It is the power (*śakti*) of Brahman. It is not *sat* (existent), not *asat* (not non-existent) and not *sadasat* (not both existent and non-existent). But it is the material cause of the universe and the apparent limiting adjunct (*upādhi*) of *Īśvara* (God). Through *Māyā* alone, God becomes the Creator of the universe. In actuality, activity belongs to *Māyā* or *Avidyā* (nescience). The *Māyā* concept of the non-dualistic Saiva philosophy is different from that of Śaṅkara Vedānta. The *Pratyabhijñā* philosophy does not recognize *Māyā* as an ontological principle. It is not the material cause of the universe. It does not impart doership and creatorship to *Paramaśiva* or *Maheśvara*. *Māyā* is His own power by which He brings about multiplicity and the sense of difference. *Māyā* is *śivamayī* or *cinmayī*, the power of the Divine and is perfectly real. *Vimarśa* or *Svātantrya* is one of the two aspects (*Prakāśa* and *Vimarśa*) of *Paramaśiva*. Activity belongs to this *Vimarśa* aspect. Hence *Paramaśiva* is ever active unlike the inactive Brahman of Advaita Vedānta.

According to Advaita Vedānta, the universe is *mithyā* or unreal. The manifestation of the universe is only *nāma-rūpa* (name and form). The multiplicity of the world is due to the appearance of multiple forms that are variously named. This doctrine is known as *vivartavāda*. In contrast to this, the Sāṅkhya propounds *pariṇāmavāda* in which *prakṛti* (the primeval nature) is transformed into the multiplicity of the world. According to the non-dualistic Śaiva philosophy, the universe, being *śiva-rūpa*, is real. It is a display of the glory of *Paramaśiva*. This doctrine is known as *ābhāsavāda*. The word *ābhāsa* means "appearance in a limited way". Whatever appears in the ever-changing world is an expression of *Cit* or *Saṁvit* (Universal Consciousness). Nothing new appears. Whatever appears is not false and unreal. It is in the analogy of the plasma of the peacock's egg (*mayūrāṇḍarasanyāya*). The peacock is beautiful with colourful variegated plumage. This beautiful plumage is not seen in the plasma of the peacock's egg. But it is potentially present there in a state of undifferentiated mass. Likewise the entire universe is potentially present in *Paramaśiva* as an undifferentiated mass.

The analogy of reflection in a mirror is used in *ābhāsavāda*.[17] Various images are reflected in a mirror. The images appear to be different from one another and also from the mirror although they are non-different from the mirror. In the same analogy, the *ābhāsas* are not different from one another and *Paramaśiva*. Here *Paramaśiva* is compared with the mirror; the manifold world with the knowers (subjects), knowns (objects) and knowledge is a variegated complex of images. But these images are not different from one another and are non-different from *Paramaśiva* or *Maheśvara*.

There are three exceptions, however, in the use of the simile of *Paramaśiva* and the mirror. In the case of the mirror, an object external to the mirror is reflected. In contrast, there is nothing external to *Maheśvara* or the Universal Consciousness. Whatever is reflected in *Maheśvara* is His own ideation. Secondly, reflection in the mirror is possible due to an external light. The *Prakāśa* aspect of *Cit* or the Universal Consciousness is its own light. It is the Light of all lights. It does not require any external light which does not exist. Thirdly, the mirror, being insentient, is not conscious of the reflections within itself. This is not the case with the omniscient *Paramaśiva*. The *Vimarśa* aspect of *Paramaśiva* knows the *ābhāsas* that are the ideations of the Divine.[18] These ideations appear external to the empirical subject, but not to the Universal Consciousness (*Cit*).

The *ābhāsas* and the Universal Consciousness are likened to the waves and the sea, respectively. The waves appear and disappear. The underlying sea remains unchanged. The sea does not gain due to the appearance of the waves; nor does it lose due to the disappearance of the waves. So does *Paramaśiva* remain unchanged even though the world *ābhāsas* appear and disappear. The waves that originate and perish are not unreal. Similarly, the *ābhāsas* are not false and unreal.

The *ābhāsas* are external projections of the ideation of *Paramaśiva*, and this projection is done by the Divine Will without the aid of any external material or agency which does not exist.[19] The pot-maker shapes clay into pots. He is the efficient cause of the pot; clay is the material cause of the pot; and the potter's wheel is the instrumental cause. The creation of the world is not done like this. There is nothing else other than *Paramaśiva*. He does not need any material or instrument to create the world. Neither do the materials and the instruments exist. The concept of creation (*sṛṣṭi*) in the *Pratyabhijñā* philosophy is the external manifestation of what is latently contained within *Paramaśiva*. In this process, the knowledge (*jñāna*) of *Paramaśiva* is materialized by His Will into objects of knowledge (*jñeya*); the "I" of *Paramaśiva* appears as "this" or the universe. There is nothing external to Him. But the universe appears as something external to the empirical subjects. *Cit* or the Universal Consciousness appears in the form of subjects and objects. This is *ābhāsa* only. But the *ābhāsa* cannot be called false.

In the monistic Śaivism of Kāshmīr, *Cit*, *Parāsaṁvit*, or *Paramaśiva* is accepted as the changeless principle of all changes. This is in contradistinction of the *kṣanikavāda* (doctrine of momentariness) and *anātmavāda* (doctrine of not-self) of the Bauddha who does not admit any permanent subject, individual or universal. Utpalācārya and Abhinavagupta have refuted the Bauddha objections against a permanent subject and an omniscient God in the *Īśvara-Pratyabhijñā* and the *Īśvara-Pratyabhijñā-Vimarśinī*, respectively.

Scope of Multiplicity in Śaiva non-Dualism

The monism in the *Pratyabhijñā* philosophy has already been presented in a nutshell. In both Advaita Vedānta and *Pratyabhijñā*, *Cit* or Consciousness is the Ultimate Reality. But, in Advaita Vedānta, *Cit* or Brahman is undifferentiated, homogeneous Consciousness which is ever immutable. Brahman is actionless and attributeless. The cosmic phenomena are ascribed to *Māyā* through which *Īśvara* (God) operates. In *Pratyabhijñā*, *Cit* or *Paramaśiva* is both transcendental (*viśvottīrṇa*) and immanent (*viśvamaya*). The immanent or creative aspect of *Paramaśiva* is called *Śiva tattva*. Thus *Paramaśiva* is not inactive. He is ever active and, through His activity, the multiplicity of the universe is possible.

The word *tattva* is hardly translatable. It means the "thatness" of a thing. Many *tattvas* come into existence from the single Ultimate Reality. Thus is explained the reality of the multiplicity of the universe.

I. The *Tattvas* of the Universal Experience

Five *tattvas* will be discussed under this head. All these are related to the universal consciousness. All these experiences are ideal, i.e., they are in the form of an idea. These five *tattvas* are *śuddhādhvan* (pure order). The real nature (*svarūpa*) of *Paramaśiva* is not veiled by the manifestation of any of these *tattvas*.

1. *Śiva tattva*. It is the first creative movement (*prathama spanda*) of *Paramaśiva*. He, by His *Svātantrya* (Absolute Will), desires the unfoldment of the universe which is unfolded in Him. The first vibration of this Will is known as Śiva.

2. *Śakti tattva*. It is the energy of Śiva. In *Śiva tattva*, the "this" is withdrawn due to the negating action of *Śakti tattva* and consequently the "I" side of the experience alone remains. *Śakti* polarizes Consciousness into *aham* ("I") and *idam* ("this")—subject and object. Of course, *Śakti* is not a second entity and not different from Śiva. The creative, active and kinetic aspect of *Paramaśiva* is *Śakti*. In *Śakti tattva*, the bliss (*ānanda*) aspect is predominant. Both the *Śiva* and the *Śakti tattvas* ever remain united whether in creation or dissolution. It is not correct to say that the *Śiva-Śakti tattva* is an *ābhāsa* (emanation). It is the seed (*bīja*) from which all emanations germinate.

3. *Sadāśiva* or *Sādākhya tattva*. The will (*icchā*) to affirm the "this" side of the Universal Consciousness is the *Sadāśiva* or *Sādākhya tattva*. In this *tattva*, the will (*icchā*) is predominant. The word *sat* (being) is present in the compound word *sādākhya*. In this state, the experience is "I am" (*ahamasmi*, *asmi* or 'am' for being). In the experience of "I am", "I am this" is implied, since one cannot experience "I am nothing". At this stage, the "I" (*aham*) side of experience is clear and dominant and the "this" side is hazy (*asphuṭa*). *Paramaśiva* works like an artist. Before portraying a picture, the details about the picture are hazy in the mind of the

artist. Similarly, the universe in *Sādākhya tattva* is hazy. It is still in an ideal state (in the state of an idea). The ideal universe is experienced by the Supreme as an indistinct something in the depth of consciousness. Hence this experience is called *nimeṣa* (*nimeṣo'ntaḥ sadāśivaḥ*). The *Sādākhya tattva* is the first manifestation (*ābhāsa*). There cannot be any *ābhāsa* without a subject (perceiver) and an object (perceived). In the first *ābhāsa* which is the *Sādākhya tattva*, both the subject and object are Consciousness since there is nothing else other than Consciousness at this stage. Consciousness is perceptible to Consciousness itself in the *Sadāśiva* or *Sādākhya tattva*.

4. *Īśvara* or *Aiśvarya tattva*. In this stage, the "this" side of the total Divine experience becomes a little more distinct (*sphuṭa*). The *Īśvara tattva* is *unmeṣa* or distinct blossoming of the universe. The experience of *Sadāśiva* is "I am this" whereas the experience of *Īśvara* is "This am I". In this *tattva*, knowledge (*jñāna*) is predominant.

5. *Sadvidyā* or *Śuddhavidyā tattva*. In this *tattva*, the "I" and the "this" sides of the Divine experience are equally balanced. In this experience, there is diversity-in-unity (*bhedābheda-vimarśanātmā*). At this stage, the power of activity (*kriyā-śakti*) is predominant. *Paramaśiva* has the I-experience (*ahaṁ vimarśa*) in *Śiva tattva*, I-this experience (*ahamidaṁ vimarśa*) in *Sadāśiva tattva* and this-I experience (*idamahaṁ vimarśa*) in *Īśvara tattva*. The emphasis is on the first term in each of these experiences. In *Śuddhavidyā tattva*, the emphasis is equal on both "I" and "this" (*ahamaham—idamidam*), the experience becoming "I am I and this is this". This experience is called *parāpara daśā* since it is intermediate between the higher (*para*) and the lower (*apara*).

II. The *Tattvas* of the Limited Individual Experience

The first five *tattvas* were *śuddhādhvan* (pure order) in the manifestation of which the real nature (*svarūpa*) of *Paramaśiva* is not veiled. From this stage onward, the *tattvas* are *aśuddhādhvan* (impure order) in which the real nature of *Paramaśiva* is concealed. The concealment is done by *Māyā* and her five coverings (*kañcukas*). From the *Śiva tattva* to the *Sadvidyā tattva*, the experiences were universal, the "this" meaning "all-this"—the total universe. When *Māyā* starts operating, the meaning of "this" is limited; "this" means "this" distinct and different from everything else. *Māyā* severs "this" from "I" and "I" from "this" and excludes things from one another. *Māyā* draws a veil (*āvaraṇa*) on the Self. Due to this veiling effect, the Self forgets its own nature and knowledge gets limitations (*saṅkoca*). Thus *Māyā* generates a sense of difference.[20]

Māyā has five products known as *kañcukas* or coverings. Their functions are given below:

(i) *Kalā*. It brings about limitation in the universal authorship (*sarvakartṛtva*) of the Universal Consciousness.

(ii) *Vidyā*. It reduces the omniscience (*sarvajñātṛtva*) of the Universal Consciousness.

(iii) *Rāga*. By reducing the all-satisfaction (*pūrṇatva*) of the Universal, it brings about desire for this or that.

(iv) *Kāla*. It reduces the eternity (*nityatva*) of the Universal. Thus is time divided into past, present and future.

(v) *Niyati*. By reducing the freedom (*svatantratā*) and pervasiveness (*vyāpakatā*) of the Universal, it brings about limitation in respect of cause and space.

III. The *Tattvas* of the Limited Individual Subject-Object

Puruṣa. Śiva subjects Himself to *Māyā*. By putting on the five *kañcukas* or cloaks which limit His omniscience and omnipotence, He becomes *puruṣa* or the individual subject. Every sentient being that is thus limited is a *puruṣa*. In this philosophy, *puruṣa* is also called *aṇu* because of the limitation of the divine perfection (*pūrṇatvābhāvena parimitatvādaṇutvam*).

Prakṛti. In the "I am this" experience of *Sadvidyā*, *puruṣa* is the subjective manifestation and *prakṛti* is the objective manifestation. *Prakṛti* is the objective effect of *kalā*.[21] While *puruṣa* is the subject (*vedaka* or knower), *prakṛti* is the object (*vedya* or known). *Puruṣa* is the experient (*bhoktā*) and *prakṛti* is the experienced (*bhogyā*). *Prakṛti* is constituted by three *guṇas* (threads or constituents), viz., *sattva* (serenity), *rajas* (activity) and *tamas* (inertia), and exists in a state of equilibrium of these *guṇas*. There is a difference in the Sāṅkhya and the Śaiva concepts of *prakṛti*. In the Sāṅkhya system, *prakṛti* is one and universal for all the *puruṣas*, whereas in the Śaiva system each *puruṣa* has a different *prakṛti*.

IV. The *Tattvas* of Mental Operation

Differentiation takes place in *prakṛti*, resulting in the production of the psychic apparatus (*antaḥkaraṇa*), senses (*indriyas*) and matter (*bhūtas*). Under the present heading, the three *tattvas* that constitute the *antaḥkaraṇa* are being discussed.

The literal meaning of *antaḥkaraṇa* is "inner instrument". It is the psychic apparatus of the individual. It consists of three *tattvas*, viz., *buddhi*, *ahaṅkāra* and *manas*. The mind operates by means of these three *tattvas*.

Buddhi. It is the first *tattva* of *prakṛti*. It is the intelligence that ascertains. It receives two types of reflections, viz., external and internal. The external reflections are from objects received through the sense-organs.

The internal reflections are from within the *antaḥkaraṇa*; they are from images imprinted in the *saṁskāras* (the impressions on the *manas*).

Ahaṅkāra. It is the product of *buddhi*. It is the I-consciousness in the individual. It is the power of self-appropriation.

Manas. It is the product of *ahaṅkāra*. It is the perceiving organ that receives external information through the senses and builds up mental pictures that are called perceptions. It also makes concepts and creates ideas.

V. The *Tattvas* of Sensible Experience

Jñānendriyas. These are the five powers of sense-perceptions, corresponding to the five sense-organs, viz., eyes, ears, nose, taste-buds in the mouth, and skin-receptors. The *indriyas* are not really the sense-organs. They are the powers which operate through the sense-organs. The five powers of sense-perceptions are seeing (*darśanendriya*), hearing (*śravaṇendriya*), smelling (*ghrāṇendriya*), tasting (*rasanendriya*) and feeling by touch (*sparśanendriya*).

Karmendriyas. These are the five powers of action. These are also the products of *ahaṅkāra*. These are the powers of handling (*hastendriya*), locomotion (*pādendriya*), speaking (*vāgindriya*), excreting (*pāyvindriya*) and sexual action (*upasthendriya*).

Tanmātras. The word *tanmātra* literally means "that only". A *tanmātra* is a primary element of perception. It is a general element of a particular sense-perception. There are five *tanmātras* which are also products of *ahaṅkāra*. These *tanmātras* are: colour-as-such (*rūpa-tanmātra*), sound-as-such (*śabda-tanmātra*), odour-as-such (*gandha-tanmātra*), flavour-as-such (*rasa-tanmātra*) and touch-as-such (*sparśa-tanmātra*).

VI. The *Tattvas* of Materiality

The five gross elements (*pañca-mahābhūtas*) are the products of the five *tanmātras*. Solid matter (*kṣiti* or *pṛthivī*), liquid matter (*āpaḥ*), energy-matter (*tejas*), gaseous matter (*vāyu* or *marut*) and space (*ākāśa* or *vyoma*) are the five *bhūtas*. *Ākāśa*, *vāyu*, *agni* (*tejas*), *āpaḥ* and *pṛthivī* are produced from the *śabda-tanmātra*, *sparśa-tanmātra*, *rūpa-tanmātra*, *rasa-tanmātra* and *gandha-tanmātra*, respectively.

Jīva, Its Bondage and Liberation

Jīva. The individual self or *jiva* has a gross body (*sthūla śarīra*) and a subtle body (*sūkṣma śarīra*). The gross body is made of the five *mahābhūtas* that are highly organized. The subtle body is a *puryaṣṭaka* (group of eight) consisting of *antaḥkaraṇa* (the inner instrument) and the five *tanmātras*. As has been discussed, *buddhi*, *ahaṅkāra* and *manas* are combinedly called the *antaḥkaraṇa*. The *jīva* discards the *sthūla śarīra* at the time of death; but it retains the *sūkṣma śarīra* in which it leaves the body.

The *prāṇa śakti* is a type of divine energy that works both in the universe and the individual. Everything is sustained and maintained by this *prāṇa śakti*.

There is *kuṇḍalinī* in every individual being. This is a form of *śakti* that ordinarily lies dormant.

Every individual being has *caitanya* (consciousness) that is Śiva. Thus every *jīva* is Śiva. Although intrinsically he is Śiva, he becomes an *aṇu* or a limited individual because of *āṇava mala* (innate, impure, limiting condition).

Bondage. Śiva is ever free. But the *jīva* is in bondage. The bondage is due to the innate, impure, limiting condition (*āṇava mala*). *Paramaśiva* brings about limitation of His *icchā śakti* (will power) and thereby the universal consciousness becomes limited to an *aṇu*. The *āṇava mala* is the primary limiting condition of the *jīva*. Through the operation of the *āṇava mala*, the *jīva* considers himself as an individual entity separate from the unitary universal consciousness.

In addition to the *āṇava mala* which is primary, two other types of *mala* (impure limiting condition) bind the *jīva*. These are the *māyīya mala* and the *kārma mala*. *Paramaśiva* limits His *jñāna śakti* (power of knowledge) and, as a result, the *māyīya mala*, brought about by *Māyā*, generates the consciousness of difference. The *kārma mala* originates from the *vāsanās* or impressions left behind in the mind due to the *karma* or action of the individual. The *jīva* is carried from one life to another by the force of the *vāsanās*.

Liberation. Mokṣa or liberation is the recognition (*pratyabhijñā*) of one's true nature. It is the attainment of the original, innate, pure I-consciousness (*akṛtrima-ahaṁ-vimarśa*). The pure I-consciousness is free from *vikalpa* (involvement of alternatives, dualities and relations) and is the immediate awareness.[22] When one has the pure I-consciousness, one knows one's real nature, and that is one's liberation. Abhinavagupta defines liberation as the awareness of one's own nature.[23] By attaining liberation, one's *citta* (individual mind) is transformed into *Cit* (Universal Consciousness).

Liberation is achieved by the *anugraha* (grace) of *Paramaśiva*. This comes through *śaktipāta* (the descent of divine power). There are four means (*upāyas*) through which one earns the grace of the Supreme. These are *āṇavopāya, śāktopāya, śāmbhavopāya, anupāya*. These means are to be adopted to get rid of the *malas* (impure limiting conditions).

The *āṇavopāya* includes the regulation of *prāṇa*, worshipping rituals, concentration on one's chosen deity, etc. The *śāktopāya* is the means of the *mantra śakti*. One mentally repeats a *mantra* (such as *śivo'ham*) and meditates on it. By this practice, the feeling of duality gets less and less and the individual consciousness merges in *Parā-saṁvit*, the Universal Consciousness. When one attains liberation, one feels that the whole universe is only an expansion of one's Self which is nothing else other than *Paramaśiva*. In the *āṇavopāya*, the practice of *prāṇāyāma* helps the *kuṇḍalinī* (latent energy stored in spiral form at the base of the spinal cord) rise up from the *mūlādhāra* (the basal, astral centre in the spinal cord). But, by the *śāktopāya*, the *kuṇḍalinī* ascends from the *mūlādhāra* without much effort of the practice of *prāṇāyāma*.

The *śāmbavopāya* is meant for the advanced aspirant. Through *dhyāna* and *samādhi*, he meditates on Śambhu or the *Śivatattva*. He meditates on *pañcakṛtya*[24] and practises *vikalpa-kṣaya*. The five-fold act of Śiva, viz., *sṛṣṭi* (creation), *sthiti* (preservation), *saṁhāra* (destruction), *vilaya* (dissolution) and *anugraha* (grace) is to go on constantly even in the individual. He is to meditate on the esoteric meaning of this five-fold act (*pañcakṛtya*) in order to rise to the Universal Consciousness. *Vikalpa-kṣaya* is another method for getting rid of the mental agitation (*kṣobha*) and immersing to the underlying Consciousness. As on the surface of the sea, waves appear one after another, so also does the mind generate bizarre ideas. These are the *vikalpas* of the mind. By deep meditation, one stills the mind, stops the generation of the *vikalpas* and remains in a thoughtless condition without losing awareness.

The *sādhaka* (aspirant) meditates on the idea that the universe is only a reflection of *Cit*. He practises *krama-mudrā*,[25] by which his experience of the identification of his individual consciousness with the Universal Consciousness is carried out into the experience of the outer world. The *yogī*, in this system, does not limit his *samāveśa* (immersion into the divine consciousness) to the period of his *samādhi* (contemplation). Even after getting up from the contemplative state, the *samāveśa* continues and he achieves a state of constant awareness of *Paramaśiva*. On attaining the state of pure I-consciousness, the universe becomes an expression and play of the Universal Consciousness. In the state of *akṛtrima-ahaṁ-vimarśa*, the identity of *Paramaśiva, jīva* and *jagat* (universe) is fully realized. Thus the world is not something to be shunned; it is an eternal delight (*jagadānanda*).

In contrast to the three means that have been described here, the *anupāya* is hardly a means. The word itself means, "It is not a means". This entirely depends on the grace (*anugraha*) of *Paramaśiva*, either directly, or indirectly through a *guru* (spiritual teacher).

A summary of the *Pratyabhijñā* philosophy has been given in the foregoing pages. It is a monistic system with its own peculiarities. The world with its matter and energy and diverse forms and names is rooted in a single principle—*Cit, Parāsaṁvit* or *Paramaśiva*. *Cit* is the Universal Consciousness. In this system, consciousness is not a product of matter or energy-matter. Rather the reverse is true; energy-matter is a product of the Universal Consciousness. Of course, it is not a simple case of transformation (*pariṇāma*) unlike the clay being transformed into a pot. The universe is the reflection of *Cit*; it is the expansion of the Universal Consciousness. Hence the universe is not unreal; it is not negated; it is not a thing to be despised and shunned. The Universal Consciousness or *Cit* or *Parā-saṁvit* limits its omniscience and omnipotence; differentiates Its unity into multiplicity through Its power of *Māyā* and thus manifests Itself as the universe and the *jīvas* (individual selves). Nothing, whether matter and energy or the *jīva*, is ever separate from *Paramaśiva*, although omniscience and omnipotence are drastically reduced in the former.

The world-process has a beginning from the pure I-consciousness of *Paramaśiva*. Although man himself is Śiva, he ignorantly alienates from the Supreme and identifies himself with his physical and psychic coverings. This is due to the effect of the *Māyāśākti* of Śiva who imposes restrictions and limitations on Himself. The world which is the *ābhāsa* of *Paramaśiva* stands as something different and undivine. The Pratyabhijñā philosophy says that man has to recognize the pure I-consciousness and re-establish his identity and the identity of the world with the Divine Supreme. When he recognizes the pure I-consciousness and re-discovers himself, he becomes free from bondage. That is his liberation.

Vibration

The Kāshmirī Śaivite uses the word *spanda* or *spandana* for vibration (pulsation or throbbing). The Absolute Consciousness (*Paramaśiva* or *Maheśvara*) vibrates and, as a result of that vibration, the manifestation, maintenance and dissolution of the universe are possible.

The definition of *spandana*, as given by Abhinavagupta, is reproduced here. "*Spandana* is some sort of movement. If there is movement from the essential nature (of *Paramaśiva*) towards another object, the movement is definite and not some sort. Otherwise there is no movement. Hence, *spanda* is only a throb, a heaving of spiritual rapture in the essential nature (of the Absolute Consciousness) without any reference to all types of succession and simultaneity. This is the meaning of the word *kiñcit* in *kiñcit calanam*. Its interpretation is "movement as it were' and not 'movement' in the ordinary sense".[26]

Elsewhere we find a similar definition of *spandana* by Abhinavagupta. "*Spandana* is somewhat (*kiñcit*) of a movement. The significance of *kiñcit* (somewhat) lies in the fact that even the immovable appears 'as if moving'. Though the own aspect of *Prakāśa* (Light of Consciousness) does not change at all, it appears to be changing as it were. The immovable appears as if it has a variety of manifestation".[27]

A proposition like "The immovable moves" is self-contradictory and hence cannot be true. The *spanda* philosopher uses the word *spanda* in a special sense. If the technical meaning of *spanda* is taken into consideration, the contradiction involved in the said proposition is apparent only. 'Movement' is a term which ordinarily implies change in space and time. One position in space is A and another is B. An entity changes its position from A to B in time t. This is the usual concept of movement. In *spanda* philosophy, the Absolute Consciousness (*Paramaśiva* or *Maheśvara*) pulsates without any reference to space and time. This pulsation (expansion and contraction of Consciousness) does not entail spatial and temporal changes. Hence the statement "The immovable moves" does not contradict itself.

Paramaśiva is bipolar. The male pole is Śiva and the female pole is *Śakti*. The Śiva or *Prakāśa* aspect is the light of Consciousness. He is self-luminous by virtue of this *Prakāśa* aspect. The dynamic aspect is *Śakti* or *Vimarśa*. The *jñānaśakti* (power of knowledge) and *kriyāśakti* (power of activity) of *Paramaśiva* are due to the *Vimarśa* aspect. *Spanda* is another name of *Vimarśa*. *Svātantrya*, *Aiśvarya*, *Kartṛtva*, *Sāra*, *Hṛdaya*, *Vimarśa*, *Sphurattā* and *Spanda* of *Maheśvara* or *Paramaśiva* are synonymous. The vibration or pulsation (throbbing) of *Śakti* is *spandana*. *Paramaśiva*, being motionless, is ever in a state of pulsation.

In the ordinary sense of the term "movement" (*calana*), expenditure of energy is unavoidable. Motion is not possible without expenditure of energy. But it does not happen in the case of the divine vibration. In reality, nothing new comes into being and nothing decays. Nothing really appears and disappears. Only the *Divine Spandaśakti* (the vibrating power of the Supreme), which, though free of succession, appears differently as if arising and subsiding.[28]

The creative power of *Maheśvara* is ever full. There is no quantitative reduction nor qualitative change in this power. The full reservoir is ever replete and is never depleted. This power is the wave of the ocean of Consciousness, the volitional power of the Almighty. This idea has aptly been depicted by visualizing this ever full reservoir of power as a goddess.[29]

Spanda (*sphurattā*) has no distinction of space and time (*deśakālāviseṣiṇī*[30]). It is free from sequences (*krama*) whereas the world of diversity has sequences of time and distinctions of space.[31] Locations or directions (*deśa*), dimensions (*dik*) and time (*kāla*) are not real entities; they are mental constructs[32] only. If two or more events occur, the sequence of event B is expressed with reference to event A. This is the concept of time. Such a concept is generated by the mind and is mentally meaningful. Otherwise there is no real entity like time that exists. Regarding space, the Śaiva philosophy makes a clear distinction of *ākāśa*, *deśa* and *dik*. *Ākāśa* or space is an entity. It is one of the five great elements (*pañcamahābhūtāni*). It is material although this matter is very subtle (*sūkṣma*). The apparent, so-called void is *ākāśa* which is full instead of being empty. It produces all sorts of micro-particles and reabsorbs them. The word *deśa* is used here with the meaning of location. It carries a geometrical meaning. A thing A occupies a location L_1 and a second thing B occupies a second location L_2. The different locations may not necessarily refer to areas or volume in *ākāśa*; they may also refer to those in solids or liquids like stone-slabs, metal-instruments, human body and water-mass. The locations are mental constructs. They are generated by the mind. They are mentally meaningful. But they don't exist as real entities. *Dik* (dimension) is another mental concept which is not an entity. Length, breadth and thickness (depth or height) are three dimensions. No action is possible without changes in the four dimensions of length, breadth, thickness and time. In the Indian philosophical systems there are ten *diks*. Thus there are altogether eleven dimensions which include time as one dimension. All those eleven dimensions are relative. Being mental constructs, they quantitatively vary from zero to infinity. Their motions or changes are involved in activity. These dimensions with reference to one activity are not fixed without reference to another activity. Thus all the eleven dimensions of *deśa* and *kāla* are relative. This relativity, however, is confined to the multiplicity and diversity of the cosmic processes. *Paramaśiva, Parāsaṁvit* or *Maheśvara* is absolute and free from any type of relativity.

The vibration (*spandana*) or pulsation of *Śakti* of the Supreme Lord creates (*sṛṣṭi*) the universe, maintains (*sthiti*) it and dissolves (*pralaya*) it. The Śaiva philosophy uses the term *unmeṣa* for the emanation and *nimeṣa* for the dissolution.[33] The *unmeṣa* or *udaya* refers to the emergence of the world; the *nimeṣa* or *pralaya* refers to the submergence of the world. The Śaiva philosophy does not support the concept of creation out of nothing (*creatio ex nihilo*). Whatever is produced (*kārya*) has come forth from *Paramaśiva*, the Absolute Consciousness.[34] The world-products were present in *Paramaśiva* in latency like the banyan tree in the banyan seed[35] or the peacock in the peacock's egg.[36] Emergence (*udaya*) is the manifestation of what was potentially present. When *Paramaśiva* opens His eyes, the world manifests; when He closes His eyes, the world retracts to its latent state within Him.[37] The universe actualizes when *Paramaśiva* awakes and dissolves to remain in its sleeping or latent state when He sleeps.[38] Consciousness evolves out of itself; the pre-existent potential is actualized, resulting in the diversified universe of experience; this is *unmeṣa* or *udaya*.[39] *Unmeṣa* is one phase that does not continue for ever; it alternates with a second phase which is *nimeṣa*, the phase of involution. In the state of *nimeṣa*, all things mingle with one another and contract to a potential state to rest in the all-embracing egoity (*pūrṇāhantā*) of the nature of *Paramaśiva*.[40]

The one and the single entity becomes the perceiver and the perceived, the subject and the object. Again He becomes the subject only. His *Śakti* vibrates and these pulsations embrace the endless cycles of creations and dissolutions. Bliss (*ānanda*) is the nature of *Vimarśa* and pulsation is the inherent nature of bliss.[41] *Paramaśiva*'s nature is an undivided unity. But He veils His undivided nature to enact the cosmic play of diversity and multiplicity. The Consciousness expands. This is the *unmeṣa* phase of the pulsation. Again, when He withdraws the veil, the Consciousness contracts and thereby the universe is dissolved. This is the *nimeṣa* phase of the pulsation.[42]

Kṣemarāja maintains that the state of expansion of Consciousness (*unmeṣa*) is identical with the state of cosmic contraction (*nimeṣa*).[43] Cosmic lysis (*pralaya*) is the same as the genesis of Consciousness (*udaya*) and genesis is the same as lysis.[44] The two phases of the pulsation are sequential for the world of experience. But succession (*krama*) and simultaneity (*yugapat*) have no relevance for *Paramaśiva*. He transcends all talk of succession.[45]

So far has the Divine Pulsation been discussed with reference to the creation and the dissolution of the world. But it is also true for the maintenance (*sthiti*) of the world. All the diverse and the multiple entities of the world owe their existence and activities to the Divine Pulsation. The *Śakti* of *Paramaśiva* ever pulsates. Everything in the universe is the product of the vibration of the single *Śakti*. Although *Paramaśiva* is motionless (*nistaranga*), through the pulsation (*spanda*) He tends towards manifestation. The *spanda* simultaneously operates everywhere and so is the cosmic multiplicity.[46] Absolute Consciousness (*Saṁvitattva*) is manifest everywhere (*sarvataḥ*). It is everywhere full and perfect. The pulsation of *Śakti* is the cause of all things since the emergence (*udaya*) of each manifest entity is the product of the vibration of the Divine Energy. Abhinavagupta[47] says that Consciousness does not issue forth in succession unlike the sprout from the seed and the stalk from the sprout. He contends that whatever manifests in the cosmos is a direct product of the vibration of *Śakti*. The whole world is the objectification of the Absolute Consciousness.

It has already been said that the *Pratyabhijñā* and *Spanda* philosophy is both idealistic and realistic. It accepts an undivided unitary Consciousness as the Reality and hence is idealistic. But, at the same time, it accepts the world of diversity and multiplicity as real. The world is not different from *Paramaśiva* whose Consciousness expands and actualizes as the world as a result of the vibration of the Divine Power (*Śakti*). The cycles of creation and dissolution are infinite. All the cosmic entities undergo constant changes. In spite of the perpetual changeability of the cosmos, in no circumstances is *Paramaśiva* subject in this way to change, either apparent or real.[48]

The entire universe of being and non-being is one with *Paramaśiva*. The Absolute Consciousness as Unity is full (*pūrṇamadaḥ*); the world of diversity and multiplicity is full (*pūrṇamidam*). Maharishi Mahesh Yogī says that the two fullnesses complement each other. In reality, they are not two; they are one only. The Maharishi may be quoted here:

> There is one hundred percent diversity and one hundred percent unity, both performing their work at the same time. That is the nature of the work of creation—this is true reality. To us, one seems real and the other unreal. The reality is that both are real at the same time. As water is true, so ice is true. Both are quite opposed to each other, and their affinity is so great that the ice cannot exist without the water—it is water and nothing but water. So unity and diversity are there together and at the same time.[49]

The Doctrine of Vibration very successfully explains the monistic concept of the Śaiva philosophy along with its concept of realism and that of unity-cum-multiplicity. Although this Doctrine has been conspicuously elaborated in the Śaiva system, its brief mention has also been made in Vedānta. Gauḍapāda holds that the world-appearance is due to the vibration of *prāṇa*[50] or *citta*[51] or *vijñāna*.[52] *Sabdabrahman*[53] is a synonym of *Prakṛti* or *Māyā*. The concept of vibration is implied in this word. The world of diversity and multiplicity is produced as a result of the vibration of the *Māyā-śakti*, the power of Brahman. The Upaniṣads use the term *Sūtrātman*[54] for Brahman. The whole universe is the vibration of the single string (*sūtra*), the Self of which is Brahman. The *Brahma-Sūtra* traces the manifestation (*vyakta*) of the unmanifest (*avyakta* or *Māyā*) to the origination of *prāṇa*[55] and its subsequent vibrations (*kampana*[56]). Thus the Śaiva Doctrine of Vibration gets support from the Vedāntic scriptures.

But, there are some salient points of differences between the Śaiva monism and the Vedāntic non-dualism. Brahman in Advaita Vedānta is motionless and actionless. According to the logic of Advaita Vedānta, motion is an activity and any activity necessitates an expenditure of energy. If Brahman has activity, it cannot be permanent and unmodifiable. Hence, says Advaita Vedānta, Brahman, the Absolute Being, is devoid of becoming. Its power (*Māyāśakti*) which is indescribable (*anirvacanīyā*) has attributes and activity. The three strings (*sattva, rajas* and *tamas*) produce the empirical universe. Vedānta holds that *Māyāśakti* vibrates whereas Brahman is completely unmoving (*niḥspanda*). In the process of the activity of *Māyāśakti*, there is a perpetual degradation (entropy) of energy. Hence, in order that the available energy of *Māyāśakti* is not rendered zero and the cosmic process is not brought to a stand-still condition, the world-energy is recycled through the process of *pralaya* (dissolution). The totality of the manifest universe is dissolved in *Māyā*, to be manifested in the next cycle of emanation, maintenance and dissolution.

In the Śaiva view, a pulsation (*spandana*) consisting of two phases (a phase of expansion and another phase of contraction) is not a motion. Of course, it is not a motion in the sense of change of position, movement from position P_1 to P_2. But it cannot be denied that pulsation is a movement. Any movement needs expenditure of energy and pulsation (vibration) is not possible without expenditure of energy.

By "pulsation", we refer to the cosmic cycles of emanation, sustenance and dissolution and also the perpetual pulsations with regard to the sustenance of the universe. The atoms, the molecules, the galaxies and the super-galaxies are all products of the pulsations of the second type. There is no loss of energy in any pulsation; there is, however, degradation of energy (conversion of utilizable to non-utilizable) in the second type. The existence and the activities of the universe necessarily involve degradation of energy. This degraded energy is reconverted to utilizable energy in the process of the cosmic dissolution (*pralaya*). If considered from this point of view, the Doctrine of Vibration is free from any conceptual defect.

In Advaita Vedānta, Brahman is functionless and *Māyā* is active. This is, however, not the case in Śaiva philosophy, in which *Paramaśiva*, the Universal Consciousness, is ever active. He is the self-luminous light (*Prakāśa*); He is also the self-conscious and active agent. He is the *Svātantrya Śakti* (the Absolute Freedom of the Divine), otherwise known as *Vimarśa*, appearing as the Power of Will (*Icchāśakti*), the Power of Action (*Kriyāśakti*) and the Power of Knowledge (*Jñānaśakti*). In reality, *Śakti* is one, although Her manifestations are many. The Śaiva holds that the power (*śakti*) is non-different from the possessor of the power (*śaktiśaktimato-rabhedaḥ*). There is no *Śiva* without *Śakti*; nor is *Śakti* without *Śiva*. Like fire and heat, *Śiva* and *Śakti* are ever non-different.[57] *Prakāśa* is the *Śiva* polarity and *Vimarśa* is the *Śakti* polarity of the undivided unity of the Universal Consciousness. In fact, *Śakti* vibrates, but the agency of the vibration is attributed to *Paramaśiva* Who is free from duality. Thus, in both Advaita Vedānta and the *Spanda* philosophy, it is *Śakti* that vibrates. The details of the concepts of *Māyā* and *Śakti* in the two systems are not identical; there are subtle differences which are not insignificant. But, at least on the surface, the one common factor that needs emphasis here is that the active agent is *Śakti*, named as *Vimarśa* or *Māyā*. Even though the *Pratyabhijñā* and *Spanda* philosophy is monistic, the *Spandaśakti* (the Energy of Creative Pulsation) has been termed as *Śāṅkarī* (of Śaṅkara or Maheśvara) in Kṣemarāja's propitiatory verses in his *Spandanirṇaya*. Vasugupta, in his *Śivasūtra*, has prayed to Śaṅkara in the first verse and has used the term *śāṅkaraṁ caitanyam* for the same *Svātantrya-śakti*. Thus, as *Māyā* is the power of Brahman, so also is *Śakti*, the power of Śaṅkara (Maheśvara).

There is both idealism and realism in *Pratyabhijñā* philosophy. Reality is Universal Consciousness. Without undergoing any change and affecting its undivided, unitary existence, it manifests as the world of diversity and multiplicity. It reflects on its own mirror.[58] This is the doctrine of appearance (*ābhāsavāda*) in the *Pratyabhijñā* philosophy. But, in spite of this concept of *ābhāsana* (appearance), the world is real in this system.

Advaita Vedānta is absolute idealism. Brahman is Pure Consciousness and is the Reality. The world is an illusion; it is not real although not non-existent. A rope is mistaken, due to ignorance, as a snake. In this case, the rope is the substratum (*adhiṣṭhāna*) and the snake is the illusory appearance. And so is the world which is the illusory appearance of the substratum, Brahman. The whole cosmos is ever-changing. But all these changes are apparent only. Any change is not real since there is nothing other than Brahman that does not change. As gold takes forms of a ring, a necklace, a bangle and still remains as the same gold, the change being in the form and name (*nāma-rūpa*) only without changes in the substance, so does Brahman appear as the manifold world of names and forms without undergoing any modification. This is the *vivartavāda* (doctrine of apparent change) of Advaita Vedānta. There is *pratibimbavāda* (doctrine of reflection) in Advaita Vedānta. According to this doctrine, the one Brahman (Self or Consciousness) is reflected on its power, *Māyā* and also on the empirical subtle bodies (*liṅga-śarīras*). The former reflected image is *Īśvara* (God) and latter reflected images are the empirical shelves (*jīvas*). Although the source of the reflected images (*jīvas*) is one Brahman only, each *jīva* is different from the others. One Sun is reflected on many water-reservoirs to appear as many Suns and so is Brahman.

If the fundamentality of the *ābhāsavāda* of *Pratyabhijñā* and the *pratibimbavāda* of Advaita Vedānta is considered at the exclusion of the minute details of the two systems, there seems to be more commonness and less distinctions. Realism, in its rigorous form, does not operate in the *Spanda* philosophy. Reality (the Universal Consciousness) is one and one only. Due to the vibration or pulsation of one of its bipoles, the world of diversity and multiplicity appears. As different musical tones are produced by the vibration of the string of the violin, so appears the manifold world as a result of the vibration of the *Śakti* of the Self. This is the essence of the *Spanda* philosophy. It does not stand the rigours of strict realism. Thus it is not much meaningful to say that Advaita

Vedānta is illusionistic and *Spanda* philosophy is realistic. There has been much confusion over the use of the word "illusion". Śaṅkara's concept of illusion has already been explained in Chapter II of this book. Śaṅkara does not deny the existence of the world. He recognizes the absolute existence of Brahman and refutes the absoluteness of the existence of the world. And so is Śaiva monism that recognizes *Paramaśiva* as the Absolute Universal Consciousness and the world with its phases of manifestation, sustenance and dissolution as the reflection of the Consciousness. Gauḍapāda in his Advaita Vedānta contends that the *prāṇaśakti* vibrates. The Śaiva monism maintains that the *spandaśakti* vibrates. Except the difference in the philosophical jargons, basically the concept seems to be one and the same.

The *tāṇḍava* dance of Śiva is a symbolic expression of the creative pulsation (*spanda*). The beating of His drum (*ḍamaru*) is the further confirmation of the doctrine of vibration. The image of the *Naṭarāja* (the king of dance, the dancing God) is a symbolic exhibition of the vigorous steps of the divine dance with the vibrating sounds of the drum. The cosmic creative pulsation comes into being as an external manifestation of the supernal creative joy (*ānanda*) of *Paramaśiva*. The *ānanda* wells up (*ucchalat*[59]) from the Universal Consciousness and vibrates rhythmically to be manifested as the universe.

NOTES

1. *Śiva-Sūtras*, by Vasugupta, with Vimarśinī Commentary by Kṣemarāja, translated and edited by Jayadeva Singh, Motilal Banarsidass, Delhi, 1979.
2. *Pratyabhijñāhṛdayam*, by Kṣemarāja, translated and edited by Jayadeva Singh, Motilal Banarsidass, Delhi, 1987.
3. *Spanda-Kārikā*, by Vasugupta, with *Spanda-Nirṇaya* Commentary by Kṣemarāja, translated and edited by Jayadeva Singh, Motilal Banarsidass, Delhi, 1991.
4. *Īśvara-Pratyabhijñā-Vimarśinī*, with original text of *Īśvara-Pratyabhijña-Sūtra* of Utpala, *Īśvara-Pratyabhijñā-Vimarśinī* Commentary by Abhinavagupta and *Bhāskarī* Commentary by Bhāskarakaṇṭha, Edited by R.C. Dwivedi, S. Ayer and K.C. Pandey, Motilal Banarsidass, Delhi, 1986.
5. M.S.G. Dyczkowski, *The Doctrine of Vibration*, Motilal Banarsidass, Delhi, 1989.
6. K.C. Pandey, (Gen. Editor, R.C. Dwivedi), *An Outline of Śaiva Philosophy*, Motilal Banarsidass, Delhi, 1986.

7. Kṣemarāja in *Parāpraveśikā*, p. 2 (*akṛtrimāhamiti visphuraṇam*).
8. *Ibid.* (*yadi nirvimarśaḥ syāt, anīśvaro jaḍaśca prasajyeta*).
9. *Ibid.*
10. BSŚB, II.1.14.
11. *Tantrāloka*, III. 100.
12. Maheśvarānanda in *Mahārthamañjarī*, p. 52.
13. *Parātriṁśikā*, 24.
14. *Īśvara-Pratyabhijñā*, I, pp. 203-4.
15. *Ibid.*, I. pp. 207-8.
16. *Ibid.*, V.V.Pt. I, p. 9.
17. *Paramārthasāra*, 12-13.
18. Quoted by Yogarāja in *Paramārthasāra*, p. 39.
19. *Īśvara-Pratyabhijñā*, I.5.7.
20. *Ṣaṭtriṁsattattvasandoha*, V.5.
21. *Tantrāloka*, Āhn. 9.
22. *Utpaladeva's Īśvara-Pratyabhijñā*, I.6.1.
23. *Tantrāloka*, I, p. 192.
24. Kṣemarāja's *Pratyabhijñāhṛdayam*, Sūtra, 11.
25. *Ibid.*, Sūtra, 19.
26. *Parātriṁśikā-Vivaraṇa*, p. 207.
27. *Īśvara-Pratyabhijñā-Vimarśinī*, I.5.14.
28. Kṣemarāja's *Spandanirṇaya*, the Commentary on Abhinavagupta's *Spandakārikā*, Ist *Kārikā*.
29. Quoted by Kṣemarāja in *Spandanirṇaya*, the Commentary on the Ist *Kārikā* of Abhinavagupta's *Spanda-Kārikā*.
30. *Īśvara-Pratyabhijña-Kārikā* of Utpala, I.5.14.
31. *Ibid.*, II.1.2; II.1.4.
32. *Ibid.*, II.1.3; II.1.5-7; II.2.3-4; II.2.6.
33. *Spanda-Kārikā* of Vasugupta, I.1.
34. *Ibid.*, I.2.
35. *Parātriṁśikā*, 24.
36. *Mahārthamañjarī*, p. 75.
37. Kṣemarāja's *Spanda-Nirṇaya*, Commentary on Vasugupta's *Spanda-Kārikā*, I.1.
38. Abhinavagupta's *Mohopadeśaviṁsatikā*, V.11.
39. *Śivadṛṣṭi*, I.7b-8.
40. *Spandasandoha*, p. 7.
41. *Spandanirṇaya*, pp. 3-4.
42. *Spandasandoha*, p. 4.
43. *Ibid.*, pp. 5-6.

44. *Spandanirṇaya*, pp. 5-6.
45. *Tantrāloka*, IV. 179 b - 180 a.
46. *Spandapradīpikā*, p. 84.
47. *Tantrāloka*, X. 220 b - 2.
48. *Spandapradīpikā*, p. 85.
49. Quoted in *Quantum Healing* by Deepak Chopra, Bantam Books, New York, 1989, p. 228.
50. GMK, I.6.
51. GMK, IV. 72.
52. GMK, IV. 51.
53. MTU, VI. 22; BG, VI. 44.
54. BU, III. 7. 1; BUŚB, III. 7. 1.
55. BS, I. 1. 23.
56. BS, I. 3. 39.
57. Quoted in *Īśvara-Pratyabhijñā-Vimarśinī*, Vol. II, p. x.
58. Kṣemarāja's propitiatory verses in *Spandanirṇaya*.
59. *Śiva-Sūtra*, Ist verse.

IV

PLURALISM IN INDIAN PHILOSOPHY

In the first three chapters of this book, monism or non-dualism, as presented in Indian philosophical systems, has been described. All Indian philosophical schools, however, do not subscribe to the monistic or non-dualistic concept. Many Indian philosophical schools are in favour of realism[1] instead of idealism and all the realistic schools are pluralistic.

Vijñānavāda

Yogācāra Vijñānavāda, one of the Buddhistic schools of philosophy, was founded by Maitreyanātha (*c.* A.D. 270-350), developed by his illustrious disciple Asaṅga and renowned brother Vasubandhu, and later elaborated and diversified by others.[2] This school pleads for subjective idealism and is anti-realistic. It does not accept the existence of an external world. It holds that the so-called external object is an unreal appearance (*saṁvṛta satya*) and that the only reality is cognition or *vijñāna* (synonymous with *citta, manas,* or *vijñapti*[3]). Thus the *Vijñānavādin* maintains two contentions,[4] viz., (1) *Vijñāna* is real; it is not apparent; and (2) *Vijñāna* alone is real; the external world is unreal; no object is real. The cognition manifests itself. It is self-aware (*svasaṁvedya*). It does not depend upon any other cognition for its revelation. But, unlike the eternal (*nitya*) *Cit* (consciousness) or Brahman of Advaita Vedānta a cognition in *Yogācāra Vijñānavāda* is momentary (*kṣaṇika*). It appears for a moment (*kṣaṇa*) and disappears the next moment. One cognition is preceded by other cognitions and also succeeded by some others. Although an individual cognition is momentary, the different cognitions of an individual are related to one another and form a stream of consciousness (*santāna*). In *Vijñānavāda*, the world is negated and the individual is regarded as nothing but a stream of consciousness. Every individual differs from other individuals. They are an irreducible plurality. Thus the anti-realistic subjective idealism of *Vijñānavāda* is pluralistic.

Sarvāstivāda

Sarvāstivāda (all-exists-theory) is a branch of the Buddhist school of the Elders (*Theravāda*). It maintains that everything exists at all times. It is an ultra-realistic school that accepts the past and the future events as equally existent as the present. Its adherents are realists of an extreme type. They steadfastly hold that the world exists and is real.

According to the Abhidharmakośa[5] of Vasubandhu, everything is a *dharma*. This philosophy is a radical pluralism which denies any substance and accepts discrete momentary *dharmas* which are the ultimate elements of existence. Each *dharma* is discrete (*pṛthag*) and simple, not compounded of simpler entities. The *dharmas* are impermanent (*anitya*); they are momentary and durationless. They are not properties of any substance. There is no substance apart from qualities; there is no matter beyond the separate sense-data; there is no *ātman* (soul) beyond the separate mental data.[6] According to the *Sarvāstivāda* philosophy, a thing like a chariot, a tiger, a man or a tree is an aggregate (*skandha*) of the *dharmas*, and the whole (*avayavin*) is not an additional reality.

Sarvāstivāda has a long list of seventy-five *dharmas*. Out of these, seventy-two are conditioned phenomena (*saṁskṛta*) and three unconditioned noumena (*asaṁskṛta*). The *saṁskṛta dharmas* are conditioned by *avidyā* (ignorance) and its satellite *kleśas* (passions) and flow as a stream (*sāsrava*) of phenomenal life (*saṁsāra*). These conditioned *dharmas* are pain (*duḥkha*) or cause of pain. The three unconditioned *dharmas* are *ākāśa* (space), *apratisaṅkhyānirodha* (the cessation of existence that is not observed by the mind) and *pratisaṅkhyānirodha* (the cessation of existence which is attained by the knowledge of the ultimate truth). In *Sarvāstivāda*, space (*ākāśa*) is eternal and omnipresent; it is defined as non-obstruction.[7] *Apratisaṅkhyānirodha* is not produced by knowledge unlike in *nirvāṇa*; it is produced by lack of necessary conditions.[8] An example of this kind of cessation of existence[9] is the entrance of unconscious impressions into the mind and their disappearance into the past. *Pratisaṅkhyānirodha* is the cessation of existence attained by spiritual practice (*mārga*), culminating in the knowledge (*prajñā*) of the ultimate truth which reduces everything to a state of quiescence (*nirvāṇa*[10]).

The conditioned (*saṁskṛta*) *dharmas* are classified objectively and subjectively. Objectively they are of four kinds, viz., matter (*rūpa*), mind (*citta*), mental states and characteristics (*caitta* or *cetasika*) and the forces which are neither mental nor material but common to both (*cittaviprayuktasaṁskāra*).[11] Matter is of four kinds —earth, water, fire and air. Each of these four kinds is made of atoms that are the final constituents. Mind is the contentless consciousness (*vijñāna*). It is self-conscious and self-revealing and conscious of all sense-perceptions. The 'mentals' (*caittas*) are the psycho-ethical qualities that represent the many states of mind such as love, hatred, conation, attention, inattention, etc. These are forty-six in number.[12]

The conditioned *dharmas* are subjectively classified[13] into *skandhas* (aggregates), *āyatanas* (the bases of our experience) and *dhātus* (the elements of our being) as given by the school of the Elders (*Theravādins*).

The *skandhas* (aggregates) are five in number, viz., *rūpa* (material or bodily factors), *vedanā* (feeling), *saṁjñā* (conception and generalization), *saṁskāra* (will and other forces) and *vijñāna* (pure awareness).[14] The *āyatanas* (the bases of our experience) are enumerated as twelve — the six sense-organs including the *manas* (mind) and the six sense-data including the objects of thought.

The Sarvāstivādins analyze away the 'I' (*ātman*) into the aggregates (*skandhas*), bases (*āyatanas*) and elements (*dhātus*) and thus show the 'I' to be void (*śunya*) and unreal. But they hold that the *skandhas, āyatanas* and *dhātus* exist as real *dharmas*. For them, time exists. The past, the present and the future constitute one time only. All belonging to the past, present and future exist in the view of the *Sarvāstivādins* who are also *anātmavādins* (those who reject the existence of the soul) like the followers of the other schools of Buddhist philosophy.

The philosophy of the *Sarvāstivādins* was codified in the form of aphorisms (*sūtras*). Kaniṣka ordered commentaries (*vibhāṣas*) to be written on the original aphorisms. Those who followed the *vibhāṣas* were known as *Vaibhāṣikas*. Some others who were reluctant to follow the *vibhāṣas* and stuck to the original aphorisms were known as the *Sautrāntikas*. The *Sautrāntikas* rejected all the three unconditioned *dharmas*, including *nirvāṇa*, which were declared nominal. They also rejected the past and the future phases and the non-mental forces (*citta-viparyukta saṁskāras*). They reduced the long list of *dharmas* drawn by the *Vaibhāṣikas*. The list of *dharmas* drawn up by them included forty-three elements under five heads.[15] This comprises:

(1) Matter (*rūpa*)—four primary forms (*upādāna*) and four derivatives (*upādāya-rūpa*).

(2) Feelings (*vedanā*)—pleasure, pain and neutral.

(3) Signs, sense-organs (*samjñā*)—five sense-organs and mind (*citta*).

(4) Consciousness (*vijñāna*)—six in number corresponding to the six signs.

(5) Forces (*saṁskāras*)—ten good and ten bad.

Mīmāṁsā

The Pūrva-Mīmāṁsā, shortly known as Mīmāṁsā, is a system of Indian philosophy which investigates the nature of *dharma* propounded in the *karma-kāṇḍa* (former section dealing with ritualism) of the Vedas. According to this system, the ethical action is the supreme governing force of the universe. *Dharma* is the ethical potency (force or power) of merit and demerit. Jaimini, the author of *Mīmāṁsāsūtra*, defines *dharma* as the good which impels or directs man to act.[16] It controls the universe and hence forms the core of the Mīmāṁsā concept. The Mīmāṁsā is a school of realism. Ethical action is real; the agent of ethical action is real; the universe as the field of action is also real.

According to the Mīmāṁsā, the universe had no beginning and will have no end. It is as it was and will be as it is (*na kadācid anīdṛśaṁ jagat*). Its reality is both qualitatively and quantitatively pluralistic.

The Mīmāṁsā refutes the subjectivism and nihilism of the Buddhists and establishes the objective reality of the universe. Five categories, viz., substance (*dravya*), quality (*guṇa*), action (*karma*), generality (*sāmānya*) and non-existence (*abhāva*), are accepted. Among these, the first four are positive and the fifth one is negative. The negative categories are four: prior negation (*prāgabhāva*), posterior negation (*pradhvaṁsābhāva*), absolute negation (*atyantābhāva*) and mutual negation (*anyonyābhāva*).

That which possesses a size is a substance (*dravya*). The substances are eleven in number. These are: earth, water, fire, air, *ākāśa*, space, time, *ātman*, mind (*manas*), darkness, and sound (word, letters). Kumārila enumerates thirteen substances by the addition of two more, viz., force or potency (*śakti*) and similarity (*sādṛśya*). *Ākāśa*, time, space, soul, mind, and sound are eternal and omnipresent. All of them except mind are perceptible.

The Mīmāṁsā enlists fourteen qualities (*guṇas*), viz., colour, taste, smell, touch, magnitude, separateness, conjunction, disjunction, priority, posteriority, gravity, fluidity, viscidity, and number.

There are five types of activities (*karmas*). These are: upward and downward movements, side-ward movement, bending or contraction and stretching or expansion. These activities are the same as those of the Nyāya.

The universal (*sāmānya*) is of two kinds, the higher and the lower. Man and cow are both animals. Animal-ness is a higher universal whereas man-ness or cow-ness is a lower universal. But such a distinction is only relative. Man-ness is a higher universal with reference to Englishman-ness. Being (*sattā*) is the highest universal which is not lower than any other. The lowest universal is the individual like Plato or Socrates. The Mīmāṁsā does not accept the reality of the particular (*viśeṣa*). The particulars of the Vaiśeṣika are nothing other than individuals in the Mīmāṁsā which does not recognize the particulars and the individuals as a separate category.

Prabhākara and Kumārila do not agree with each other on the categorization of reality. Prabhākara does not accept non-existence (*abhāva*) as a separate category. Negation is a category for Kumārila; but Prabhākara rejects it by saying that *abhāva* does not belong to reality itself. Prabhākara presents a list of eight positive categories, viz., substance (*dravya*), quality (*guṇa*), action (*karman*), universal (*sāmānya*), inherence (*paratantratā*), potency (*śakti*), similarity (*sādṛśya*), and number (*saṅkhyā*). He differs from Kumārila who includes force and similarity under substance and number under quality.

The Mīmāṁsā accepts the reality of *ātman* or soul. But unlike Advaita Vedānta, where there is only one Ātman that is equated with Brahman, the Mīmāṁsā accepts a plurality of *ātmans*. The individual *ātmans* are innumerable. Each *ātman* is responsible for its own actions and has to enjoy the fruits of its actions. Thus the *ātmans* are the agents (*kartṛ*) and enjoyers (*bhoktṛ*). They are different from the body, senses and knowledge. The *ātman* by itself is unconscious. Consciousness is an adventitious quality of *ātman*; it is not its essential nature. When the mind (*manas*), along with some information, comes in contact with the *ātman*, consciousness arises in the latter.

Jaimini is silent about the existence of God and soul. Kumārila and Prabhākara accepted souls as permanent substances, but did not need the existence of God to explain the world phenomena. According to their opinion, the universe is beginningless and endless, although its constituent units have both beginning and end. There is no necessity of God's interference in the production of animate and inanimate bodies.

Thus *dharma*, instead of God, is the central problem of the Mīmāṁsā. It is *dharma* that supports the universe and holds the plurality together. Without it, the manifold units of the universe will fall apart. If the action of the individual is ethically right, it produces results that are enjoyable. If the action of the individual is ethically wrong, it produces results that cause suffering.

Dharma is a potential force (*śakti*) of merits and demerits. The merits and demerits are not qualities (*guṇas*). They constitute the potential force which is called *apūrva* (extraordinary) or *adṛṣṭa* (unseen). This force resides in the *ātman* of the agent. It is the *apūrva* or *adṛṣṭa* that determines the future lives in the transmigratory existence. Thus, in the Mīmāṁsā philosophy, the doctrine of *karma* (action) is the doctrine of *dharma*.

Nyāya-Vaiśeṣika

The Nyāya-Vaiśeṣika metaphysics is pluralistic realism. It does not accept a single Being as the Reality. It admits many realities that are independent of one another. It broadly divides the realities into two classes, viz., being (*bhāva*) and non-being (*abhāva*). The positive realities (*bhāvas*) are of six kinds: substance (*dravya*), quality (*guṇa*), action (*karman*), universal (*sāmānya*), particular (*viśeṣa*), and inherence (*samavāya*). Each category is called a *padārtha* in the Vaiśeṣika. Thus, inclusive of non-being or *abhāva*, there are seven *padārthas* in the Vaiśeṣika.[17]

The Vaiśeṣika defines a substance as that in which qualities and actions inhere (*samaveta*). A substance (*dravya*) is the substratum (*āśraya*) of qualities and actions and is the material cause of composite things. Neither a substance without qualities and actions nor qualities and actions without a substance are possible. The Vaiśeṣika enlists nine kinds of substances, viz., *pṛthivī* (earth), *jala* (water), *tejas* (fire), *vāyu* (air), *ākāśa* (space), *kāla* (time), *dik* (dimension), *ātman* (soul), and *manas* (mind). Earth, water, fire, and air are made of atoms. The atoms are eternal, while the compounds made of them are non-eternal. The words *pṛthivī*, *jala*, *tejas*, and *vāyu* have been symbolically used for solid, liquid, energy and gaseous substances, respectively.

Kaṇāda, the founder of the Vaiśeṣika philosophy, laid the foundations of an ultimate pluralism. His discovery of the category of the particular (*viśeṣa*) favoured the manifoldness of the universe and antagonized the monistic unity. He was the father of the Indian concept of atomism. The word *kaṇā* means 'particle' and the suffix *da* (from the verb root *dā*) means 'giver' or 'propounder'. If we go on dividing a composite thing, we reduce it from larger to smaller and smaller parts till we obtain the smallest parts which cannot be further sub-divided. These minute, indivisible parts are called *paramāṇus* or atoms. The atoms are not ordinarily perceived; their existence is proved by inference. Kaṇāda thought that the atoms are eternal entities, not destructible through any means. He conceived of different kinds of atoms by virtue of their qualitative difference from one another. In this respect, the Nyāya-Vaiśeṣikas differ from the Jainas and the Greek atomists who hold that atoms differ in quantity and not in quality. It may be mentioned here that, in Kaṇāda's conception, *tejas* or energy was constituted of atoms (quanta, photons). The three categories of substances, viz., *ākāśa*, *dik*, and time (*kāla*), are not composed of atoms. Each of them is unitary, all-pervading and eternal.

The soul is an eternal, all-pervading and immaterial substance. Its qualities are cognition, desire, volition, aversion, pleasure, pain, merit, demerit, etc. It is distinctly separate from the body, senses, mind, and the stream of consciousness. Only the embodied soul is conscious, while the liberated soul is not. Thus consciousness is an accidental attribute of the soul; it is not an essential one. As there are many individuals, so is the plurality of souls.

Four terms are involved in the cognition of an external object. They are: the *ātman*, mind, senses and objects. Even if the *ātman*, the senses and the object are present, the absence of the mind does not generate a cognition.

There are twenty-four qualities in the Nyāya-Vaiśeṣika system. They are: colour (*rūpa*), taste (*rasa*), odour (*gandha*), touch (*sparśa*), sound (*śabda*), number (*saṅkhyā*), magnitude (*parimāṇa*), distinctness (*pṛthaktva*), conjunction (*saṁyoga*), disjunction (*vibhāga*), remoteness (*paratva*), nearness (*aparatva*), cognition (*buddhi*), pleasure (*sukha*), pain (*duḥkha*), desire (*icchā*), aversion (*dveṣa*), effort (*prayatna*), heaviness (*gurutva*), fluidity (*dravatva*), viscidity (*sneha*), tendency (*saṁskāra*), merit (*dharma*), and demerit (*adharma*).

Action (*karma*) is physical movement. Only a limited corporeal substance can act. There are five kinds of action. They are: throwing upward (*utkṣepaṇa*), throwing downward (*avakṣepaṇa*), contraction (*ākuñcana*), expansion (*prasāraṇa*) and locomotion (*gamana*).

The Nyāya-Vaiśeṣika defines a universal (*sāmānya, jāti*) as that which is eternal (*nitya*) and inheres in many. It is the common essence of all the individuals of a class. It exists in substances, qualities and activities. Although the universal is real, it is not a kind of being (*sattā*) and it is dependent on our cognition (*buddhyapekṣyam*). A universal does not exist in another universal, but exists only in individuals. Being (*sattā*) is the highest (*para*) universal, that is all-pervading. It is never an individual. Substance-ness, quality-ness and action-ness are universals lower than Being (*sattā*). They are intermediate (*parāpara*) universals. Universals like man-ness, red-ness and throw-ness are lower than substance-ness, quality-ness and action-ness. They are the lowest (*apara*) universals. No individuals are ever universals.

The particular (*viśeṣa*) is defined as that which is ultimate and exists in eternal substances. It is the ultimate differentiator. Particulars exist in eternal substances, viz., earth-atoms, water-atoms, fire-atoms, air-atoms, *ākāśa*, *ātmans* (souls), minds, *dik*, and time. They are different from the substances in which they exist. All the earth-atoms are alike; so also are all the water-atoms, fire-atoms and air-atoms. The atoms of each of these four substances, although alike, are differentiated from one another by virtue of a particular present in each. The *ātmans* (souls), being ultimately alike, are differentiated from one another by having a particular in each. Similar is the case with the minds. *Ākāśa*, *dik*, and time are all-pervasive. Each one of these three is different from the others by having a particular. Since there is a particular for each of the ultimate entities, there is a plurality of such particulars.

Inherence (*samavāya*) is the eternal relation between two entities, of which one is in the other. In this definition, 'eternal' means a kind of inseparability. The whole is in parts; a quality or an activity is in a substance; the universal is in the individuals, i.e., the universal is in substances, qualities or activities. This type of inseparable relation is expressed by saying: the whole inheres in its parts; qualities and activities inhere in substances; universals inhere in substances, qualities and activities. Inherence is different from conjunction (*saṁyoga*). The latter is a temporary relation between two substances that can exist separately, whereas the former is an eternal relation between two entities, one of which cannot exist without the other. A higher universal does not inhere in a lower universal; it directly inheres in the individuals. As an example, Being (*sattā*) inheres in man, but not in substance-ness (*dravyatva*) and man-ness (*mānavatva*). In any individual man, Being, substance-ness and man-ness inhere together. Being is a higher universal than substance-ness, which in turn, is higher than man-ness. Hence, Being cannot inhere in substance-ness which also cannot inhere in man-ness, although all these three universals can inhere together in an individual man.

The Nyāya-Vaiśeṣikas combine pluralistic realism with theism. They believe in the existence of God who is one, infinite, eternal, omniscient and omnipotent. He is the Supreme Self and is the efficient cause of the world. He creates, maintains and destroys the world. He does not create the world out of nothing. He uses the eternal atoms, space, time, *ākāśa*, minds and souls as the materials for the creation of the world. He is the moral ruler of the world and the impartial dispenser of the fruits of our good and bad actions.

Substances like space, time, atoms, etc., that are not parts of other composite substances are not effects and hence are uncaused. This is, however, not the case with all composite objects like earth, water, etc., that are effects and have causes. Their material causes like atoms need some intelligent cause for the co-ordination and order of the worldly process. No individual soul possesses omniscience and omnipotence for becoming the efficient cause of the universe. God, the Supreme Self, is the efficient cause of the world.[18]

According to the Sāṅkhya conception, the effect pre-exists in the material cause. The Nyāya-Vaiśeṣikas do not agree to this view. The latter school holds that the subsequent is a new one different from its antecedents, that the effect cannot pre-exist in its material cause and that the effect is not cognized before its production. Such a causal doctrine of the Nyāya-Vaiśeṣika school is called *ārambhavāda* (the doctrine of beginning) or *asatkāryavāda* (the doctrine of no pre-existence of effect).

Sāṅkhya-Yoga

The Sāṅkhya is the oldest philosophical system in India. It is definitely pre-Buddhistic. Kapila was the founder of this system. Unfortunately, the works of Kapila, Āsuri (who was the direct disciple of Kapila) and Pañcaśikha were lost. The *Sāṅkhya-Kārikā* of Īśvarakṛṣṇa who was not earlier than the Christian era has escaped extinction and is the basis of the Sāṅkhya philosophy which we know today.

The Sāṅkhya system is qualitatively dualistic. It recognizes *prakṛti* and *puruṣa* as two ontological Beings. *Prakṛti* is one whereas *puruṣas* (spirits) are infinite in number. *Prakṛti* is insentient (*jaḍa*); but *puruṣa* is pure consciousness, eternal and immutable.

Prakṛti is the primeval stuff of all the matter and psychical manifestations of the world. It has three constituents (*guṇas*), viz., *sattva* (serenity, tendency to manifestation), *rajas* (activity) and *tamas* (inertia, obstruction to manifestation). *Prakṛti* continues to remain in dormancy as long as its three constituents are in equilibrium (*samatā*). This is the original state of *prakṛti*, when there is no world of forms. When somehow the reflection of *puruṣa* is thrown in *prakṛti*, the latter is disturbed. This disturbance upsets the original equilibrium of the three constituents or attributes of *prakṛti*. As a result, any one constituent dominates over the other two and evolution ensues. *Prakṛti* evolves the world through its three constituents.[19]

The Sāṅkhya is atheistic. It does not need the existence of God to explain the evolutionary processes. According to this system, the one *prakṛti* and the multiple *puruṣas* were never created; they are eternal, beginning-less and endless; and both are real ontological entities.

Twenty-five categories (*tattvas*, ultimate thats, thatnesses) are enumerated in the Sāṅkhya system. Out of these, the class of *puruṣas* is one category. All the categories of the Sāṅkhya are given in the form of the following chart:

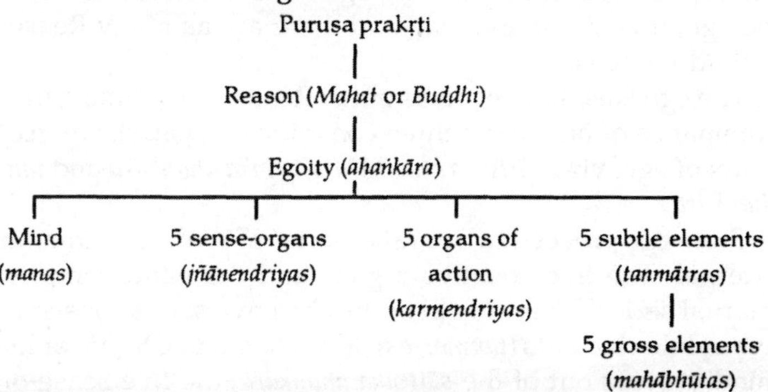

Unlike in the Nyāya-Vaiśeṣika, where categories are meanings of words (*padārthas*), they are ontological entities in the Sāṅkhya-Yoga.

Puruṣa which is pure consciousness seemingly comes in contact with *prakṛti*. This is only a seeming contact which is not at all real. The sun reflected in water, with ripples and waves, moves in the water. So is *puruṣa* which is reflected in *prakṛti* without coming in real contact.[20] The *puruṣa* does not get involved in the actions of *prakṛti*; he remains unchanged (*kūṭastha*), becomes the knower and the witness (*sākṣī*), but does not become the doer, enjoyer or sufferer.

The primal *prakṛti* (*mūlaprakṛti*) is indeterminate and imperceptible. It is the equilibrium (*sāmyāvasthā*) of the three constituents (*guṇas*) which are opposing in nature. At this stage of the absolute equilibrium of the *guṇas, prakṛti* is absolutely homogeneous. Although the primal *prakṛti* is not unchanging, the change is homogeneous from similar to similar. *Prakṛti* evolves as a result of the disturbance of the equilibrium of its three attributes and the evolution consists in transition from general to particular, unspecialized to specialized and simple to complex. *Prakṛti*, being the simplest entity, is the ultimate prius in accordance with the Sāṅkhya conception of cause which is the unspecialized state of the specialized effect.

After getting the reflection of the *puruṣa, prakṛti* becomes conscious and agitated. This agitation disturbs the equilibrium of the three constituents of *prakṛti* and thereby evolution becomes operative. First of all, the *sattva* constituent becomes dominant and

Reason (*Buddhi*) appears. It has cosmic significance and hence is called the Great (*Mahat*). Although Reason is cosmic and above the ego, it is still individual, and there are as many Reasons as individual egos.

The ego (*ahaṅkāra*) evolves out of Reason. Depending upon the dominance of one of the three constituents (*guṇas*), we get three kinds of ego, viz., *sāttvika ahaṅkāra, rājasika ahaṅkāra* and *tāmasika ahaṅkāra*.

From ego proceed two parallel series of evolutes—internal and external. The five conative organs and the mind comprise the internal series. The external or the objective series consists of the five subtle elements (*tanmātras*). In the opinion of Vijñānabhikṣu,[21] mind evolves out of the *sāttvika ahaṅkāra*, the five sense-organs and the five organs of action from the *rājasika ahaṅkāra* and the five subtle elements out of the *tāmasika ahaṅkāra*. Īśvarakṛṣṇa[22] differs from Vijñānabhikṣu and contends that the mind, the five sense-organs of action evolve out of the *sāttvika ahaṅkāra* and the five subtle elements from the *tāmasika ahaṅkāra*, the *rājasika ahaṅkāra* supplying energy to all these transformations.

The five subtle elements (*tanmātras*, thats-only) are sound (*śabda*), touch (*sparśa*), colour (*rūpa*), taste (*rasa*) and smell (*gandha*). The five gross elements or great elements (*mahābhūtas*) evolve out of the subtle elements. *Ākāśa*, gaseous matter or *vāyu*, energy or *tejas*, liquid matter or *āpaḥ* and solid matter or *pṛthivī* evolve out of *śabda-tanmātra, sparśa-tanmātra, rūpa-tanmātra, rasa-tanmātra*, and *gandha-tanmātra*, respectively. Unlike in Vedānta which favours sequential evolution (*ākāśa* → *vāyu* → *agni* → *āpaḥ* → *pṛthivī*), Sāṅkhya holds that all the five gross elements appear simultaneously from the five subtle elements.

In the Nyāya-Vaiśeṣika system, space (*dik*) and time (*kāla*) are substances different from *ākāśa*. The Sāṅkhya does not accept this view.[23] According to *Yoga-Bhāṣya*, time does not correspond to any real entity, but is a product of mind, following the result of perceptions or words (*sa khalvayaṁ kālo vastuśūnyo'pi buddhinirmāṇaḥ śabdajñānānupātī*[24]). Both the Sāṅkhya and the Yoga schools maintain that space (*dik*) and time (*kāla*) have no existence apart from *citta* (mind). Both of them are mental constructs only. Mental concepts of extension such as right or left, east or west, length, breadth or depth give rise to *deśa* or *dik*. In terms of Einstein's relativity, *dik* may be better translated as 'dimension' and not as 'space'. Where there are at least two events, the concept of succession or simultaneity is to creep in. That concept is time. Dimensions (*dik*) and time (*kāla*) are two forms of modes of activity of the *citta* (mind). Activity, movement or transformation is basic to changes in the *dik-kāla* matrix.

The processes of evolution involve transformation (*pariṇāma*). In the case, C is evolved to E, C is the material cause and E is the effect; C is transformed into E. After the transformation is over, C no longer remains as C, but becomes E. The antecedent continues as the consequent; C continues as E. It may not be misconstrued that, in transformation, the prior stage is annulled in the posterior. This doctrine of the Sāṅkhya is called *pariṇāmavāda* (the doctrine of transformation) which holds that the effect is existent (*sat*) before it is born.[25] The Sāṅkhya rejects the idea of the origination of an effect (*kārya*) from non-Being. Something can be transformed into something else. Something cannot come out of nothing. It is also a fact that something cannot be reduced to nothing. When C is transformed into E, C is a positive, real entity and E is also a positive, real entity. The effect must be pre-existent in the causal stuff. Since the effect is only a transformation of the material cause, both of them are existent alike and must be identical in substance. This is called the *sat-kārya-vāda* (the doctrine of existent effect) in the Sāṅkhya philosophy.

The world is not unreal like a man's horn; nor is it real in the sense of being unchangeable.[26] It is also not regarded by the Sāṅkhya as indescribable.[27] It is not a reflection of what is not.[28] It is not a mere idea.[29] It exists in its eternal form of *prakṛti*.[30] The world, undergoing transformations, has a phenomenal reality.[31] The world undergoes alternate evolution and involution. Evolution is the unfoldment of the latent state of *prakṛti* and the manifestation of the world from the successive evolutes. Involution is the reverse process of evolution. At the close of the world-period, the products return by a reverse movement into the preceding stages and finally get dissolved in *prakṛti*. There is a latent period when *prakṛti* remains in the unmanifested (*avyakta*) condition. When the equilibrium of the three constituents of *prakṛti* is disturbed, evolutionary processes again operate for the development of a new universe. This cycle of evolution and involution is beginningless and endless. Even if individual *puruṣas* attain release, the processes of evolution and dissolution of the world do not cease.[32] The rhythmic activity of *prakṛti* is a continuous phenomenon and *saṁsāra* (the worldly phenomena) will never reach its end.[33]

Jaina Concept of Pluralistic Realism

Jaina philosophy is atheistic, realistic and pluralistic. It is an ethics of self-conquest which does not need God's help or intervention.

The comprehension of three doctrines of the Jaina philosophy is useful for the full understanding of the Jaina metaphysics. These are: (1) the doctrine of multiple modality (*anekāntavāda*), (2) the doctrine of modalities (*nayavāda*), (3) the doctrine of conditioned predication (*syādvāda*).

Ultimate reality is complex in structure. Its nature cannot be comprehended unless it is examined from various points of view. A particular aspect of reality to the exclusion of other aspects may be examined for a definite purpose. But to insist on that single aspect as the end-all of reality is erroneous. It is like the fabular examination of an elephant by six blind persons and their descriptions of the animal with reference to the part of the animal each examined. The Jainas reject the over-emphasis on one aspect of reality to the exclusion of its other aspects. They recognize the complex nature of the ultimate reality and try to describe it in its completeness after viewing it from many aspects. This is their doctrine of multiple modality (*anekāntavāda*). On the basis of this doctrine, they developed the other two doctrines, viz., *nayavāda* and *syādvāda*.

The doctrine of modalities or the doctrine of standpoints is called *nayavāda*. Knowledge of a thing in its relation is *naya*. The Jainas believe in the relativity of knowledge. To hold a particular standpoint is not to deny the others. The particular standpoint is true for a definite purpose. Some other standpoints may be true for other purposes also. That truth is relative to our standpoints is a fundamental principle in Jaina philosophy. If this is accepted, the possibility of accepting two contradictory propositions relating to the same object cannot be ruled out. This is *asti-nāsti-vāda* (the doctrine of 'is' and 'is not'). One may describe an object from one point of view that it exists and from another point of view that it does not. If the different points of view are stated, an object may be affirmatively and negatively described and both descriptions are true with their respective qualifications.

The doctrine of conditioned predication (*syādvāda*) holds all knowledge to be only probable. Every proposition gives us a sense of probability (maybe or *syāt*) and not of certainty. The nature of reality is extremely complex and hence absolute or categorical predication is not correct. Predications of an object may be too many. But we cannot affirm or deny any predication absolutely. All predications are to be conditional. Every proposition is true, but only under certain conditions.

The *syādvāda* is also known as *saptabhaṅgī*. There are seven different ways of predicating an object or its attributes according to the point of view. A substance or its attribute may be predicated as (1) is (*syād asti*), (2) is not (*syād nāsti*), (3) is and is not (*syād asti nāsti*), (4) is unpredicable (*syād avyaktavya*), (5) is and is unpredicable (*syād asti avyaktavya*), (6) is not and is unpredicable (*syād nāsti avyaktavya*), and (7) is, is not and is unpredicable (*syād asti nāsti avyaktavya*).

According to the Jaina metaphysics, reality which is complex in nature is permanence in the midst of change, identity in the midst of diversity and unity in the midst of multiplicity. Reality is characterized by origination, decay and permanence (*utpāda-vyaya-dhrauvya-lakṣaṇaṁ sat*[34]).

In the Jaina view, everything is a substance (*dravya*). A substance is defined as that which possesses qualities (*guṇas*) and modes (*paryāyas*)—*guṇaparyāyavad dravyam*.[35] A substance is a *dharmī* (possessor of characteristics). The characteristics (*dharmas*) are the *guṇas* and the *paryāyas*. The qualities or *guṇas* are the essential characteristics and the *paryāyas* are the changing modes. Substances undergo modifications and such changes are the *paryāyas*. In the Advaita Vedānta definition of reality, permanence and unchangeability are implied. But the Jainas hold that both change and permanence are real. Furthermore, they hold that every object has both positive and negative characteristics. From one point of view, an object has the characteristic P, and from another, the characteristic not-P.

The Jaina classification of categories may be presented in the chart on page 148.

In the Jaina metaphysics, time (*kāla*) is a substance that has no extension. Time is accepted as real. The Jaina thinkers maintain the reality of change, motion, growth and development. The concept of change implies that of time. The former being accepted

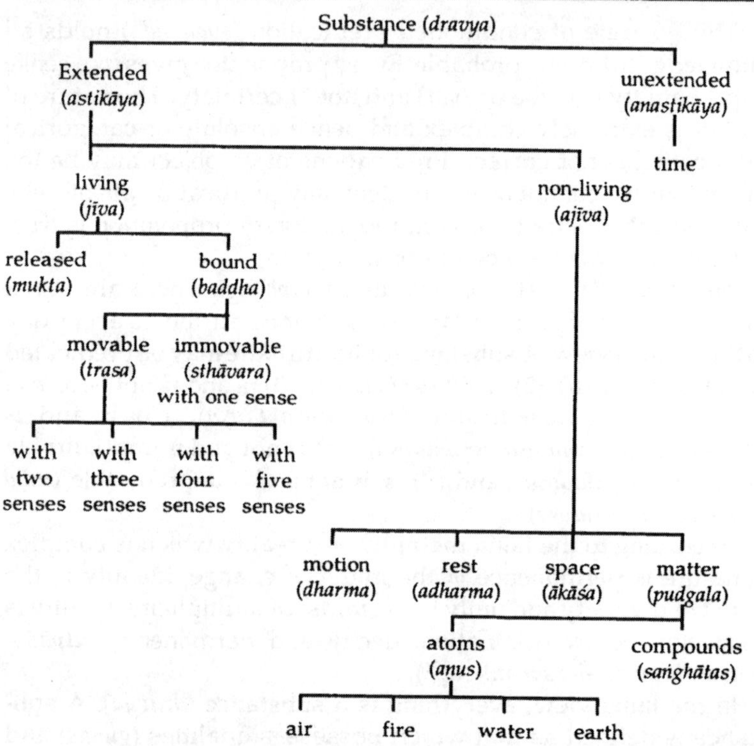

as real, the latter cannot be explained away as illusory. In the Jaina view, this *kāla-dravya* is constituted by atomic moments of time.

The extended substances are divided into two classes, viz., conscious (*cetana*) and non-conscious (*acetana*). The former are animate whereas the latter are inanimate. The *jīvas* are divided and sub-divided as shown in the foregoing chart. *Jīva-dravya* (living being) is one of the most important categories of reality. It is a sentient substance.

The *ajīvas* or inanimate substances have four sub-groups, viz., *dharma*, *adharma*, *ākāśa* and *pudgala*. The two words, *dharma* and *adharma* have technical meanings in the Jaina philosophy. Unlike in Indian ethics, *dharma* is not virtue and *adharma* not vice. For the purpose of the Jaina metaphysics, *dharma* and *adharma* are the principles of motion and rest, respectively. These two imperceptible principles pervade the whole of *loka-ākāśa* (mundane space). The Jaina thinkers assert the reality of space or *ākāśa*. That portion of space that accommodates physical objects is *loka-ākāśa*, beyond which is infinite space where there is no physical object.

Material objects (*pudgalas)* are constituted by atoms (*paramāṇus*). There are four *pudgalas* whose constituent units are atoms. They are: air, fire, water and earth. These words are used in symbolic senses—air for gaseous matter, fire for energy, water for liquid and earth for solid. The Jaina thinkers conceived of the particulate nature (quanta) of energy. The compounds (*saṅghātas*) of matter are constituted by the conglomeration of the atoms of different elements. These aggregates are called *skandhas*, the whole physical world being a mighty aggregate (*mahāskandha*).

The aggregates and the atoms of the physical world are in motion. There is no motionless object. By virtue of the motion (*dharma*) of the objects, they are to disperse in the vast space, disintegrate and go away from one another. It is *adharma* or gravity that antagonizes the motion of the objects. *Adharma* is the steadying principle that helps stabilize the materials of the world. The Jaina thinkers anticipated Newton's law of motion and law of gravitation in their concepts of *dharma* and *adharma*, respectively.

Evaluation of Indian Pluralism

It is not the intention here to present a critical review of the pluralism in Indian philosophy. An analytical probe into the matter will need a big volume. As has been discussed in the foregoing pages of this chapter, the Indian philosophical schools that advocate realism and pluralism are diverse and their concepts of reality are also varying. With their uncommon concepts of reality, their categorization is bound to vary.

Vijñānavāda is a school of subjective idealism. The world is unreal for the Vijñānavādins. Still they are pluralists since they hold that the streams of consciousness are different from one another and innumerable. Subjective idealism has been successfully refuted by many philosophers.[36] This author agrees to their view-points.

Sarvāstivāda is a realistic school that holds that the world exists and is real. This is a philosophy of radical pluralism. But the peculiarity of this pluralism is that it denies both the unity and the plurality of substances. It accepts the reality of *dharmas* only. It denies all substances of the world and accepts everything as a *dharma* (phenomenal property). The *dharmas* are discrete, impermanent and momentary. This philosophy can hardly be supported since it fails to present an integral explanation of the world.

"Being as an ontological entity is one or many" is the central question of this discussion. The Indian philosophical schools that uphold realism and pluralism have mixed up issues and ended in confusion. Qualities, actions, emotions, negation, etc., cannot be entities. Many diverse categories have been enumerated as real. In one sense, such categorization is not wrong. My upward or downward movement is real for me. My body colour and my feelings are also real for me. But these meanings of "real" are not right, if considered in an ontological sense. My *vedanā* (feelings) cannot be an ontological entity.

Speculation has played a prominent role in the categorization of reality by the Indian pluralists. To cite an example, one philosopher says that potency, similarity and number are categories of reality while another rejects this notion. The Sāṅkhya holds that reason (*Mahat* or *Buddhi*) evolves out of *prakṛti* and that it is both cosmic and individual. How the individual *buddhis* are evolved out of the cosmic *Buddhi* has not been elaborated in the Sāṅkhya system. *Mahat* or *Buddhi* is the first evolute of *prakṛti*, as given in the Sāṅkhya. Someone may place another evolute between *prakṛti* and *Mahat*. The Sāṅkhya view needs logical substantiation to be established as a fact so that it can refute other assertions. Diverse categories have been enumerated in the metaphysics of the Sāṅkhya, the Nyāya-Vaiśeṣika, the Jaina, and the other Indian pluralistic schools. We have to accept the categories on some logical basis. If we are to accept a category as a fact, we have to state the basis for our acceptance. If we are to reject a category, we have also to cite our criteria and desiderata for the rejection. Such a logical approach is lacking in the works of the pluralists.

Many pluralists contend that the world is beginningless and endless. In the ancient past, the Mīmāṁsā philosophers anticipated the steady-state-theory postulated in 1948 by Hermann Bondi, Thomas Gold and Fred Hoyle. The logical untenability of this theory will be discussed later in this book. Even the empirical findings of the twentieth-century astrophysicists conclusively prove that the world had a beginning and that space and time had beginnings. There are mathematical predictions to the effect that the universe will implode and be subjected to a big crunch. It would be reduced to a point-like singularity. The mathematics tends to show that the singularity will finally attain zero volume. To express it otherwise, *this* world will have an end. Hence, the eternality of the world, as advocated by many realists and pluralists cannot be upheld.

Most realists-*cum*-pluralists deny the existence of God. They do observe order (*ṛta*) in the universe (although disorder or *anṛta* is not non-existent). The laws of nature and the functioning of the universe are empirical facts and undisputable. They observe co-ordination among the diverse units of the universe. The intelligent functioning of the insentient nature is quite obvious. They are fascinated by the beautiful architecture of the universe. The teleology behind the functioning of the different units of the universe cannot be effectively explained away. In spite of all these empirical observations, most realists and pluralists are strong advocates of atheism. They have a right to cherish their atheistic notions. But they have to justify their atheism, if not empirically, but at least logically. It cannot be said that the pluralists with atheistic conviction have successfully justified their non-acceptance of the existence of God.

Some pluralistic schools have accepted the existence of God, individual souls and other multiple categories. In their opinion, all the rest categories are co-eternal with God. Such a concept of pluralism does not explain how God is able to control and co-ordinate the diverse categories that are different from Him and independent of Him. They are satisfied by saying that God is omniscient and omnipotent. This is again speculation. Is it a necessary truth for God to be omniscient and omnipotent? No self-contradiction is involved if a negative proposition is stated. Hence the omniscience and omnipotence of God is not necessary in pluralism. The fact is, however, different in non-dualism, in which only Brahman exists and nothing else other than Brahman exists. The non-dualist can say that Brahman (consciousness) is all-knowledge (omniscient), and being all, is all-potential (omnipotent). With this concept of the non-dualist, it would be self-contradictory if a statement is made, "Brahman is not omniscient and omnipotent". Unless we accept the monistic or non-dualistic concept, we cannot explain the governance of the universe by God.

Whether consciousness or matter is primary is a moot point in philosophy and science. The materialists believe that matter is primary and that consciousness is a manifested symptom of matter at a particular stage of the development of the latter. This materialistic concept fails to explain the integral cosmology and cosmogony. Before life was generated on the Earth and consciousness was manifested, the insentient matter had existed and functioned in meaningful ways. The appearance of the cosmic egg, the big-bang explosion, the evolution of micro-particles, elements and compounds, stellar evolution, galactical evolution, inorganic evolution, organic evolution, DNA and RNA evolution and species evolution were meaningful steps in the long ladder of the development of nature. How can we say that a Cosmic Intelligence was not essential for the guidance of this development? So far we know of the origin of intelligence on the Earth. We are still to discover planets of stellar systems in our galaxy and other galaxies where intelligent beings have been evolved. It is, however, a fact that majority of the stellar systems are devoid of life. In spite of this fact, the non-living world maintains order, functions meaningfully and is not chaotic. Whatever chaos is apparent in the world is finally subservient to an integral order. We cannot explain the cosmological and cosmogonical order unless we accept consciousness as primary. Matter, in its diversity, is secondary to consciousness. Many realists-cum-pluralists of Indian philosophy have not realized this fundamentality of Being. They could not explain the intelligent functioning of the different categories of matter. Some of them had to introduce God as one of the realities. Some others introduced infinite number of souls as a category class. A third group spoke of God and souls in addition to other categories of the multiple reality. To some, these souls are unconscious, and to others, they are multiple entities of pure consciousness. How these infinite number of souls appeared is a mystery. Some say that they are beginningless and endless. How the multiple conscious entities such as souls and God, being unrelated and independent of one another, still function in harmony cannot be satisfactorily explained. Monism or non-dualism provides a satisfactory explanation of the cosmic processes and hence is preferred to pluralism.

The Sāṅkhya initiates the evolutionary process by the disturbance of the equilibrium of the three constituents of *prakṛti*. It is said that the seeming reflection of *puruṣa* on *prakṛti* brought about, in the latter, agitation that disturbed the equilibrium. *Puruṣas* are infinite in number. There are chances of such reflection at all the times. Why reflection takes place at a particular moment and not at other times is not answered by the Sāṅkhya.

The eternality of the universe is contended by most pluralists. In their opinion, the universe is beginningless and endless. The question is: Is it possible for the universe to be eternal? All the worldly processes involve expenditure of energy. There is no exception to this statement. The universe cannot function and cannot maintain its existence even for a single moment without the expenditure of energy. It is a fact that the different energy systems are in a dynamic state of flux, one type of energy being converted into another. But, in spite of the inter-conversion of energy, the process itself has to pay a price. This price is the conversion of the utilizable energy into non-utilizable energy which is called entropy. With the continuous rise of entropy, the utilizable energy declines in quantity. This trend may be extrapolated to a point at which the entropy is maximum and the utilizable energy is zero. There can be no universe at this point with zero utilizable energy. Thus the concept of the eternality of the universe is untenable. The world-energy which is kinetic and dynamic must be converted into its original form, the potential and latent form. Through this process is the entropy dissolved to be again utilizable. Hence a dissolution of the world is necessary in order that the creation of a new universe is possible. The Sāṅkhya has the cycle of evolution and involution to meet this requirement. But, it has no cosmic co-ordinator, controller and architect. This is another serious lacuna in the Sāṅkhya system. The Mīmāṁsā supports the theory of the steady-state-universe. It has already been discussed that such a theory is logically and empirically untenable.

The universe is empirically pluralistic. There is no doubt in it. Both the inanimate and the animate objects, the insentient stone and the sentient man are constituted of atoms. The atoms are constituted of micro-particles whose constituent units are quarks. The quarks may not be the primary units. The primary unit may be the unified field, *ākāśa*, *prāṇa* or *āpaḥ*. Thus all the diverse objects of the manifold universe boil down to one principle only, i.e., *āpaḥ* or the primal waters. Is that also the final state of matter-energy or energy-matter? Advaita Vedānta negatively answers this question. *Āpaḥ* dissolves in *Māyā-śakti* and loses its identity with the termination of this world-period. This *āpaḥ* is again manifested from *Māyā-śakti* with the beginning of the next world-period. It may be deduced from this that *Māyā* is the unitary substance from which the world originates and into which it again dissolves to repeat the unending cycles. Advaita Vedānta says that it is true but not the whole truth. *Māyā* is the power of Brahman and indescribable (*anirvacanīyā*). It cannot be said that it exists; it cannot be said that it does not exist; and it cannot be said that it exists and does not exist. *Māyā* is not an independent entity. Its substratum is Brahman which alone exists. This is the summary presentation of Advaita Vedānta. Even in modern empirical science, the concept of realism and pluralism has been outdated and discarded. The quantum physicist is speaking of the unbroken whole, the one homogeneous substratum below the surface of the manifold phenomenal macro- and micro-world. The post-quantum physicist is presenting his mathematical panorama of the superstring. The violin is being played by the master musician. From only one string are generated various musical tones. The musical tones are phenomenal entities, not noumenal. The string and only one string vibrates; the manifold universe appears as a result of this vibration. The universe is the vibration (*jhaṅkāra*) of the string of the *vīṇā* (a musical string instrument). If *Māyā* is the *vīṇā*, *Īśvara* (God) is the musician. The superstring physicist probes into the phenomenal vibrations. Will he be able to detect the *vīṇā* ? *Īśvara* is touch-me-not entity in science. Will the physicist touch that entity ? Will he ponder over the musician ?

The musician and the *vīṇā* will be discussed later in this book. It is stressed here that pluralism and realism cannot be logically and empirically upheld.

NOTES

1. J. Sinha, *Indian Realism*, Motilal Banarsidass, Delhi, 1986.
2. *History of Philosophy, Eastern & Western*, Vol. I., George Allen & Unwin Ltd., London, 1967, p. 209.
3. Vasubandhu in *Viṁśatikārikā*.
4. *Triṁśikā-bhāṣya*, p. 15.
5. Vasubandhu's *Abhidharmakośa*, edited by Rāhula Saṁkṛtyāyana.
6. *Central Conception of Buddhism*, p. 74.
7. AKV of Yośomitra, edited by Woghihara, Tokyo, p. 15.
8. *Ibid.*, p. 17.
9. P.T. Raju, *Idealistic Thought of India*, p. 211; and Y. Sogen, *Systems of Buddhistic Thought*, pp. 164 fol.

10. AKV, p. 16.
11. AKV, pp. 24 ff.
12. Y. Sogen, *Systems of Buddhistic Thought*, pp. 155 fol.
13. *Ibid.*, pp. 111-12.
14. AKV, p. 42.
15. Commentary by Aruṇandi on *Śiva-Jñāna-Siddhi*.
16. MSS, I. 1. 2.
17. VS, I. 1. 4.
18. NS, IV. 1. 19-21; VS, II. 1. 17-19.
19. SK, 2.
20. SD, VI. 28.
21. SD, II. 18.
22. SK, 25.
23. SD, II. 12.
24. YB (*sa khalvayaṁ kālo vastuśūnyo'pi buddhinirmāṇaḥ śabdajñānānupātī*).
25. SK, 9.
26. SPS, V. 52-53.
27. SPS, V. 54.
28. SPS, V. 55.
29. SPS, I. 42.
30. SPS, V. 56.
31. SPB, I. 26.
32. SPS, III. 66.
33. YS, II. 22; SPB, I. 67; I. 159; II. 4; VI. 68-69.
34. TTAS by Umāsvāmī.
35. TTAS by Umāsvāmī.
36. J. Sinha, *Indian Realism*, Motilal Banarsidass, Delhi, 1986, pp. 225-73.

V

MONISM, DUALISM AND PLURALISM IN WESTERN PHILOSOPHY

MONISM

THE MOST ANCIENT Western philosophy was the Greek philosophy. It began with Thales who was a native of Miletus in Asia Minor in the sixth century B.C. He said that everything was made of water.

Anaximander, the second philosopher of the Milesian school was sixty-four years old in 546 B.C. He did not accept water as the single primal substance, as held by Thales. Nevertheless, he also held that all the substances of the world came from a single primal substance which is infinite, eternal and ageless. He conceived of many worlds out of which our world is one only. His primal substance which is common to all the worlds is transformed into the various substances that we experience. That these transformed substances are also transformed into each other was predicted by Anaximander. Unlike in Jewish or Christian theology, his worlds were not created, but evolved. There was an eternal motion, in the course of which originated the worlds.

Anaximenes, the last of the Milesian triad, who flourished before 494 B.C., said that the fundamental substance of the world was air.

Xenophanes, an Ionian by birth, believed all things to be made out of earth and water. Heraclitus, an Ionian, regarded fire to be the primordial element, out of which all objects had arisen. He conceived of the world as ever in motion. He propounded the doctrine that everything is in a state of flux. "You cannot step twice into the same river" was his famous statement. In spite of the doctrine of the perpetual flux, Heraclitus allowed something everlasting. His primordial substance, fire, never dies. "The world was ever, is now, and ever shall be, an ever-living Fire" he said.

Parmenides

Parmenides, a native of Elea, flourished in the first half of the fifth century B.C. For Heraclitus, everything changes while for Parmenides, nothing changes. "It is 'the One' which is infinite and indivisible and is the only true being", declared Parmenides. He condemned the sense-perceptions as mere illusion. He thinks of 'the One' as material and extended, as a sphere which is present everywhere and cannot be divided. The Primordial Being of Heraclitus is a union of opposites. On the contrary, Parmenides thinks that there are no opposites.

Spinoza

The foregoing discussion presents the Greek thought on the unitary nature of the primordial substance of the world. After a long interval, Spinoza (1632 - 77) deliberated on the same topic. He was a Jewish philosopher. By substance he meant what can exist by itself. He asserted that there is only one substance, the whole of reality. This whole of reality is God, only one God, absolutely infinite Being. Nothing finite is self-subsistent. God, being infinite, exists without any extraneous help. He exists necessarily; His essence implies His existence. He is eternal, not temporal. He is His own cause, *causa immanens* and *causa sui*. For Spinoza, God and substance mean the same thing. Descartes's mind and matter were defined, respectively, by the attributes of thought and extension. For Spinoza, thought and extension are both attributes of God who also has an infinite number of other attributes. All the separate pieces of matter in the world and all the individual souls are not considered as things by Spinoza. He accepts them as adjectival and different aspects of the Divine Being. Unlike the Christians, he does not believe in personal immortality. His concept of immortality is impersonal. It is becoming more and more one with God.

Spinoza's philosophy is strictly deterministic. There is nothing like free will in the mental sphere. There is no scope of chance in the physical world. All events of the world, both psychical and physical, are ruled by an absolute logical necessity. Whatever happens is the manifestation of God's inscrutable nature. No events other than the ones that are happening can happen. This is the rigid determinism of Spinoza. This is bound to be the corollary of his one-substance theory that equates the unitary substance with God.

From the early Greek period to the seventeenth century, a number of philosophers have been speaking of monism. But the term "monism" was not in usage until Christian Wolff (1679-1754) coined it. Monism is a metaphysical view which holds that the world must be composed of one basic entity. Parmenides and Spinoza represent substantial monism, i.e., the view that whatever exists is part of a single substance.

Democritus

Attributive monism is the view that however many substances may exist they are all of a single kind. Democritus, Leibniz and contemporary atomic theory represent this attributive monism.

The founders of Greek atomism were Leucippus and Democritus (460 - 370 B.C.). Leucippus and Democritus flourished about 440 B.C. and 420 B.C., respectively.[1] Historically Democritus has gained more prominence than Leucippus; but, for a discussion of the Greek atomism, it is difficult to disentangle them.

Amongst the Greek philosophers, Parmenides was a monist and Empedocles was a pluralist. The Greek atomism was an attempt to mediate between monism and pluralism. The atomists held a number of concepts about the atoms. Everything of the universe is ultimately composed of atoms, which are physically, but not geometrically, indivisible. The atoms are indestructible. There is empty space between the atoms, but not inside them. They are internally solid, simple, homogeneous and without void. They are infinite in number and kinds. The kinds are due to their differences in shape, size and velocity. Thus their differences are quantitative, but not qualitative. The Democritean idea of the void is empty space, in which nothing exists and through which existent things can move. There are atoms and void in the world. All composite things are combinations of atoms in the void.

Motion is a natural and inherent property of atoms. They are ever in chaotic motion. They move about and collide. In the process of collision, they combine when they have shapes capable of interlocking. Such combination takes place in the analogy of hook-and-eye. Through collision of atoms, vortices are set up. Worlds are generated out of these vortices. Democritus imagined many worlds in the process of formation and many others in the process of dissolution. In his opinion, worlds are destroyed by collision with larger worlds.

In his contemporary society, Democritus was reproached for his so-called fault of attributing everything to chance. This was, however, a misconception. The atomists were, on the contrary, strict determinists. They believed that all events are caused and whatever happens is in accordance with natural laws. That nothing can happen by chance was the explicit assertion of Democritus. Leucippus held the same view. "Naught happens for nothing, but everything from a ground and of necessity", he said. Democritus did not account for the original motion of the atoms. He did not assign a cause for the initial datum. But he held that the further developments in nature were strictly determined by causation and were in strict adherence of the mechanical principles.

The Greek atomists, unlike Socrates, Plato and Aristotle, did not uphold teleology. They did not explain the world-phenomena by introducing the notion of *purpose* or *final cause*. They wanted to know the "why" of the world-events. But they did not seek teleological explanation or final causes of whatever is happening in the world. They were in search of mechanistic explanation. They asked mechanistic questions; they gave mechanistic answers.

Democritus was a die-hard materialist. He visualized the development of life out of the primeval slime. He held that the soul was composed of atoms. Perception and thought were physical processes for him. Thought was a kind of motion which was able to cause motion elsewhere. He did not believe in personal immortality. His ethics was hedonistic—seeking pleasure and avoiding pain.

The concept of Democritus on void needs some elaboration here. All composite things, he said, are combinations of atoms in the void. Thus the two ultimate explanatory principles for him are atoms and the void. Atoms are the existent things. The void is non-being; it is the idea of empty space in which nothing exists and through which existent things can move. Parmenides was against the idea of not-being. He recognized the plenum and vehemently refuted the idea of nothingness or void. The atom of Democritus did not contain any internal void and hence, he argued, it was impenetrable and indivisible. He presumed that anything bereft of internal void was infinitely hard and therefore physically indivisible. He presumed that the cutting or slicing instrument was able to pass through the inter-atomic void and not through any atom inside which the void did not exist. Thus he explained the indivisibility of the atom. The Democritian atoms were internally unchanging, but were not externally inactive. The only action the atoms were supposed to do was movement, thereby hitting each other. For such an action, a void instead of a plenum was visualized necessary by Democritus.

This concept of void of the Greek atomists with the subsequent history of its development in the Western philosophy and science has generated much confusion and misconception. The void preoccupied the mind of Aristotle and tormented Descartes, Galileo and Newton. The fuller development of the concepts of quantum physics in the twentieth century has dispelled most of the confusion. But the field of vision is still somewhat foggy and more light is to be thrown for fully clearing the mist.

Parmenides conceived of the plenum of the unchanging world. But the other Greek philosophers explained the motion of objects by introducing the concept of the void since they cherished the idea that a thing could move only into an empty place. In a plenum there are no empty places and hence it was thought that the Parmedian concept could not explain the motion of objects. This concept that a thing moves only into empty place (void) is basically wrong. A fish moves inside the ocean water. In this example, motion does not take place in an empty place or void. A relatively grosser object can move in a relatively subtler medium. The fish which is solid in texture moves in water which is a fluid medium. Both the moving object and the medium are material; but the former is relatively grosser than the latter. If the so-called void is considered as subtle, as was done by the Indian atomists (the *Vaiśeṣikas*), the problem altogether vanishes.

The dichotomy of matter and space in the Western view is the main source of the problem. According to this view, space is of the nature of a receptacle or a container and matter is the content. Some part of space may be filled with matter whereas some other part may be empty. Aristotle[2] says: "The theory that the void exists involves the existence of place: for one would define void as place bereft of body".

The Aristotelian notion of space was further elaborated by Newton with the utmost explicitness. He asserted the existence of absolute space and accordingly distinguished absolute from relative motion. This notion of space as void (emptiness or nothing) is absolutely wrong. Furthermore, all motion is always relative and never absolute. Einstein's theory of relativity disproved the Newtonian concept of absolute space. But, here too, there was a serious confusion. The three dimensions of space, viz., length, breadth and depth, were equated with space itself. These dimensions may belong to any solid, liquid or gaseous mass, or to space (*ākāśa*). The dimensions are not absolute; they are "relative" to some arbitrarily chosen frame of reference.

For Descartes, extension is the essence of matter. Therefore he conceived of matter existing everywhere. But he considered extension as an adjective, not substantive. Matter is the substantive of extension and therefore extension cannot exist without matter. In the opinion of Descartes, the concept of empty space is absurd. He believed in the plenum, but not in the substantiality of space.

Leibniz also believed in the plenum. For him, space is merely a system of relations. He had sharp differences with Newton who maintained that space is absolute and void, functioning as a container or receptacle of all material objects. Einstein's theory of relativity gave support to Leibniz, but not to Newton. It is generally believed that Einstein's theory conclusively proved the relativity of space or rather space-time. This is, however, not correct. What Einstein called space was really dimension(s). The three dimensions of space and the one dimension of time, or the four dimensions of space-time are relative. That space is a substance was not a consideration in the relativity theory of Einstein.

Space or *ākāśa* is a form of matter in most philosophical systems of India. The Indian atomists or the *Vaiśeṣikas* considered *ākāśa* as a *dravya* or substance. The Advaita Vedānta also regarded *ākāśa* as a form of matter, the subtlest form of matter from which other forms evolved in succession. Nothingness, void, absolute vacuum, *śūnya* are meaningless terms for the Advaita Vedānta that recognizes plenum (*pūrṇa*) only. But this plenum concept of Advaita Vedānta is different from that of the Western philosophers. *Ākāśa* is not an inert container; it is not a mere place to hold matter. *Ākāśa* itself is matter along with the other four forms of matter (solid form, liquid form, gaseous form and energy form). Among all these forms, *ākāśa* is the subtlest. Any form of matter that is relatively more subtle can hold any other form of matter that is relatively less subtle. The ocean-water can hold a submarine and so is *ākāśa* that functions as a receptacle for relatively grosser forms of matter. In the view of the Vedānta philosopher, *ākāśa* is not inert; it can generate particles (*reṇus*) and again absorb them. It is the source of all the gross objects and also of energy; at the time of dissolution, it is the receptacle of all other forms of matter. *Ākāśa* is an evolute in the Vedānta philosophy. It is created in the beginning of the world-period and dissolved at the end of the world-period. The whole universe of gross material bodies and *ākāśa* (space) is limited in volume (although vast) and full everywhere. The Vedānta philosopher does not conceive of a void anywhere; for him, the so-called empty space is not empty, but is full. 'Place' is a mental concept of extension with reference to any form of matter including *ākāśa*. Hence, in the Vedānta, the so-called void is something and something full.

The atomic concept of Democritus is historically important. It is a revolutionary thought that could profoundly influence the notions of later philosophers and scientists. But many ideas of Democritus on the atom have been discarded in the light of later discoveries. The atom is not indivisible. It is constituted of micro-particles, viz., neutrons, protons and electrons, the former two being subject to further sub-division. Secondly, the atom is not absolutely solid. Most of the volume of the atom is *ākāśa* or the so-called empty space or void. Thirdly, motion in the so-called inter-atomic *void* is not the only function of the atom. The atomic constituents inside the atom are ever in motion. The atom is not inert and unchanging. It is constantly active and ever in change. Both the so-called unchanging atom and the empty space (void) of Democritus are the beehives of activity.

Democritus is seemingly a pluralist. But such an estimate is not exactly true. He represents attributive monism, the view that however many substances may exist they are all of a single kind. All objects of the world are constituted of innumerable atoms, each of which is separate from the others. But all these atoms are not qualitatively different; they are all of one kind only. If considered from this point of view, Democritus is a monist and not a pluralist.

Leibniz

Leibniz (1646-1716) was a German philosopher who contributed, in a way different from that of Democritus, to attributive monism. Like Descartes and Spinoza, Leibniz based his philosophy on the notion of substance. Descartes conceived of three substances, viz., God, mind and matter. Spinoza, as a monist, recognized God alone as the sole substance. For Descartes, extension, being the essence of matter, is the attribute of the latter. For Spinoza, both extension and thought are attributes of God. Leibniz rejected the idea that extension is an attribute of a substance. In his view, each single substance is unextended; extension involves plurality; and an aggregate of substances instead of a single substance can have extension. He believed in an infinite number of substances for which he used the term "monads". Each monad is a soul. Thus Leibniz denied the reality of matter and, instead, accepted the existence of an infinite family of souls.

The Democritean atom is the smallest particle of matter. This atomic concept is meaningless for Leibniz who argues that matter is divisible as long as it is characterized by extension. By taking the Zeno paradox seriously, he deprived matter of its extension. His ontological unit which he called "monad" is primarily a centre of force. These extensionless units are the simple substances out of which everything else is made. Since they lack extension, they are not in space. They are not composite things; they don't have constituent units; being partless, they cannot be sub-divided into simpler substances.

Leibniz thinks that monads cannot interact. According to this view, no two monads can ever have any causal relation to each other. To use his words, "monads are windowless". He holds that every monad mirrors the entire universe and hence is a microcosm. What appears to be interaction among monads is a "pre-established harmony". Many clocks may strike at the same moment because each has been accurately made by their maker. God has given the monad a nature which spontaneously produces the result. The harmony between the changes in one monad and those in another have been pre-established by God and this harmony produces the semblance of interaction. Leibniz believes that the infinite number of monads have been arranged by the Creator to function harmoniously, not because they affect each other, but because God has set or pre-established the mechanism with perfect accuracy. Leibniz thinks that this "pre-established harmony" is an admirable evidence of the existence of God.

In the opinion of Leibniz, the human body is entirely composed of monads. Each of these monads is a soul which is immortal. One of these monads is dominant and is called the soul of the individual man. The soul is a monad of higher grade controlling a colony of monads of lower grade. The ruling monad is the entelechy of the body. Monads form a hierarchy in which some are superior to others. The superiority lies in the clearness and distinctness in mirroring the universe. No two monads are exactly alike.

In Leibniz's philosophy, space does not seem to be real. It is the "order of possible co-existences", the arrangement of the monads in a three-dimensional order. In this system, there is no such thing as a vacuum. From an abstract point of view, every possible point is filled by an actual monad and by only one.

Unlike space, time is the order of possibilities which cannot coexist. It exists successively. Space and time are relative. They have only a phenomenal existence depending upon our perception of the monads. They depend upon the possibilities and incompatibilities of the monads.

The attributive monism of Leibniz, as described in the foregoing paragraphs, has its own peculiarities. It allows the existence of God as the Creator of the monads. It asserts the existence of infinite number of monads, no two of which are identical. Again, these monads are windowless and do not interact. This description gives a picture of apparent pluralism. But all the multiple monads are of a single kind (although not alike) and hence the philosophy of Leibniz represents attributive monism. It is a reflective and speculative philosophy. The existence of monads and their attributes cannot be empirically verified nor logically established. There should be a logical basis for claiming something in metaphysics. The descriptive metaphysics should be able to present an integral picture of the universe and explain, without self-contradiction, the world phenomena. The speculation of Leibniz does not satisfy these conditions.

Bertrand Russell

Bertrand Russell was a pluralist. But he adhered for a long time to a position he called neutral monism. According to this concept, reality is neither mental nor physical but some neutral stuff capable of either type of organization.

In 1904, William James published an article called "Does consciousness exist?" This became the first chapter of his book *Essays in Radical Empiricism*[3] which was published in 1912. He developed his view further in the same book in the second chapter under the title "A World of Pure Experience". Explicitly basing on the suggestion of James, Russell made further elaboration on this concept in his book *The Analysis of Mind*.[4] It was not James but Russell who gave the general notion of a neutral stuff. For James, experiences are the basic entities from which everything is composed. He further insists that there is no general stuff of which experiences are made. Russell suggested one basic stuff or kind of substance which can be called neutral stuff. This neutral stuff underlies the whole of the material world as well as all mental phenomena. This is a summary of the neutral monism of Russell.

DUALISM

Dualism is the metaphysical view that holds the world to be composed of two basic kinds of entities. Thomas Hyde introduced the term "dualism" in 1700. He did it to characterize the good-evil conflict of Ormazd and Ahriman in Zoroastrianism. This term has been used in a religious context to describe the good-evil opposition in Manichaeism and Gnosticism. It has also been used in the Taoist and neo-Confucian contrast of Yin and Yang. Christian Wolff (1679-1754) was the first to apply this term to the metaphysical opposition of mind and matter.

Plato

In the Western philosophy, Plato (428 - 348 B.C.) propounded the earliest complete metaphysical dualism. His philosophy rests on the distinction between reality and appearance. Before we understand his notion of reality *versus* appearance, we are to be acquainted with his universals and particulars. When we say "man", we don't mean any individual man such as Socrates, Plato or Aristotle. "Man" is a universal term whereas Socrates is a particular man. When we say, "This is a cat", we refer to a particular cat. There are many individual cats and each is a particular cat. The universal cat participates in a general nature common to all particular cats. But the reverse is not true. Any particular cat is not identical to the universal cat. The word "cat" means something which is not this or that cat, but some kind of universal cattiness. This is not born when a particular cat is born. Neither does this die when a particular cat dies. All universals have no position in space or time. They are eternal.

What has been said about cattiness and particular cats has logical implications. But there is also a metaphysical part in Plato's doctrine of "ideas" or "forms". The word "cat" means a certain ideal cat, "*the* cat", created by God. Particular cats partake of the nature of the ideal cat, but more or less imperfectly. The ideal cat is one only; it is unique and perfect. The particular cats are imperfect and that's why many. In Plato's opinion, the ideal cat is real and the particular cats are only apparent. All particular things, this man or that man, this dog or that dog, this cat or that cat, always partake of opposite characters. They can be both beautiful and ugly, good and bad. All particular sensible objects, contends Plato, possess contradictory characters and are thus intermediate between being and not-being. This is, however, not the case with the universals that are free from contradictions and are absolutely perfect. Men are many in number; they are born; they die. All the men who are dead, who are living, and who will be born have a common "idea" or "form". This "idea" or "form" has been created by God in a perfect manner and is eternal. This "idea" or "form" is real. All particular men are only reflections of the real man that is an "idea". As the image of a man reflected in a mirror is apparent but not real, so also are all particular men who are apparent. What has been said about man here is true of all particular animate and inanimate things. This is the metaphysical dualism of Plato who attributes true existence to ideas, but nonetheless recognizes an inferior but opposing principle.

Plato's dualism of "form" or "idea" and matter concerns the

created world. He has also God or the Creator who is a different ontological entity. The "ideas" or "forms" created by God are many although attributively they belong to one kind. The metaphysics of Plato is purely speculative and there are no grounds for its acceptance. To consider an universal as an ontological entity is erroneous. All particulars exist relatively, if not absolutely; but all universals are concepts or ideas only, ideas that appear in the mind, but not created by God. To attribute eternal existence to universals is a sheer speculation, not based on any acceptable standard of reasoning. This philosophical error has engendered confusion in the kingdom of thought for not less than two millennia.

Descartes

René Descartes (1596-1650) distinguished mind from matter. It was he who gave prominence to the philosophy of dualism. We may introduce his philosophy by explaining the method of "Cartesian doubt". In order to search for a firm basis for his philosophy he made himself doubt everything that he could manage to doubt. He asked himself: What is the certainty that I have a body? What is the certainty that I am sitting on a chair? What is the certainty that I see a dog, listen to music, feeling the sweetness of sugar, smelling the fragrance of a flower or touching the soft fingers of a lady? Am I not deceived by my senses? Am I not deceived by a cunning demon, an evil genius? From these premises Descartes concluded: "Only one thing is certain that nothing is certain".

Descartes continued to think on his doubts. If one is doubtful of everything, one must exist to do the doubting. "I think, therefore I am (*Cogito, ergo sum*)". This is the single proposition that can stand against the scepticism of doubt. This is known as Descartes' cogito.

Plato gave the notion of the dualism of "idea" and matter. Descartes laid a strong foundation of the dualistic philosophy by distinguishing mind from matter. He drew a dividing line between the *res extensa* (extending thing) and *res cogitans* (thinking thing). Matter is extended, a *res extensa*, that has reference to space, time and motion. All of space is filled with matter corpuscles, and yet motion of the corpuscles is possible. Mind is just the opposite of matter. It is a *res cogitans* (thinking thing). It has no extension. It is in no way essentially connected with space and time. Most ancient and medieval Western philosophers equated the soul with the mind. Soul is a spiritual substance which does not have extension and hence does not occupy space. Thought is the attribute of mind and extension is the attribute of body. Thus Descartes holds that thought and extension are the two chief attributes of reality. He tries to adduce evidence to prove the existence of God. He contends that minds and bodies are substances created by God, who alone is the self-subsistent Being and is *the* substance in the fullest sense.

One will not be wrong if one uses the term "triadism" instead of "dualism" for Descartes' philosophy. In his ontology he describes three substances, viz., divine substance, spiritual or intellectual substances and material substance. The divine substance (God) exists by its very essence; It is uncreated and infinite. God has created the other two types of substances. The spiritual or intellectual substances are angelic and human; they are finite and numerous. Descartes rejects the notion of the plurality of the material substance. He regards the entire material universe as a single substance. But the material bodies (both animate and inanimate) are numerous and of diverse types. A satisfactory explanation is necessary for the plurality of the material bodies out of a single material substance. He regards the numerous material bodies as "modes" of a single material substance. In his view, the one material substance which constitutes the physical universe as a whole is locally modified or qualified. He contends that all material things share the same essence which is the property of being extended in space. The modes of extension, viz., motion, rest, size, shape, etc., explain the differences observed in physical objects. According to Descartes, different human minds or souls are indeed different substances; but they belong to one type only since they share the same essence which is thought or consciousness.

The exclusiveness of the mind-body dualism in Cartesian philosophy posed a problem. Soul and body, being utterly unlike, cannot interact. But it is a fact that interaction does take place. A philosophical theory called occasionalism was evolved in the seventeenth century to explain the soul-body interaction. According to this theory, God is intermediary between soul and body. God moves the body whenever the soul gives consent to a given action. God also delivers to the soul the awareness of any physical modification of the body. Malebranche, Geulincx, Johannes Clauberg and Louis de la Forge were some of the occasionalists.

Cartesianism is rigidly deterministic. According to it, living organisms and non-living matter are strictly governed by the laws of physics. In this system, both material and mental events are equally determinate and hence Cartesians face difficulty to explain the free will. Descartes allowed the soul to man only. However, in the mechanical interpretation of his system, the soul did not receive much functional role. Many followers of Descartes, being influenced by his science, regarded animals as automata. They did not hesitate to extend this concept of automata to even man.

The Cartesian division of mind and matter influenced Western thought until about the middle of the twentieth century. It misguided the common man's thought; moreover, it did not fail to confuse the intellectuals. What Heisenberg said in this connection may be quoted here:

> If one follows the great difficulty which even eminent scientists like Einstein had in understanding and accepting the Copenhagen interpretation of quantum theory, one can trace the roots of this difficulty to the Cartesian partition. This partition has penetrated deeply into the human mind during the three centuries following Descartes and it will take a long time for it to be replaced by a really different attitude toward the problem of reality.[5]

It gave an impression that the subject and the object are two distinct entities, the "I" as the subject here perceiving the world as the object out there. The discoveries of quantum physics in the twentieth century rejected this dualism of subject and object and distinction between mind and matter. The modern analytical philosopher like Bertrand Russell vehemently criticized the "I" in Descartes' *cogito* (I think, therefore I am). Russell said:

> Here the word 'I' is really illegitimate; he ought to state his ultimate premiss in the form 'there are thoughts'. The word 'I' is grammatically convenient, but does not describe a datum. When he goes on to say 'I am a *thing* which thinks', he is already using uncritically the apparatus of categories

handed down by scholasticism. He nowhere proves that thoughts need a thinker, nor is there reason to believe this except in a grammatical sense.[6]

The mind-matter dichotomy of Descartes is classically famous as the philosophical dualism. It is often interpreted as the soul-body dichotomy. There is no such parallel notion in Indian system of philosophy, in which soul or *ātman* is different from the mind or *manas*. Most of the schools of Indian philosophy regard mind as a category of matter.[7] It is not gross matter like the earth, water or air. The subtle body (*sūkṣma śarīra*) comprises *manas* or mind as its principal component. Hence the mind-body dichotomy is not acceptable to Indian philosophy.

PLURALISM

Pluralism is the metaphysical view which holds that the world is composed of more than two kinds of entities. In the Western philosophy, pluralism was born in Greece as early as the fourth century B.C. Still now it has many adherents, although it has been disfavoured in the twentieth century after the discoveries in quantum physics have been known.

Anaxagoras

Anaxagoras, the Greek philosopher who was born in Ionia in 500 B.C. was a pluralist. He held the number of qualitatively different substances to be indefinitely great. He further held that everything is infinitely divisible. He did not consider any matter to be purely constituted of any single element (earth, water, air and fire). Even the smallest portion of matter contains some of each element. A thing is known by the element which is the most predominant one in it. We may take the example of fire. All the elements, viz., earth, water, air and fire, contain fire. But the one in which fire preponderates is called by that name. Like Empedocles, he rejected the existence of the void. He was the first to suggest mind as the primary cause of physical changes. In everything, he says, there is a portion of everything, with the single exception of the mind, which does not contain anything else. In his view, all things except mind contain portions of all opposites. He was an atheist and hence God does not find a place in his philosophy.

Empedocles

Empedocles, another Greek philosopher, flourished about 440 B.C. He established four basic forms of matter, viz., earth, air, fire and water. These are the four classical elements, combinations of which form all types of material bodies. Empedocles used the term "element" in a special sense and the meaning of this word is not the same as that in modern chemistry. All these four elements of Empedocles are everlasting. They are mixed in different proportions to produce various types of compound-matter that we find in the world.

This doctrine of the four elements may be compared and contrasted with that of the five elements (*pañcamahābhūta*) of the Indian Vaiśeṣikas. There is an additional element, viz., *ākāśa* (space) in the Indian system. These elements are forms of matter. Kaṇāda, the founder of the Vaiśeṣika philosophy, used the word *tejas* (heat or light) as a symbolic representation of all forms of energy. That energy is a form of matter was somehow appreciated in the ancient past. Secondly, *ākāśa* or space was considered by the Indian Vaiśeṣikas as a form of matter which is interconvertible into the other forms, viz., solid, liquid, gaseous and energy. Kaṇāda held that all the four elements other than space are constituted of atoms. That energy is not continuous but corpuscular was somehow appreciated by him. Empedocles did not include space as the fifth element. He also did not say anything about the atomic constituents of these elements. Democritus, another Greek philosopher, gave the atomic theory.

Empedocles made an attempt to explain the changes in nature. He made use of the two principles of Love and Strife for this purpose. Love and Strife were primitive substances for Empedocles on a level with the four elements. He postulated that the elements were combined by Love and separated by Strife.

Being a pluralist, Empedocles was a vehement critic of monism. He rejected teleology and explained the course of nature as regulated by chance and necessity.

Herbart

Johann Friedrich Herbart (1776-1841), the German philosopher, describes his ontology as a "pluralistic realism". He defines ontology as the study of Being, which is non-contradictory in his opinion. He terms his point of view as "pluralistic realism" for the purpose of explicating the non-contradictory nature of Being. He holds that reality is constituted of simple qualitative units, called "reals". These simple units interrelate in various ways. They form syntheses, leading to the world we experience.

William James

The American philosopher and psychologist, William James (1842-1910), is a modern pluralist. He rejects monism and tries to establish his doctrine of pluralism. He is of the opinion that ours is not a block universe and that it is not absolutely unified. There is looseness among the different units of the world. The looseness in the world is sufficient to keep the future open. James contends that the relations of the world are not those of entailment. He observes external relatedness in the functioning of the universe.

Evaluation

Monism of Western philosophy is not as developed as the non-dualism of India. The rigours of logic are lacking in Western monism. Furthermore, it does not provide an integral explanation for the operation of the cosmos.

The dualism of both Plato and Descartes has arisen mainly from speculative metaphysics. Neither empirical nor logical proofs can be made available to substantiate such metaphysical claims. Dualism has definitely done disservice to philosophical thinking. It has confused and misguided intellectual thought for many centuries.

The pluralism in Western philosophy is naive. It does not need a philosopher to observe the plurality of the world. The world is apparently plural. One may not be able to observe the plurality of the micro-world of molecules, atoms, sub-atomic particles like protons, electrons and neutrons, neutrinos, photons and quarks. But one does observe the sun, stars, moon, different species of plants and animals, rivers, mountains, etc. One does observe earth, water, air and fire. Hence any person,without any formal or informal education in philosophy and science, can easily assert that the world is pluralistic. But, what is apparent is not necessarily true. Empirical evidences have been forthcoming from the science discoveries of the twentieth century to conclusively prove that the plurality of the world is rooted in unity and that all the apparent diversity is substantially one only.

The non-dualistic philosophy of India that has already been discussed in the second chapter of this book has logically derived its conclusions without any reference to empiricism. The Upaniṣadic seer has aptly said: "In the beginning, my dear, this was Being alone, one only without a second (*sadeva, saumya, idamagra āsīd ekamevādvitīyam*[8])". "It thought, 'May I be many' (*tadaikṣata, bahu syāṁ prajāyeyeti*[9])". The seer does recognize the pluralistic universe. But he stresses the primacy of the Being that is one alone. Not only has the manifold universe its origin from the Being, but also it is dissolved in the same source at the end of the world-period. "Seek to know that from which these beings are born, by which they live during life and into which they enter while departing. That is Brahman (*yato vā imāni bhūtāni jāyante, yena jātāni jīvanti, yat prayantyabhisaṁviśanti, tad vijijñāsasva, tad brahmeti*)."[10] From both empirical and logical points of view, absolute existence (*sat*) refers to Being which is one alone, although a pluralistic concept is bound to creep in with reference to becoming.

NOTES

1. B. Russell, *History of Western Philosophy*, George Allen & Unwin Ltd., London, 1975, p. 82.
2. Aristotle, *Physics*, 208 b.
3. W. James, *Essays in Radical Empiricism*, Longmans, London, 1912.
4. B. Russell, *The Analysis of Mind*, Allen & Unwin, London, 1921.
5. W. Heisenberg, *Physics and Philosophy*, Penguin Books, London, 1989, p. 69.
6. B. Russell, *History of Western Philosophy*, George Allen & Unwin Ltd., London, 1975, p. 550.
7. CUŚB, VI. 5. 1; S. Chennakesavan, *Concept of Mind in Indian Philosophy*, Motilal Banarsidass, Delhi, 1980, pp. 44-45.
8. CU, VI. 2. 1.
9. CU, VI. 2. 3.
10. TU, III. 1. 1.

VI

PLURALISM IN SCIENCE

PLURALISM WAS THE dominant thought in science up to the middle of the twentieth century. The macro-world was pluralistic; so also was the micro-world.

The Earth is an entity, distinct from the Moon. The Moon is distinct from the Sun. Each individual star has an identity different from the Sun and the other stars. The blue sky is simply a hard canopy in which the shining celestial bodies are set like diamonds. The *Bible* refers to the sky as the "firmament", a word derived from the Latin root as the word "firm". During the period from the sixth to the fourth century B.C., Greek astronomers visualized more than one canopy. It was thought that the "fixed" stars that moved around the Earth in a body without changing their relative positions were studded to one canopy. The Sun, the Moon and the other five bright objects (Mercury, Venus, Mars, Jupiter and Saturn) were wandering in the sky. Each one moved on a separate path. Each one was set in an invisible spherical vault. The vaults were nested one above the other.

The Earth contains many objects which are distinct from one another. All these are constituted of four basic substances, viz., earth, air, water and fire. There is a plurality of plant and animal species on the Earth. Each species has many individuals. According to the *Bible*, each man has a separate soul, whereas the plants and animals are soulless. The ancient Western man assumed an anthropocentric world whose centre was man. God created Heaven and the Earth; stars in Heaven; water and air on the Earth; plants, birds and beasts on the Earth; God created man (man and woman) and created everything else for the pleasure of man. This is the seminal principle of anthropocentrism.

The world of the early Greek astronomers was geocentric. The Earth which was regarded as motionless was the centre of the universe. The Greek astronomer, Aristarchus (320 - 250 B.C.) made an attempt to calculate the size of the Earth and that of the Sun. According to his estimate, the Sun must be at least seven times larger than the Earth. He could not believe the large Sun circling the small Earth and so he stated that the Earth revolved around the Sun. This was the first Western blow to the concept of geocentrism.

What Aristarchus said was heliocentrism, i.e., the Sun is the centre of the universe. But he was unheeded during his lifetime and a number of subsequent centuries during which later Greek astronomers, beginning with Hipparchus (170-125 B.C.) and ending with Claudius Ptolemy (90-170) held geocentric views with a stationary Earth at the centre and the movement of the heavenly bodies around the Earth. Nicolaus Copernicus (1473-1543), a Polish astronomer, rejected the geocentric model of Ptolemy and proposed a heliocentric cosmology in which Earth and the planets rotate about the Sun. He circulated this idea privately in a short manuscript in 1514. He wrote a complete book on it. Although this book, *De revolutionibus orbium coelestium* (The Revolution of the Heavenly Spheres), was completed in 1530, its publication was intentionally delayed until 1543, the year in which Copernicus died. He perhaps had seen the book just before he closed his eyes.

The ideas of the early astronomers were drastically changed after the invention of the telescope. The first telescope that had the shape of an "optical tube" was invented by the Dutch scientist Hans Lippershey. That this could bring distant objects close was demonstrated at an exposition in Venice in 1609. The Italian astronomer and physicist Galilei Galileo (1564-1642) observed it and set out to reinvent such an instrument. In 1610, Galileo used the telescope made by him and observed for the first time mountains on the Moon, four satellites around Jupiter and numerous stars. With the help of his telescope he made other astronomical discoveries. His observations of the heavenly bodies confirmed the Copernican idea that the Sun and the planets do not circle the Earth. His book *Dialogue* on the Two Chief World Systems, Ptolemaic and Copernican, published in 1632, strongly supported the heliocentric views of Copernicus. It brought him into conflict with the Church. He was before the Inquisition in 1633. The torture chamber was shown to him. He was given the option either to be tortured to death or to denounce his discovery. He had to recant to save his life. But he was sentenced to house arrest for life at the age of sixty-nine. He died in 1642, the year in which Newton was born.

Since Galileo's time, telescopes have been improved and vast areas of the fathomless space have been probed into. The world's first mountaintop telescope (the Lick 91-cm refracting telescope) was installed on Mount Hamilton near San Francisco on 31st December, 1887. Newton designed and built a reflecting telescope which used a parabolic mirror, instead of a lens, to magnify an image. The giant telescopes of today are of this reflecting variety. In 1948, the five metre Hale reflecting telescope was installed on Palomar mountain and is the largest in use today in the United States. In 1976, the Soviet Union built and located a telescope with a mirror that is six metres in diameter in the Caucasus mountains. The construction of the world's largest telescope, the Keck, with a 10-metre mirror, has begun in 1985 on Mauna Kea in Hawaii. So far has been said about the progress made in designing and building optical telescopes. Interferometry has been made use of in designing radio-telescopes, that have more specific use in radio-astronomical probes. Space-telescopes have also been launched. They may be more powerful than the land-based telescopes and may be able to supply us information such as planets circling nearby stars.

Through the sophisticated instrumental aids, we now know the planets of our solar system. Our Sun is only one star out of innumerable stars, some of which we observe and some we cannot observe at present. There are many stars, much bigger than our Sun. Many stars may be having planets like our Sun. Many planets of other stellar systems may be congenial to the development of life. It may not be necessary for life to evolve according to the pattern that has actualized on the Earth. Life might have evolved differently in different habitable planets of different stellar systems. It might happen that more intelligent living beings are inhabiting some planets elsewhere in other stellar systems. With our present knowledge, we cannot answer questions pertaining to these topics. But this much we know that the universe is vast with a plurality of stars, stars with planets and satellites, stellar clusters, galaxies, with multitudinous stellar clusters, galactic clusters, and so on.

Before the beginning of the twentieth century, we had no knowledge about the existence of multi-galaxies in the universe. At the beginning of the twentieth century, astronomers got the idea that our Sun was one of the many stars comprising the Milky Way that was thought to fill the entire universe. The German philosopher Immanuel Kant wrote in 1755 in his book *General Natural History and Theory of the Heavens* that our solar system belongs to an "island universe" which is only one out of the many that exist in the universe. But no experimental verification was made to confirm the statement of Kant. Many fuzzy patches had been observed since the introduction of better telescopes at the end of the eighteenth century. During the first decades of the twentieth century, astronomers realized that these patches in space were huge systems of stars like ours.

Astronomers wanted to know the distances of the different galaxies from us. They were assessing the distance of stars by measurement of stellar parallax. But, by this method, only distances of up to about a hundred light-years could be measured. In 1912, Henrietta Swan Leavitt (1868-1921), an American astronomer, discovered period-luminosity relationship of Cepheid variable stars. According to her observations, the brighter were the Cepheid variable stars, the longer their period of light variation.

In 1915, the American astronomer, Harlow Shapley (1885-1972) discovered the structure of our galaxy (the Milky Way). By using Leavitt's "Cepheid variable" method of estimating stellar distances, he presented the first reasonable picture of the structure and size of the Milky Way galaxy. According to his estimate made in 1920, our Sun is about 50,000 light-years away from the centre of our disc-shaped galaxy. He roughly estimated the overall diameter of our galaxy to be about 300,000 light-years.

The Swiss-American astronomer, Robert Julius Trumpler (1886-1956) discovered interstellar light absorption. The dust grains in interstellar space absorb light and, as a result, brightness of the starlight is decreased by about twenty per cent for every thousand light-years travelled. In 1930, he discovered that the more distant stars generally appeared to be larger than the nearer ones. This discovery of Trumpler revised Shapley's estimate of the diameter of the Milky Way galaxy and the distance of the Sun from the galactic centre and reduced these estimates by a factor of three or more.

We are within the Milky Way, though towards its outer reaches. That is why we do not observe this galaxy as a disc or spiral. But we are able to observe a broad band of stars in a very large number towards its centre. From above the galaxy, one would see the spiral structure, with two arms at the centre and four arms in the outer regions. One would see the disc shape of this galaxy if one were to observe from the edge.

If we travel by a starship at a speed of 14 km per second, we would take over 80,000 Earth years to reach Alpha Centauri, one of the nearest stars from us. For measuring interstellar distances, we use the unit "light-year". One light-year is the distance travelled by light at its speed of 300,000 km per second in one year. Light takes about 8 minutes to travel from the Sun to the Earth. It reaches the Earth from Alpha Centauri in 4.3 years. Our galaxy is 100,000 light-years across. To express it otherwise, a person is first to convert himself to light and then to travel from one end of the Milky Way galaxy to the opposite end in 10^5 light-years. Our galaxy is not a sphere and hence its diameter does not remain constant by joining all possible opposite points. But one may get a rough idea about its size from its diametrical distance given here.

Even if telescopes have been immensely improved by this time, it has not been possible for the astronomer to view the totality of the universe. What fraction of the universe has been viewed is not known. It has been guessed that the universe may contain 10^{11} galaxies each with, on the average, 10^{11} stars. Majority of the stars do not have planets. It is roughly estimated that all the galaxies in the universe have 10^{22} planets. There are many galaxies that are much bigger than our Milky Way. The astronomical distances at which the stellar bodies within a galaxy are distributed pose unsurmountable problem for interstellar space travel. Intergalactic space travel is still more a puzzling fiction. The Andromeda nebula which is one of our neighbouring galaxies is two million light-years away. The light which now reaches our telescope from the Andromeda galaxy has left that galaxy two million years ago. Even if that galaxy has disappeared during this long span of two million years, we still can see the light that emanated from the then present galaxy.

These are the glimpses of only one aspect of the brief story of the macro-world. The vast "empty" space contains innumerable material objects, widely separated from one another. Not only the ordinary man, but also the "wise" scientist held the world to be pluralistic. Up to the early decades of the twentieth century there was no trace of any monistic notion in science.

Is "empty" space an object amongst the plurality of objects? This question has been baffling philosophers and scientists alike since the early Greek period. This idea of void occupied an important place in the classical mechanics of Sir Isaac Newton (1642-1727). According to Newton, all celestial bodies are immersed in an absolute vacuum which is identical throughout, having no differences at all. Newton's space was absolute; his time was absolute; his space and time were independent of each other. He discovered the three laws of motion. His discovery of the general theory of gravitation is an important milestone in the annals of science. All matter, without exception, is subjected to this force of gravity. By virtue of this force all material entities attract each other. Newton gave the following equation from which the gravitational force can be calculated:

$$F = G\, m_1\, m_2 \,/\, d^2$$

Here F is the gravitational force, G is a universal constant, m_1 and m_2 are the masses of the interacting bodies and d is the intervening distance between them.

The Sun attracts the Earth which, in turn, attracts the Sun. Such attraction is mutual and universal. One thing is puzzling here. How does action at a distance take place? Early theories of motion did not allow such a concept of action at a distance. Aristotle assumed that some physical object must push or pull on another to cause motion. No such pull or push can be conceived of to explain the mutual attraction of the material bodies located at great distances in space. Newton made no hypotheses as to how gravitational force was transmitted. He said: "I frame no hypotheses". One may say that Newton's theory of gravity really involved action at a distance.

In the sixteenth and seventeenth centuries, scientists tried to solve the problem of action at a distance by postulating various subtle media through which the action is transmitted. The transmitting medium was named "aether" or "ether". Different scientists postulated different ethers such as one ether for heat, another for gravity, another for magnetic force, and so forth. Newton's opinion on the existence of ether was not consistent. He sometimes affirmed and sometimes denied the existence of ether as a universal medium. He says: The stars, the Sun and the planets are surrounded by absolute nothing which fills universal space. On other occasions he says: Space is filled with some material medium which is not nothing; it is something about which one should not guess. His third opinion seems to posit ether as a material substance. He says: Everything in the universe, from empty space between objects to the objects themselves, is permeated with ether. In the second edition (1713) of the *Mathematical Principles of Natural Philosophy*, usually referred to as the *Principia*, Newton wrote: "And now we might add something concerning a most subtle spirit which pervades and lies hid in all gross bodies, by the force and action of which spirit the particles of bodies attract one another at near distances, and cohere, if contiguous; the electric bodies operate to greater distances, as well repelling as attracting the neighbouring corpuscles; and light is emitted, reflected, refracted, inflected and heats bodies; and all sensation is excited, and the members of animal bodies move at the command of the will, namely, by the vibrations of this spirit, mutually propagated along the solid filaments of the nerves, from the outward organs of sense to the brain, and from the brain to the muscles. But these are things that cannot be explained in a few words, nor are we furnished with that sufficiency of experiments which is required to an accurate determination and demonstration of the laws by which this electric and elastic spirit operates".[1] According to Newton's concept of absolute space, the fabric of space itself (the ether presumably) was at rest. Because of this assumed absolute rest, he could speak of absolute space. The ether was imagined to be motionless. Basing on this imagination, one could conceive of the absolute motion in relation to the ether.

Another discovery of Newton was also in connection with the pluralism of the world. Basing on his experimental work, he proposed a corpuscular theory of light, which was described in his *Optics*, published in 1704. The wave theory of light had been established before Newton announced his own. The English physicist Robert Hooke (1635-1703) published his book *Micrographia* in 1665. It included the idea that light might consist of waves. Christiaan Huygens (1629-95), the Dutch physicist and astronomer, expounded his wave theory of light in 1678. According to this theory, light as a vibration spreads through an all-pervading "ether" which consisted of microscopic particles. Contrary to the wave theory of Hooke and Huygens, Newton's experimental conditions proved the particulate nature of light. Both these concepts were later proved to be correct. But, one thing was obvious from the corpuscular theory of light that even energy is composed of a plurality of particles.

Newton's universe was pluralistic. Matter was made of indivisible and indestructible atoms that were eternal in absolute space and absolute time. All the multiple entities of the Newtonian universe were functioning in strict adherence to the causal law. Every effect, without a single exception, had some cause. Such a universe was deterministic and mechanistic. It was a mega-machine whose component parts were causally determined. If all the initial conditions were known, the final outcomes were thought to be accurately predicted.

Newtonian classical mechanics was unchallenged until the advent of the twentieth century in which quantum mechanics flourished. In 1900, the German physicist Max Planck (1858-1947) published a paper which, together with Einstein's paper of 1905, initiated quantum theory. From studies of the distribution of radiation emitted by a black body, Planck discovered the formula, $E = h\upsilon$, where E stands for energy, υ (the Greek letter nu) for the frequency of radiation and h for the Planck's constant (6.626×10^{-34} J Hz^{-1}). As physicists define action as energy multiplied by time, Planck's constant is thus measured in units of action. Although this theory later developed holistic ideas, Planck's discovery contained fertile seeds of pluralism. Planck suggested that radiation is emitted in energy packets called quanta ("quantum" is a Latin word for "how much", the Sanskrit equivalent being *katama*). As matter is made up of atoms, so also is energy that is radiated in small units of packets. The equation suggests that the amount of energy in a quantum is inversely proportional to the wavelength. The shorter the wavelength, the more energetic the quantum. It is also understood that the frequency (the number of waves emitted in one second) is inversely proportional to the radiation's wavelength. These relationships have been expressed in Planck's equation. Planck's theory served as a watershed in the history of physics. The year 1900 (Planck's equation was announced on December 14, 1900) is the dividing line between classical physics and modern physics. In classical physics, energy was assumed to be continuous. Modern physics took quanta into account and in this concept, energy is discontinuous or discrete. This notion of corpuscular energy provided one fertile seed-bed to the pluralistic philosophy of science. Max Planck was awarded the Nobel Prize in physics in 1918 for this brilliant discovery of the quanta.

Albert Einstein (1879-1955) was the second quantum physicist in order of historical sequence. One of his papers, published in 1905, advanced an explanation for the photoelectric effect by the use of Planck's quantum theory. Light effects the ejection of electrons from metal surfaces. This phenomenon is known as the photoelectric effect. Einstein maintained that light was not only radiated in quanta, as Planck had stated, but that it was absorbed in quanta also. When light fell upon a metal surface, the electrons, bound to the surface, absorbed energy by one quantum at a time. If the absorbed energy suffices to overcome the forces that bind the electron to the metal surface, it is set free. Otherwise the electron cannot be ejected even though light falls on the metal surface. The energy content of the quantum increases as frequency increases. As the frequency of light increases, or in other words, as the wavelength of light decreases, part of the energy of the absorbed light breaks the electron bond and the surplus is applied as the kinetic energy for the electron to be emitted. Einstein suggested the following equations:

$$\frac{1}{2} mv^2 = h\upsilon - w$$

Here $\frac{1}{2} mv^2$ is the kinetic energy of the emitted electron, $h\upsilon$ (Planck's constant time frequency) the energy content of the quantum being absorbed by the surface and w the energy required to break the electron bond.

Thus quantum becomes analogous to an "atom of energy". Energy is particulate. It can be radiated or absorbed only in whole numbers of quanta. Energy in all its forms is quantized; it is made up of indivisible quanta. The discovery of Einstein unhesitatingly showed that light consists of particles (eventually called "photons" from the Greek word for light).

Robert Andrews Millikan (1868-1953), the American physicist, studied the photoelectric effect during the period from 1912 to 1916. He confirmed Einstein's deduction of the equation on the photoelectric effect. For his accurate measurements of e (the charge on an electron) and h (Planck's constant) he was awarded the Nobel Prize for physics in 1923. Einstein won the Nobel Prize for physics for his discovery of the law of photoelectric effect in 1921.

Since 1916, the quantum theory has been universally recognized by physicists. As matter is composed of atoms, so also is energy which is made up of quanta or energy atoms. The world is plural. All its constituent entities are discrete and distinct from one another.

In 1905, Einstein published two papers on his special theory of relativity. This theory was restricted to bodies moving with uniform velocity with respect to one another. It rejected the notion of absolute motion and absolute rest. It declared that it is impossible to determine the absolute motion of a moving object and that only speed relative to some other object can be measured. Aristotle (384-322 B.C.), the Athenian (Greek) philosopher and naturalist, held the view that bodies outside the sphere of the Moon were perfect and unchanging. This idea was challenged after the telescope was invented and the motion of the celestial bodies was observed. But again ether was considered as a subtle substance that was at absolute rest. Absolute motion could be thought of with the ether (which was supposed to be at absolute rest) as the frame of reference. Einstein declared that all motion is relative. He denied the existence of absolute space and absolute time. He laid emphasis on the selection of a frame of reference to which the events of the universe can be related. Any frame of reference is equally valid and, for any particular event, the most convenient frame may be chosen. Thus the measurements of space and time are relative to some arbitrarily chosen frame of reference. From the special theory of relativity, two important derivations were made by Einstein himself. The first one was regarding the velocity of light. The speed of light in a vacuum is the same in all frames of reference moving relative to one another. It remains constant no matter how fast the observer or light source moves. The velocity of light in a vaccum is 299,792.8 kilometres per second, or roughly 3×10^{10} centimetres per second. This is the maximum velocity that can be attained in the universe. The second derivation was regarding the mass : energy equivalence. Mass and energy are related in accordance with the equation, $E = mc^2$, where E is the energy in ergs, m the mass in grams and c the velocity of light, i.e., 3×10^{10} cm/second.

The mass of any particular object does not remain constant at all speeds. The higher its velocity, the larger its mass; the lower its velocity, the smaller its mass. From the mathematical relation, tau $= \sqrt{1 - v^2 / c^2}$, it may be calculated that the mass of an object grows towards infinity as its velocity v comes closer to c, the velocity of light. While the object is in motion, some kinetic energy is converted into mass. It is impossible for any material body with positive mass to travel at the speed of light. All the massless particles can exist only while they travel exactly at the speed of light. Physicists say that the photon has zero "rest mass". Unless understood in its proper perspective, it would be sheer misleading, since a photon cannot exist at rest without being destroyed.

Einstein's recognition of the light quanta in his studies on the photoelectric effect went in favour of the doctrine of pluralism. But his mass-energy equation in his special theory of relativity worked as an important step towards monism. Matter and energy are interconvertible. They are not distinct entities exclusive of each other. Factually, any matter is a packet of energy.

Einstein's special theory of relativity did not deal with accelerated motion or gravitation. This was treated in his general theory of relativity, formulated in 1915 and published in 1916. For this formulation, he introduced the principle of equivalence which says that acceleration forces and gravitational forces are not distinguishable from each other. This can be otherwise expressed by saying that the inertia of an object is proportional to its mass. This principle of equivalence was already known to Galileo. According to this general theory of relativity, gravity is a property of space. Newton viewed gravity as a force between bodies. But Einstein held gravity bound up with the shape of space itself. The presence of mass curves space. A gravitational field is really a curving of space. The greater the mass, the larger the curvature of space in its vicinity. Mass distorts the "flatness" of the four-dimensional space-time continuum and produces "hollows" that give rise to the notion of curved space. The more massive the matter, the deeper the hollow.

One of the consequences of the equivalence of gravitation and acceleration force is the bending of light rays by the presence of huge masses such as stars or planets. Gravity bends light waves. For instance, the light of stars passing very close to the Sun would bend inward towards the solar centre. This would happen since the light beam would be affected by the geometry of space in the vicinity of the Sun.

The Russian-German mathematician Hermann Minkowski (1864-1909) suggested in 1908 that relativity theory makes more sense if the universe is regarded as four-dimensional. He took the three dimensions of space and added time as the fourth dimension. Einstein adapted this idea of Minkowski (who was his mathematics teacher) to the general theory of relativity. Gravitation corresponds to the amount of curvature in a non-Euclidean, four-dimensional space-time continuum. As space is more curved near a large mass, any matter or energy passing near that mass follows that curvature of space. For Newton, space was absolute, time was absolute and space and time were exclusive of each other. His time was an ever-flowing stream without a beginning and an end. His time flowed homogeneously for any place and any person in any frame of reference. Time was considered to be a fundamental property of the universe, experienced by every part of the universe at the same rate. The Newtonian time was an objective phenomenon. This solid view of time has been completely eroded by the theory of relativity. Time, said Einstein, has no independent existence apart from the order of events by which one measures it from one's own frame of reference. Einstein's time is relative; his space is relative. He does not recognize any separate space or separate time. He refers to space-time continuum. This space-time can stretch, bend and distort almost like a sheet of rubber. Time which is never absolute but variable is distorted in the region of large masses. In Einstein's theory, time does not exist in the absence of space; time and space invariably go together; and it is impossible to consider time as a thing in itself. One can deduce from the relativity equations that time has a beginning and an end. In the light of the relativity theory, temporal terms like "before", "after", "simultaneous", etc., have little meaning unless the frames of reference are specified.

Without going into the details of the mathematics and physics of Einstein's discoveries, we may do conceptual analysis and compare and contrast Einstein's concepts of space and time and the corresponding Vedāntic concepts. The Vedānta does not recognize time as an ontological entity. Time does not find a place in the Vedāntic cosmogonical sequences. The Vedāntin holds that time is a mental construct and that it is a subjective appreciation of the sequences of events. The time concept cannot be born in the mind of an individual in the absence of the occurrence of events. In consideration of the cyclic cosmogony advocated by the Vedānta, every world-period (*para* or *mahākalpa*) has a t_0 (beginning of time) and a t_m (end of time or maximum time). The t_0 corresponds to the emanation of the universe and the t_m to its dissolution. Einstein's concept of time has some similarity with that of the Vedānta. Time, in the concept of Einstein, is relative. It has no independent existence apart from the order of events that one measures.

Einstein's time is born with the appearance of the singularity or the monoblock or with the big-bang explosion; it ends at the termination of the process of big crunch and re-appearance of the singularity or the monoblock.

Energy multiplied by time is action. From this definition of action, it may be deduced that there cannot be any concept of time in the absence of action. Time is inextricably associated with change or motion. There is no change or motion without events. With the occurrence of events, time concept is generated in the mind.

Energy is defined as that which can do work. There can be no work without utilization of energy. Again, work is defined as the product of force and distance in the direction of the force. The energy associated with motion is kinetic energy and is mathematically expressed as $\frac{1}{2} mv^2$ (where m is mass and v is velocity). Thus, action, which is energy X time, has an implied meaning with reference to motion. The concept of time cannot arise in the absence of a motionless and actionless universe.

In the concept of motion, there is change in location and displacement with reference to the three spatial dimensions, viz., length, breadth and depth. These three spatial dimensions along with the one temporal dimension constitute an inextricable web. All these four dimensions are not independent of one another. Moreover, being relative, they are not invariable. As time is a mental construct, so also are the three spatial dimensions. The former is sequential whereas the latter are extensional. Location which is placement of a body with reference to the x-, y- and z- axes is also not independent of the time axis. All locational concepts are mental constructs.

Vedānta uses the term *jagat* for the universe. It is derived from the Sanskrit verb root *gam* (*gam* + *kvip*) which means "to go". Thus changeability is an invariant notion associated with the universe. There is nothing in the universe that is changeless, motionless and actionless. The whole universe is expanding. The galaxies are in motion. Each star is rotating around its own axis and revolving. Each planet is rotating around its own axis and revolving around its star. So also is the satellite. Similar is the situation in the micro-world. Inside the atom, each electron spins and revolves around the nucleus. Inside the nucleus of the atom, the protons and neutrons are not stationary. No micro-particle is at complete rest. No matter or energy particle can exist without motion. Nothing in the universe is immobile. Rest is suicidal to existence in the manifested universe.

There is no motion without reference to the four dimensions, viz., length, breadth, depth, and time, all of which are relative. All these dimensions are not ontological entities. They are mental constructs only. Even mind is not an ontological entity in the Vedānta. Hence to consider these four dimensions as something real is fallacious.

The space-time, says Einstein, is relative. It has been said here that the three spatial dimensions and the one temporal dimension are relative. That space is not to be made equivalent to the three dimensions of length, breadth and height has already been discussed in some of the previous chapters. Irrespective of the nature of the material object (solid, liquid, gaseous, energy and space), it has the dimensions of length, breadth and height. Space (*ākāśa*) is a form of matter, says the Vedānta. It is the subtlest of the five forms of matter and still it is matter itself. Hence it is not correct to say that space is relative. It is more appropriate to reparaphrase the statement as "The dimensions of space are relative".

Here we may try to answer the question, "Is space an entity? Is it something?" According to Einstein's general theory of relativity, the presence of mass curves space; gravity is a property of space. One may conceptually analyze such statements and come to the conclusion that space is something. It is not a fictitious creation of mass. The Upaniṣadic seers[2] declare that *ākāśa* (space) is a created thing, that it is an evolute prior to the evolution of other forms of matter and that it is the material cause of solids, liquids, gases and energy. It is also declared that, in the process of involution, all the matter and energy forms of the universe are sequentially converted back to *ākāśa*.[3] The Vedas view *ākāśa* or *aditi* as both parents and offspring of micro-particles (*reṇus*).[4] According to this Vedic concept, micro-particles are generated from *ākāśa* and again re-absorbed into *ākāśa*. Thus *ākāśa* and micro-particles are in a dynamic state of flux. The Vedic and the Vedāntic *ākāśa* is not static and not nothing. Neither is it eternal. The emanation of *āpaḥ* (cosmic waters), *prāṇa* (vital entity) and *ākāśa* sequentially takes place from *Māyā*. At the time of dissolution, *ākāśa* merges into *prāṇa*, *prāṇa* into *āpaḥ* and finally *āpaḥ* into *Māyā*. The cosmic processes are cyclic and *ākāśa* cannot remain as such at the termination of a world-period (*para* or *mahākalpa*).

What has been said by the Vedic and the Upaniṣadic seers on the dynamic state of flux between *ākāśa* and micro-particles has been confirmed by the quantum physicists in the later half of the twentieth century. Einstein could realize the significant role played by *ākāśa* during the last years of his life. He considered field as the reality in the following statement:

> We may therefore regard matter as being constituted by the regions of space in which the field is extremely intense.... There is no place in this new kind of physics both for the field and matter, for the field is the only reality.[5]

But his reality shifted from field to *ākāśa* or space during the concluding period of his life. This is obvious from the following statement which Einstein made shortly before his death:

> Space has devoured ether and time; it seems to be on the point of swallowing up also the field and the corpuscles, so that it alone remains as the vehicle of reality.[6]

What Einstein means by space in the foregoing paragraph is not the same thing as he said in his theory of relativity.

Thus it is seen that the concept of space and time as visualized by the Western philosophers and scientists has undergone a radical change. The old conceptual edifice has collapsed and new ones have emerged in its place.

Einstein discarded the concept of "action-at-a-distance". He had also no need to accept "ether" as a pervading substance or as a substance at all. The background and the evolution of the concept of ether may be briefly presented here before Einstein's thesis is discussed.

Aristotle (384 - 322 B.C.), the Greek philosopher and naturalist, visualized four shells of the world, viz., earth (the solid ball), water (the ocean), air (the atmosphere) and fire (an invisible outer shell that occasionally becomes visible through the flashes of lightning). He imagined a fifth element (quintessence) that he called "ether". The universe beyond the four shells, he said, was constituted of ether. It filled the heavens. Aristotelian ether was unearthly, perfect, unmoving and unchanging. There was no room for emptiness in his scheme. His ether continued to the end of the universe. "Nature", he said, "abhors a vacuum".

Aristotle's concept of ether underwent some modification, but was retained in science up to the time of Einstein. Ether made up the fabric of space. It filled up all that was considered vacuum. It was also conceived that ether permeated into the innermost recesses of all forms of matter.

Physicists were very much puzzled with a nagging question regarding the transmission of light waves through a vacuum. Other kinds of waves require a material medium for their transmission. To the contrary, light, being a wave, reaches us from galaxies, billions of light-years away, through a vacuum. There is nothing in empty space. Then what is there to wave? This was the question which puzzled the physicists.

Newton did not worry about the transmission of light through a vacuum since he supposed light to consist of speeding particles. However, he worried over "action-at-a-distance" with reference to his theory of gravitation. Although he did not frame any hypothesis about how the force of gravity operates through space, he adopted the Aristotelian concept of ether as a possible explanation. He thought the force of gravity might somehow be conducted by the ether.

In 1678, the Dutch physicist and astronomer Christiaan Huygens (1629-95) expounded the wave theory of light. He thought that something must necessarily be doing the waving. He considered light as a vibration which was spreading through an all-pervading "ether" which consisted of microscopic particles. Thomas Young (1773-1829), the English physiologist and physicist, established the wave theory of light that was first proposed by Huygens.

Aristotle's concept of ether was old and fragile. Newton who did not need the ether for the propagation of his corpuscular light but did need for his gravitational force did not frame hypotheses on ether. But Huygen's theory gave a truly new life to the concept of ether. Physicists speculated the presence of the "luminiferous (light-carrying) ether" to explain the conduction of light-waves through space. But soon they faced a serious trouble. Huygens and Young had suggested that light consisted of longitudinal waves just like sound waves. Longitudinal waves vibrate back and forth in the direction of travel. The French physicist Augustin Jean Fresnel (1788-1827) established that light waves are transverse. Transverse waves undulate at right angles to the direction of travel. Only a solid medium can convey transverse waves. Water waves are exceptional in the sense that, being transverse, they travel on the water surface but cannot penetrate the body of the fluid. Moreover, to be a medium for the motion of transverse waves of light that travels at the highest possible speed, ether would have to possess a fantastically high elasticity. Elasticity is primarily a property of solids. Hence physicists started tailoring their theory according to their need. Their imaginary, invisible and weightless ether had to be a super-rigid solid. It filled the vacuum of space and moreover it had to permeate ordinary matter like glass, water and transparent substances. It had also to be perfectly frictionless.

Thus physicists had to speculate the properties of their imaginary ether. Such vague speculations were contrary to the philosohy of science. Nevertheless, the mind-made ether was useful to explain some important observations other than the conduction of light-waves. Michael Faraday (1791-1867) was the creator of the classical field theory. He observed the lines of force in a magnetic field and explained these as the elastic distortions of the ether. James Clerk Maxwell (1831-79) produced the unified theory of electromagnetism. He had to take the help of the ether to explain the transmission of the electromagnetic wave which also included the light-wave.

The classical physicists assumed that the ether was not moving under any circumstances. However, by the nineteenth century, it was clearly known that the Earth, the Sun, the stars and, in fact, all objects of the universe were in motion. If ether which was at absolute rest could be taken as a fixed reference point, a method could be devised to determine the absolute motion—the foundation on which Newton's laws of motion were based. In the 1880s, the American physicist Albert Abraham Michelson (1852-1931) conceived an ingenious method to determine the absolute motion of the Earth. He invented the interferometer that allowed the speed of light to be compared in two pencils of light split from a single beam. He sent a beam of light in the direction of the Earth's motion and another beam at right angles. Both the beams were allowed to be reflected back. He reasoned that the beam of light sent out in the direction of the Earth's motion should travel a shorter distance than the other one, if the Earth moved through a motionless ether.

In 1887, Michelson associated the American chemist Edward Williams Morley (1838-1923) in this experiment. They stationed their instrument on a stone floating on mercury. By doing that, they could turn the instrument in any direction easily and smoothly to project their beam in various directions with respect to the Earth's motion. They could find no difference. The interference bands were virtually the same no matter in what direction the instrument was pointed.

According to the old concept, light wave was transmitted through the ether medium. If the ether moved, it should carry its own vibrations with it. But the results of the Michelson-Morley experiment concluded to the contrary. Either the Earth was moving with the ether or there was, perhaps, no such thing as ether. The first alternative made no sense at all. Hence the second alternative was accepted. Thus the experiment showed that the hypothetical ether probably did not exist. By this, the foundations of physics tottered. It was conclusively proved that there was no absolute motion or absolute space (space as usually understood by physicists). Michelson was awarded the Nobel Prize in 1907 (He was the first American to be awarded the Nobel Prize.)

In 1905, Einstein dispensed with the need of the ether. He perceived that the same physical laws must be true in all frames of reference in steady motion with respect to each other. This requirement necessarily implies that light must have the same speed no matter how a body is moving. Einstein rejected any fixed frame of reference against which the Earth moves. Furthermore, he showed the wave-particle duality of light in a separate paper. Unlike waves, particles do not need a medium for their movement.

It was the year 1905 in which the curtain in the long drama of ether finally dropped. Einstein's special theory of relativity played an important role in conclusively proving that the hypothetical ether was not necessary for explaining the motion of light through space.

From the time of Aristotle to 1905, both scientists and philosophers were very much confused with the misconceived ether. In Indian philosophy, there has never been any concept such as the ether of Aristotle. Nevertheless, the modern Indian philosophers were not less confused with the ether concept. Most modern Indian philosophers translate *ākāśa* (space) as the ether. Such a translation is totally wrong and based on sheer misconception. *Ākāśa* is a subtle form of matter. It is not a void, not a vacuum. It is a positive entity, not nothing. It is not at absolute rest; it is not at rest at all. Like other forms of matter and energy, it is ever in motion. It is active, not inert. It interacts with other forms of matter and energy. If this concept of *ākāśa* is accepted, all the pseudo-problems concerning the ether automatically vanish. The twentieth-century physicists have already obtained empirical evidences regarding the generation of particles from space and the dissolution of particles into space. When space itself is matter, question does not arise on the separation of the celestial bodies by vast expanses of empty space. We may take the simile of two icebergs floating in the ocean at two distant spots. One person stands on one iceberg and a second person on the second one. Both the persons on the two icebergs think that the icebergs are two isolated blocks separated by a water-mass by a distance of many kilometres and completely different from the intervening water. But, as a fact, the ice-blocks and the intervening water are all made of H_2O, and the two icebergs are connected, not separated. Similar is the situation with the galaxies, stars, planets and satellites that seem to be separated by a void but are really connected by the *ākāśic* matter. As the floating ice and the water are essentially made of the same substance, so also are the celestial bodies and the intervening *ākāśa* that are substantially identical. Everything in the universe is intimately connected with the rest; nothing in the universe is separate from the rest. If this is accepted in principle, there is nothing like action-at-a-distance. After 1915, scientists have been complacent with the notion that everything about space has been finally settled. This is, however, not correct. Since 1905, we very confidently say that light travels in a vacuum at the speed of 3×10^{10} cm per second. There is nothing like a vacuum, declares the Vedānta, that recognizes the plenum (*pūrṇa*) and rejects the void (*śūnya*). It may be correct to say that light travels in *ākāśa* at the speed of 3×10^{10} cm per second. There is difference between pure, distilled water and water in which salt has been dissolved. The so-called empty space also contains molecules, atoms, ions, neutrinos, photons, etc., although in traces. As a fact, we do not exactly know if substances like neutrinos and all sorts of radiations are abundantly present or present *in traces* in space. Hence the concept of light passing through space or a vacuum seems to need a revision.

What has been so far said in this chapter is on the macro-constituents of the universe, although discussion on some micro-constituents has not been avoided. We may now probe into the building blocks of matter. What are the smallest units of which matter is constituted? Are the micro-particles made up of a single micro-entity? Is the micro-world monistic or pluralistic? An attempt will be made to answer these questions in the remaining part of this chapter.

The Greek atomic concept remained in dormancy for about twenty-two centuries after Leucippus and Democritus, the authors of the Western atomic concept. In the seventeenth century, Robert Boyle (1627-91) believed that gases must be constituted of small particles to behave as they do when compressed. In 1797, Joseph Proust (1754-1826) stated that the ratios of one element to another in a given chemical compound remain constant. This law of definite proportions was further clarified by Dalton. John Dalton (1766-1844), the English chemical theorist, proposed an atomic theory linked to quantitative chemistry. In 1803, he put forward his atomic theory of matter. From the fact that chemicals combine only in integral proportions, he deduced that atoms must exist. His atom was the indestructible particle that could not further be sub-divided.

In 1855, the German scientist Heinrich Geissler (1814-79) developed his mercury pump which he used to produce vacuum tubes. During the 1870s, Sir William Crookes (1832-1919) modified these vacuum tubes and used them to produce cathode rays. He offered convincing evidences to prove that the cathode rays were streams of invisible charged particles. In 1881, the English physicist George Stoney (1826-1911) gave the name "electron" to this particle. In 1897, J.J. Thomson (1856-1940) discovered the electron. He measured the deflection of the cathode rays in an electric field, indicating that they were composed of particles. These particles were electrons. Sir J.J. Thomson received the 1906 Nobel Prize for physics. He proved the electron to be a particle. His son Sir G.P. Thomson (1892-1975) won the Nobel Prize for physics in 1937 (jointly with Davisson) for demonstrating that the electron possessed both particle-like and wave-like behaviour.

Cathode rays emanated from materials and hence electrons came from materials. From this it was assumed that electrons must be components of atoms. In 1898, Sir J.J. Thomson came forward with the suggestion that the atomic model might be compared with a raisin-pudding. This model was visualized to be a sphere of positive charge embedded with electrons like raisins in a pudding.

The German physicist Phillipp Lenard (1862-1947) did not agree with J.J. Thomson who proposed a solid model of the atom. In 1903, he deduced from his experimental results that the atoms contained much empty space and both positive and negative charge. He received the 1905 Nobel Prize for physics for his work to show that cathode rays are an electron beam.

Sir Ernest Rutherford (1871-1937), the New Zealand-born British physicist, who worked as the first research student of J.J. Thomson in Cambridge, was the founder of nuclear physics. In 1911, he presented his theory of the atom. He suggested his atomic model with a positively charged nucleus surrounded by negative electrons. The Rutherford model was like the solar system with a central positive nucleus and a few electrons orbiting it in circles. The Rutherford model was the simplest model to be visualized, but it was later proved not to be the accurate one. It was not stable, since electrons orbiting a nucleus were to give off radiation constantly, leading to the falling of the electrons into the nucleus. Scientists like Niels Bohr, Arnold Sommerfeld, Wolfgang Pauli, Werner Heisenberg, Louis de

Broglie, Erwin Schrödinger and Max Born worked on this problem. Many modifications were done to the original atomic model of Rutherford. The modified picture of the atom contains cloudy regions in which electron wavicles are present in accordance with the laws of probability and quantum mechanics.

Scientists were busy in their studies on radioactivity. In 1896, the French physicist Antoine Henri Becquerel (1852-1908) discovered radioactivity in uranium. The radiation given off by uranium and thorium was not homogeneous in its properties. In a cloud chamber with a magnetic field, part of the radiation was deflected in one direction by a very slight amount, a second part was deflected in the opposite direction by a considerable amount and a third part remained undeflected. In 1899, Becquerel identified some of the radiation as consisting of electrons, the negatively charged particles like the ones in the cathode rays. The studies of Ernest Rutherford revealed in 1898 that the radioactive emission consisted of at least two kinds of rays. He gave the name "alpha rays" to the less penetrating emission and "beta rays" to the more penetrating one. Two years later he discovered the third type of radioactive emission which was more penetrating than the beta rays. He called it "gamma rays". The gamma rays were not deflected by the magnetic field.

The gamma rays were as penetrable as the X-rays; the beta rays were much less penetrable; but the alpha rays had hardly any penetrability.

It came to be realized that the radioactive emissions must originate from within the nucleus of the atom and that there are nuclear energy levels within the nucleus. Unlike the alpha and the beta rays that are particles, the gamma rays are not particles but are electromagnetic radiations of shorter wavelengths. The alpha rays were deflected in the direction opposite to that of the beta rays. This showed that the alpha rays must consist of positively charged particles. J.J. Thomson suggested that the alpha rays be called positive rays. The same magnetic field deflected the alpha rays slightly, but the beta rays considerably. From the amount of deflection, Rutherford's calculation showed that the alpha particles were much more massive than the beta particles or electrons.

What was the nature of the alpha particles was a big puzzle for Rutherford. He measured the ratio of mass to charge in alpha particles. In 1906, he concluded from his results that alpha particles are the nuclei of helium atoms. In 1908, he designed a skilful set of experiments in collaboration with T.D. Royds to probe into the nature of alpha particles. These studies confirmed the earlier suggestion of Rutherford that alpha particles are helium nuclei. In 1911, Rutherford presented his theory of the atom, according to which a positively charged nucleus is surrounded by negative electrons. In 1914, he discovered the proton. In 1919, he reported on his discovery which he made two years earlier that alpha particles striking nitrogen knock out protons. This experiment proved that protons are the constituents of the nucleus of the atom. Rutherford received the Nobel Prize for chemistry in 1908.

With the discovery of the electron and the proton along with that of the atomic model, concepts about the atom became somewhat clearer. The nucleus carries the positive charge whereas the electron in the orbit around the nucleus carries the negative charge. The number of positive charges is equal to that of negative charges in the whole atom. The nucleus is massive. It contains more than 99.9 per cent of the mass of the atom. The mass of an electron is 9.1091×10^{-28} grams. It is 1/1836 that of the proton. The atom is practically empty. Its nucleus has a diameter in the range of 10^{-13} to 10^{-12} of a centimetre. The volume occupied by the nucleus is an insignificant portion of the atom (a little more than 1/100,000).

It was thought that a helium atom contained four protons. But the nucleus of a helium atom carries two units of positive charge. This cast doubt on the supposition that the nucleus of a helium atom consisted of protons only. But this doubt was explained away by the imagination of the existence of neutralizing electrons inside the atomic nucleus. This was the genesis of the proton-electron theory of nuclear structure. In 1920, the American chemist William Draper Harkins proposed the existence of the neutron, an uncharged particle, inside the atomic nucleus.

In 1930, two German physicists, Walter Bothe (1891-1957) and Herbert Becker bombarded beryllium atoms with alpha particles and thereby released from the nucleus a new radiation of unusual penetrating power. Two years later the Bothe-Becker discovery was followed by the French physicists Frédéric and Irène Joliot-Curie. They bombarded paraffin (composed of hydrogen and carbon) with the new-found radiation from beryllium. By this, protons were knocked out of the paraffin.

In England, James Chadwick (1891-1974) was doing research under Rutherford. While re-interpreting the experimental findings of the Joliot-Curies, he got evidence for the existence of the neutron with charge 0 and mass 1. Rutherford had foreseen it in 1920. Chadwick devised his own experiments to confirm his deduction. His experimental results confirmed the existence of the neutron in 1932. In 1935, he won the Nobel Prize for his discovery of the neutron.

By the discovery of the neutron, an important puzzle of the atomic theory was solved. The theoretical physicists had a serious doubt about the proton-electron model of the nucleus. The German physicist, Werner Heisenberg announced that a proton-neutron model of the nucleus was acceptable instead of a proton-electron model. It was finally resolved that the nucleus of any atom does not contain any electron at all.

This finishes the history of the discovery of the atomic constituents which are three in kind, viz., proton, neutron and electron. The former two are inside the nucleus and are called nucleons. The electrons revolve around the atomic nucleus in definite orbits. The positive charges in the nuclear protons are equal to the negative charges in the orbital electrons and thus an unionized atom is neutral in charge. When beta rays are emitted from an atomic nucleus, the electrons come out of the nuclear neutrons. A neutron is disintegrated into a proton, an electron and an anti-neutrino. A proton is 1836 times as heavy as an electron whereas a neutron is 1839 times as heavy as an electron.

In the early 1930s scientists were content with their discovery of "all" the particles of nature. These were the proton, neutron and electron. But physicists could not rest in this Eden of simplicity for a long time. Even before the neutron was discovered, the existence of anti-particles had been indicated.

The concept of anti-particles was born in 1930 from the theoretical treatment of the properties of the electron, worked out by Paul Adrien Maurice Dirac (1902-84). In 1928, he developed an equation that combined the ideas of quantum mechanics with special relativity. This was the relativistically invariant equation of the electron. It may be interesting to briefly state here the genesis of the brilliant idea of Dirac. Einstein expressed the energy of a particle with mass m and momentum p by the following equation:

$$E^2 = m^2c^4 + p^2c^2$$

When the momentum of the particle is zero, the equation is reduced to $E = mc^2$. Strictly speaking, it becomes $E = \pm mc^2$. The "negative roots" are generally ignored; but Dirac, being a genius, deeply pondered over it. He mathematically reasoned the theoretically possible positive and negative energy states of the electron. Since electrons are fermions, only one electron can go into each possible state (two per energy level, one with each spin). Dirac reasoned that the electrons did not fall into the negative energy states because all those states are already full. If an electron in the negative energy sea is given enough energy, it will jump up the ladder of energy states. The two energy-states of the electrons are diagramatically represented in Figure 6.1.

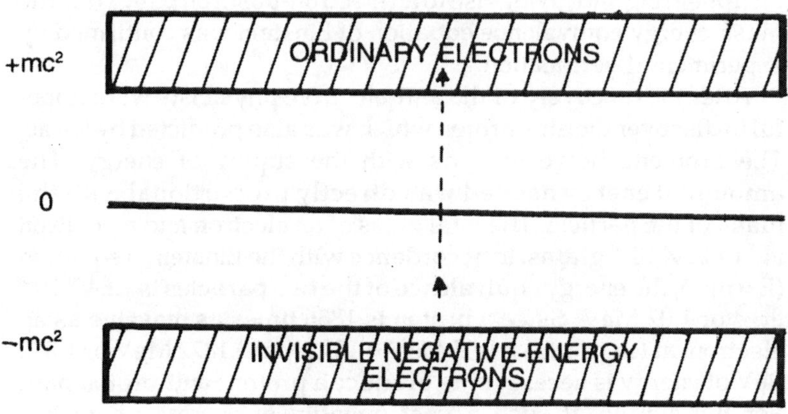

Fig. 6.1:Two energy-states of electrons.

Since the negative states are filled with particles of negative energy, other electrons cannot enter them. A sufficiently energetic photon can knock an electron out of one of these negative energy states, thus leaving a positively charged hole. This positively charged hole is the anti-particle of the electron (anti-electron or positron). When the electron and the anti-electron meet, they annihilate each other releasing energy in the form of gamma rays.

Dirac's argument applies to all particles without being restricted to the electron. Thus all particles possess corresponding anti-particles. In 1933, the Nobel Prize for physics was shared by Dirac and Schrödinger.

The predictions of Dirac were verified experimentally by the American physicist C.D. Anderson (1905-) in 1932. He discovered the positron while studying cosmic rays. This positively charged electron or positron was the first form of anti-matter to be discovered. Anderson shared the 1936 Nobel Prize for physics with Victor Francis Hess (1833-1964) who discovered cosmic rays (Millikan in 1925 named the high-energy particles from the extraterrestrial source "cosmic rays").

The electron-positron pair is very unstable. It remains in existence at most for only a ten-millionths of a second. The momentary dance of the pair-particles ends in their combination and mutual annihilation with the release of energy. Anderson also observed the reverse phenomenon—gamma rays suddenly disappearing and giving rise to an electron-positron pair. Thus the mass-energy equivalence equation of Einstein was confirmed by experimental verification.

After the discovery of the anti-electron, physicists were hopeful to discover the anti-proton which was also predicted by Dirac. The problem, however, was with the supply of energy. The amount of energy needed was directly proportional with the mass of the particle. The total mass of an electron and a positron is 1.822×10^{-27} grams. In accordance with the Einstein's equation ($E = mc^2$), the energy equivalence of the two particles is 1.64×10^{-6} ergs or 1.02 MeV. Since a proton is 1836 times as massive as an electron, at least (1836 x 1.02 MeV = 1872 MeV) 1872 MeV or 1.872 BeV of energy is necessary to produce a proton : anti-proton pair. For the supply of such a vast quantity of energy, physicists became busy in devising particle-accelerators. Different types of particle-accelerators such as cyclotron, synchrotron, bevatron, etc., were planned to reach acceleration capacity of 1,000 to 20,000 BeV. In 1955, Owen Chamberlain (1920 -) and Emilio Gino Segrè (1905 -), by conducting experiments with the bevatron particle-accelerator at Berkeley, discovered the anti-proton with the same mass as the proton, but of opposite charge. They shared the 1959 Nobel Prize for physics for this discovery. Attempts were made to experimentally verify the reverse process, i.e., production of proton : anti-proton pair from energy. This was done in 1965 by concentrating enough energy for this purpose. An energy of 6 BeV was necessary to do this job.

According to Dirac's prediction, no particle can be produced without the simultaneous production of its corresponding anti-particle. This principle was verified for the electron : positron and proton: anti-proton pairs. It was the next attempt for the physicists to obtain experimental verification for the existence of anti-neutron. In 1956, B. Cook, G.R. Lambertson, O. Picconi and W.A.Wentzel discovered the anti-neutron.

The question arises here: The anti-electron has a positive charge as opposed to the electron with a negative charge. The anti-proton has a negative charge as opposed to the proton with a positive charge. But the neutron has no charge. What is the difference between the neutron and the anti-neutron then? This question can be answered by introducing the spin concept. The particle : anti-particle pairs exhibit equal and opposite spins. It is a well known fact that a spinning electric charge sets up a magnetic field with a north magnetic pole and a south magnetic pole. The proton and the electron, having electric charges, behave this way. Although the neutron has no electric charge, it does have a magnetic field associated with it. The neutron is surrounded by a cloud of virtual charged pions (Figure 6.2) which endow it with electric properties. The net charge of the neutron is zero since the overall neutrality is achieved by having an equal number of positive and negative pions. The charge in the pion clouds associated with the neutron and the anti-neutron are opposite in kind. Hence the neutron and the anti-neutron have the same mass, but the orientation of the magnetic field of one is opposed to that of the other.

The photon and the graviton are massless particles. From theoretical consideration, the massless particles may be regarded to be their own anti-particles. Particles in nature are not limited in kind. But whatever may be the particle, it necessarily has an anti-particle. They are created together; they are annihilated together.

The particles are characterized by their mass, electric charge, spin and lifetime. Among the particles carrying electric charge, the electron or the positron has the lowest mass. The electric charge carried by an electron is taken as one unit. All other known

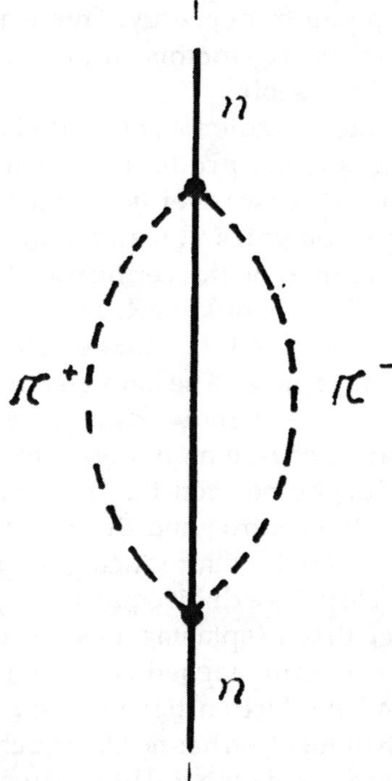

Fig. 6.2: A neutron surrounded by a pion cloud.

particles with electric charge carry the charge in simple multiples of the fundamental unit of charge carried by the electron.

Many particles possess a type of internal rotation called spin. The angular momentum or the spin of the subatomic particle is a quantum mechanical property. It is quantized, i.e., it comes in fixed discrete units that are integer multiples of ½ $\hbar$, where $\hbar$ is Planck's constant h divided by 2 π. For the sake of simplicity, spin ½ $\hbar$ is commonly expressed as "spin ½". The electron has spin ½ and the photon has spin 1. Particles with an even number of spin units (½ $\hbar$) are referred to as *bosons* while those with an odd number of spin units as *fermions*. No two fermions can occupy the same quantum state. In other words, fermions are subject to the Pauli exclusion principle propounded by Wolfgang Pauli in 1924. (For this idea of the exclusion principle, Pauli was awarded the Nobel Prize for physics in 1945.) Such a restriction is not applied to bosons.

All the subatomic particles are grouped into two distinct classes, viz., leptons and hadrons. The light particles are leptons and the heavy particles are hadrons. Leptons that have so far been known are six in number. They are the electron, the muon, the tauon and the three neutrinos. All the six leptons are fermions, with spin ½.

The muon is a particle that is about 207 times as heavy as the electron. It is unstable; it decays into electrons in about two microseconds. In 1932, Carl David Anderson discovered the mu-meson (which is now known as muon) by observing cosmic ray tracks in the cloud chamber. In 1937, he conducted further studies on this particle for the confirmation of some of its characteristics. The Anderson's particle was called meson since its mass was in between that of the proton and the electron. It was mistaken as the Yukawa pi-meson (now known as pion) that mediates the strong froce. In 1942, Shoichi Sakata and T. Inoue presented their two-meson theory—the mu-meson discovered by Anderson and the as yet unobserved meson predicted in 1935 by Yukawa. In 1945, M. Conversi, E. Pancini and O. Piccioni demonstrated that the mu-meson discovered by Anderson interacts too weakly with protons and neutrons to be the Yukawa particle. In 1947, R. Marshak and Hans Bethe, independently of S. Sakata and T. Inoue, rediscovered the two-meson theory. Now it is established that the mu-meson discovered by Anderson in 1937 is really a "fat electron". It is renamed as muon. Now muons are not considered as mesons. They are included in the lepton class.

The tau lepton or tauon was discovered in 1975. It is a "fat muon" just as a muon is a "fat electron". The mass of a tauon is about 3500 times that of an electron. Both the muon and the tauon have properties of the electron. Both are very unstable.

The electron, the muon and the tauon are charged leptons. There are three types of neutrinos that are the uncharged leptons. Each type of neutrino is associated in its behaviour with one of the charged leptons. Thus there are electron-neutrinos, muon-neutrinos and tauon-neutrinos (tauon-neutrinos have not yet been detected).

The historical background behind the discovery of the neutrino is very interesting. Lise Meitner (1878-1968), the Austrian-Swedish physicist and radiochemist was working on nuclear fission. In 1922, she was concerned with the missing energy in the process of the emission of the beta particle from the neutron of the atomic nucleus. By 1930, Niels Bohr (1885-1962) was ready to abandon the law of the conservation of energy at least for the subatomic particles. In 1931, Wolfgang Pauli (1900-58) made an attempt to save the sacrosanct law of the conservation of energy. In order to find out a solution to the riddle of the missing energy, he conceived of a very light neutral particle that carried the missing energy while coming out of the atomic nucleus along with the beta particle. This particle has rather strange properties. It has no mass and no charge. It exists as a certain amount of energy and always speeds along at the velocity of light. The Italian-American nuclear physicist, Enrico Fermi (1901-54) gave the name neutrino (Italian for "little neutral one") to this strange, mysterious particle. In 1933, he established the theory of radioactive beta decay, whereby a neutron emits an electron (beta particle) and an anti-neutrino and becomes a proton. For his outstanding discoveries in nuclear physics, Fermi received the Nobel Prize in 1938.

The anti-neutrino is necessary in the beta decay also for maintaining the conservation of spin. The amount of spin is expressed in multiples of one-half, plus or minus, depending on the direction of the spin. The neutron has a + ½; the proton also has a spin + ½; but the electron has a spin – ½. The law of conservation of spin is violated if it is presumed that a neutron is converted into a proton and an electron. For this purpose, the anti-neutrino with a spin + ½ comes to the rescue. With the introduction of the anti-neutrino in the beta decay equation, the law of conservation of spin is maintained.

A proton is converted into a neutron, a positron and a neutrino. Here also the law of conservation of spin is maintained. Neutrinos with spin ½ are fermions. In both conversions (neutron to proton and proton to neutron) another conservation law, i.e., the conservation of particle/anti-particle, is also saved.

The neutrinos were still fictitious particles up to 1955 although they were predicted by Wolfgang Pauli in 1930. Clyde Lorrain Cowan (Jr.) and Frederick Reines observed neutrinos for the first time in 1955.

Neutrinos virtually do not interact with matter. With ease they can pass through the Earth. An average neutrino can pass through a 100-light-year-thick solid lead with only a 50 per cent chance of being absorbed.

In contrast to the leptons which are six in kind, the hadrons (from the Greek word meaning "heavy") are too many. They are heavy particles. The nuclear particles (proton and neutron) and the particles formed as a result of nuclear interactions are collectively known as *hadrons*.

The heavier hadrons tend to be fermionic. Those hadrons that are fermions are called *baryons* (meaning heavy ones). The proton and neutron are baryons, both having spin ½. Those hadrons that are bosons are collectively called *mesons*, after their mass intermediate between the mass of leptons and that of baryons. The lightest meson is the pion.

The discovery of mesons was associated with the strong nuclear force. The Japanese physicist Hideki Yukawa (1907-81) first described the strong nuclear force and proposed that this force involved the exchange of a particle between the nucleons. In 1935, he predicted the existence of a meson that caused the attraction between particles in the atomic nucleus. He was the first Japanese to be awarded the Nobel Prize in 1949. In 1937, C.D. Anderson detected in cosmic ray a particle with similar mass as that of the Yukawa particle. But it did not interact with the nucleons sufficiently strongly. In 1942, Shoichi Sakata and T.Inoue suggested that Yukawa's meson was different from Anderson's. In 1947, R. Marshak and Hans Bethe, independently of Sakata and Inoue, rediscovered the two-meson theory. They declared that the meson found by Anderson in cosmic rays was not the same as the one predicted by Yukawa. In the same year (1947), Cecil Frank Powell (1903-69) discovered the new particle pi-meson or pion with mass 273 times that of an electron. This was the particle predicted by Yukawa in 1935. It acts as the exchange particle in the strong nuclear interaction among nucleons and is different from the muon discovered by Anderson. Powell won the Nobel Prize in 1950.

Two Polish physicists, Marian Danysz and Jerzy Pniewski detected the K-mesons or kayons in 1952. These are about 970 times as massive as an electron. Both the positive kayon and the neutral kayon have their corresponding anti-particles. They break down to pions in about a microsecond. There are three pions: an electrically neutral one, π^o, with a mass of 264.1 electron masses, a positively charged one, π^+, with a mass of 273.1 electron masses, and a negatively charged one, π^-, also with a mass of 273.1 electron masses. The positively charged pion is the anti-particle of the negatively charged pion. All these three pions have zero spin.

Hadrons proliferate to many kinds. Some of the more common hadrons are the pion, kaon, eta, proton, neutron, lambda, sigma, xi, omega, etc. Of all the hadrons, only the proton is stable. The others decay either into lighter hadrons or leptons. Even it is not correct to say that the proton is absolutely stable. In 1973, Jogesh C. Pati and Abdus Salam suggested theoretical reasons why protons might decay into other particles.

Until the 1950s, the proton and the neutron were the only baryons. Beginning in 1954, a series of still more massive baryons were discovered. It is the baryon particles that have particularly proliferated in the 1950s and afterwards. The proton and neutron are the lightest of the large variety of baryons.

There is a law of conservation of baryon number. More massive baryons break down to less massive particles. In this breakdown process, the net number of baryons (baryons minus anti-baryons) remains the same. The proton and the anti-proton are the lightest baryons and the only stable ones.

A number of baryons heavier than the proton and neutron have been discovered. These heavier particles have the group-name "hyperons". The lambda particle, the sigma particle, the xi particle and the omega-minus particle are worth mentioning here. There is only one variety of the lambda particle; it is a neutral particle. The sigma particle has three varieties, positive, negative and neutral. The xi particle is in two varieties, negative and neutral. Each one of these has an associated anti-particle. All these particles are unstable. None can live for more than a hundredth of a microsecond. The neutral sigma particle breaks down after a hundred trillionths of a microsecond.

In 1960, Luis Walter Alvarez (1911-88) discovered in bubble chambers very short-lived particles, which were termed resonances. He received the Nobel Prize in physics in 1968. The half-lives of these ultra-short-lived particles (resonance particles) are something of the order of a few trillionths of a trillionth of a second. With the availability of higher energies in the particle-accelerators at the disposal of physicists, more and more hadrons were produced until 150 or more were known. The resonance particles are so short-lived that it is not possible to directly detect them. Their existence can only be deduced from the necessity of accounting for their breakdown products.

A problem with which physicists grappled was the fundamentality of the particles. Are they really elementary or fundamental? Are they constituted of still smaller components? The leptons are assumed to be fundamental; they are not made up of smaller components. In contrast, hadrons are not elementary particles. They are constituted of still smaller particles called quarks.

In 1953, the American physicist Murray Gell-Mann (1929-) introduced a system assigning isospin to particles that led to the concept of "strangeness". In the same year, the Japanese physicists T. Nakano and Kasuhiko Nishijima introduced the concept of the strangeness in quantum number independently of Murray Gell-Mann. Strangeness is a new quantum number which is conserved in events involving strong nuclear interactions. The graviton and the photon, all the leptons, the pion, the eta (η) meson and the nucleons have a strangeness number of zero. The particles, with strangeness numbers other than zero, are lumped together as *strange particles*. By using this strangeness, in 1961, Gell-Mann and the Israeli physicist Yúval Néeman (working independently) fitted the elementary particles into a classification scheme, somewhat like the earlier periodic table. The elementary particles were neatly classified into multiples of 1, 8, 10 or 27 members. The members of the multiplets were then related by symmetry operations in a pattern that Gell-Mann called the *eightfold way* (a pun on the Buddhist eightfold route to *nirvāṇa*). This is formally referred to by the group-theoretic designation as SU (3). One such grouping needed one more particle for completion. This predicted particle was christened "omega-minus". In 1964, the omega-minus particle was detected with just the predicted set of properties. In 1971, its anti-particle, the anti-megaminus, was detected.

Murray Gell-Mann and George Zweig introduced the concept of quarks in 1964. The word "quark" has no scientific significance. Gell-Mann adopted it from Joyce's novel *Finnegan's Wake*: "Three quarks for Muster Mark!" Quarks are the bricks out of which all hadrons (baryons and mesons) are made. For the quark theory, Gell-Mann was awarded the Nobel Prize for physics in 1969.

Quarks are postulated to have spin ½, fractional charge of either 1/3 or 2/3 of the fundamental quantity e, and baryon number 1/3. Three quarks combine to form a baryon. Two quarks, i.e., a quark and an anti-quark combine to form a meson. All baryons are fermions which have half integral spins (½, 3/2, 5/2, et cetera). Three quarks must therefore combine to give a spin of either ½ + ½ + ½ = 3/2 or ½ + ½ - ½ = ½. Thus the resulting baryon is a fermion. In contrast, all mesons are bosons that have integral spin (0, 1, 2, et cetera). The quark-anti-quark combination gives a spin of either ½ + ½ = 1 or ½ - ½ = 0. Thus the resulting meson is a boson.

To account for all the baryons, there have to be different varieties or *flavours* of quarks. A total number of six flavours have so far been known. They are: up (u), down (d), sideways or strange (s), charm (c), top or truth (t) and bottom or beauty (b). These are whimsically named without any reference to the literal meanings.

Gell-Mann introduced three quarks, viz., u,d and s, in his quark theory. In 1964, Sheldon Lee Glashow (1932-), in collaboration with James D. Bjorken, introduced a particle property called "charm". He adopted Gell-Mann's theory that hadrons and mesons are made up of smaller particles called quarks. He postulated a fourth "charmed" quark which was necessary for a group of particles described by SU4 (Unitary Symmetry of Dimension 4).

In 1974, Burton Richter (1931-) and Samuel Chao Chung Ting (1936-), working independently, experimentally demonstrated the existence of charmed quarks. Richter discovered the psi (ψ) hadron, a new heavy elementary particle whose unusual properties supported Glashow's hypothesis of charmed quarks. The same particle was christened by Ting as J. This particle is now called the J/psi. Richter and Ting shared the 1976 Nobel Prize for physics for their parallel discovery of the J/psi particle. This is a spin 1, non-strange, electrically neutral meson with a huge mass (3097 MeV). The three-flavours quark model could not account for the psi particle. It was theorized to have been made of a charmed quark and an anti-charmed quark ($c\bar{c}$).

In 1977, Leon Lederman discovered the upsilon (γ) meson. This is the product of the combination of a bottom quark and an anti-bottom quark ($b\bar{b}$). In 1984, Carlo Rubbia at CERN announced that his group discovered evidence for the top quark, the heaviest of all the quarks. We are not sure if all the quarks have already been discovered. But, the six flavours of quarks that have so far been known can account for all the known hadrons. The quarks are in pairs such as u and d, s and c, and b and t.

Quarks have fractional electric charge as opposed to leptons with integral charge. Expressed in units of e, they have charges as follows: u, + 2/3; d, – 1/3; c, + 2/3; s, – 1/3; t, + 2/3; b, – 1/3. Notwithstanding the fractional charge of the quarks, the products of their combination, viz., baryons and mesons, have integral or no charge.

All quarks must have baryon number 1/3. The s quark carries – 1 strangeness. The arrangement of quarks for any particular hadron can be determined by specifying the spin, charge, baryon number and strangeness. For example, the proton is composed of uud, having spin ½, charge + 1, baryon number +1 and strangeness 0. The anti-proton is formed by $\bar{u}\bar{u}\bar{d}$. A combination of udd makes a neutron. The anti-neutron is formed by $\bar{u}\bar{d}\bar{d}$. In contrast to the nucleons (protons and neutrons), the hyperons (baryons heavier than the nucleons) contain strange quarks in their quark composition. The lambda (Λ) particle is neutral in charge. The sigma (Σ) particle is both charged and neutral (Σ^o, Σ^+, Σ^-). The xi (Ξ) particle has both neutral (Ξ^o) and negative (Ξ^-) varieties. The omega (Ω) particle has negative charge (Ω^-). All these hyperons have also anti-particles. Their quark compositions are as follows: **Λ = uds, Σ^+ = uus, Σ^0 = uds, Σ^- = dds, Ξ^0 = uss, Ξ^-= dss, Ω^- = sss.** The mesons are constructed of quark-anti-quark pairs. For example, a positive pion (π^+) is u$\bar{d}$ whereas a positive kaon (K^+) is u$\bar{s}$.

In 1965, Moo-Young Han and Yoichira Nambu introduced a new concept for quarks. It was later named "colour". Each different flavour of quark possesses three varieties of the colour property. These three colours are *red, blue* and *green*. When the quarks combine, they follow definite colour rules. In the combination of three quarks to form a baryon, one must be red, one blue and one green. Thus the baryon constituted of three quarks is colourless or white. When a quark and an anti-quark combine to form a meson, one is a particular colour and the second one that particular anti-colour, the combination being colourless or white. Quarks are coloured; but the final product or the particle, constituted of quarks, is colourless. The study of quark combination which was initiated by Murray Gell-Mann in 1972 is known as quantum chromodynamics (QCD).

In 1973, David Politzer and, independently, David Gross and Frank Wilczek showed that quarks must exhibit asymptotic freedom. The farther apart they are, the more they attract each other. Conversely, their mutual attracting force becomes weaker as they come closer, and they ignore each other when they touch.

Discussions have so far been made on leptons and hadrons. There is a third distinct class of particles known as messenger particles. These are otherwise known as exchange particles with reference to the interactions of the fundamental forces.

Hadrons are either fermions or bosons. Quarks, the constituents of hadrons, are fermions. Leptons are also fermions. The fundamental particles of atoms are all fermions. The photon differs from either quarks or leptons in being a boson. It has a spin of one unit. It is a massless particle that travels at the speed of light. It is the exchange particle in the electromagnetic interaction. When two charged particles like proton A and proton B approach, the electromagnetic fields of A and B interact, causing a repulsive force. When two charged particles like a proton A and an electron B approach, the electromagnetic fields of A and B interact, causing an attractive force. In the electromagnetic interaction, the particle photon is exchanged. This exchange process involves exchange of momentum and perhaps energy between the particles. Both the momentum and energy are quantized instead of being continuous. The emission and the absorption of the photon between the two charged particles may be compared with the to-and-fro movement of a tennis ball between two players. In the case of the tennis ball, the direction of its passage can be discerned. But this is not the case with the photon whose emission and absorption events occur within the interval Δt over which the time is uncertain (vide Heisenberg's uncertainty principle).

In the case of the gravitational force, the analogue of the photon is called the graviton. It is a massless boson with a spin of two. Photons couple only to charged particles whereas gravitons couple to all particles, although too weakly. Gravitons also couple to gravitons and thus they interact with each other.

The nucleons (protons and neutrons) inside the atomic nucleus are bound together by the strong force. Back in 1935, the Japanese physicist Hideki Yukawa predicted the existence of the exchange particle of the strong force binding the nucleons. In 1947, the British physicist Cecil Frank Powell detected this particle in cosmic ray. (Yukawa was awarded the Nobel Prize in physics in 1949 and Powell received it in 1950.) This particle is the pi meson or pion. It has three varieties, viz., positively charged (π^+), negatively charged (π^-) and electrically neutral (π^0). The positive pion acts as an exchange particle in the strong force binding protons and protons, neutrons and neutrons and protons and neutrons. The negative pion performs a similar function for anti-protons and anti-neutrons. Both are very short-lived with an average lifetime of about 1/40 microsecond. The neutral pion breaks down in less than a quintillionth of a second to form a pair of gamma rays.

The quarks inside nucleons are also glued together by the strong force. The messenger or exchange particles for the strong force are collectively called the *gluons.* All gluons are bosons. There are no less than eight gluons. In 1979, four groups of physicists observed the gluon at the Deutsches Electronen Synchrotron in Hamburg. Gluons have spin 1. Like the graviton, they also couple to themselves. The quarks of the hadrons are bound by the strong force that is carried by the gluons. Most forces decline with distance. But the gluon force increases with distance and fades out at close range. For the gluon force only, the quarks can never come out of their hadronic prisons.

The weak force is associated with the emission of the electron from the nuclear neutron in the process of beta decay. Three messenger particles, viz., W^+, W^- and Z carry the weak force. These particles were discovered in 1983 by Carlo Rubbia of Italy and Simon van der Meer of the Netherlands. For this discovery they won the Nobel Prize for physics in 1984. All the three particles are bosons with spin 1. They have a non-zero mass. The Ws are as heavy as about 80 protons and the Z is as massive as 90 times the proton. This is the peculiarity of the particles carrying the weak force in that they are massive whereas photons and gravitons are massless and pions are mesons with masses intermediate between protons and electrons. For this reason only, the weak force acts in a very short range. Both W^+ and W^- have one unit of charge like the electron. In fact, W^- is the anti-particle of W^+. Unlike the Ws that are electrically charged, the Z is a neutral particle and resembles the photon in all respects other than the mass.

We have now reached the concluding part of this chapter. The micro-world is bizarre. Particles and subatomic particles are too many in kind. Among the diverse particles, physicists have been searching for the fundamental ones. They think that they have found them. The leptons and the quarks are the fundamental particles. They are point-like and structureless. They are not made up of smaller components. They do not have internal structure. They are the smallest building blocks of nature.

Can't we conceive of components of leptons and quarks? Are we finally certain that the leptons and quarks are really structureless? We pause a while, ponder over these questions and express our reluctance to answer. Once upon a time, the atom was structureless and the smallest unit in nature. That was falsified. The proton and the neutron were also once structureless. Now we say that the nucleons are made up of quarks. To conceive of leptons and quarks as micro-structures constituted of still smaller components does not involve any self-contradiction. Hence the possibility of detecting component parts of leptons and quarks cannot be ruled out.

Finally, we do appreciate the rapturous utterance of the Upaniṣadic seer "smaller than the smallest, bigger than the biggest (*aṇoraṇīyān, mahato mahīyān*[7])". We tried to fathom the macro-world. We could voyage a great surface area. We could dive into a great depth. But it seemed, the entirety of the macro-world was unknowable for us. We tried to dissect out nature. We made all attempts to do micro-analysis for the detection of the smallest components of nature. We got the leptons and the quarks. The question is: Can't we dissect them further? Such a question is so far unanswerable.

We may conclude this chapter by focusing on its title "Pluralism in Science". Is nature pluralistic? The pluralism of nature is apparent only. The surface is plural, the bottom is singular. There is a unity underneath the diversity. Both the macro - and the micro-world are constituted of particles—hadrons, leptons, messenger particles. All these particles, irrespective of their sizes and properties, are material entities. But matter is a packet of energy. There is no difference between matter and energy. Although there are different forms of energy, all the forms are interconvertible. Energy is both continuous and discrete. When considered as a field or a wave, it is continuous. As energy-quanta, it is discrete. Whether continuous or discrete, energy may be regarded as a single entity. Thus nature is monistic instead of pluralistic. Nature manifests at the surface level as pluralistic. But, at the bottom level it is monistic. This kind of monism in science is known as attributive monism.

Is energy the rock-bottom of nature? Can't we blast it and reach still deeper level? Can't we break it open? Can't we bore it to reach some level that is the real substratum of everything conceivable? These aspects will be dealt with in the succeeding chapters.

NOTES

1. Quoted by R. Podolny, *Something Called Nothing*, Mir Publishers, Moscow, 1986, pp. 37-38.
2. TU, II. 1. 1.
3. BS, II. 3. 14.
4. ṚV, I. 89. 10.
5. A. Einstein, quoted by M. Capek, in *The Philosophical Impact of Contemporary Physics*, D. Van Nostrand, Princeton, New Jersey, 1961, p. 319.
6. A. Einstein, quoted by R. Thiel, in *And There was Light*, 1958, p. 345.
7. KTU, I. 2. 20.

VII

UNCERTAINTY AND PROBABILITY

THE STATEMENT "A is A" is certain. It is an analytical statement and necessarily true. The statement "A is B" or "A is C" is synthetic. Such a statement may or may not be true. Whether it is true or not can be ascertained only by verification, which is empirical and depends upon our sense-perception. Again, there is no way of being sure of the correctness of the sense-perception. Hence the truth or the falsity of the verification of a synthetic statement is a matter of probability.

If B and C are exclusive of each other, A cannot be both B and C simultaneously. A is B and A is C. Physicists have grappled with this problem for some centuries. We shall begin this chapter with the wave-particle duality of light.

The English physicist Robert Hooke (1635-1703) published his book *Micrographia* in 1665. This book included the idea that light might consist of waves. The next scientist who significantly contributed to the wave theory of light was the Dutch physicist and astronomer Christiaan Huygens (1629-1695). He expounded his wave theory of light in 1678. He described light as a vibration which spreads through an all-pervading "ether", consisting of microscopic particles.

The English physicist and mathematician Sir Isaac Newton (1642-1727) published his book *Optics* in 1704. In this book he proposed a corpuscular theory of light. He based his theory on the results of his ingenious experiments conducted in 1666.

Controversy arose over the issue of the particulate or the wave theory of light. Particles are discrete units whereas a wave is a continuous entity. These two are exclusive of each other. How can light be both particle and wave then?

If considered in detail, both the wave theory and the corpuscular theory had some limitations since none could explain all the properties of light. In addition, the wave theory faced a peculiar problem. Water waves and sound waves can go around obstacles whereas light waves cannot. Furthermore, a medium is necessary for the transmission of a wave. Light reaches the Earth from the Sun and the stars through a vacuum. What medium does light wave through a vacuum? This was the question which puzzled the wave-theorists. And so did they try to solve it by their speculation of an "ether" medium. This topic has already been discussed in chapter VI.

For about a century the two rival theories contended with each other. Of course, scientific opinion tilted more towards the corpuscular theory because of the great name and fame of Newton. In 1801, opinion suddenly changed in favour of the wave theory due to the results of an experiment performed by the English physician and physicist Thomas Young (1773-1829). He projected a narrow beam of light through two closely spaced holes on a screen. A series of bands of light alternating with dark bands were observed on the screen. If light consisted of particles, brighter regions would have been produced on the screen where the two beams overlapped and less bright regions where they did not. When the observation and the argument contradicted each other, Young had to reject the corpuscular theory of light. He tried to explain the observation by the wave theory. When waves of the two beams of light emerging through the two holes were in phase, they reinforced each other and so produced the bright bands. On the other hand, the dark bands were produced at places where the two sets of waves were out of phase. At such places, the trough of one wave cancelled the crest of the other. The dark bands represented the areas where the two sets of waves interfered with each other instead of mutual reinforcement. As a result, the net effect of light energy at the areas of the dark bands became zero.

In the first decade of the twentieth century, the pendulum again swung to both sides. Evidences forthcame to prove that light is corpuscular as well as wavy. In the last two decades of the nineteenth century, it had been discovered that electrons were ejected from metal surfaces when a beam of light fell on the metal. The electrons were bound to the structure of the metal. Light energy broke this bond and set the electrons free. More and more light could provide sufficient kinetic energy by which the electrons could dart off at great velocities. This effect of light on the electrons bound to the atoms of some metals is known as the photoelectric effect which was discovered in 1902 by the German physicist Philipp Lenard (1862-1947). For this discovery, Lenard received the Nobel Prize for physics in 1905. He observed a limiting thereshold frequency of light, above which the electrons were kicked out of the atoms of the metal. Each metal surface, out of the ones that exhibited the photoelectric effect, had its own specific threshold frequency. At that time physicists were surprised at the fact that any increase in the intensity of light did not affect the electrons whereas changes in the wavelength of light did. No explanation could be provided for this observation by the physical theories of the nineteenth century.

In 1905, Albert Einstein (1879-1955) advanced an explanation for the observed photoelectric effect. He did this by making use of Max Planck's (1858-1947) quantum theory which was only five years old and so far neglected. Planck maintained that energy is radiated in quanta. Einstein said that energy is radiated and absorbed in quanta. When light energy fell upon a certain metal surface, the electrons bound to the atoms of the surface absorbed the energy one quantum at a time. The shorter the wavelength and the higher the frequency of the light energy, the larger is the quantum, according to the Planck's equation, $E = h\upsilon$. If the energy of a quantum of light was sufficient to overcome the force that bound the electron to the surface, the electron was set free. The frequency of the light wave was to be higher than the threshold one so as to leave excess energy to act as kinetic energy for the ejection of the electron from the metal surface. The quantum of light which Einstein recognized in 1905 for the first time in the history of science was given the name "photon" by Gilbert N. Lewis in 1926. By his explanation of the photoelectric effect, Einstein recognized light as both a particle and a wave. He said in 1909: "It is my opinion that the next phase in the development of theoretical physics will bring us a theory of light that can be interpreted as a kind of fusion of the wave and the emission theory... (The) wave structure and (the) quantum structure ... are not to be considered as mutually incompatible."[1] He was awarded the 1921 Nobel Prize for physics for his work of the photoelectric effect. The American physicist Robert Andrews Millikan (1868-1953) made further studies on the photoelectric effect during the period from 1912-16. He confirmed Einstein's deductions on the said effect. Millikan was awarded the 1923 Nobel Prize for physics for his measurement of the elementary electrical charge and his accurate measurement of h of the Planck's equation. It was the year 1916 (the year of the announcement of Millikan's results) when the quantum theory was universally accepted by physicists.

As it is obvious from the foregoing discussion, Einstein did not reject the wave theory of light. If light is a wave, what medium is it waving? This question again came up and Einstein did not find any relevance to answer this question. In 1887, the classical experiment of Michelson and Morley had already confirmed the null result on the ether. Einstein did not need the ether to explain the propagation of light through the vacuum. Light is made up of particles that do not need a medium for their transmission. Thus a full-stop was given to the age-old problem of the nature of light and the existence of an all-pervading ether.

In 1923, the American physicist Arthur Holly Compton (1892-1962), through his discovery of the Compton effect, came to the conclusion that photons (electromagnetic waves) behave as particles as well as waves. He observed that X-rays, on being scattered by matter, lose energy and become longer in wavelength. As $\upsilon = c/\lambda$, where c is the velocity of light and λ is its wavelength, Planck's equation may be rewritten as $E = hc/\lambda$. Both h and c being constant, λ must increase with decrease of E. This Compton effect provided evidence for the wave-particles dualism. Compton and C.T.R. Wilson received the Nobel Prize for physics in 1927.

The French physicist (Prince) Louis-Victor de Broglie (1892-1987) established the existence of matter waves. In 1923, he announced the relationship, $\lambda = h/mv$, where h is Planck's constant, m is the mass of a moving particle, v its velocity, mv its momentum, and λ (lambda) is the wavelength associated with its wave-like properties. He submitted his doctoral thesis in 1924 and published it in 1925. De Broglie originally applied this equation to the electron. But, in theory, it applies to any moving body.

In 1925, the American physicist, Clinton Joseph Davisson (1881-1958) accidentally created large nickel crystals that exhibited X-ray diffraction. In this experiment, Lester Halbert Germer (1896-1971) was the coworker of Davisson. In 1927, they obtained conclusive evidence that electron beams were diffracted on reflection by nickel crystals and had the wavelength as predicted by de Broglie. In 1927 the English physicist George Paget Thomson (1892-1975), working independently of Davisson, discovered experimentally the interference (diffraction) of electrons by atoms in crystals. He passed the electrons through a thin gold foil instead of a nickel crystal. Davisson and Germer used slow electrons whereas Thomson used fast electrons in their respective experiments. Thus de Broglie's theory that particles always have waves associated with them was experimentally confirmed. Davisson and Thomson shared the 1937 Nobel Prize for physics. De Broglie received the Nobel Prize for physics in 1929.

Albert Einstein, in his studies on the photoelectric effect in 1905, proved the corpuscular nature of light. In 1924, the Indian physicist Satyendra Nath Bose (1894-1974) introduced new statistics for light quanta (photons). By applying the Bose statistics to matter, Einstein deduced that matter should exhibit wave properties. In 1928, the Indian physicist Chandrasekhara Venkata Raman (1888-1970) discovered the scattering effect. He showed that light scattered by molecules of matter exhibits lower and higher frequency components (the Raman effect). One thing is deduced from this observation that light is scattered because of its particle nature. Raman received the Nobel Prize for physics in 1930. His discovery led to one of the earliest confirmations of quantum theory. Not only the electron is both particle and wave, but light also. As a matter of fact, everything in nature, whether matter or energy, has both corpuscular and wave nature. Everything is both continuous and discontinuous.

In spite of the discoveries that have already been mentioned, the matter-wave dualism was a controversial problem in the physics world for a number of years. The German physicist Werner Karl Heisenberg (1901-76) formulated his theory of matrix mechanics in 1925 when he was only twenty-four years old. At the age of twenty-three, the German physicist Ernst Pascual Jordan (1902-) collaborated with Max Born, and then Heisenberg, to set out the theory of quantum mechanics, using matrix methods. Heisenberg, in presenting his own model of the atom, abandoned all ideas that visualized the atom as composed either of particles or of waves. He made an attempt to extricate from the web of the wave-particle duality. He preferred basing his ideas on tangible quantities to intangible entities like "orbits". He described the energy levels or orbits of electrons purely in terms of numbers, without a trace of picture. He used a mathematical device called a matrix to manipulate his numbers and hence his system got the name "matrix mechanics". He received the Nobel Prize in physics in 1932 for his contribution to matrix mechanics.

In 1926, the Austrian physicist Erwin Schrödinger (1887-1961) took another look at the atom in the light of the de Broglie theory of the wave nature of particles. In the planetary model of the atom, the electrons, as particles, circle around the nucleus in the analogy of the planets circling around the Sun. Schrödinger did not accept this planetary model of the atom. He considered the electron as a wave that curves all around the nucleus. In such a view, the electron is a standing wave in all parts of its orbit at once. The different energy levels of the electrons in an atom represent different standing waves. Schrödinger analyzed this point of view mathematically and, in 1926, worked out an equation which is now called the Schrödinger wave equation. The analysis of the details of atomic behaviour on the basis of the Schrödinger wave equation is termed "wave mechanics". For this work of wave mechanics, Schrödinger shared the 1933 Nobel Prize for physics with Dirac.

Some critics asked the question: "What is waving in the wave equation?" Schrödinger answered this question in the following way: "A particle is in reality nothing but a group of waves of relatively small dimensions in every direction."

From a psychological point of view, Schrödinger's wave mechanics was more satisfactory than Heisenberg's matrix mechanics. Wave mechanics offered a picture of wave forms, whereas matrix mechanics provided an array of pictureless numbers. It was hard to grasp the numbers especially when the mind sought images for easy grasping.

In 1944, the Hungarian-American mathematician John von Neumann (1903-1957) presented arguments to show the mathematical equivalence of the matrix mechanics and the wave mechanics. In his opinion, anything that could be demonstrated by the matrix mechanics could be equally well demonstrated by the wave mechanics. Dirac, in 1964, raised doubts in the conclusion of Neumann. The two theories are not mathematically equivalent for him. He suggests that matrix mechanics more accurately fits reality.

The German physicist Max Born (1882-1970) who was the advisor of Werner Heisenberg and Ernst Pascual Jordan invented matrix mechanics. There is an interesting historical background behind this invention. Heisenberg, while working on his quantum-mechanical series, discovered a distressing asymmetry. His new quantum theory seemingly violated the commutative law of mathematics. According to this law, A X B always equals B X A. But quantum-mechanical series A multiplied by quantum-mechanical series B did not give him the same answer as quantum-mechanical series B multiplied by quantum-mechanical series A. The paper submitted by Heisenberg was seriously pondered over by his Professor Max Born who was perhaps the only European physicist with a good knowledge of matrix mathematics. By rewriting Heisenberg's equations as matrics, he explored a whole new world of applications of matrix mathematics. He figured out the noncommutativity in the quantum-mechanical series of Heisenberg. The matrix q for position and the matrix p for momentum are noncommutative in a special way. Firstly, pq is different from qp. Secondly, the difference between pq and qp is always the same irrespective of whatever p or q is chosen. Born gave a mathematical shape to these ideas and the equation he formulated is as follows:

$$pq - qp = \hbar/i$$

Here $\hbar$ is Planck's constant divided by twice pi and i is the square root of minus one. For the further development of the theory of matrix mechanics, Born sought the help of his student-scientists. Pauli, a former student of Born, declined to be associated. In 1925, Born turned to another pupil, Pascual Jordan who eagerly collaborated. They finalized the theory of matrix mechanics in 1926. In 1954, Born shared the Nobel Prize for physics with W. Bothe, the former for his work in quantum mechanics and the latter for his work in cosmic radiation. Dirac subsequently showed interest in the theory of quantum mechanics. In 1926, he blended the quantum mechanics and Schrödinger's wave mechanics into a single theory.

In 1926, Born also put forward the probability interpretation of the wave function. He worked on the wave mechanics of

Schrödinger for whom the waves were real. Born did not consider these waves as real three-dimensional ones. For him, they were probability waves, rising and falling with the likelihood that a particle might be in a given location. He conceived of the electron as a real particle, but in some sense guided by the wave. The important thing in Schrödinger's equation is the wave function which is denoted by the Greek letter psi (Ψ). The strength of the wave (more precisely, the value of Ψ^2) at any point in space is a measure of the probability of finding the particle at that particular point. It is not possible for us to locate a particle like an electron with a certainty. An electron might be anywhere. It cannot be said for sure that the electron is at point A and not at point B. According to the statistical rules, it is extremely likely to be in some locations and very unlikely to be in other. The wave function is made use of to work out the probability of locating the particle in case an experiment is designed for its location. The quantum world was already uncertain. Born's interpretation of psi (Ψ) removed some of the certainty from that uncertainty.

Born's probability interpretation of the wave function is not confined to the electron or any other single particle. It has universal implications. Nature functions statistically. Huge numbers are involved in the micro-world. Statistical laws are well applicable to large numbers. We observe the occurrence of an event. After the occurrence, it is a practicality, but before the occurrence it was a probability. It was one of the many probabilities. We cannot be sure that a certain event will occur before the actual occurrence of the event. We are able to predict the probability of the occurrence of an event.

Classical physics had a concept that an outcome can be known with certainty provided all the initial data are known. With the known initial conditions and the known cause(s), the effect is bound to be accurately known. This was the prevalent notion of all scientists before the advent of the twentieth century. Such a notion inspired Laplace to invent his famous demon calculator:

> In intelligence knowing, at any given instant of time, all forces acting in nature, as well as the momentary positions of all things of which the universe consists, would be able to comprehend the motions of the largest bodies of the world and those of the smallest atoms in one single formula, provided it were sufficiently powerful to subject all data to

> analysis; to it, nothing would be uncertain, both future and past would be present before its eyes.[2]

Such a notion of certainty, as cherished by Laplace and Newton, is no longer tenable in the age of quantum physics. It is incompatible with Born's idea of probability. The idea of certainty is expelled from the quantum world in which all things are probable.

Born's introduction of probability in quantum theory was a big blow to the concept of classical causality. It went against the philosophical concept of determinism. It gave the idea that all events in nature are purely random and that chaos reigns the universe, especially the microcosm. The word "chaos" began to be accepted in quantum physics with the definition that it is merely a synonym for randomness. The following statement of Max Born unequivocally presents his concept of indeterminism in the micro-universe:

> One does not get an answer to the question, What is the state after collision? but only to the question, How probable is a given effect of the collision? ... From the standpoint of our quantum mechanics, there is no quantity (Grösze) which causally fixes the effect of a collision in an individual event. Should we hope to discover such properties later ... and determine (them) in individual events? ... I myself am inclined to renounce determinism in the atomic world, but that is a philosophical question for which physical arguments alone do not set standards.[3]

Born's probability interpretation began with his observation in June, 1926 that the absolute square of a Schrödinger's wave function (Ψ^2) is to be interpreted as a probability density. Schrödinger did not like such a meaning of psi square on which Born built up the whole edifice of his concept of indeterminism in the events of the microcosm. Thinking that it is a misinterpretation of his wave function, Schrödinger told Niels Bohr: " I might not have published my papers had I been able to foresee what consequences they would unleash".

In Einstein's reply to one of Born's letters, the following paragraph was included:

> Quantum mechanics is very impressive. But an inner voice tells me that it is not yet the real thing. The theory produces a good deal but hardly brings us closer to the secret of the Old One. I am at all events convinced that He does not play dice.[4]

Einstein was never satisfied with the chance events of the quantum world. It was not a fact that he did not have faith in statistics. He published important papers on the random events of the molecular world and used statistics in his own theories. But he had a realization that there is something (or somebody) else below the surface phenomena of the confused randomness and the utter disorder. He made the following statement as a seer but not as a physicist:

> It seems hard to look in God's cards. But I cannot for a moment believe that He plays dice and makes use of 'telepathic' means (as the current quantum theory alleges He does).[5]

Born's probability theory and Heisenberg's uncertainty principle jointly contributed to the rise of the concept of indeterminism in quantum physics. Einstein, however, felt that the understanding of quantum phenomena did not damand a weakening of classical causality, as was done in quantum mechanics. On the contrary, he had a strong urge to strengthen classical causality as evident from the following statement:

> Natural phenomena seem to be determined to such an extent that not only the temporal sequence but also the initial state is fixed to a large extent by (physical) law. It seemed to me that I should express this idea by searching for overdetermined systems of differential equations. ... I strongly believe that we will not end up with a Subkausalität (subcausality) but that, in the indicated sense, we will arrive at an Überkausalität (supercausality).[6]

In a letter written to Einstein, Heisenberg communicated his strong favour for indeterminism by the following sentences:

> I would nevertheless like to write once more why I believe

> that indeterminism, that is, the nonvalidity of rigorous causality, is *necessary* and not just consistently possible.[7]

But Einstein adhered to the classical concept of determinism. Overdetermination continued to remain his hope for an answer to the quantum problem.

Quantum mechanics deals only with group behaviour. This theoretical system cannot account in detail for individual happenings. Einstein did not accept this concept and believed that the quantum theory was incomplete. In this connection he said: "The following requirement for a complete theory seems to be a necessary one: *every element of the physical reality must have a counterpart in the physical theory*".[8]

The wave-particle duality was an established concept in the 1920s. It was mathematically proved to be true. No physicist had any doubt in this duality of matter-wave or wave-matter. In spite of this fact, scientists could not free themselves from the puzzlement of the so-called violation of the Aristotelian logic. How can A be both B and not-B? Is it correct to violate the sacrosanct law of non-contradiction of classical logic? This confusion persisted in the science world for some decades. Einstein was the first physicist to suggest a synthesis of the apparent opposites. He said: "What nature demands from us a synthesis of these two views which thus far has exceeded the mental power of physicists".[9] This suggestion of Einstein perhaps influenced Niels Bohr (1885-1962) who came forward with his "principle of complementarity" in September, 1927. This holds that B and not-B which are properties of A and which are apparently mutually exclusive of one another are complementary. A single concept such as B or not-B describes a single aspect of A like the head or the tail of a coin. To provide complete description of A, both (B and not-B) concepts are necessary. For such a complete description of A, B complements not-B and *vice versa*. At the Volta meeting in Como, on the 16th September, 1927, Bohr enunciated for the first time the principle of complementarity. He stated: "The very nature of the quantum theory ... forces us to regard that space-time co-ordination and the claim of causality, the union of which characterizes the classical theories, as complementary but exclusive features of the description, symbolizing the idealization of observation and definition, respectively".[10] Of course, a single experiment cannot be designed to demonstrate both the corpuscular and the wave nature of light or an electron. If we want to prove that A is B, we have to design a special set of experiments. If we want to prove that A is not-B, we have to design a different set of experiments. We cannot demonstrate simultaneously that A is both B and not-B. But B is not the whole picture of A; so also is not-B. Each one of the contradictory pair of characteristics of A complements the other. In this regard, what is true for the electron or light is universally true for everything in the universe. Thus Bohr's principle of complementarity is an important contribution to the philosophy of quantum physics.

The ideas of both Bohr and Born tied in very well with the uncertainty principle (principle of indeterminancy) enunciated by Werner Heisenberg (1901-76) late in 1926. We may again consider the noncommutative mathematical relation, $pq \neq qp$, where p is the momentum of a particle (say, an electron) and q is its position. Heisenberg says that we can never be certain just what p and q are. The amount of "mistake" in our measurement of p may be called Δ p (the Greek letter delta, Δ, symbolizes small pieces of variable quantities) and the corresponding mistake in q is Δ q. Heisenberg showed that $\Delta p \times \Delta q$ must always be bigger than $\hbar$, Planck's constant divided by 2π. His famous uncertainty principle may be mathematically phrased as follows:

$$\Delta p \times \Delta q \geq \hbar$$

The more accurately we know the position of a particle, the less certain we are of its momentum, and *vice versa*. One can never quite succeed to accurately measure both the position and momentum of a particle. The uncertainty principle is not confined to the electron only; nor is it confined to the position and momentum. It is a principle which is universal to everything. It is also applied to any pair of conjugate variables, having the units of action (energy X time).

We may generalize a statement like this: There is no absolute truth at the quantum level. Such a concept clashed with the classical view of science. The classical scientist was sure of predicting the future and confident in the certainty of his empirical knowledge. Quantum physics did not agree to this idea. The future is inherently unpredictable and uncertain.

In the 1930s the philosophers took up the implications of the principle of indeterminancy to build up their concept of acausality. The classical physics maintained that every effect is necessarily caused and that the event which is an effect is preceded by another event which is the cause. It further maintained that, all conditions being common, identical causes must produce identical effects without any exception whatsoever. These concepts of causality were outright rejected by the quantum physics. The micro-world is chaotic. Everything happens there randomly. A particle appears from *nowhere*; it proliferates and suddenly disappears. A particle dashes against another one; other particles are produced out of this collision; in a fraction of a microsecond, all of them disappear. In a certain condition, effect x is observed; again in the same condition, effect y or z is observed. It is impossible for the quantum physicist to account for all the phenomena of the micro-world on the basis of strict adherence to causality.

In September, 1927, Niels Bohr presented a lecture in Como, Italy to a wide audience. Through this lecture, he conveyed two fundamental concepts to the intellectual magnets of physics; one was the principle of complementarity and the second one was the interaction of the observer and the object observed. Bohr's interpretation of quantum mechanics, as presented in this lecture, is known as the "Copenhagen interpretation". In a broader sense, this interpretation relates to a collection of ideas—Heisenberg's uncertainty principle, Born's probability theory and Bohr's complementarity and his notion of the disturbance of the system being observed by the observer. The concepts of indefiniteness, chance, probability and entanglement are implicit in the Copenhagen interpretation of quantum theory.

The uncertainty principle was the source from which Bohr developed the idea of the observer's interaction with the process observed. An electron can be detected as a particle or as a wave. Experiments designed to detect the electron as a particle always detect it as a particle. Experiments designed to detect the electron as a wave always detect it as a wave. But no experiment can show the electron behaving like a particle and a wave at the same time. The observer asks a question of the quantum world and accordingly devises an experiment to get his answer. He has to interfere with the atomic processes in order to observe the properties of the atoms and the subatomic particles. From this premise, Bohr deduces that it is meaningless to ask what atoms are doing when nobody is looking at them.

Bohr's subjectivism took a philosophical leap, leaving behind the objective outlook of classical physicists like Galileo and Newton who held that the laws of physics exist objectively, apart from the affairs of humans. A question sometimes puzzles the layman: "Does a falling tree in the forest make a sound if there is nobody to hear it?" To such a question, the solipsists and the eighteenth-century philosophers like Berkeley would answer 'no'. To such a question, the classical physicists would answer 'yes'. The quantum physicists, however, state that a falling tree in the forest does not make a sound in the absence of any one to hear it. They would rather add that there are no trees to fall if there is no one to see them. According to Bohr, reality does not exist without a measurement taking place, i.e., without someone to observe it, since the observation process creates the reality. Many traditional physicists were skeptical of this new worldview. Even the founders of quantum mechanics expressed their concern. Werner Heisenberg had conversation with Niels Bohr late into the night in 1927. He left Bohr almost in despair, walked alone in the park at about the mid-night and repeated to himself the question: "Could nature possibly be as absurd as it seemed in these atomic experiments?" Of course, the absurdity of nature is quite apparent. But, the mathematical formulas on which the quantum physicists base their new worldview are valid and resoundingly successful. This, however, could not convince the celebrated mathematician-physicist Albert Einstein who had a belief in the existence of the objective world.

Quantum mechanics does not accept anything like absolute objectivity. According to the Copenhagen interpretation, there is no reality independent of the observation of the observer. The quantum "reality" is altered by an observation and whatever appears as the reality is a product of the interaction of the observer with the process observed. The observer is therefore part of the reality he is probing. The element of conscious choice in observing reality as x or not-x implies that any picture of an observed phenomenon must include the observer's mind. In this connection, the Nobel-Prize-winning physicist Eugene Wigner deduced the following conclusion: "It was not possible to formulate the laws of quantum mechanics in a fully consistent way without reference to the consciousness (of the observer)... (Remarkably) the very study of the external world led to the conclusion that the content of the consciousness is the ultimate reality".[11]

The concept of the "participatory universe" is found as a clear exposition in John Wheeler's article contributed to the proceedings *Some Strangeness in the Proportion.*[12] Wheeler stresses the fundamental concept of quantum physics that no elementary phenomenon can be accepted as a phenomenon until it is a recorded phenomenon and that our process of recording influences reality. He considers the whole universe as a participatory, self-excited circuit. He does not recognize anything as reality in the absence of the participation of an observer. The concept of the participatory universe may not be strictly applicable to the macro-world. But everything in the macro-world is made of particles that obey the quantum rules. We call the macro-entity real; the paradox in this case is that the micro-constituents of the macro-entities cannot be regarded as real.

The double-slit experiment shows the importance of the observer in actualizing the micro-universe. Richard Phillips Feynman (1918-1988) who received the 1965 Nobel Prize for physics stresses the importance of the double-slit experiment by the following words: "The basic element of quantum theory is the double-slit experiment. Because this is a phenomenon which is impossible, *absolutely* impossible, to explain in any classical way, and which has in it the heart of quantum mechanics. In reality, it contains the *only* mystery ... the basic peculiarities of all quantum mechanics."[13]

When a light beam or an electron beam passes through a single slit, it produces a distribution on the screen with most "particles" detected in line with the slit. It has been presented in Figure 7.1.

In the double-slit experiment, the source of photons may be a lamp and that of electrons an electron-gun. The photon or the electron beam is allowed to pass through two slits or small round holes in a screen placed between the source of the beam and the detector screen. If the experiment is conducted with light, the detector may be a white surface on which light and dark bands can be seen. Alternatively, the detector may be a photographic plate which may be developed later. If the experiment is conducted with electrons, the screen may be covered in an array of electron-detectors.

When one of two holes is blocked off in turn, we get the usual pattern on the screen for single-hole experiments. When both the holes are open, we do not get the pattern produced by adding up

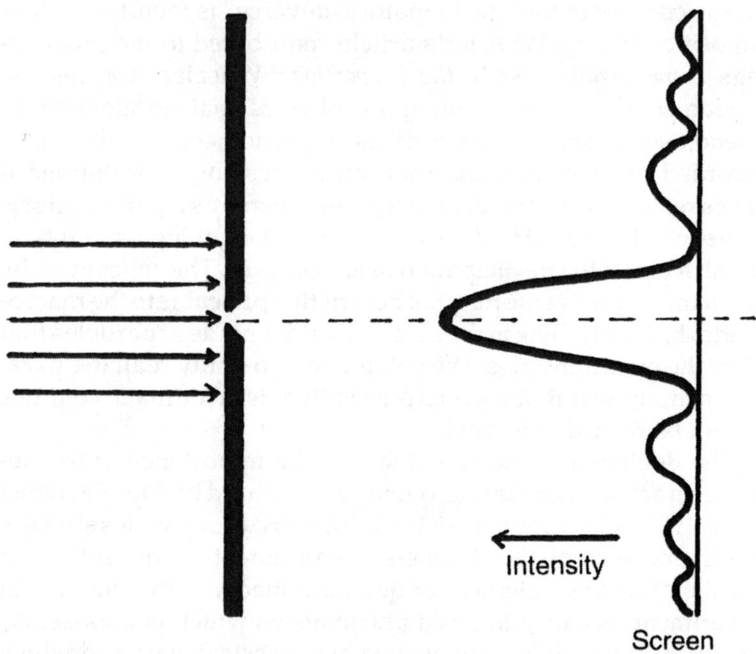

Fig. 7.1. Electron or photon beam passing through a single slit and projected on a screen.

those two patterns. Instead, a pattern for interference by waves is obtained. The pattern observed on the screen when both the holes are open has been shown in Figure 7.2. The pattern is the same for both electrons and photons.

A wave is a spread-out thing. It can pass through both the holes. But an electron is a point-like particle although it has associated wave-like properties. It is natural to expect that each individual electron must pass through one hole or the other even if both the holes are open. But, contrary to our expectation, we still get the pattern for interference by waves. We may slow down our electron gun and allow only one electron at a time. After enough electrons pass through, the pattern that builds up on the detector screen is the diffraction pattern for waves. It is interesting and surprising that a single electron or a single photon, on its way

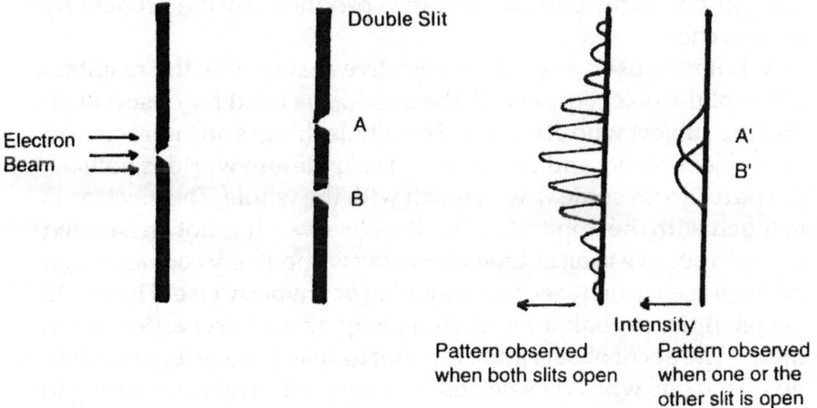

Fig. 7.2. A doublt-slit experiment with electrons or photons.

through one hole, strictly adheres to the statistical laws which are only appropriate if it "knows" whether the other hole is open or closed. Feynman emphasized this central mystery of the quantum world.

Even if we try to cheat the electron or the photon by shutting or opening one of the holes while the particle is in transit through the apparatus, the pattern on the screen is still the "right" one for the state of the holes at the instant the particle passes through.

We may devise an experiment to record which hole the particle (electron or photon) passes through. In that case, the particle is seen passing through one hole or the other, but never both at once, and the pattern that builds up on the detector screen does not show any trace of interference. The particles know whether one hole or both holes are open. They also know if someone is watching them and they adjust their behaviour accordingly. When some observer looks at the spread-out electron wave, it collapses into a definite particle and passes through only one hole. When nobody is looking, it keeps its options open. This experiment provides the clearest example of the interaction of the observer with the experiment.

The observations of the two-hole experiment may be interpreted in terms of Born's probabilities. The electron is forced to choose one course of action out of an array of available possibilities. It has a certain probability tc pass through one hole. It has an equivalent probability to pass through the other hole. The diffraction pattern on the detector screen is produced by the probability interference.

What we observe is not an objective reality. It is the resultant effect of the object observed, the apparatus used for observation and the subject who observes. The whole thing is an interaction of the subject, object and instrument. The quantum world is holistic; the parts are in some way in touch with the whole. The electron is in touch with the apparatus and the observer. It is not an isolated entity to behave in an independent way without any consideration of the presence or absence of anything or anybody else. The world keeps all its probabilities open as long as an observation is not made. The act of observation forces it to select one of its probabilities. That one which is selected becomes real. Thus, according to the Copenhagen interpretation of the quantum mechanics, the act of observing a system actualizes it.

The interference of probabilities in the double-slit experiment needs some interpretation. The electron that leaves the gun vanishes once it is out of sight. It is replaced by an array of ghost electrons, each of which traverses a different path to the detector screen. The ghosts interfere with one another. The probability interference which we observe on the detector screen is an evidence of it. The ghosts interfere with one another only when we do not look at them. When we look, all the ghost electrons except a single one vanish and this one ghost materializes as a real electron. In terms of Schrödinger's wave equation, each ghost electron corresponds to a wave or rather a packet of waves. Max Born interpreted these waves as a measure of probability. When we do not observe, all the ghost electrons correspond to the array of probability waves. The act of observation makes all the probability waves except a single packet disappear. That single packet of waves is actualized by our observation as one real electron. This phenomenon of the disappearance of the probability waves (except a single one) on our observation is called "the collapse of the wave function", which is at the heart of the Copenhagen interpretation. In Bohr's opinion, the only real things are the results of our experiments. He further adds that the way we make measurements influences what we measure. "What we see is what we get; we get what we want to see; nothing else is real". Nothing is real unless and until we look at it. What is real as long as we observe it ceases to be real as soon as we stop looking at it. Hence quantum mechanics recognizes the event only. A set of initial and final conditions is an event. In the example of the double-slit experiment, an event constitutes the leaving of the electron from the gun and its arrival on the detector screen. We cannot say if there is an electron in the interval between its leaving the gun and arriving at the detector. This concept of quantum mechanics has similarity with the phenomenalism of John Stuart Mill (1806-73). It is the view that we know only phenomena, and that there are no things behind phenomena causing their appearance. In quantum mechanics, the probability of an event is expressed by Ψ^2, the square of Schrödinger's wave function. When both the holes are open, the electron has the option of passing through either of the holes if and only if nobody is looking at it. In such a situation, the probability of each possible event is given by the square of the sum of the Ψs. There is interference in this case. But if we make an observation to know the specific hole through which the electron passes, the wave function collapses and the interference term disappears. In this situation, the probability distribution is the sum of the squares of the Ψs.

John Wheeler came up with another thought experiment, which was a variation on the double-slit experiment. He combined the two slits with a lens that focused light passing through the system. A second lens that replaced the standard screen caused photons coming from each of the two slits to diverge. A photon-detector was placed below the second lens. The second lens was covered with a photographic film arranged in strips like a venetian blind. The strips could be closed to prevent the photons from passing through the lens and being deflected. Alternatively, the strips could be opened to allow the photons to be deflected either to the left or the right and recorded by the detector. Figure 7.3 is a diagramatic presentation of Wheeler's delayed-choice double-slit experiment.

When the strips in the second lens were closed, the photons arrived at the screen just as in the classic two-hole experiment. There was no way of ascertaining the hole through which a

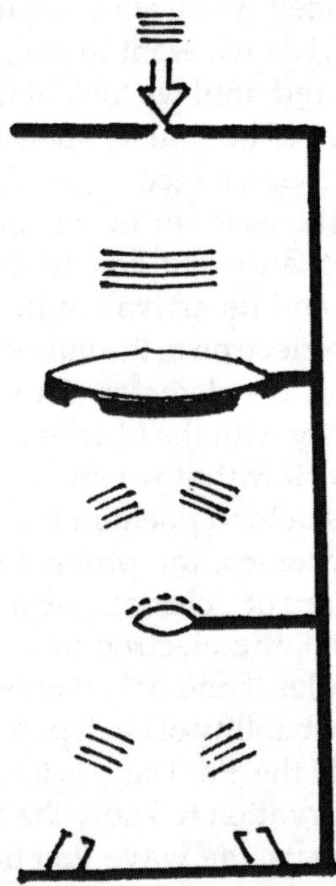

Fig. 7.3. Wheeler's delayed-choice double-slit experiment.

particular photon passed. An interference pattern was also obtained to indicate that each individual photon went through both slits at once. In a second set of experiments, the strips were open from the beginning of the experiment. In a third set of experiments, the strips were closed after the photon had passed through the first lens and was in between the first lens and the second lens. The photon behaved in the same way when the strips in the second lens were closed before or after it passed the hole(s) in the first lens. It was impossible to deceive the photon that could *know* in advance what the experimenter was going to do with the strips.

The delayed-choice experiment gives a clear indication that what we do now has an irretrievable influence on the past. Wheeler emphasizes the fundamental axiom of quantum theory that no elementary phenomenon is a phenomenon until it is a recorded phenomenon and that the process of recording decides what is to be recorded. "We have no right to say what the photon is doing until it is registered"—says Wheeler.

Wheeler and other quantum physicists who share his philosophy do not recognize anything as objective reality. The observer or participator and his process of observation influence the nature of reality, both present and past. This concept of Wheeler and similar thinkers is rejected by critics who brand it as philosophical speculation. The critics feel that such a concept is not applicable to the everyday, macroscopic world. But everything in the macroscopic world is made of particles that obey the quantum rules. The so-called real things of the macroscopic world are made of microscopic units which are not real.

Wheeler considers the whole universe as a participatory, self-excited circuit. It cannot be said whether the universe had existed before man (the observer or the participator) appeared. According to Wheeler, the universe without a participator is meaningless. Man observed the photons of the cosmic background radiation, the echo of the big-bang. By this act of observer-participancy, man gave tangible "reality" to the universe, which seems to be real now and real back in time, reversing to the singularity and the big-bang. The past of the universe, prior to the appearance of man (observer), may be explained in the light of the delayed-choice experiment.

The Copenhagen interpretation did not go unchallenged. Thinkers of the calibre of Einstein questioned the veracity of this interpretation. Einstein was the second scientist who contributed to quantum physics. Notwithstanding this historical truth, he came forward with the EPR paradox to vehemently criticize and refute the Copenhagen interpretation. The Bohr-Einstein debate on the interpretation of quantum theory began in 1927 at the fifth Solvay Congress. Einstein made correspondence with Born on the subject and the polemical nature of the exchange of ideas may be evident from a perusal of *The Born-Einstein Letters.* He continued to cherish his critical attitude towards the Copenhagen interpretation until his death in 1955.

Einstein devised some "thought experiments" to refute the Copenhagen interpretation. These were not real experiments carried out in the laboratory. Through a series of imaginary tests, Einstein made an attempt to theoretically prove that it is possible to precisely measure two conjugate variables at a time such as the position and mass of a particle. In response, Bohr and Born were trying to disprove the contentions of Einstein.

In 1934 and 1935, Einstein worked in Princeton with Boris Podolsky and Nathan Rosen to prepare a paper[14] that presented what is known as the "EPR Paradox". A pair of particles, say an electron (e^-) and a positron (e^+) interact with each other and then fly apart. After this, they do not interact with anything else until the experimenter works on one (e^-) of them. Without violating the rules of quantum theory, one can precisely measure the total momentum of the two particles and the distance between them when they are close together. When they are wide apart, one can precisely measure the momentum of one particle (e^-) which is near the experimenter. Since the total momentum must be unchanged, the momentum of the second particle (e^+) can be known by calculation. Now the position of the first particle (e^-) can be precisely ascertained. (Position and momentum can be accurately determined if measurement is done at different times.) This precise measurement of the position of particle, e^-, disturbs its momentum; but it does not disturb the momentum of the particle, e^+, which is far away. From the position measurement of particle e^-, the present position of particle e^+ can be deduced on the basis of the momentum of e^+ and the original separation of the pair. Thus both the position and the momentum of the particle e^+ can be accurately deduced in violation of the uncertainty principle. There also may be an alternative interpretation of the thought experiment. The measurements done on particle e^- here affects its partner particle e^+ there without any interval of time duration. If this is a fact, it involves a violation of causality. Secondly, "action-at-a-distance" is to be recognized if the phenomenon of an instantaneous "communication" travelling across space is accepted.

The EPR paper concluded: "It makes the reality (position and momentum in the second system) depend upon the process of measurement carried out on the first system which does not disturb the second system in any way. *No reasonable definition of reality could be expected to permit this*".[15] Einstein and his collaborators considered the Copenhagen interpretation as *incomplete*. They accepted reality as some underlying clockwork that keeps the universe running. The objective reality is at the substratum of everything. The uncertainty and unpredictability of the quantum world are appearances at the surface level only. Einstein rejected Born's introduction of probability by saying, "God may be subtle, but He is not malicious". He expressed his reluctance to accept the "chance" functioning of the quantum world. He rejected the concept of chance, randomness or chaos as the guiding principle of the universe by his famous statement, "God does not play dice". The real, objective world exists irrespective of the observation of any observer. Each particle has both position and momentum that are precisely defined even when nobody is looking at it. Bohr and his colleagues did not accept these interpretations of Einstein.

Erwin Schrödinger was another critic of the Copenhagen interpretation. He wanted to show the absurdity of the subjective implication of the Copenhagen interpretation by his imaginary experiment of the cat paradox. His cat-in-the-box paradox first appeared in print[16] in 1935. He imagined a live cat closed in a box that also contained a phial of poison and a lump of radioactive material. There was a precise 50 : 50 chance for one of the atoms of the radioactive material to decay in a certain time. A detector (say, a Geiger counter) was fitted to register the decay if it did happen. The occurrence of the radioactive decay would break the poison-container, and, if that happened, the cat would die. A person, unacquainted with quantum physics, would expect that the cat was either dead or alive, since there was fifty-fifty chance for the decay to occur. The quantum physicist, with belief in the Copenhagen interpretation, would, however, reject this "either-or" business. Without opening the box and observing the decay and the cat, the two possibilities open to the radioactive material (to decay or not to decay) as well as to the cat (to be alive or to be dead) had no reality. Without the actual observation of an observer, the atomic decay had neither happened nor not happened, and the cat had neither been killed nor not been killed. The radioactive material was in a superposition of states, and so was the cat. Once the quantum physicist looked into the box, the atom was forced into one state or the other (either decayed or not decayed); and the cat was forced to be dead or alive. The Copenhagen interpretation says that the cat inside the box existed in some indeterminate state (neither dead nor alive) until an observer observed what was going on inside the box. Schrödinger did not accept such a subjective implication of the Copenhagen interpretation.

Those physicists who argued against the Copenhagen interpretation were supporters of the hidden variables theory. It is a class of physical theories which deny that the quantum mechanical description of a physical system is a state in the sense of a complete specification. This theory does acknowledge that a system prepared in a given way is correctly described by one quantum state and not by others; but it asserts that even the correct one gives only an incomplete description. Those properties which are specified by the complete state but not by the quantum state are expressed as the "hidden variables". It is not a fact that the hidden variables are in principle inaccessible to experimental investigation. The theory does not intend to introduce a radically non-empirical element in physics.

The controversy between Bohr and Einstein persisted for about three decades. The first conceptual breakthrough came in 1964 when John Bell, a physicist working at CERN, published his paper[17] which contained what is known as the Bell's inequality. Bell's inequality concerns the probabilities of the joint occurrence of certain events in the two well separated parts of a composite system, implied by any hidden variables theory which satisfies an appropriate locality condition. The "local realistic" view of the world is based on three assumptions. First, things objectively exist regardless of whether they are observed. Second, it is proper to draw general conclusions from consistent observations. Third, no influence can propagate faster than the speed of light. This third assumption was called "locality" by Bell. If Bell's inequality is violated, the local realistic view of the world is false and the Copenhagen interpretation of quantum mechanics is true.

To test Bell's inequality, one has to do the spin measurements of material particles or measurements of the polarization of photons. Both are difficult; but the latter is relatively easier to carry out. Most of the tests of Bell's inequality carried out so far have been done by measurements of the polarization of photons.

The first tests of Bell's inequality were conducted at the University of California, Berkeley, using photons. These were reported in 1972. In the 1970s more tests were carried out by varying the details of the techniques, but by the same principle of the measurement of the polarization of photons. Majority of the tests produced results that violated Bell's inequality. Some loopholes in the experimental design remained in a few tests that could not prove the violation of Bell's inequality.

A team of physicists at the Saclay Nuclear Research Centre in France reported the results of their experiment in 1976. By using measurements of proton spins in these experiments, they obtained results that violated Bell's inequality. It was, therefore, a proof in support of the quantum view of the world.

In 1982, Alain Aspect, J. Dalibard and G. Roger at the University of Paris-South devised and conducted experiments[18] which closed the last major loophole for the local realistic theories. They placed the bits of the apparatus far apart in order to prevent any "signal" between the detectors that might produce a spurious correlation. Any signal from photon γ_1(gamma-1) to the counterpart photon γ_2 (gamma-2) must not travel at a speed faster than light. If the correlated responses of γ_1 and γ_2 cannot be mediated by any signal that cannot traverse the distance between the two photons within that short time, the question of the propagation of any signal is ruled out (unless we speculate faster than light travel, and we cannot do that since we do not have any proof that photons use the hypothetical tachyon for the purpose of sending signals). We may also think of a second loophole in the experimental design. We set up the experimental apparatus before we *create* the photons. Our apparatus may establish an overall wave function that affects the photon-pairs at birth. The photon-pairs know our experimental apparatus even when they are born. They correlate with each other because they already know and hence faster than light signal is not necessary for the correlative functions. In order to avoid this complication, the structure of the experiment is changed while the photons are in flight.

Aspect and his coworkers, before 1982, had already conducted tests of the inequality by using photons from a cascade process. They found that Bell's inequality was violated. They made an improvement to their experimental design by the use of a switch that changed the direction of a beam of light passing through it. An automatic device changed the direction of the light beam every ten nanoseconds (10×10^{-9} s). The beam was directed towards either one of the polarizing filters, each measuring a different direction of polarization. There was one photon-detector behind each polarizing filter. A photon was to take twenty nanoseconds to travel from the atom in which it was born in the heart of the experiment to the detector placed behind the polarizing filter. Hence there was no scope in this experimental set-up for any signal to travel from one photon to the other unless faster than light travel was speculated.

Without going into the experimental details, we may summarize the events that took place in Aspect's test of the inequality. Two photon-detectors were situated far apart in space. Photons generated in a central source flew off to each of these detectors. During the flying off process, the polarization of one beam of photons was changed. This resulted in changes in the polarization of the other beam of photons at the second photon-detector situated far away from the first one. The results showed that Bell's inequality was violated. Thus the Copenhagen interpretation of quantum mechanics was conclusively proved to be true and Einstein's objections could not be upheld.

When many photons are produced from a central source, they appear in pairs, one particle being the antiparticle of its interacting partner. Properties like the spin or the polarization of the particle-pairs may be considered. Before the appearance of the particle-pair, there was zero manifestation of the spin. After the appearance of the particle-pair, the total of the spins of the two partners is also zero, since the spin of one particle is always equal and opposite to the spin of its antiparticle. Any change in the spin of one particle must be simultaneously reflected in a corresponding change in its antiparticle irrespective of whether they stay close together or far away at a distance of billions of light-years. The distribution of spins in the newly generated particles results from random quantum processes. The particle-pairs fly apart in opposite directions. In spite of the spatial separation, there is a non-separability in the quantum world. When the polarization of one beam of photons is changed, that of the second beam is correlatively changed although the numerous photons in the second beam do also display random behaviour. What is true with regard to the spin or polarization is in principle universally true for the other pairs of conjugate properties of particles.

How do we explain the results of Alain Aspect and his colleagues? How does a signal propagate from photon γ_1 to photon γ_2? If an information passes from γ_1 to γ_2, it must do so at supraluminal speed. But that is not possible. No particle can travel at a speed faster than light. *Tachyon* is the particle that is postulated to always travel at a speed faster than light. However, all the particles we speak of, including the photon, are not tachyons. And we do not have any evidence for any possibility of the use of tachyons as signals by photons. Alternately, we are to accept action-at-a-distance without the mediation of any signal. No norm of rationality can entertain such a concept of action-at-a-distance. We can explain the quantum phenomenon by the holistic concept of Reality as an unbroken whole. All the macro-objects of the universe are made up of particles. All the particles that were once together in an interaction continue to remain as parts of a single system which responds together to further interactions in complete synchronicity and harmony. Immediately after the big-bang, all the micro-entities that newly appeared were in close proximity since space was also created with the big-bang and its volume was too small. The interacting particle-pairs in the new-born universe were in harmonious coordination, beginning with time t_o, and they would continue to be responsive partners of a single system until the maximum time t_m is reached. David Bohm contends that reality is holistic and that everything is connected to everything else. He postulates subquantum models in which pulses like shock waves propagate superluminally in a kind of ether and establish correlations among separated systems. In order to explain the results of the experiments of Aspect *et al.*, we have to take the help of Advaita Vedānta. The multitudinous, separate and discrete particles are seemingly unconnected at the surface level; but everything is connected with everything else at a deeper level which is the substratum of the apparent manifoldness. The substratum is a single one, homogeneous, unbroken and all-pervading. The unbroken whole is not matter; nor is it energy; it is not particulate; nor is it wavy. It is Consciousness. It is not Consciousness of somebody or something. It is Consciousness itself. It cannot be described in language. It is what it is. It cannot be said what it is. It can be indicated in deep silence as THAT (*TAT* in Sanskrit).

We cannot disregard the propagation of a signal simply by postulating an unbroken whole. The human body may be taken as an example. It is one body whose parts are seemingly connected. In spite of this apparent connectedness, electrical signal passes from the toe to the brain through the nerve if a scorpion stings. It takes some time for the signal to reach the brain. This is, however, not the case with the homogeneous and undifferentiated Consciousness which does not send a signal to Itself. In contrast, the body lacks homogeneity and is differentiated. The concept of nonlocality of the quantum physicist is applicable to Consciousness only. Advaita Vedānta uses the term Brahman for this Consciousness.

Now we may discuss the philosophical implications of the Copenhagen interpretation of quantum mechanics. We may draw parallels between the philosophy of Advaita Vedānta and that of the quantum physics.

Heisenberg's uncertainty principle is universal in application for the micro-world. We may take any pair of conjugate variables. It is impossible to precisely know both the members of the pair simultaneously. The more certain we are about one, the more uncertain does the other become.

Śaṅkara, the famous exponent of Advaita Vedānta, contends that the world is illusory. Of course, he has his own technical meaning of the word "illusion". In his opinion, anything which is illusory cannot be cognized with precision. In this context, his views on the uncertainty may be noted from the following: "Its form, as described here, cannot be determined with any degree of certainty. It is apparent like a dream, water of a mirage or a city in the sky. It is fugitive, its own form being evinced and not evinced. Therefore, it has no end, no fixity, no determinancy; it never stays as a particular form exclusive of other forms; it can never be determined conclusively. Similarly, it has no beginning; nobody can determine it as starting from something and becoming something definite. Nobody can determine it as having any definite existence or intermediate existence".[19]

The micro-entities of the micro-world are numerous. Each micro-entity functions randomly. Chance plays a dominant role in the functioning of the micro-world, where nothing is determined and caused. The outcome of any individual event of the micro-world cannot be predicted with any degree of certainty. All entities and all events of the micro-world are chaotic. There prevails disorder instead of order. But, in spite of the utter chaos of the micro-world, the probability of the outcome of the totality can be predicted without any reference to an individual micro-entity. Nature obeys the rules of the statistical probabilities.

Werner Heisenberg's principle of indeterminancy and Max

Born's theory of probability prompted philosophers to develop a concept of acausality. According to this acausal theory, our observations on the cause and effect relationship are merely empirical; but there is no logical necessity for an event to be caused. The quantum physicists observe the functioning and the behaviour of the micro-entities of the micro-world. Particles suddenly appear from *nowhere*. They proliferate into a number of particles with larger and smaller mass with the violation of the *sacrosanct* law of conservation of mass and energy. They rush madly and randomly. They collide against other particles. They annihilate one another with the liberation of energy. They suddenly disappear. One cannot say wherefrom they appear and why they do so. One cannot guess why they run a mad race. One cannot ascertain the reason of their erratic, random behaviour. It does not seem that each micro-event of the micro-world is caused. A chaotic play of chance reigns supreme in the world of the micro-entities. There does not seem to be any rule or law in the micro-world; if there is any, it is the rule of the jungle, unsystematic, uncoordinated and irrational.

Advaita Vedānta does recognize the chaos (*anṛta*)[20] prevalent in the universe. But it holds that order (*ṛta*),[21] functioning amidst disorder (*anṛta*), is the guiding principle of the universe. Order and disorder are coupled in the proper functioning of the world (*satyānṛte mithunīkṛtya*).[22]

It was a wrong conception of some quantum physicists who mistook the disorder of the micro-world as lawless behaviour. The whole science of statistics has been evolved on the foundation of chance events. Whether it is normal distribution, or any other distribution, the random behaviours of the multitudinous entities follow a statistical equation and conform to a definite pattern. What superficially seems to be a chaos is really a cosmos at the deeper level. A popular non-quantum example may be cited here to show that what seems to be a disorder is really a meaningful order. Every ovum carries the sex-chromosome X whereas every sperm carries the sex-chromosome X or Y. On the fusion of an ovum and a sperm to make a zygote, the sex-chromosome combination is either XX or XY. The former is a girl whereas the latter is a boy. Many millions of sperms are present in the semen of a single ejaculation. All of them run a race, swim up the female genital tract to fertilize the ovum in one of the two uterine tubes.

Only one sperm succeeds to first reach and penetrate the ovum. It is purely a chance action for any sperm to get the success. It is impossible to definitely predict which particular sperm will fertilize the ovum. But the 50 per cent probability of getting a daughter or a son can be predicted. All the random events in this particular example obey the binomial equation that was discovered by Isaac Newton. If one observes the random behaviour of the sperms while they swim up the genital tract, one is awed at the sheer chaos. But for this chaos, the 50 : 50 (approximate) male : female ratio in a zoological species would have been upset. A built-in disorder is meant for a necessary order. The study of chaos is an important activity of many mathematicians at present. What seem to be unpredictable and apparently random structures are studied by using topology and computers in modern mathematics. Such studies reveal universal and fundamental laws of a remarkably simple kind.

From the macro-world we plunge into the micro-world, where everything is chaos, nothing is determined and all events happen randomly. From these premises, the materialists draw their general conclusions that the whole universe is rooted in chaos and the existence as well as the functioning of the universe is simply fortuitous. The biological philosophy of Jacques Monod (who shared the Nobel Prize of 1965) on the primacy of chance may be quoted here:

> Among all the events possible in the universe the *a priori* probability of any particular one of them occurring is next to zero. Yet the universe exists; particular events must occur in it, the probability of which (before the event) was infinitesimal ... It offends our very human tendency to believe that everything real in the world is necessary, and rooted in the very beginning of things. We must be constantly on guard against this notion, this powerful feeling of destiny. Immanence is alien to modern science. Destiny is written as and while, not before, it happens.[23]
>
> The ancient covenant is in pieces; man at last knows that he is alone in the unfeeling immensity of the universe, out of which he emerged only by chance. Neither his destiny nor his duty have been written down. The kingdom above or the

darkness below: it is for him to choose.[24]

Some philosophers, both scientists and non-scientists, stretch the quantum chance events too far. They do not care to study nature in its entirety. Without getting a total vision of the underlying as well as the overlying processes of the micro-world, they rush to the naive conclusion that everything exists and functions in the universe by chance. They lose sight of the hidden factor, the substratum that guides and coordinates both the disorder and order of the universe. Scientists who are profound thinkers spot out the mystery of the order of the disorder.

The Vedāntic concept of causality is not the same as in science and Western philosophy. Vedānta recognizes two types of causes, viz., efficient cause (*nimitta kāraṇa*[25]) and substantial or material cause (*upādāna kāraṇa*[26]). Every verb has a subject, whether expressed or understood. If there is an action (*kriyā*), there must be a doer (*kartā*) of the action. Such a statement is analytical. The doer of the action is the efficient cause of the action. A particle suddenly appears and moves at a high velocity. No event, precedent to this event, is evinced, and hence the quantum physicist says that the action of the particles is uncaused. Vedānta does not agree to this view. The efficient cause of the action of the particle is the particle itself.

No transformation is involved in many actions. In such cases, the action has its efficient cause only. But, in some other actions, something is converted into something else. If C is converted into E, C is the material or substantial cause. In each event of transformation, something C is transformed into something E. Such a statement is also analytical. A neutron is transformed into a proton, an electron and an antineutrino. In this case, the neutron is the material cause of the three products mentioned.

In the causal concept of the Vedānta, there is nothing else other than what has been said here. There is no commitment here regarding sufficient reasons, sufficient justifications and an adequate rationality of the occurrence of an event. An action may be absurd, unreasonable, unjustifiable and irrational and still it has necessarily some efficient cause(s). If transformation is involved in the action, it has necessarily some material cause(s). Of course, it needs empirical verification to identify the efficient as well as the material cause. The identification is not *a priori*. Nevertheless, it is a necessary truth that all events are caused (in the Vedāntic sense discussed here). Actions that do not involve transformations are acted by something or somebody. That something or somebody may or may not be external to the agent of the action. What we call agent of the action is the efficient cause. In actions involving transformations, the precursor substance that becomes the product is the substantial or material cause. In such actions, the efficient cause may be identical to the material cause, or alternatively, both the causes may not be the same. All manifested entities are ever in motion and they cease to exist when they cease to move. All manifested entities are ever mutable. Only Brahman is timelessly motionless, actionless, formless, attributeless and immutable. Only Brahman is beginningless and endless. Such a Being without becoming is uncaused and is not a cause of any entity or event. This is the causal and the acausal concepts of Advaita Vedānta.

What chaotic picture has been presented in quantum physics holds good for the micro-events of the micro-world only. However, it would not be correct if the universe in totality is considered as chaotic. The Vedas declare a deterministic, cyclic universe.[27] Both determinism and indeterminism can be accommodated in the Vedic and Vedāntic concepts. The chaos or randomness observed by the quantum physicist is accepted as a fact. The apparent acausality in the quantum world is also accepted as a fact. Advaita Vedānta does not have any conflict with quantum physics on this point. But the bone of contention centres around the core concept of reality. The term "reality", as used in quantum physics, is at variance with that used in Advaita Vedānta. An in-depth analysis of quantum physics reveals that there is really no reality. In contrast, Brahman or Absolute Consciousness is the Absolute Reality for the nondualist for whom the empirical universe is a relative reality for empirical purposes only. The Vedāntic concept of Unmanifest (*avyakta*) is not prevalent in science or in the Western philosophy. Concepts like field or space in the twentieth-century physics cannot be accepted by the Vedāntin as Unmanifest, although these entities cannot be directly observed by our senses. All entities that have been created, that have manifested in perceptible or imperceptible forms and that have beginnings and ends are manifested becomings (*vyaktabhūtāni*). *Māyā*, the power of Brahman, is the Unmanifest (*avyakta*) in Advaita Vedānta. Brahman, the Absolute Existence, cannot be grasped by our senses. *Avyakta* or *Māyā* or the Unmanifest is also sense-imperceptible. Although attributeless Brahman is neither the efficient nor the material cause, *Īśvara* (Brahman with attributes) is the efficient cause of the universe. *Māyā*, the power of Brahman, is the material cause of the universe. Quantum physics does not recognize the Unmanifest; it does not accept a Being (Brahman) beyond the phenomenal becomings. Here lies the problem of the fallacy of acausality. The quantum physicist observes the micro-entities of the micro-world; he observes the micro-events of the micro-entities. These are the consequent entities and events. The antecedent entities or events remain unobserved. And so does the quantum physicist infer that there is no necessary cause of an event and there is no precursor substance of an entity. Such an inference is not valid, however.

Advaita Vedānta considers the universe as an illusion. It is not non-existent. But it exists illusorily. It is not real in the sense that it is ever mutable, that it evinces mutually exclusive contradictory properties and that it cannot be ascertained with an accuracy. *Māyā*, the precursor of the universe, is indescribable (*anirvacanīya*[28]); it cannot be said that it exists; it cannot be said that it does not exist; and it cannot be said that it exists and does not exist. This Vedāntic concept of illusion and indescribability implies that utter absurdity prevails in any state of the functioning of the universe. That everything in the universe is neat and mathematically precise and that every event occurring in the universe is strictly caused, as understood in Newtonian physics or the classical Western philosophy, are not expected to conform to the psychedelic concept of the Vedāntic illusion.

According to quantum physics, all the micro-entities of the micro-world are not real. They cannot be measured with precision. They cannot be accurately described. Their actions cannot be precisely predicted. They live as ghost entities, as myriads of potentialities. On the observation of an observer or on the participation of a participator, one of the potentialities actualizes and the rest vanish. The particles or the ghost particles are *conscious* of our observation and accordingly they change their behaviour. They are *conscious* of our would-be actions before the actual occurrence of our actions and, because of this prior knowledge of the particles about our would-be manipulation of the instruments of measurements, they cleverly change their course of action in order to avoid being cheated. This type of psychophysics that has been discovered in the later half of the twentieth century is compatible with the philosophy of Advaita Vedānta. Śaṅkara holds that the so-called insentient particles are conscious (*cetanāvantaḥ sthāvarāḥ*[29]).

Consciousness is inseparably associated with willing. A volitional action is not necessarily preceded by any event. Although it is outrageous to express something like "volition of a quantum particle", such expression is not unacceptable to Śaṅkara's Advaita Vedānta according to which nonliving entities, in which the Universal consciousness (*Cit*) is reflected, gain consciousness. A person X wills to stand up and he stands up. In this example, no precedent event is the cause of the consequent standing up of X. Similar is the situation of a photon or an electron that jumps out of the unobserved field and dips into the same field. If quantum physics accepts the Vedāntic contention that particles are conscious, its problem of the interpretation of the behaviour of the microcosm would vanish.

The many-worlds interpretation of Hugh Everett may be mentioned here. He developed this idea in his Ph.D. thesis while he was a graduate student at Princeton University in the 1950s. John Wheeler encouraged Everett in this development of the many-worlds interpretation of quantum mechanics as an alternative approach to the collapses of the wave functions in Schrödinger's theory. Everett's interpretation implies the existence of an infinite number of worlds existing parallel to our universe but for ever cut off from it. In contradistinction to Schrödinger's collapsing wave functions, Everett thinks that the overlapping wave functions of the whole universe do not collapse. All of them exist in their own parts of superspacetime and are equally real. When we make a measurement at the quantum level, we are forced by the process of observation to select one of these alternatives. What we select becomes our own "real" world. Each of the other alternatives is a world which we do not see. The act of our observation cuts the ties that bind alternative realities together. And so they are not real for us since they go on their own separate ways through superspacetime, to be observed not by us but by other observers for whom they become real.

Some physicists are sceptical of Everett's many-worlds interpretation. It may be a fact; it may not be. Whatever may be the case, Schrödinger's collapse of the wave function or Everett's multi-worlds, each one of these psychedelic quantum phenomena is compatible with the doctrine of illusion of Advaita Vedānta. One cannot question why a magical trick shows W_1, W_2, W_3, ... W_∞. After all, these Ws are not real and are apparent to the psyche only. Each W is a world in Everett's interpretation. Of course, the difference lies in Everett's use of the word "real". He contends that each world out of the infinite number of worlds is real for its respective observer. Perhaps his use of the word "real" is different from that of Advaita Vedānta.

Bohr says that only that thing which is observed is real. With reference to the quantum world, his concept of reality is restricted to what is recorded or registered in experiments. An electron appeared in space at point A; it disappeared; it then appeared at point B. According to Bohr's interpretation, we cannot say that an electron, e^-, that appeared at point A jumped to point B; we cannot say that it is the same electron which appeared at both the points. He bewares of intrapolation and extrapolation. We have no right to say that the electron exists when it is not observed.

Bohr was very much influenced by Ernst Mach (1838-1916). Bohr's emphasis was on reality, only when it was observed, and our noncommitment or silence about what was not observed, what was not experimentally registered or recorded. Mach was the Austrian theoretical physicist who fundamentally reappraised the philosophy of science. He was the father of logical positivism. Mach recommended to discard the abstract and untestable models and concepts of science. He believed that all information about the world come through sensations and anything that is not sensed or that is not observable is meaningless and hence is to be discarded. This idea of Mach was adopted by the philosophers of the Vienna Circle who propounded the doctrine of the logical positivism that laid excessive stress on the verification principle. Mach influenced the authors of quantum mechanics, particularly the Copenhagen school of Bohr.

Bohr's philosophy of subjectivism denies an objective world. His views may be compared with those of George Berkeley (1685-1753) whose philosophy is perhaps the simplest version of idealism. For him the universe consists of the infinite mind of God, the finite minds created by God and the ideas possessed or experienced by these minds. He does not accept the existence of material things that exist independently of minds. He declares: *Esse est percipi* or "to be is to be perceived". He calls his views "immaterialism", claiming that nothing material exists. He agrees with Locke on the point that all ideas originate in sense experience. When he says that he perceives an object which is red, he perceives just the red colour which he actually experiences and not some unknown substratum in which this sensory quality is supposed to inhere. He asserts that qualities are sensations or mental entities and that it must not be inferred that they belong to some substance which is altogether different in character. Hence he concludes that nothing exists but thinking minds and their thoughts. Berkeley rejects conceptualism. He does not recognize the universals. In his opinion, abstract ideas do not correspond to any reality external to themselves. He carries the nominalistic doctrine to its extreme. His denial of abstract ideas leads to his denial of matter.

The French philosopher Destutt de Tracy coined the word "ideology" to characterize his philosophy that trusts sense impressions akin to the impulses of British empiricism. Both Berkeley's idealism and Tracy's ideology contain some amount of empiricism.

Bohr's subjectivism and Berkeley's idealism have common elements. But Bohr, being a physicist, does not commit anything on the infinite mind of God and the finite minds created by God. He does give emphasis on the consciousness of the observer, his instrumentality of observation, the device of his experimentation and the object observed, all of which interact to create the reality. As in idealism and ideology, Bohr's emphasis on sense experience contains the element of empiricism.

The Copenhagen interpretation rejected anything like the objective world. According to it, there is no object without a subject, without the consciousness of the subject. The observer, his instrumentality as well as his device of observation and the object observed interact or participate in the creation of reality. Hence Bohr's philosophy is one type of subjectivism although it may not be equated with solipsism. Bohr's subjectivism does not suggest relativity with reference to the individual observer, because whatever irreversible registration occurs at the conclusion of a measurement is accessible to many observers, and the available information can be unambiguously communicated.

According to the Copenhagen interpretation, there is no reality without an observer and his observation. A pertinent question pops: Had there been a world before man was evolved? The big-bang occurred about fifteen billion (15×10^9) years ago. Less than ten million years ago, creatures who closely resembled human beings evolved. Only a few million years ago, the first true humans emerged. Then how could there be a world without an observer? John Wheeler considers the whole universe as a participatory self-excited circuit via the mechanism of the delayed-choice experiment. By observing the photons of the cosmic background radiation, the echo of the big-bang, man created the big-bang and gave tangible "reality" to the universe.

In the Copenhagen interpretation, much emphasis is laid on the consciousness which is a property of the observer. The *consciousness* of the particles that are observed is also referred to. But this has no connection with the universal consciousness (Brahman) of Advaita Vedānta. The Consciousness (*Cit*) of Advaita Vedānta is not a property of anything and is the primary, fundamental entity which is the substratum of the whole universe and on which the existence of the empirical universe depends.

According to Advaita Vedānta, anything that has manifested in the universe is bound to be bipolar. The unmanifested condition is the zero-property state. On manifestation, every pair of the manifested entity possesses plus and minus properties so that the total is zero. Each member of the pair is also not unipolar. Its two poles are opposite to each other. It is like a coin with a head and a tail side. It cannot be said if any one of the two sides is the real coin. In order to comprehend the entity in its entirety, one has to consider the two poles which are exclusive of each other. Bohr's principle of complementarity is in conformity with the bipolar (*dvandva*) concept of Advaita Vedānta.

The principle of complementarity is, however, confined to the illusory, phenomenal world. It is not applicable to the noumenon that is the substratum (*adhiṣṭhāna*) of everything that is phenomenal. Quantum physics (with the exception of the private beliefs of some quantum physicists) does not recognize the substratum which is free from dualities (*nirdvandva*). Brahman or *Cit* or the Absolute Consciousness is the substratum that is the only Reality for the non-dualist. Brahman is neither unipolar nor bipolar. Nor is It multipolar. It is in fact apolar. According to Advaita Vedānta, we cannot say that Brahman is X, that Brahman is not-X and that Brahman is both X and not-X. Hence Bohr's principle of complementarity is not applicable to Brahman.

The use of the word "real" in Bohr's philosophy is at variance with that in Advaita Vedānta. Under the influence of Mach, Bohr stresses that what is observed, recorded or registered in experiments is real. In his theory of knowledge, sense-perception is depended upon. Reality is defined in Advaita Vedānta as that which exists timelessly in an unchangeable or immutable condition, which is in the nature of pure consciousness, which cannot be cognized by our senses, and which is immeasurable, illimitable and indescribable. Reality, as defined here, is designated by the word "Brahman". Bohr measures his "reality" and verifies it with sense-perception. Advaita Vedānta asserts that "reality" cannot be measured, that it cannot be perceived by senses and that it cannot be verified. The quantum physicists are confused over the use of the word "reality". The observed particle is real, as said by Bohr. But, again, the quantum theory says that all the particles, all the micro-entities of the micro-world are not real. According to Advaita Vedānta, Brahman or Consciousness is reflected in the entities that are manifestations of *Māyā*, and consequently, the created entities acquire varying degrees of consciousness, depending upon the level of their evolutionary development. Man, being the highest evolved species on the Earth, is the most conscious animal. But, the so-called insentient (*jaḍa*) entities like the particles are not completely devoid of consciousness. Everything is known through Brahman or Consciousness,[30] but there is no way to know Consciousness itself. "Who can know the Knower?" This question is posed by the seer of the Bṛahadāraṇyaka Upaniṣad in a number of places.[31] Brahman cannot be perceived by our senses and thought of by our mind; rather our senses and mind function through Brahman.[32] The fundamental entity, Brahman, is necessarily indeterminable (*aparimeya*,[33] *aprameya*[34]) since it is dimensionless (*amātra*[35]), spaceless (*anākāśa*[36]), timeless (*akāla*[37]), without inside (*anantara*[38]) and without outside (*abāhya*[39]).

No language can accurately describe the reality as conceived of in the Advaita Vedānta. A language is used to describe something that has attributes, functions, forms, dimensions, etc. Brahman, being objectless (*aviṣaya*[40]), attributeless and functionless, cannot be described by the language. Hence says the *Taittirīya*

Upaniṣad, "Whence words recoil" (*yato vāco nivartante*[41]).

The Upaniṣadic seer, while describing Brahman in a negative language,[42] expresses his sheer inability in using any language for Brahman. A contradictory language[43] is also used for the description of the indescribable reality. The correct attitude of the seer is appropriately expressed by "not this (*neti*[44])" when he is provocatively urged by his disciple to describe Brahman in a positive way. In this connection, Śaṅkara says, "That can be indicated, but not expressed (*tallakṣyate, na tūcyate*[45]).

The classical logic is inapplicable to Brahman. The law of non-contradiction and the law of excluded middle of the Aristotelian logic are not adequate for proving or disproving the validity of statements used in Advaita Vedānta as well as quantum physics. The logic which is applicable to the psychedelic phenomena of quantum physics is called quantum logic. A great deal of similarity exists between Advaita (non-dualistic) logic and quantum logic.

Quantum physics recognizes the surfs, bubbles and ripples that appear on the surface water of the deep ocean. But the water at the deep level of the ocean is not a subject-matter of science in general and quantum physics in particular. The particles that are experimentally observed, registered or recorded are discussed as "real" or "unreal". Some quantum physicists do realize within themselves the underlying substratum (*adhiṣṭhāna*) of the phenomenal micro-universe, but they shy away from uttering anything about the noumenon, or they think it unscientific to do so. The failure of the recognition of the deep-level substratum is *the* reason for the lack of success in explaining three important obervations of quantum physics. First, the microparticles are created from a vacuum or a void and the whole universe is created from nothing. Second, a particle like a photon or an electron *knows* whether an observer is watching it and playing any trick with it. Third, the conjugate particles that are separated by a distance send message to each other at a speed faster than that of light; or, alternatively, they are interconnected at a deeper level.

The *ex nihilo* concept of creation can be rejected outright by logical considerations. The statement "Something is nothing" or "Something = Nothing" is self-contradictory and hence cannot be a fact. This is not a synthetic statement and does not need experimental verification for proving its truth or falsity. If the statement is self-contradictory, i.e., if the subject and the predicate contradict each other, it cannot be true. That something cannot be nothing and nothing cannot be something has been clearly mentioned in the Bhagavadgītā (*nāsato vidyate bhāvo nābhāvo vidyate sataḥ*[46]). Again, Vedānta considers that "nothing" or "a void" is a nonsensical concept. The concept of existence implies something existing. "The void (*śūnya*) exists" is a meaningless statement. Some X may exist at spacetime Y_1 and may not exist at Y_2. This may be accepted. But the statement "A vacuum exists" or "Nothing exists" cannot be accepted. It has already been discussed in some previous chapters of this book that space or *ākāśa* is an entity. It is ever in interaction with other forms of matter (including energy). According to the Vedāntic view, *ākāśa* is born at the beginning of the manifestation of the universe and has an end at the dissolution of the universe. Particles do originate from space; but they do not originate from nothing, since space is something.

Advaita Vedānta has its own concept of Consciousness (*Cit*) and consciousness (*cetanā*). Brahman that is pure Consciousness is primary and fundamental. This Consciousness is reflected in everything that is manifested. As a result, all manifested entities, without exception, acquire consciousness. In the Vedāntic view, matter (including energy) is a product of the power (*śakti*) of Consciousness (without the process of conversion or *pariṇāma*). But Consciousness is not a product of matter and energy. Depending on the evolutionary stage and consequently on the structural development, the nature and degree of consciousness vary from entity to entity. Nevertheless, it is not confined to man or the animals. Whether it is a proton, an electron or a photon, it is not deprived of consciousness. The sentience or insentience is relative. A comparatively less conscious entity is insentient when considered relative to a highly developed conscious entity. But, in absolute sense, it is not totally devoid of consciousness. All manifested entities are functional and they cannot be functional without the possession of something of consciousness. The *Bible* assigns a soul to each human being and declares that all animals, plants and non-living things are soulless. The Western tradition associates consciousness with the soul. The Vedāntic view is different from that of the *Bible*. According to Advaita Vedānta, everything in the universe is pervaded by Brahman and the individual self (*ātmā*) is not different from the cosmic Self (*Paramātmā* or Brahman). Irrespective of the living or non-living, everything has a self (*ātmā*). It may be called *jīvātmā* in the case of a living being (human or non-human) or *bhūtātmā* in the case of a lifeless entity. The electron or the photon has a *bhūtātmā*. The *ātmā* or self is identified with Self which is Brahman or Consciousness. Hence a particle with a *bhūtātmā* cannot be devoid of consciousness. If this concept which is outrageous in the world of science is accepted, the consciousness of the electron or the photon in the double-slit experiment may be very well explained.

It has experimentally been verified that two members of a photon pair separated by a long distance communicate with each other at superluminal speed. As a fact, they work synchronously as two sympathetic partners of a total entity in observance of the laws inherent in their existence of the totality. If it is presumed that they send signals at superluminal speed, the special theory of relativity (the speed of light in a vacuum is the maximum attainable) of Einstein is violated. Hence this concept is to be rejected. The alternative concept that everything in the universe is connected to everything else may be examined. Quantum mechanics does not identify the connecting medium of all the separate entities. Even if we presume that there is a cementing medium, we cannot rule out the necessity of sending signals from one particle to its companion particle located at a distance. There is a necessity to send signals from the stomach to the brain or from the brain to the lungs of an individual person whose organs, tissues and cells are connected in his body. Hence this alternative concept cannot be upheld since it does not satisfactorily explain the observed phenomena.

Quantum mechanics gets an explanation if it adopts the Brahman concept of Advaita Vedānta. Brahman is pure Consciousness which is one, nondual, unbroken (*akhaṇḍa*) and undifferentiated (*avyākṛta*). The example of an individual body given in the foregoing paragraph is one that is differentiated into billions of units (cells). It is not necessary for the nondualistic,undifferentiated Consciousness to send signals to itself. Brahman or Consciousness is the substratum (*adhiṣṭhāna*) of everything in the universe. This substratum is the Reality and everything else is an appearance. The substratum is the absolute existence (*satya*) and all the manifested entities have relative existence dependent on the Absolute. The substratum is formless, attributeless and functionless and hence is immutable and space-time-less. The manifestations are transient and modifiable. They appear; they undergo modifications; they disappear. This substratum is to be recognized by quantum mechanics and then only it can get an integral picture of the whole and a coherent explanation of all the bizarre phenomena of the quantum world.

Quantum mechanics was born in the year 1900 when Max Planck discovered the quanta nature of radiation. What was hitherto considered as continuous was proved to be discrete or discontinuous. Thus quantum mechanics started with the concept of pluralism. In the same twentieth century, it has undergone a complete metamorphosis from pluralism to non-dualism. Now it is accepted that matter is not primary, that the particles of matter are not primary, that energy is not primary, that the quanta of energy are not primary, and that the fundamental reality is Consciousness which is not related to anything (*nirviṣaya*) in the absolute sense.

NOTES

1. A. Einstein, quoted by Gribbin J., In: *In Search of Schrödinger's Cat,* Wildwood House, London, 1984, p. 82.
2. Quoted by P.C.W. Davis and J. Brown, In : *Superstrings*, Cambridge University Press, Cambridge, 1988, p. 3.
3. M. Born, quoted by A. Pais, In : *Subtle is the Lord*, Oxford University Press, London, 1982, p. 442.
4. A. Einstein, quoted by A. Pais, *idem.*, p. 443.
5. A. Einstein, quoted by A. Pais, *idem.*, p. 440.
6. A. Einstein, quoted by A. Pais, *idem.*, p. 465.
7. A. Einstein, quoted by A. Pais, *idem.*, p. 444.
8. A. Einstein, B. Podolsky and N. Rosen, "Can Quantum Mechanical Description of Physical Reality be Considered Complete ?", *Physical Review*, 1935, Vol. 47, pp. 777-80.
9. A. Einstein, quoted by A. Pais, *idem.*, p. 443.
10. M. Born, quoted by A. Pais, *idem.*, p. 444.
11. E. P. Wigner, In: E.P. Wigner, ed., *Symmetries and Reflections,* Indiana University Press, Bloomington, Indiana, 1967, p. 172.
12. J. Wheeler, Article contributed to the Proceedings "Some Strangeness in the Proportion", *Proceedings of the Centenary of Einstein's Birth*, ed., Harry Woolf, Ch. 22, Addison-Wesley, Reading, Massachusetts, 1980.
13. R. Feynman, R. Leighton, and M. Sands, *The Feynman Lectures on Physics*, Vol. III, Addison-Wesley, Reading, Massachusetts, 1981.

14. Same as reference 8.
15. A. Einstein, Quoted by A. Pais, In : *Subtle is the Lord*, Oxford University Press, London, 1982, p. 456.
16. *Naturwissenschaften*, 1935, Vol. 23, p. 812.
17. J.S. Bell, *Physics*, Vol. 1, p. 195, 1964.
18. *Physical Review Letters*, Vol. 49, p. 1804, 1982.
19. BGŚB, XV.3.1.
20. BU, V. 5.1; CU, I.2.3; VI.16.1; VII.2.1; VII.7.1; VIII.3.1-2; MTU, VI. 34; VII.10-11; MUU, IIII.1.6; PU, I.16; VI.1; TU, II.6.1; GMK, I.12.
21. ṚV. X.90.1; KTU I.3.1; II.2.2; MNU, I.6; II.6-7; V.5; VIII.1; XII.1; TU, I.1.1; I.9.1; I.12.1; II.4.1; III.10.6.
22. BSŚB, Intr.
23. J. Monod, *Chance and Necessity*, Collins Fontana Books, Glasgow, 1974; p. 136-37.
24. *Ibid.*, p. 167.
25. BS, II.2.2; BSŚB, I.1.2; I.1.5; I.1.10; I.1.11; II.2.1; II.2.2; ŚU, VI.9; BGŚB, XIII.19; XIV.3; Bhā, III.5.25.
26. BSŚB, I.2.22; I.4.2; I.4.3; II.1.14; ŚU, I.3; ŚUŚB, I.3; BGŚB, IV.6; VII.6; VII.14; VII.25; IX.7; IX.8; XIII.5; XIII.19; XIII.29; XIV.3-4; XV.1; XV.4; XV.16; Bhā, III.5.25; VC, 108-109.
27. ṚV, X.190.3; BS, I.3.30; BSŚB, I.3.30; VPu, I.5.59-61; MBh, ŚP, 231.48-49.
28. ŚUŚB, I.9.
29. CUŚB, VI. 11.2.
30. KTU, II.1.3; KTUŚB, II.1.3; KNU, I.2.
31. BU, II.4.14; III.4.2; III.7.23; IV.5.15.
32. KNU, I.3; I.5-9; KTU, II.2.15; MUU, II.2.11; ŚU, VI.14.
33. BG, XVI.11.
34. BU, IV.4.20; MTU, V.1; VII.1; BG, II.18; XI.17; XI.42.
35. BU, III.8.8; MAU, 12; GMK, I.23; I.29.
36. BU, III.8.8.
37. MTU, VI.14.
38. BU, II.5.19; III.8.8; IV.5.13; GMK, I.26.
39. BU, II.5.19; III.8.8; IV.5.13; GMK, I.26.
40. BSŚB, I.1.4; BGŚB, II.25.1.
41. TU, II.9.1.
42. BU, III.8.8.
43. IU, 4 & 5; MUU, III.1.7; BG, XIII.15.
44. BU, II.3.6; III.9.26; IV.2.4; IV.4.22; IV.5.15.
45. TUŚB, II.6.1.
46. BG, II.16.

VIII

UNIFICATION

NOT ONLY IN philosophy, but also in science, man has been in search of a unity. Diversity is ubiquitous. Plurality seems to be the rule. But, amongst the seeming diversity, there is an underlying unity, which is not apparent at the surface level. Fields, forces and their unification will be the subject-matter of this chapter.

Michael Faraday (1791-1867), the English chemist and physicist, is credited as the creator of the classical field theory. In 1845, he developed the idea that the forces of electricity, magnetism, light and gravity are connected. He was able to demonstrate that polarized light is affected by a magnetic field.

Faraday developed his field theory from simple observations of magnetic behaviour. In 1831, he took a bar magnet, placed a sheet of paper over it, sprinkled iron filings on the paper and jarred the paper. The iron filings moved about and took up an orientation, as shown in Figure 8.1. The filings followed lines that curved from one pole of the magnet to the other. They crowded together near the poles and spread apart at greater distances. Each line began at one pole and ended at the other, without crossing of any two lines. Faraday called these lines as the magnetic lines of force. He believed them to have real existence. He visualized them to be made of some elastic material that was stretched when extended between two unlike poles and that exerted a force tending to shorten itself. In the opinion of Faraday, this shortening tendency accounted for the magnetic attraction.

Another observation of Faraday was very important in the development of science. An electrically charged object also behaved like a magnet. He discovered electric lines of force just like the magnetic lines of force.

The French physicist Charles-Augustin Coulomb (1736-1806) made precise measurements of the forces between charged

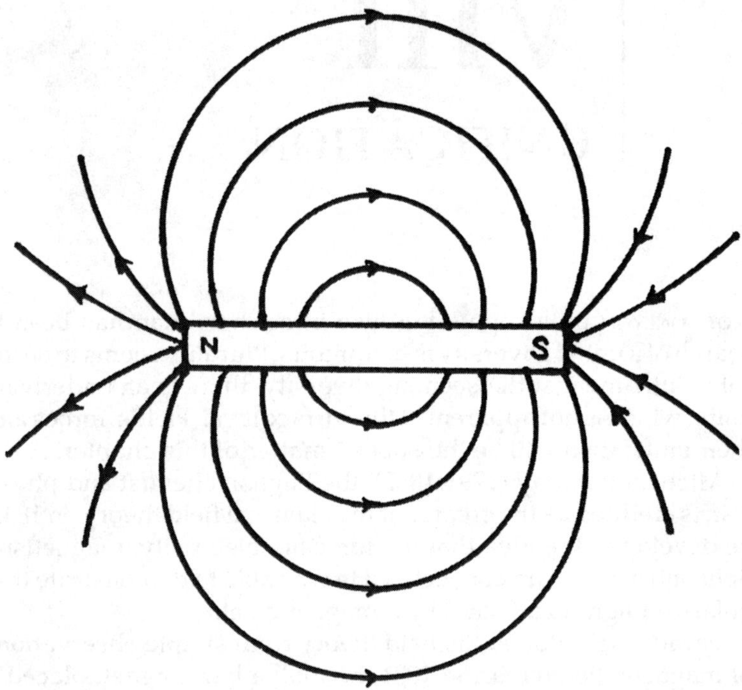

Fig. 8.1: Magnetic lines of force.

bodies and between magnetic poles and demonstrated conclusively that electric charge and magnetism obey the inverse square law like Newton's law of gravitation. The strength of the force diminishes with the increase in the distance between the magnetic poles or the electric charges. The force between point charges of magnitude e_1 and e_2 has the following mathematical relation:

$$F = Ke_1e_2 / r^2$$

Here F is the force, K is a constant and r is the distance between charges e_1 and e_2.

In the early part of the nineteenth century, the Danish scientist Hans Christian Oersted (1777-1851), and French physicists André Ampère (1775-1836), Jean Baptiste Biot (1774-1862) and Felix Savart (1791-1841) discovered important mathematical relations between electric currents and magnetic fields. Thus by the mid-nineteenth century, the connection between magnetism and electricity was well established. An electric current invariably produces a magnetic field and a magnet can be made to produce an electric current. Both electric charges and magnetic poles set up fields consisting of lines of force. In the 1860s, the Scottish physicist James Clerk Maxwell (1831-1879), who was a great admirer of Faraday, produced the unified theory of electromagnetism. Faraday viewed electric and magnetic effects as stemming from fields of lines of force about conductors or magnets. The material existence of lines of force, as viewed by Faraday, did not survive long. By mid-nineteenth century, the ether concept had already been developed in connection with light. The magnetic lines of force were now considered as distortions of the ether. In 1856, Maxwell showed that the flow of an incompressible fluid would behave in the same way as the fields. In 1861-62, he used the field concept for developing a model of electromagnetic phenomena. The magnetic intensity and the electric current represented vortices in the fluid. He introduced elasticity into the model and showed that the electromagnetic wave is a transverse wave. He also calculated the speed of the electromagnetic wave and found it very close to the measured speed of light. He inferred that light consists of transverse electromagnetic wave in a hypothetical "ether" medium. In 1864, he devised a set of four fundamental equations of electromagnetism, known ever since as Maxwell's equations. Thus, in the study of electromagnetic waves, he took over the fluid analogy into a purely mathematical description of electromagnetic fields.

According to Maxwell's equations, an electric field or a magnetic field cannot be considered in isolation. The two are always present together, directed at right angles to each other. As a fact, both these fields constitute two components of a single electromagnetic field. A changing electric field has to induce a changing magnetic field, which in turn has to induce a changing electric field, and so on. The electromagnetic field progresses outward in all directions. In other words, it is a radiation possessing the properties of a wave-form. The whole wave progresses in a direction at right angles to the electric and the magnetic components of the field. The frequencies of the electromagnetic waves are equal to that in which the electromagnetic field waxed and waned. Maxwell calculated the velocity of the electromagnetic wave and the value turned out to be 300,000 kilometres per second, the same as the velocity of light (light is itself an electromagnetic radiation). Out of the several general functions of Maxwell's equations, the field-view of the universe is the most spectacular.

Maxwell's equations implied that electromagnetic waves longer and shorter than those of light could be produced by moving electric currents. The German physicist Heinrich Rudolph Hertz (1857-94) was the first to demonstrate the existence of radio waves, generated by an electric spark. In 1888 he showed that electromagnetic waves were emitted by the spark. The discovery of Hertz was an important verification of Maxwell's ideas. Infrared radiation was also explained as electromagnetic waves. The transmission of heat through space was accounted for by the infrared radiation.

Maxwell was wedded to the ether hypothesis. This ether was a mysterious fluid which was supposed to permeate all of space. Maxwell believed that electromagnetic waves travelled through the ether. It seemed the oscillation of the electromagnetic field consisted of wave-like distortions of the ether.

The concept of a field removes the necessity of action-at-a-distance. It is not a fact that a magnet attracts iron over a distance. A magnet gives rise to a field that influences a piece of iron within itself. What has been said with reference to the magnet holds good for an electrically charged body.

From Newton's time onward, four different phenomena, viz., electricity, magnetism, light and gravity, have seemed to involve action-at-a-distance. Maxwell's equations showed the first three to be different aspects of a single phenomenon. Since his time, electricity, magnetism and light have been all included in the electromagnetic field. He recognized some important differences between gravity and electromagnetism and did not make any attempt to include the gravitational field in his equations.

Maxwell also suggested the Michelson-Morley experiment to search for an absolute electromagnetic medium (the ether). The experiments were actually performed in 1881 and 1887 and their results proved the absence of the ether. The findings of Michelson and Morley prompted Albert Einstein to do research on the special theory of relativity. In 1905, Einstein showed that electromagnetic fields are associated with quanta (photons) that act as agents of the field. His work on the photoelectric effect proved the corpuscular nature of light. He recognized both the particle and the wave form of light. Since particles do not need a medium for their propagation, he did not find the necessity of the ether for the propagation of light. Anyway the ether hypothesis passed away, but Maxwell's electromagnetic wave remained. The presence of any matter was not required for the propagation of the electromagnetic wave. Nothing had to wave in order to form electromagnetic waves.

The discovery of the general theory of relativity by Einstein in 1916 changed the concept of space-time. In the light of this theory, it became possible to view the oscillating changes in the geometry of space. The field that represents the space geometry touches both the interacting bodies and hence the necessity of action-at-a-distance is eliminated.

Einstein, during the later part of his life, made a serious attempt at finding a unified theory of electromagnetic and gravitational fields. But he could not be successful in doing so.

The field theory initiated by Faraday and later developed by Maxwell is called the classical field theory. This was followed by the quantum field theory which is being subsequently discussed.

Paul Adrien Maurice Dirac (1902-84), the British theoretical physicist and major contributor to quantum mechanics, propounded the first real quantum field theory. His principal tool was an old idea of a field. He considered the interaction of matter and electromagnetic radiation, that of the atom and the field. Through an appropriate mathematical procedure, he worked out the probability of the absorption or release of a photon by an atom present in a given state of a particular field in a particular configuration. This had reference to a law which Einstein had already discovered. Dirac linked the quantum theory with the dynamics of electromagnetic fields and hence it got the name "quantum field theory". He called it *quantum electrodynamics.* He submitted his paper[1] on "The Quantum Theory of the Emission and Absorption of Radiation" for publication to the *Proceedings of the Royal Society* in the last days of January of 1927.

In an attempt to quantize the electromagnetic field, Dirac hypothesized that his oscillators went into a "zero state" when the field disappeared. Associated with zero-state oscillators were zero-state photons. In the absence of the electromagnetic field, both the zero-state oscillators and the zero-state photons could not be detected. Dirac's mathematics had the implication that so-called empty space contains billions of invisible photons.

The uncertainty principle of Werner Heisenberg applies equally well to both particles and fields. The energy of a field over any given time cannot be determined exactly. The less the time of measurement, the greater the margin of error. Hence a vast amount of energy may escape detection if measurement is done in a very short time such as a few trillionths of a trillionth of a second, during which the zero-state oscillators of a field might not actually be at the zero-state. According to the uncertainty principle, any small area can contain undetectable energy and thus contain undetectable matter. Any space might harbour particles for a short time. If one interprets Dirac's theory in the light of uncertainty principle, the zero-state photons do show up.

Dirac emphasized that *virtual particles* are a central feature of quantum field theory. A virtual particle exists only temporarily while being exchanged between other particles. It need not satisfy the usual relationship between energy, momentum and mass because of Heisenberg's uncertainty relation. The fact that it need not conserve energy or momentum implies that it can come and go randomly. Basing on these concepts of the uncertainty principle, quantum field theory and virtual particles, Dirac suggested that the spaces around and within atoms were not empty but were filled with a boiling soup of ghostly particles. This idea introduced a dreadful picture of chaos in the micro-universe.

Dirac's idea of a negative-energy state was transformed into a triumph for a quantum electrodynamics. The famous equation of Einstein, $E = mc^2$, is a square root. Dirac's genius was not satisfied with the mathematical notation of this equation. As for example, the square root of 64 is ± 8, because 8×8 and -8×-8 equal 64. In the same analogy, E is both $+ mc^2$ and $- mc^2$. But negative mass seemed to be an absurd impossibility. Nevertheless Dirac accommodated the negative energy states in his theory. He set up a new picture of the vacuum in which all the negative energy states are filled up.

Dirac's idea of negative energy states created the concept of anti-matter in 1929. He introduced the notion of hole theory. Because of quantum randomness, photons may hit some of the particles in the negative energy states in the bottomless sea of the vacuum. If they hit with enough energy, they make the particles of the negative energy states jump out it, leaving a hole in their former location. Dirac incorrectly identified a hole of negative energy in a sea of electrons with a proton. He later corrected this idea and predicted the existence of anti-electron or positron.

Dirac's discovery of the hole in space, coupled with Heisenberg's uncertainty principle completely changed our notion on the so-called emptiness of space. Particles may arise spontaneously from the vacuum so long as they disappear before violating the uncertainty principle. The quantum vacuum is ever a beehive of activity, with all sorts of particles appearing and disappearing. The "empty" space is not at all empty. We get a lot out of "nothing".

Quantum field theory developed further after the Second World War. In 1943, the Japanese physicist Sin-Itiro Tomonaga (1906-79) developed a renormalizable quantum electrodynamics (QED). He created the idea that two particles interact by exchanging a third virtual particle between them. This interaction is likened to the momentum exchange when one rugby player passes the ball to another.

In 1947, Willis Lamb discovered that two states of the hydrogen atom differ in frequency. He observed a shift (the Lamb shift) in the lowest energy levels of the hydrogen atom, away from the previously predicted levels. This discovery of the Lamb shift led to the development of quantum electrodynamics. In 1948, the American physicist Richard Phillips Feynman (1918-88), independently of Tomonaga and the American physicist Julian Seymour Schwinger (1918 -), developed renormalizable quantum electrodynamics. Feynman, Tomonaga and Schwinger shared the 1965 Nobel Prize for physics.

The British-American theoretical physicist Freeman John Dyson (1923 -) unified independent versions of quantum electrodynamics. It has already been mentioned that shortly after the Second World War several physicists began to apply quantum mechanics to system in which particles (particularly electrons) interact with electromagnetic radiation (photons). Dyson showed how the ideas developed by Tomonaga, Lamb, Feynman and Schwinger are related to each other. By this he produced a single general theory of quantum electrodynamics.

With the development of QED, the details of how electrons

interact with electromagnetic fields are clearly understood. Because this topic is necessarily heuristic, we shall resort to diagramatic presentation. A pictorial representation cannot substitute for detailed mathematics. Diagrams cannot mirror the real microcosmos, but still are invaluable for a schematic description.

The simplest process in electrodynamics is the emission of a photon by an atom. This is illustrated in Figure 8.2. An excited atom is shown by a heavy line. It makes a transition from the excited state to the ground state. In this process, a photon is emitted to the right and the atom recoils to the left. The path of the photon is shown by a wavy line and that of the recoiled atom by a solid line. This whole phenomenon is a single event, occurring at one space-time point, marked on the diagram with a little dot, called a vertex.

One cannot predict the emission of a photon. This unpredictability is common with all quantum processes. What quantum theory can do is to provide the probability of such an incidence. The key quantity that enters into the probability is the

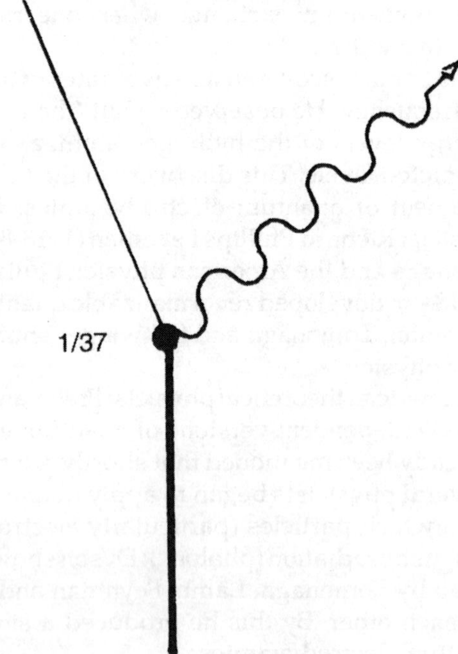

Fig. 8.2: Photon emission in the de-excitation of an excited atom.

factor $Ke^2/\hbar c$, usually abbreviated as alpha (α). This is a dimensionless quantity, i.e., a pure number, having a value of approximately 1/137. The likelihood of the photon emission process, illustrated in Figure 8.2, is regulated by the number 1/137. This alpha enables us to treat the coupling between the electromagnetic field and a charged particle such as an electron as a small perturbation. Figure 8.2 is an example of a first order perturbation process. In the second order perturbation process two photons are emitted rather than one. This would be regulated by the quantity α^2. The double-photon emission is, therefore, considerably less probable than the single-photon emission.

Now we study a second situation, depicted in Figure 8.3, where two charged particles interact at a distance. If the particles are with like charges, they repel each other. The two particles shown in Figure 8.3 are negatively charged electrons. While they approach each other, they suffer mutual repulsion and are deflected, a process known as scattering. In classical physics, the scattering of similar electrically charged particles is described as

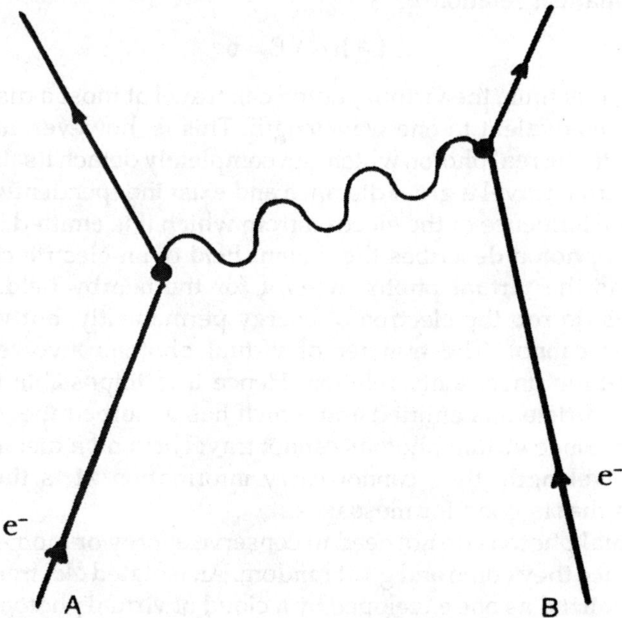

Fig. 8.3: Transfer of virtual photons between two electrons.

a continuous transfer of energy and momentum between the two particles through the electromagnetic field, thus causing the particles' trajectories to curve away from each other.

The quantum description of scattering of electron A and B, depicted in Figure 8.3, involves a transfer of virtual photons that play the role of messengers to convey the electromagnetic force to the two participating charged particles. Electron A emits a virtual photon which travels across to electron B where it is absorbed. Similarly, electron B emits a virtual photon which travels across to electron A, where it is absorbed. This process of emission and absorption is continuous. The virtual photons are short-lived and are not seen explicitly during scattering. The electrons' motions are disturbed due to the effect of the emission and the absorption events and thus is caused scattering.

The concept of virtual photons, as distinguished from the ordinary photons, needs a clarity. An ordinary photon possesses definite values for energy and momentum. A virtual photon can live for a short time, Δt, that is regulated by the following mathematical relation:

$$\Delta t \approx h / \Delta E \approx \upsilon^{-1}$$

During this time, the virtual photon can travel at most a distance of c/υ, equivalent to one wavelength. This is, however, not the case with the real photon which can completely detach itself from an electron, travel a great distance and exist independently, free from the influence of the electron from which it is emitted. Thus, the real photon describes the distant field of an electric charge whereas the virtual photon does it for the nearby field. Real photons do rob the electron of energy permanently, but virtual photons cannot. The transfer of virtual photons involves the energy-time uncertainty relation. Hence it is impossible to tell which particle has emitted and which has absorbed the virtual photon. Since virtual photons cannot travel beyond a distance of one wavelength, they cannot carry information. It is the real photon that is good for messages.

Virtual photons do not need to conserve energy or momentum and hence they come and go at random. An isolated electron may be visualized as one enveloped by a cloud of virtual photons that are continuously being produced and reabsorbed again within the duration allowed by the uncertainty principle. This process is represented in Figure 8.4.

Fig. 8.4: Emission and reabsorption of a virtual photon by a charged particle.

The same holds good for all other charged particles.

Diagrams of the type used here are known as Feynman diagrams. The American physicist Richard Phillips Feynman (1918-88) used them as an aid to computation in QED (quantum electrodynamics). Such diagrams are used for all types of messenger particles.

Not only photons, but also all quantum particles can exist in virtual forms. An example of this process is furnished in Figure 8.5 in which a virtual electron-positron pair appears briefly. A photon, during its flight, is suddenly converted temporarily into an electron and a positron that annihilate again within the duration permitted by the uncertainty principle. Thus two photons can scatter from each other through the interaction of virtual electron-positron pairs. The vacuum polarization is effected through this process since all photons, real and virtual, spend part of their time as electron-positron pairs.

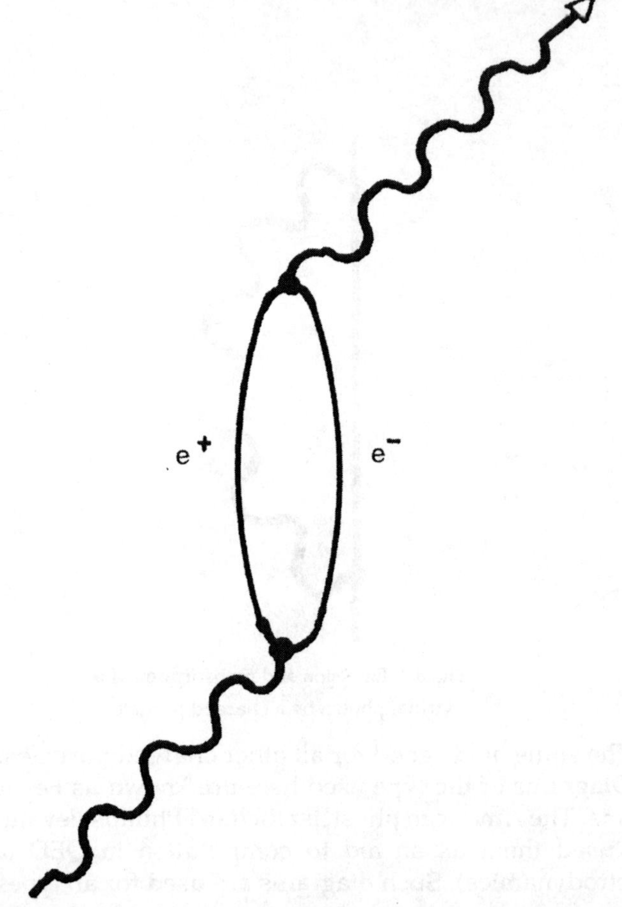

Fig. 8.5: Brief transmutation of a photon into a virtual electron-positron pair.

The discovery of the quantum field effects has revolutionized the concept of a vacuum. The so-called "empty" vacuum is not really empty. What we call "real" particles are like the froths and bubbles on a sea of quivering vacuum activity. Even if a hypothetical case of the absence of real particles is imagined, still apparently empty space teems with a ferment of virtual particles of all varieties. As a fact, space does not teem with particles. it would be more appropriate to say that the particles are the phenomenal appearances of space itself. Particles are the bubbles; space is the underlying sea water.

The next important milestone following the work of Tomonaga, Feynman and Schwinger in the development of the field concept was the Yang-Mills theory. In 1954, the Chinese-American physicist Chen Ning Yang (1922 -) and the American physicist Robert Mills published a short paper "Gauge Invariance and Isotopic Spin" in the *Physical Review*. Here they established the basis for modern quantum field theory by developing the mathematical characteristics of fields. Such a mathematical technique was needed to allow symmetry to produce new particles. The Yang-Mills gauge-invariant fields do account for almost every particle and force in existence. Through their theory, Yang and Mills strongly suggested that the clue to the diversity of the world lays in symmetry.

The quantum field theory is not restricted to the electromagnetic force only. There are four types of fundamental forces, viz., strong force, weak force, electromagnetic force and gravitational force. Each force is associated with a separate field and different types of exchange particles. We may have a brief description of the fundamental forces after which we shall come back to the topic of fields and the unification of the fields.

A force is something that can move an object. Magnetism is a force because it can move a compass needle. Electricity is a force because it can move a motor. Gravity is a force because it can pull an object. Gravity and electromagnetic forces have been known to man since time immemorial. In contrast, the nuclear forces, called weak and strong, were discovered only in the twentieth century when physicists were able to make subatomic probes.

Gravity is an attractive force that holds the whole universe together. It causes the apple to fall to the ground. It keeps our feet anchored to the floor. It binds together the solar system and all planetary systems of other stars. Because of it, our Earth and other planets are in their respective orbits around the Sun. It prevents the stars from exploding and disintegrating. It binds the stars in a galaxy. It binds the galaxies in a galactic cluster. It prevents the universe from disintegrating and running away from one another.

Gravity is the only universal force. It acts between all particles without exception. The source of gravity is the mass of the particle concerned. The heavier the mass, the stronger the gravity. The strength of the force between two idealized point masses is given by Newton's famous inverse square law which is mathematically expressed as follows:

$$F = G\, m_1\, m_2 / r^2$$

Here m_1 and m_2 are the masses of the two bodies, r is the distance separating them and G is a universal constant.

Gravity is a long-range force. It can act over macroscopic distances. It functions in both the macro- and the micro-world. But it cannot play a direct role in sub-atomic particle physics. The absolute strength of gravity is exceedingly small. For example, the gravitational force between an electron and a proton is some 10^{40} times weaker than the electromagnetic force. This is the reason of the insignificant role of gravity in the micro-cosmos.

The electromagnetic force makes the negatively charged electrons orbit around the positively charged nucleus of the atom. But for this force, the orbital electrons of the atom would run away. It determines the structure of the orbits of the electrons in the atoms and hence governs the laws of chemistry. It functions between charged particles — positive and negative, positive and positive and negative and negative.

The source of the electromagnetic force is an electric charge. Since all particles in nature are not charged, electromagnetic force, unlike the gravitational force, is not universal. But, like the gravitational force, the electromagnetic force obeys the inverse square law and hence is long-ranged.

As already mentioned, the strength of the electromagnetic force is enormously larger than that of the gravitational force. But gravity rather than electromagnetism dominates the universe on the large scale because of the cumulative nature of the former and the self-neutralizing nature of the latter. Electric charge, being both positive and negative, massive objects have a tendency for the cancellation of charges.

The nuclear forces are two in number, viz., the strong force and the weak force. Their ranges are of subnuclear dimensions and hence they are not directly observable in the daily life. They work within the nucleus. Within the nucleus of the atom, the electromagnetic force is overpowered by the nuclear forces.

The strong force is the force that binds the hadrons and the quarks inside the hadrons. It is responsible for binding the protons and neutrons together in the nucleus. Not only protons and neutrons, but also hadrons feel the strong force. Leptons, however, do not. The inter-hadron force is a remnant of the more powerful force that acts between the quarks which make up the hadrons. Being short-ranged,the strong force rapidly dwindles away beyond a distance of about 10^{-15} metres. In contrast to the gravitational and electromagnetic forces that are long-ranged, the strong nuclear force is very short-ranged in character.

All the protons in the nucleus are positively charged. Under the influence of the electromagnetic force, they have a tendency of repulsion from one another. Part of the strong force counteracts the repulsive electromagnetic force that would tear apart the nucleus, and the remaining strong force binds the nucleons together. When the proton number inside the nucleus is too large, say more than one hundred, even the strong nuclear force finds a difficulty in overcoming the repulsive electric force between the protons. This explains why there are only about one hundred known elements in nature.

The form of the inter-hadron force is very complex, since hadrons are not elementary particles but are constituted of quarks. It is the inter-quark force which is the fundamental interaction. Akin to the electric charge and the photon of the electromagnetic force, the strong force has the colour and the gluon, respectively, to play similar roles. There are three sorts of "charge" for the strong force. In this case the charge is known as *colour*, arbitrarily dubbed red, green and blue. The colour is the source of the strong force. The electromagnetic force acts between two bodies whereas the strong force binds three quarks together in baryons. Unlike the electromagnetic force whose source is one sort of electric charge, the source of the strong force are three charges (colours).

When the strong force is suddenly unleashed, the enormous amount of energy locked within the nucleus is released explosively. This type of nuclear detonation occurs when the uranium atom in an atomic bomb splits. Chemical explosives which are governed by the electromagnetic force yield significantly less energy than the strong force.

The strong force is responsible for the shining of the stars that are huge nuclear furnaces. Inside the stars including our Sun, the strong force within the nucleus is unleashed. With the production of the chemical energy, the stars would not be so bright and their spans of lives would not be so long. Without the strong force in the Sun, life on Earth would be impossible.

The weak force is another nuclear force, much weaker in strength than the strong force. It is manifested in the beta-decay. It is also involved in some radioactive decays of nuclei and neutrino interactions. Had the strong force been the only nuclear force, most nuclei would be stable. However, we do find some massive and unstable nuclei (such as uranium with ninety-two protons) that are radioactive; they automatically break apart, releasing smaller fragments and debris. The heavy nucleus of a radioactive element, being unstable, spontaneously disintegrates. The weak force governs radioactivity and is responsible for the disintegration of the nucleus of the atom.

The weak force is far weaker than the electromagnetic force, but still much stronger than the gravitational force. It acts on all quarks and all leptons. It does not exert a direct pushing or pulling effect. Its principal manifestation is evinced by its effecting the transmutation of particles. In the beta-decay which is a type of radioactivity exhibited by some unstable nuclei, a neutron turns into a proton, an electron and an antineutrino. The weak force drives this process of beta-decay in which a change of quark flavour is involved. One of the up quarks turns into a down quark within the neutron. The weak force is able to change the flavour of both quarks and leptons. Under the influence of the weak force, electrons can turn into neutrinos.

Neutrinos are not subject to the strong and the electromagnetic forces. Being subject to the weak force, they are exceedingly weakly interacting. They can penetrate many light-years of solid lead before being stopped.

The range of the weak force is extremely restricted. It is about 10^{-17} metres. With this restricted range and a feeble strength, it is, however, a useful force in nature.

The concept of force is classical. The term "interaction" rather than force is in vogue in modern physics. Every particle, without a single exception, has a field. A field is a physical quantity which varies from point to point in space. It cannot be directly observed. Its effects can be detected and hence its existence can be inferred. When we say, "Two particles interact" we actually mean thereby that two fields interact. In the concept of the working of a force between two particles or bodies was implied the action-at-a-distance. In modern physics, the force concept was replaced by the "interaction of the fields" concept which did away with a necessity of an action-at-a-distance. In this new concept, some exchange particles or messenger particles were involved. Not only these exchange or messenger particles were speculated and theoretically predicted, they were also experimentally detected. We may now describe the historical development of these messenger particles.

The role of the photon in quantum electrodynamics (QED) as an exchange or messenger particle has already been discussed. The photon is the exchange particle in the electromagnetic interaction. It is neither a quark nor a lepton. All quarks and leptons are fermions whereas photons are fundamental bosons. A photon has a spin of one unit. Its rest mass is zero and by definition it travels at the speed of light.

After obtaining a success of the quantum theory of the electromagnetic field in describing QED processes, it was conceived to extend the same principle to the other forces that were expected to possess similar quantum field descriptions. Like virtual photon of the electromagnetic force, each of the other fundamental forces was considered to possess one or more associated messenger particles.

The exchange particle of the gravitational force is the graviton which is the analogue of the photon. It too is a massless boson, but with a spin of two. Gravitons couple too weakly to other particles and hence no direct evidence has so far been obtained in the laboratory for their existence. Their existence is inferred on indirect evidence and on grounds of physical consistency. The gravitational force is a long-range one, for which the masslessness of gravitons is suitable.

Photons couple only to charged particles whereas gravitons couple to all particles, including gravitons. Thus gravitons feel gravity too. They interact with each other, with the result that graviton processes cannot be simply superimposed on each other. To express it in other words, the graviton theory is nonlinear.

An early attempt was made in 1935 by the Japanese physicist Hideki Yukawa (1907-81) to describe the strong nuclear force in this way. He proposed a new type of field that surrounds each proton and neutron which couples to the field through a nuclear "charge". This is analogous to an electron that couples to the electromagnetic field through its electric charge. Yukawa predicted that the exchange particle of the strong nuclear force was a meson. In 1936 C. D. Anderson (1905 -) discovered a particle with a mass as predicted by Yukawa and called it the mu-meson (muon). But this particle did not interact with the nucleons sufficiently strongly to correspond with Yukawa's prediction. In 1947 Cecil Frank Powell (1903-69) and his coworkers discovered the pi-meson or pion which did correspond with Yukawa's proposed particle. Yukawa was awarded the Nobel Prize in 1949. His new quantum field that surrounds a proton or a neutron has pions as quanta of excitations (virtual particles), analogous to the photons in the electromagnetic field. The exchange of pions between neutrons and protons leads to a force of attraction.

The Yukawa particle (the virtual pion) is involved in the exchanges between hadrons. Gluons are the virtual particles that exchange the strong force between quarks. The inter-quark force has no less than eight messenger bosons, known collectively as gluons. They have spin one. They couple to themselves like the gravitons and hence the resulting theory is nonlinear. Both gluons and quarks are "coloured". This colour is a charge akin to the electrical charge in the electron. There are three types of colour charge, viz., red, green and blue. Each of the six flavours (up, down, strange, charmed, top or truth, bottom or beauty) possesses all the three colour charges. As the electrical charge is the source of the electromagnetic force, so is the colour charge that is the source of the inter-quark strong force.

There are eight colour charges (gluons) and eight gauge fields. The colour gauge theory is called quantum chromodynamics (QCD). It is usual to expect a gauge force to be an infinite-range one and also its quanta to be massless particles. To the contrary, QCD produces the short-range strong force. The explanation lies in the principle called "confinement". The existence of any free particle with nonzero colour charge is forbidden. The quarks are bound to be confined. They cannot be separated from each other. Hence the question does not arise on the problem of the quarks separated to long distances where they would feel the infinite-range forces. In the same analogy, free gluons do not exist and hence there is no problem with their masslessness. Due to the fact that the particles (gluons) associated with the strong field and the quarks cannot be produced as free particles, the strong force is only rather indirectly known.

A very important property which can be derived from QCD is the asymptotic freedom. It is the principle which states that the strong forces become weaker for very close encounters between quarks. For this reason, the quarks become "free" of the forces at very short distances.

The inter-hadron forces are observed. The nucleons (protons and neutrons) are colourless compounds of quarks. The strong forces that act between the nucleons are observable. This situation is analogous to the forces between neutral atoms. Inside the neutral atom there are positively charged protons and negatively charged electrons. Any two electrically charged particles are acted upon by the electromagnetic force. Thus the force between two neutral atoms are the indirect consequences of the electric forces that operate inside the atoms. Similarly the inter-nucleon forces are complicated ones which are secondary to the inter-quark forces.

The weak force possesses three exchange particles, viz., W^+, W^- and Z^o. All these three are spin 1 bosons. They have nonzero mass whereas all other messenger particles are massless. The Ws have about 80 proton masses and the Z 90. Thus the particles are heavy and this is responsible for the very short range of the weak force. The Ws are electrically charged. Each W has one unit of charge, like the electron. The W^+ is the antiparticle of the W^-. In contrast to the Ws, the Z particle is uncharged and resembles the photon in all respects other than mass.

The four forces and the four fields, described in the foregoing pages, are distinct from one another. "Can there be a unification of all these four fields?" This is the question which is still engaging physicists in their search for a unified field theory.

Back in 1919, Einstein received a strange letter from Theodor Franz Kaluza, a mathematician of the University of Konigsberg. In this letter, Kaluza proposed a unified field theory that combined Einstein's theory of gravity and Maxwell's theory of light. He proposed a five-dimensional theory of gravity, with four spatial dimensions and one time dimension. He suggested that the fifth dimension was "curled up" like a circle.

It was already hard to understand the four dimensions of Einstein. It became harder to conceive of the fifth dimension proposed by Kaluza. Many physicists viewed the Kaluza theory of five dimensions with skepticism. In 1926, the Swedish mathematician Oskar Klein found out a possible solution to the problem. He accepted the suggestion of Kaluza that the fifth dimension was curled up like a circle. He visualized this circle to be so small in size that it could not be directly observed.

Einstein, in the later part of his life, struggled for thirty years to make some sense out of the Kaluza-Klein theory. He sought to find a unified theory of electromagnetic and gravitational fields. He tried to unite his geometric theory of gravity with Maxwell's theory of light. He spent about three decades on a quest for the unified field theory, but without a success. It was a solitary and frustrating quest which was ultimately futile. In the last years of his life he was isolated from his fellow physicists and was totally absorbed by the unified field theory. Many physicists of his time were silent bitter critics who were utterly pessimistic about the outcome of his quest for the unified field theory. A few even sneered behind his back and ridiculed his "senile" attempts. Einstein was not at all discouraged with this skepticism of his fellow physicists. It is obvious from the following comment that he considered his critics' outlook as shortsighted and narrow. He wrote: "I have little patience with scientists who take a board of wood, look for its thinnest part and drill a great number of holes where drilling is easy."[2] In spite of his failure in the unification of the electromagnetic and the gravitational fields, he was confident in the appropriateness of his attempt. In this connection, he once remarked to his secretary that physicists a hundred years later would be able to appreciate his monumental labours in trying to prove the unified field theory. His solitary search for the truth, his frustrating failure and his discomforting loneliness did not bother him too much. "The essential of the being of a man of my type", he once said, "lies precisely in what he thinks and how he thinks, not in what he does or suffers".[3]

Einstein died in 1955. His dream of the unified field theory got a concrete shape in the Glashow-Salam-Weinberg theory that unified the electromagnetic field and the weak field. In 1979, Sheldon Lee Glashow (1932 -), Abdus Salam (1926 -) and Steven Weinberg (1933 -) shared the Nobel Prize for physics for their independent work in the unification of the two fields mentioned above.

A number of scientific discoveries culminated in the first unified field theory. Here a digression is necessary to trace the background that led to the discovery of the Glashow-Salam-Weinberg theory.

First we may discuss the development of ideas on the symmetry and group theory. The most familiar example of symmetry is a crystal or a gem. When rotated at certain angles, crystals and gems retain exactly the same shape. The crystal rotates back into itself and hence it is said that the crystal is invariant under a rotation at a certain angle. A sphere is invariant under all possible rotations; it rotates into itself. And hence we say that a sphere has symmetry.

In much the same way, we apply symmetry to physics. If the equations remain exactly the same when we make certain rotations (actually shufflings) or in other words, when we change space into time, or electrons into quarks, etc., they retain a beautiful symmetry.

The mathematical study of symmetry is called "group theory". The founder of the group theory was the French mathematician Evariste Galois (1811-32). After Galois, the group theory was further developed by the Norwegian mathematician Sophus Lie (1842-99) in the late 1800s.

Sophus Lie and Elie Cartan catalogued seven Lie groups, called A, B, C, D, E, F and G. The first four groups, viz., A, B, C and D are labelled by an integer n, which can be arbitrarily large. Although a large number of papers have been written using these groups to describe elementary particles, nowhere is the value of n determined. In contrast, the value of n in groups E, F and G is limited.

Physicists have been using the groups A, B, C and D in building models of quarks and leptons. They can be rewritten in familiar notations as follows:

$$A(n) = SU(n+1)$$
$$B(n) = SO(2n+1)$$
$$C(n) = SP(2n)$$
$$D(n) = SO(2n)$$

Here the "S" stands for special (i.e., the matrix has determinant one), "O" stands for orthogonal, "U" stands for unitary and "SP" stands for symplectic. In all these groups, the value of n is arbitrary.

On the contrary, the group E, F and G come only in the following set:

G (2), F (4), E (7), E (8)

Physicists are ever in search of the smallest number of constituents of matter. Hence it is very natural for them to think that the groups E, F and G are the likely candidates to describe the symmetries of constituents like quarks.

The strangest class of Lie groups are the E (n) groups. A familiar example of E (n) symmetry cannot be cited since the E (n) groups cannot be expressed in terms of ordinary objects. For purely mathematical reasons, the highest value n can take is 8.

The atom has O (3) symmetry. The Schrödinger equation is invariant under rotations. The solutions to this equation (which are atoms) have O (3) symmetry.

Lie discovered a set of symmetries called SU (n), which rotates complex numbers. The symmetry underlying Maxwell's equations is U (1) which is the simplest example. Here 1 stands for the one photon. The next simplest symmetry is SU (2), which can rotate the proton and the neutron. Heisenberg had earlier shown that SU (2) symmetry could shuffle protons and neutrons in the Schrödinger equation.

The W-particle theory was plagued with infinities and hence was non-normalizable. This is the reason for which the theory of weak interactions languished for three decades.

As early as 1947, Chen Ning Yang (1922 -) wanted to create a theory that would be more sophisticated and general than Maxwell's. He thought of generalizing the U (1) symmetry to the SU (2) and higher. He wanted to know the result if shuffling is performed at a different angle at each point in space. He wanted to know what would happen if he created a theory that was invariant when the proton and the neutron were shuffled through an angle that was different.

In 1954, Yang, in collaboration with Robert Mills, proposed symmetry and unification. They established the basis for modern quantum field theory by developing the mathematical characteristics of fields needed to allow symmetry to produce new particles. These were called Yang-Mills gauge invariant fields. The Yang-Mills theory possessed more symmetries than Maxwell ever dreamed of. It contained a new mathematical symmetry — SU (2) X U (1).

The Yang-Mills theory (otherwise known as the gauge theory) incorporated the idea that a different rotation should occur at each point in space. By working out the details of this theory, Yang and his collaborators found that the local symmetry could be satisfied if a new meson-like particle like the W-particle of weak interactions was postulated.

The physics community was indifferent to the Yang-Mills theory for about two decades. Of course, the theory faced some genuine problems. The Yang-Mills particle possessed too much symmetry. It did not resemble any known particle in nature. The Yang-Mills particle was predicted to be massless whereas the conjectured W-particle had a finite mass. The theory was considered to be non-renormalizable.

The Yang-Mills theory that sat on the shelf for two decades gained importance in 1964 when Peter Higgs suggested a mechanism of spontaneous symmetry breaking. He could break some of the symmetries of the Yang-Mills theory and thereby obtained particles with masses. Thus the Yang-Mills theory resembled the W-particle theory. But, at that time, nobody believed that the Yang-Mills theory was renormalizable.

In 1971, a twenty-four year old Dutch graduate student Gerardus 't Hooft finally proved that the Yang-Mills theory, broken according to the method found by Higgs, was renormalizable. In his mathematical exercises on the theory, every infinity cancelled exactly. Thus this theory was made suitable for weak interactions.

't Hooft's proof of the renormalizability of the gauge theories set off a volcanic explosion in the world of physics. The theory was used with SU (2) X U (1) to describe the electro-weak force. Next it was used in the SU (3) gluon theory to bind the quarks together. Finally, it was used in SU (5) or a higher group to unite all the known particles into one family. For the first time since Maxwell in the 1860s, some of the fundamental forces of nature could be unified.

By adopting the Lie groups as the mathematical framework for unification, physicists got the key to the unified field theory.

Back in 1941, forty-two years before the discovery of the W-particle, Julian Schwinger (1918 -) of Harvard suggested to J. Robert Oppenheimer (1904-67) that the weak and electromagnetic forces could be united into one theory. Oppenheimer's response to this was very cold.

In 1956, Schwinger prepared a complete version of the

electroweak (unified theory of electromagnetic force and weak force) theory. He showed his paper to Nobel laureate Isidor Isaac Rabi (1898-1988) of Columbia University. "Everybody hates that paper" was the blunt reply of Rabi.

On the examination of some experimental data (that were really wrong), Schwinger noticed that they violated his electroweak theory. So, out of sheer disgust, he handed over his theory to his graduate student Sheldon Glashow. He did not know at that time that his theory was actually right.

Glashow and his collaborators united the electron and the neutrino mathematically using SU (2). The electromagnetic theory had U (1) symmetry. Hence the complete electroweak theory possessed the symmetry SU (2) X U (1). But the initial response of the entire physics community to this theory was indifferent. It was ignored for several years.

Referring to the work of Weinberg and Salam, their theory remains the same if the electron and the neutrino are rotated into each other. Because two particles are rotated, the theory has the symmetry group SU (2). Again, it possesses the U (1) symmetry of Maxwell. Therefore the product of these two symmetries — SU (2) X U (1) — is the complete symmetry of the Weinberg-Salam theory.

In the weak interactions, the W^{+}, W^{-} and Z^{o} particles have a mass whereas the photon of the electromagnetic interaction is massless. This was the stumbling block in the unification of these two interactions. Weinberg and Salam, working independently, found a way around. They solved the problem by Higg's mechanism of spontaneous symmetry breaking. They proposed that the W and Z particles acquire their masses through a spontaneous breaking of the underlying gauge symmetry. They introduced an additional quantum field, called a Higgs field, with massive spinless bosons as the quanta of this field. They could effect a coupling between the Higgs field and the electromagnetic-weak fields.

So was established the unification of the electromagnetic force and the weak force. In 1967, Steven Weinberg, Abdus Salam and Sheldon Lee Glashow, working independently, developed the electroweak unification in terms of spontaneously broken symmetry and group theory. Thus it was accepted that the weak and the electromagnetic forces are really two aspects of a unified electroweak force.

In 1973, Paul Musset and coworkers at CERN discovered neutral currents in neutrino reactions. The electroweak theory predicted such a phenomenon. Hence this discovery was viewed as a partial confirmation of the theory.

In 1983, the charged W^+ and W^- particles and the neutral Z particle were discovered by a team headed by Carlo Rubbia at CERN. The electroweak theory had already predicted these particles as the messenger particles of the weak interactions. These findings became the second confirmation of the electroweak theory. In 1984, Carlo Rubbia of Italy and Simon van der Meer of the Netherlands won the Nobel Prize for physics for their discovery of the W and Z particles.

Thus the electroweak theory was undisputedly accepted by the physics community. The number of the fundamental forces of nature was reduced from four to three. Next physicists began to think to unify the electroweak force with the strong force.

In the 1950s, years before Gell-Mann introduced the quarks, Shoichi Sakata and his collaborators visualized a sublayer that existed beneath the hadrons. They predicted that this sublayer obeyed the SU (3) symmetry. The SU (3) symmetry that was proposed by Sakata for the strong interactions rotate the three subnuclear particles. Such a prediction went against the prevailing opinion and hence was considered outlandish.

In 1974, Howard M. Georgi and Sheldon Lee Glashow developed the first of the grand unified theories (GUTs). These account for the strong, weak and electromagnetic forces as variants of a single force that was broken into parts when the universe began to cool down after the big-bang.

The strong force is described in terms of quantum chromodynamics (QCD). In fact, QCD is a gauge group SU (3). Since the strong force and the electroweak force are unified, the grand unified theories are based on a more embracing gauge group that embodies the SU (3) of QCD and the SU (2) X U (1) of the electroweak force. In the GUTs, the leptons are associated with the quarks and their distinctions are completely blurred.

The symmetry group SU (5) is the smallest one that the GUT theories can have. Such a group can shuffle five particles (the electron, neutrino and three quarks). If we have N quarks, the symmetry group would be SU (N), where N can be as high as desired.

Particle theorists are of the opinion that there are a definite number of quarks since the Lie groups G (2), F (4), E (6), E (7) and E (8) are small and limited. The group E (6) has successfully been used to construct GUT-type theories. Here E stands for "exceptional". The E group, instead of going on for ever, stops at E (8) and hence is exceptional. The E(8) group contains the GUT symmetry.

The proton-decay is one of the consequences of the GUTs. Previously the proton was thought to be stable and immutable. In 1973, Jogesh C. Pati and Abdus Salam suggested theoretical reasons why protons might decay into other particles ($p \rightarrow e^+ + \pi^0$). According to the prediction of the GUTs, a proton, on an average, takes at least 10^{30} years or more to decay. The proton decays ultimately into a positron. The neutral pion, being unstable, decays into two photons in about 10^{-16}s. The former is a baryon and the latter a lepton. In this transmutation of a baryon into a lepton, the laws of baryon and lepton number conservation are both violated. If this possibility of the baryon non-conservation is accepted, it would provide an explanation for the creation of matter without an equal quantity of antimatter.

The photon is the exchange particle in the electromagnetic interaction. The weak interaction has three exchange particles, viz., W^+, W and Z^0. In the GUTs, an exceedingly massive (equal to or greater than 10^{15} times the mass of a proton) particles is necessary for the interaction to take place. The superheavy particles would play a similar role to that played by photons, gluons, Ws and Zs.

The grand unification of the three forces is possible only at a very high temperature (10^{28}–10^{30}K). The relevant grand unification energy is about 10^{15} GeV which is 10^{13} times greater than the electroweak unification scale. The enormous temperature at which the grand unification takes place is far beyond the limits at which experimental test is feasible. Temperatures like 10^{28}–10^{30}K prevailed before about 10^{-35} seconds after the beginning of the big-bang. At that time the universe was but 10^{-24} centimetre in size. At the enormously high temperature, pure energy was just beginning to condense into point-like particles such as quarks and leptons, and the distinction between the leptons and the quarks and that between the strong force, the weak force and the electromagnetic force was completely lost. The grand unified force was mediated by superheavy particles, collectively called X. As the temperature fell, so the superheavies (X) decayed into more familiar, lighter particles. In this decay process, the baryon number was perhaps not conserved. As a result, the decay products showed a slight preponderance of matter over antimatter. The ratio of matter to antimatter might have been ($1 + 10^{-9}$): 1. Consequent to the annihilation of equal quantities of matter and antimatter, the residue left ($S \sim 10^9$) accounts for the presently existing matter of the universe.

The GUT model was exciting because it could unite hundreds of particles and bring down the number to a few quarks, leptons (electrons and neutrinos) and Yang-Mills particles, and it reduced the four fundamental forces of nature to only two. If we consider the six flavours and three colours of quarks along with all the antiquarks, the number of quarks is not too small. The GUT theories have to accept a minimum of forty-eight "fundamental" quarks and leptons. Physicists are not happy to recognize the grand unification as an elemental model which deals with a large number of "fundamental" units. Furthermore, the forces of nature would not be completely united because the gravitational force is still outside the GUTs. Hence the next attempt is being made by physicists to combine all the four forces into a single superforce. What is to be achieved finally is the supergrand unified theory (Super GUT).

The supergrand unified theory began in the late 1960s. A search into this area was made to meet four major requirements. First, the GUT did not include the gravitational force. The desire for unifying all the four fundamental forces of nature was still unfulfilled. Second, the GUT contained too many "elementary" particles and physicists did not favour this bizarre picture. Third, in the 1950s, hundreds of hadrons were being discovered and the list of hadrons did not seem to terminate anywhere. Fourth, quarks that are the building blocks of hadrons could not be experimentally detected.

The foundation stone of the edifice of supergrand unification was laid in 1968 by Gabriele Veneziano and Mahiko Suzuki, each working independently at CERN. At this time the S-matrix theory was still very much in vogue. While thumbing through voluminous tables of mathematical functions catalogued since the eighteenth century, they came across the Beta function, a mathematical formula first written down by the Swiss mathematician Leonhard Euler in the 1800s. They were astonished to notice that the properties of the Beta function automatically satisfied almost all the S-matrix postulates of Geoffrey Chew of the University of California at Berkeley.

The Beta function, rediscovered by Veneziano and Suzuki, established a victory of the S-matrix theory over the quantum field theory. Both the physicists independently proposed an *ad hoc* model which described the quantized motion of a string.

In 1970, the Japanese physicist Yoichiro Nambu of the University of Chicago proposed that the wonderful Beta function was due to the properties of interacting strings. He tried to dispense with the chaos of the hundreds of hadrons being discovered in the laboratories by proposing the idea of the string. He did not consider the hadrons as "fundamental" units. In his view, the strong interaction must be a reflection of some deeper underlying structure.

Nambu proposed the idea of the string to replace that of the point particles. It was assumed that a hadron consisted of a vibrating string. Each mode of the vibration of the string corresponds to a separate particle. The whole universe may be likened to the string of a violin. All the musical tones that a violin-string can produce do not exist as such. The string resonates with different frequencies, each one creating a separate tone of the musical scale. A tone created by the vibrating string is not in itself any more fundamental than any other one. The fundamental truth is that the vibrating strings of the violin can explain the laws of the musical harmony. Similar is the case with the universe in which some strings vibrate. What we call the diverse particles and the forces of nature are the expressions of the vibrations of the strings.

Nambu's string theory was restricted to describing bosons only. In 1971, John Schwarz, André Neveu and Pierre Ramond proposed a second string theory that described fermions.

Both these earlier string theories could not be mathematically worked out in four dimensions (three spatial and one temporal). Caude Lovelace at CERN declared that the string theory of Nambu had a better mathematical structure in twnety-six dimensions. Then Richard Browar and Charles Thorn at MIT showed that the string theory of Nambu completely collapsed unless it was defined in twenty-six dimensions. Some other physicists also confirmed this finding.

The concept of more than four dimensions had its origin back in 1919, when Einstein received a strange letter from Theodor Franz Kaluza, a mathematician from the University of Konigsberg. In this letter, Kaluza proposed a unified field theory that combined gravitational and electromagnetic fields in a five-dimensional universe (four spatial dimensions and one time dimension). He suggested that the fifth dimension was "curled up" like a circle while the other four were not. In 1926, Oskar Klein, the Swedish mathematician, offered a possible solution to the problem of the fifth dimension. He suggested that the size of the circle of the fifth dimension was too small to be directly observed. He even calculated a possible size of the circle. Its circumference came out to be 10^{-30} centimetres (the Planck length is 10^{-33} cm) or about 10^{-17} of the size of the atomic nucleus.

For the sake of pure mathematics, the Kaluza-Klein theory was beautiful pictorially. It had a superb mathematical elegance. Einstein could not resist the temptation of working on it for the last thirty years of his life, although he was unlucky to get a success. His time was not ripe and many related phenomena were yet to be known.

In the late 1970s, Eugene Cremmer and Bernard Julia rediscovered the truth of the Kaluza-Klein theory, which was dusted on the shelf for almost fifty years. They found that their mathematical model of the string theory for the universe became very simple if eleven dimensions were accepted with seven of them curled up. Other physicists discovered that the Schwarz-Neveu-Ramond model of the string theory was self-consistent only in ten dimensions, with six dimensions curled up.

Man has been used to three dimensions — length, breadth and height. Einstein introduced time as a fourth dimension. It was difficult to conceive of four dimensions although this concept was well established in the physics community. However, the idea of twenty-six, eleven or ten dimensions could not be accepted by many physicists in the 1970s. The string theory lost favour around 1974. Many physicists who were enthusiastic in their work on the strings unhappily deserted the model. The decade of 1974-84 was lean for the string theory.

There was a second important reason for the abandonment of the string theory in the 1970s. John Schwarz and Jöel Scherk noticed that a massless spin 2 particle, corresponding to the graviton, was involved in the theory. The graviton was outside the spectrum of particles found in the nuclear regime.

The earlier string theory was a model of strong interactions. It was meant to describe the hadrons. The quark concept was introduced by Murray Gell-Mann and G. Zweig in 1964. Hadrons such as neutrons and protons are made up of quarks. These quarks are held together by some force. The strings are a description of this force. The quarks are attached to the ends of the strings that are like bits of elastic and the whole lot whirls around in some way.

It is said that quarks cannot be observed since they do not exist in a free state. Gell-Mann and others had the suggestion that these quarks were somehow "confined" in the hadrons by a mysterious force.

Kenneth Geddes Wilson (1936 -) of Cornell University, who discovered the renormalization group technique for treating phase transitions and was awarded the Nobel Prize for physics in 1982, proposed that quarks were permanently bound together by a string-like sticky substance. He suggested that the Yang-Mills gluons which are normally particles in the quark theory, could "condense", under some conditions, into a sticky kind of taffy that would confine the quarks. According to this concept, the quarks are at either ends of the taffy-like strings, and because they are permanently confined by taffy-like strings, they can never be seen.

The string theory, as a model of strong interactions, was considered too symmetrical to be realistic. The twenty-six or ten dimensions, associated with the theory, were not acceptable to many physicists in the 1970s. The most important drawback in the theory was the discovery of the massless spin 2 particle involved in it. These were the main reasons for rejecting the string model as a strong interaction theory. When strings were thought to describe nuclear particles, they were expected to have a size typical for a nucleus, which is 10^{-13} centimetres. For gravitation, Planck's length (10^{-33} cm) was to be used. When John Schwarz and Jöel Scherk used the string for gravitation, they had to refer to Planck's length which is 10^{20} smaller than the nuclear scale. In September, 1972, Murray Gell-Mann presented the beginnings of quantum chromodynamics (QCD). In the 1970s, QCD was universally recognized as the correct theory of the strong nuclear force. Thus, inevitably the string model was practically dead in the mid-1970s. During this period of the desertion of this model, only two scientists, viz., John Schwarz of the California Institute of Technology and Michael Green of Queen Mary College in London, continued their efforts in the promotion of string research.

In 1974, five years after the string theory had been developed, the idea of using strings for gravitation and unification arose as a necessity. In 1976, John Schwarz and Jöel Scherk suggested that the string theory be reinterpreted. It ceased to be a model for strong interactions. But it could be utilized for combining gravity with quantum mechanics. The twentieth century physics stands on two strong pillars, viz., general relativity of Einstein's theory of gravity and quantum mechanics. Both these pillars are incompatible with each other. The inconsistency of gravity and quantum mechanics is well established. The inclusion of gravity in quantum field theory is impossible. If gravity is combined with quantum mechanics, it becomes nonsense from a mathematical point of view. When formulae of quantum mechanical gravity are written down, all kinds of infinities pop up. Schwarz and Scherk made an attempt to include gravity in the string theory. They got the clue from the massless spin 2 particle associated with the graviton. Thus, the factor that was responsible for the rejection of the earlier string theory as a model for strong interactions proved to be an asset for the grand unification of all the fundamental forces of nature, all particles of matter and space-time.

The development of the concepts of supersymmetry and supergravity was very helpful in the growth of the new string model. In 1971, André Neveu and John Schwarz detected a fundamental flaw in the Beta function proposed by Veneziano and Suzuki. Their theory could not describe all the spinning particles of nature. This fact drew the attention of some physicists who tried to establish some link between bosons and fermions.

All particles, without exception, have spin or angular momentum. They are divided into two classes, viz., fermions and bosons. Particles that have half integral spins (1/2, 3/2, 5/2, etc.) are fermions whereas those having integral spins (0, 1, 2, etc.) are bosons. Fermions are the particles of matter and bosons are the messenger particles that convey the forces between the particles of matter. The electron, neutron, proton, neutrino and quark (all these with spin ½) are examples of fermions. The photon (spin 1), graviton (spin 2), gluons, W-particle (spin 1), Z-particle and pion (spin 0) are examples of bosons.

The discovery of the ten-dimensional string theory in 1971 led to the birth of the supersymmetry theory. The concept of supersymmetry lies roughly in stating that fermions and bosons are amalgamated into a common description. Supersymmetry is a mathematical way of linking bosons and fermions in a single scheme. It tries to unify not only the forces, but also the forces and matter. It seeks unification by constructing family groupings and encompassing all particles with common description. It changes fermions into bosons and *vice versa*.

Nambu's string theory, which explained the origin of the Veneziano-Suzuki Beta function, described only a bosonic string. It did not account for the fermions. Schwarz, Neveu and Ramond completed the theory by inventing a fermionic string that was to accompany the bosonic one.

In 1971, Bunji Sakita of the City College of New York and Jean-Loup Gervais of the École Normale in Paris came up with the idea that the Schwarz-Neveu-Ramond theory possessed a hidden symmetry. This was the biginning of supersymmetry. This theory was also simultaneously proposed by two Soviet physicists, Yu.A. Gol'f and and E. P. Likhtman.

The supersymmetry could rotate a bosonic object into a fermionic object. This meant that each bosonic particle in the universe had a fermionic partner. The graviton which is a spin 2 boson, has the supersymmetric partner called the gravitino with spin 3/2. The photon, with spin 1, acquires the fermionic partner, the photino, with spin ½. Likewise, corresponding to the bosons — W-particle, Z-particle and gluons — the supersymmetric partners are winos, zinos and gluinos, respectively. In the same analogy, the fermions such as quarks and leptons, with spin ½, have supersymmetric bosonic companions — the squarks and sleptons, respectively.

Further work was necessary to improve the supersymmetry concept of Sakita and Gervais. Their supersymmetry was two-dimensional. When the one-dimensional string moves, it sweeps on to a two-dimensional surface. But Nambu's string theory is twenty-six dimensional and Schwarz-Neveu-Ramond string theory is ten-dimensional. Thus the supersymmetry concept of Sakita and Gervais was not yet complete.

Bruno Zumino and Julius Wess were inspired by the work of Sakita and Gervais. In 1974, they showed that the supersymmetry could be extracted from the string and be reduced to a simple point-particle theory defined in four dimensions. By taking a simple field theory involving the interaction of a spin 0 boson and spin ½ fermion, they could render it supersymmetric. The most important contribution of their work lies in the fact that supersymmetry killed many (not all) unwanted divergences found in quantum field theories of point-particles.

Basing on the successful discovery of Zumino and Wess, three physicists, viz., Peter van Neiuwenhuizen, Dan Freedman and Sergio Ferrara, who were working at the State University of New York at Stony Brook, added a fermionic partner to the graviton and thereby created a theory in 1976. They christened this theory "supergravity". Supersymmetry that includes gravity is supergravity. It provides a consistent quantum description of gravity. It produces finite results whereas non-supergravity theories run into the usual problem of infinite terms while quantizing gravity.

The orthosymplectic group Osp (N X M) and the superunitary group SU (NXM) are the underlying symmetry for supergravity and superconformal gravity, respectively. These supersymmetric groups were originally missed by Lie and Cartan.

The supergravity theory is too small to accommodate all the known particles. The largest Lie group that one can fit into this theory is O (8), which eliminate the divergences and incorporate both quarks and leptons simultaneously.

Out of the several versions of supergravity, the richest one is called N = 8, which involves eight supersymmetry operations. Each of these operations increases the spin by $\frac{1}{2}\hbar$. The mathematical operations of N = 8 supergravity are very simple in eleven dimensions rather than four.

The supergravity theory, when incorporated in the supersymmetrical string theory, is colloquially called the superstring theory. Jöel Scherk died in 1980. John Schwarz began collaborating with Michael Green in 1979-80. Both these physicists had significant contribution to the development of the superstring theory.

The string theories contained particles that travelled faster than the speed of light. These were called tachyons. This was an inconsistency. It does not seem to be possible to make sense of tachyons in a quantum theory.

The existence of tachyons is an inevitable feature in the twenty-six dimensional bosonic string theory. But it is possible to choose a version of the ten-dimensional string theory which does not contain tachyons.

The appearance of infinities in the quantum calculations of gravity was another serious problem with the superstring theory. When 1 or any such number is divided by 0 (1/0), the quotient is infinity. Such a phenomenon is a generic feature of all theories in which the fundamental particles are considered as mathematical points. In the superstring theory, the point particles were replaced by one-dimensional curves called strings. Nevertheless, the problem of infinities persisted in the calculations. Around 1982, Schwarz and Green removed the infinities from the calculations of the superstring theory. About the same time they found a couple of other superstring theories. In one of them, open strings have free ends. In a second one, closed strings form loops. The original superstring theory has both open and closed strings. Today the theory with closed strings is the favourite one.

The problem of anomalies is closely related to that of infinities. An anomaly is the name given to the breakdown of some symmetry when a classical theory is "quantized", i.e., when it is reformulated according to the rules of quantum mechanics. When a classical theory is given a quantum version, its symmetry breaks and thus it is said that the theory contains an anomaly. Symmetries and conservation laws are closely associated and hence anomalies can result in the violation of conservation laws. Anomalies were noticed to be fatal to the superstring theory. When gravity interacts with other particles, this results in fatal anomalies. This was found by Edward Witten and Luis Alvarez-Gaumé of the Princeton University.

The problem of anomalies needs some elaboration here. It is associated with parity violation. Parity in physics is a precise mathematical description of left-right symmetry or left-right-handedness. In the subatomic world, each type of particle possesses its own intrinsic parity. A perfectly symmetrical isolated system has a value of the parity which can be calculated from the wave function (Ψ). The value of parity does not alter as the system evolves. This is called the conservation of parity. Like all other conserved quantities, this is invariant.

The conservation of parity in the micro-universe was regarded as an inviolable law. In 1956, this law received a big jolt when two Chinese-Americans, Tsung Dalo Lee and Chen Ning Yang predicted that the law of conservation of parity (i.e., that physical laws are unaltered in mirror-image systems) was violated by the weak nuclear interactions. Another Chinese-American, Chien-Shiung Wu, performed a classic experiment to test the parity violation. Her experiment demonstrated directly that parity is not conserved in beta-decay. Yang and Lee were awarded the Nobel Prize for physics in 1957. This discovery of parity violation (non-conservation of parity) in weak force processes came as a great shock to physicists. Hitherto they assumed that nature would not distinguish left from right in empty space. This was, however, proved to be incorrect. When applied at low energies, the standard model of the weak and strong interactions evinces parity violation.

Thus it is correct to expect that the superstring theory should not be mirror-symmetric, or in other words, the theory should contain parity violation. Out of the few superstring theories that have been developed in ten dimensions, all but one of them have thus left-right asymmetry.

In 1984, Schwarz and Green did a calculation for one of the superstring theories. They selected SO (32) out of the infinite number of possibilities of symmetry structures. The theory in the SO (32) symmetry structure was free from anomalies. The anomaly cancelled out of the formulae for the symmetry structure SO (32) whereas this did not happen for the other symmetry structures. Thus the theory in SO (32) symmetry structure was known to be potentially consistent.

Around 1984, Schwarz and Green discovered a second symmetry structure named E_8 X E_8 that had a possibility of being consistent. But they did not develop a specific superstring theory to contain this symmetry. Shortly thereafter, four physicists at Princeton University, David Gross, Jeffrey Harvey, Emil Martinec and Ryan Rhom, discovered a new superstring theory with the symmetry group E_8 X E_8. This group of four physicists is now known as the Princeton String Quartet. They discovered two new superstring theories which they called heterotic strings. One of these theories contained the E_8 X E_8 symmetry whereas the other one was based on SO (32). The E_8 X E_8 symmetry structure has better properties than the SO (32) and is the promising candidate for a theory of the universe. With this discovery of the Princeton String Quartet, the superstring theory, which was considered dead and buried by most physicists, sprang back to life.

The supersymmetry groups were not cognized earlier and this was partly the reason for the late discovery of supersymmetry. Sophus Lie, the great Norwegian mathematician, had a mistaken idea that he had catalogued all possible types of symmetry groups. He missed the supersymmetric groups, because these are based on Grassman numbers which were not considered by Lie. In the exploration of nature, a basic, unconscious prejudice of physicists worked against the use of Grassman numbers. The mathematical relation aXb = –bXa, was not properly appreciated. Instead of being purely arbitrary, Grassman numbers are eminently practical. They describe fermions that are the constituent particles of the human body and any biological system. They are also the building blocks of all nonliving matter. Supersymmetry unites the concept of a real number with a Grassman number. Such a unification yields a "supernumber".

The present accepted superstring theory has ten dimensions, nine for space and one for time. Out of these, the extra six space dimensions are curled up into some tight little ball. When one tries to solve the equations of the superstring theory, one notices that the solution of the equations entails curling up these extra six dimensions. The curled up six-dimensional ball is too small to be observed. It is 10^{-33} centimetres across (Planck length).

The visible matter (including energy) in the universe is only ten per cent of all the matter. The rest ninety per cent of the total is invisible. This invisible matter is called shadow matter. The shadow matter is entrapped in the ball of the curled up dimensions. Even if fifty per cent of the matter of the universe is present in the six-dimensional ball, it would account for the contraction of the universe to follow its expansion.

The first E (8) of the E (8) X E (8) symmetry describes the ordinary matter. The second E (8) is for the shadow matter. This shadow matter does not interact, or only interacts extremely weakly with the ordinary matter. It does not interact with the ordinary light of the ordinary world. Hence it is bound to be invisible to us.

The E (8) symmetries break down to smaller symmetry structures. But we do not know if the two E (8) symmetries break down in an identical manner. If the symmetry-breaking pattern is the same for each E (8), both ordinary and shadow matter would have the same symmetry in the rules of physics. But it now seems more likely that the two symmetry-breaking processes are different for the two E (8)s.

Too many superstring theories have been worked out. But, a total of six theories in ten dimensions are acceptable at the present. Out of these six, three are heterotic and the other three are non-heterotic. The three heterotic string theories can be shown to be equivalent, and so we can regard them as one theory only. Further investigation may reveal that some of these theories are inconsistent. It is possible that this number may be narrowed down to one only. Thus the chance of getting one superstring theory cannot be ruled out.

Although the number of superstring theory is so far more than one, all of them accept only one type of string. This string is not a point object. It has a definite and positive size, although incredibly small. Only the Type 1 string theory has both open and closed strings. All other string theories have closed strings only, that form loops.

As a violin string vibrates at many different frequencies, called harmonics, and the different harmonics correspond to different musical sounds, the different harmonics of the superstring correspond to different elementary particles. What we call the electron, the graviton, the photon, the neutrino, and all the other fundamental particles are merely the different harmonics of a fundamental string. All the elementary particles, all the fundamental forces and the unification of all of them can be explained by the superstring theory which is claimed by someone as the Theory of Everything (TOE).

Is there really a TOE? Will there ever be a TOE? This is a big question. Everything in science is not about elementary particles, fundamental forces and their unification. There are many other branches of science that are open-ended. Hence many scientists are skeptical of this TOE claim.

To sum up this chapter, physicists are about to complete the supergrand unification of all the fundamental forces and particles. A long distance they had to travel to come to this goal. The classical field theory had a humble beginning with Faraday's work. It flourished with the ingenuity of Maxwell who unified electricity and magnetism in 1860. The quantum field theory got a good start with the brilliant concepts of Dirac in the late 1920s.

Quantum electrodynamics (QED), developed in the 1940 to 60s, and quantum chromodynamics (QCD), established about 1974, became two important milestones in the progress of the twentieth-century physics. In 1967-68, the Glashow-Salam-Weinberg theory brought about the unification of the electromagnetic force and the weak force. The electroweak force and the strong force were fused in the grand unified theory (GUTs) whose foundation was laid in 1974 by Howard M. Georgi and Sheldon Lee Glashow. The quantum field theory failed to unite the gravitational force with the other three forces. In the 1980s the supergrand unification of all elementary particles and fundamental forces has been achieved by the superstring theory. Some physicists are still skeptical of the superstring theory that has already obtained grand success at the theoretical level and needs experimental confirmation.

So the string is regarded as the final reality. The particles and the forces exist phenomenologically. The so-called elementary particles are not really elementary. Similarly, the so-called fundamental forces are not really fundamental. None of the different musical tones produced by the vibrating violin string in fundamental. Without the vibration of the string there is no musical sound. So is the case with the string. Without the vibration of the string, there are no elementary particles and no fundamental forces. In other words, the manifested world would not exist without the vibration of the string. Thus the string is the fundamental reality.

But confusion looms large without a precise definition of the word "reality". According to Advaita Vedānta, "reality" (*satya*) is that which exists timelessly without undergoing changes whatsoever. The string does not conform to the definition of reality of the Vedānta. There is expenditure of energy in the process of vibration. Since the store of energy in an entity cannot be infinite, its energy is bound to be exhaustible. Thus vibration cannot be an eternal process. At zero time (t_0) and zero space (S_0), or prior to the first cosmogonical event, the string did not exist. Again, posterior to the dissolution process, the string will not exist. Contrary to the fact of the beginning and the end of the string, the "reality" of the Vedānta, unlike the string, is beginningless and endless. It has neither the zero time (t_0) nor the maximum time (t_m). It is really timeless. Being functionless, it is bound to be timeless.

It is also spaceless and dimensionless. On the contrary, the vibrating string is active and ten-dimensional. The concept of spaceless string is self-contradictory. If the string is to be created at the time of the Big-Bang explosion or immediately after, it needs a material cause and an efficient cause, unless we assume that something comes out of nothing by chance alone. The concepts of chance origin and origin *ex nihilo* are meaningless for the Vedānta. "The string vibrates." In such a statement, the *Vedāntin* does not search for an efficient cause other than the string itself. But, similar is not the case in the *de novo* origination of the string. There must be a subject of the activity of origination, which cannot be done by a non-existing entity (the string here). Thus, we cannot say that the string is self-existent without depending on somebody or something else. The Vedānta does not accept something as "reality" if that something depends on others. Nothing is said about the consciousness of the string. It would be more appropriate if we consider it as insentient. The "reality" of Vedānta is Consciousness (*Cit*). It does not accept any insentient entity as "reality". It is also not logical to think that the insentient string is the agent responsible for the harmony and co-ordination in the functioning of the world (*saṁsāra*). Due to the main reasons cited here, the string cannot be accepted as the fundamental entity and the "reality".

The strings may be compared with the *guṇas* (strings or constituents) of *Māyā*. This will be discussed in the last chapter of this book.

The superstring theory is able to unify all the particles and forces of nature. We are made to understand that nature is perfectly symmetric. But our practical experiences are contrary to what is theoretically said here. The world is apparently pluralistic. The world is more asymmetric than symmetric. Is this contradiction apparent? If apparent, what is its cause?

At the fundamental level, nature does not just prefer symmetry in a physical theory, it *demands* it. At the same time we say that the universe is certainly not created symmetrically. The universe would be a rather dull place if symmetry were never broken. In the absence of asymmetry, there would be no atoms, no chemistry, no life, no diversity, no plants, animals and human beings. The symmetrical universe would be perfectly homogeneous and dull. It is a fact that in the beginning nature was perfectly symmetrical.

This symmetry broke down in the later processes, resulting in the asymmetric universe of today.

The universe is replete with examples where symmetry is hidden because it is broken. There was a single unified field at the instant of the Big-Bang. There was no differentiation; the manifested entity was just unitary. At the wall of the Planck time, 10^{-43} second after t_0 (beginning of time), gravity is presumed to have broken its bond with the single unified force. Up to 10^{-35} second after the Big-Bang, the strong force and the electroweak force were not separated. At that time the universe was 10^{-24} centimetre in size (this was the diameter of space). At this stage of the tiny universe, the undifferentiated, featureless, pure energy was just beginning to condense into point-like particles such as quarks and leptons. During the period from 10^{-35} to 10^{-6} second, the strong force separated from the electroweak force and subsequently the weak force separated from the electromagnetic force. Quarks and leptons were in abundance during this period.

At the beginning of time, the temperature was so high that all four forces were merged into one. The concerned temperatures were in the range of 10^{28} to 10^{32} K. These temperatures prevailed at 10^{-43} second after the beginning of the Big-Bang. At energies of 10^{19} GeV, (giga electron volt), all four forces merged in identity and the superstring theory achieved this unification. The grand unification energy was about 10^{15} GeV, at which the strong force, the weak force and the electromagnetic force were identical. These three forces were merged into one in the GUT era (10^{-35} second). The weak and the electromagnetic force merged at energies of about 10^{2} GeV. This electroweak unification temperature was prevalent at about 10^{-12} second. As the heat of the universe decreased, one by one the symmetry holding together the four forces broke down. Like the downhill flowing of water in an attempt to reach a lower energy state, quantum transitions in nature had a similar preference. The world system started in a "false vacuum" and tried to make a transition to a lower energy state.

The superstring theory has the symmetry E (8) X E (8). When this symmetry is broken, it perhaps breaks down to E (6), which later breaks down to SU (3) X SU (2) X U (1), which is the symmetry of GUTs. The complete symmetry of the Glashow-Weinberg-Salam theory for the electroweak force is SU (2) X U (1). The strong interactions, the weak interactions and the electromagnetic interactions are represented by the symmetry group SU (3), SU (2) and U (1), respectively.

The universe originally existed in ten dimensions. Only at the origin of the universe, it was possible to travel between such higher dimensions. The state of ten dimensions was unstable and hence the universe "cracked" into two pieces. The four-dimensional universe that peeled off from the rest was small, only ten per cent of the whole. The other six dimensions were curled up into a tiny ball that contained our "sister universe". Our sister universe co-exists with our universe. The matter in the sister universe is totally invisible. It is called the "dark matter". It has weight like the ordinary matter. The original fissioning of the universe was so violent that it created a gigantic explosion called the Big-Bang. Thus, according to the superstring theory, the Big-Bang is a byproduct of a much more violent transition, the cracking of the ten-dimensional universe into two pieces one four-dimensional and another six-dimensional.

The details of the Big-Bang and some other cosmological models will be discussed in the next chapter.

NOTES

1. P.A.M. Dirac, *PRSA* (*Proceedings of the Royal Society of Astronomy*) 114, no. 747 (1 March 1927) : 243.
2. A. Einstein, quoted by M. Kaku, and J. Trainer, In: *Beyond Einstein*, Bantam Books, New York, 1987, p. 35.
3. A. Einstein, quoted by M. Kaku, and J. Trainer, *Idem.*, p. 36.

IX

THE INVERTED PIPAL TREE

THE UNIVERSE is compared with an inverted pipal (*aśvattha*) tree, with roots above and branches below (*ūrdhvamūlamadhaḥśākhamaśvatthaḥ*[1]). Below and above spread its branches, nourished by the strings (*guṇas*); sense-objects are its buds (*adhaścordhvaṁ prasṛtāstasya śākhā, guṇapravṛddhā viṣaya-pravālāḥ*[2]). The *Kaṭhopaniṣad* also uses the same simile; it compares the world with an inverted pipal tree (*ūrdhvamūlo 'vākśākha, eṣo'śvatthaḥ*[3]). An infinitesimally tiny seed germinated; a sprout appeared; it grew and became the world-tree.

What has been said here will be elaborated in the last part of this chapter. Nonetheless, Vedic cosmogony is not akin to vegetative germination. It begins with ovogenesis. The egg that appears explodes into two parts. An excessive quantity of heat is formed as a result of this explosion. The Universe expands. In the superheated condition of the early Universe, different forms of matter and energy evolved. The expansion will be followed by a contraction. The evolution will be followed by an involution. The whole Universe will come back to the original state of the primeval egg that will ultimately disappear. The world-cycle will again operate.

The Vedas declare the formation of the cosmic embryo.[4] The seer of the Upaniṣad[5] gives a clear description of the formation of the cosmic egg, its subsequent explosion and splitting into two parts. Śaṅkara[6] says that a cosmic egg was produced from *Māyā* and that everything of the Universe was produced from the cosmic egg. References to the cosmic egg have been given in a number of other scriptures.[7] The fissioning of the cosmic egg into *rajatam* and *suvarṇam*[8] or *rayi* and *prāṇa*[9] is analogous to the ordinary matter and dark matter of the superstring theory. The superstring theory[10, 11] says that six dimensions out of the total of ten were curled up into a tiny ball which contained ninety per cent of the total matter, referred to as dark matter. This dark matter is invisible to us. The rest ten per cent of the total matter is the ordinary matter of our Universe with which its sister Universe of dark matter exists. The *Praśna Upaniṣad*[12] says that *rayi* is the ordinary matter.

The Vedic and the Vedāntic cosmogony invariably refers to the superheated[13] condition that prevailed during the period immediately following the explosion[14] of the cosmic egg. The creation of matter and energy would not have been possible without the generation of an excessive quantity of heat (*tapas*). Very often this word *tapas* is erroneously interpreted as "austerity" or "meditation", for which the word *tapasyā* is the most appropriate one. *Tapas* is the word for the physical heat which was a prerequisite for cosmogenesis. According to the Vedas[15] and the Upaniṣads,[16] the expansion of the Universe is brought about by heat (*tapasā*, which is the singular, instrumental case of the word *tapas*) and the initial explosion. This version is misinterpreted by the notion that the Universe expands by the austerity or meditation of Brahmā. Had it been the case, the word *tapasyayā* should have been used for the expression "by meditation".

The primordial superheated soup of the early Universe has been given the name *apāṁ napāt*[17] in the Vedas. The concept of the unified field in the twentieth century physics is analogous to that of *aditi* in the Vedas.[18] Space and field are differentiated in physics whereas *aditi* includes both. The role of *aditi*, as stated in the Vedas, in the genesis-flux[19] between matter-particles and radiation-quanta and between matter (energy) and field gives the impression that *aditi* is both parents and offspring. Quanta are generated from the field and reabsorbed into the field. Space gives rise to particles that are again reconverted into space. *Aditi* (the Sanskrit verb root *ad* means "to eat") eats all quanta and particles and so is this word etymologically constructed.[20] The vigorous as well as chaotic dance and collisions of micro-particles (*reṇus*)[21] in the superheated soup have been allegorically and symbolically expressed.

The Universe has a beginning and an end. It emanates from *Māyā* or *Svadhā*.[22] Thus the process of creation is that of a manifestation from an unmanifested condition (*avyakta*). A *de novo* creation or *creatio ex nihilo* is rejected by the Vedānta. As water is the material cause (*upādāna kāraṇa*) of ice, so is *Māyā* that is the precursor substance of the Universe (*jagat*). Before the manifestation of the Universe, there was neither nothing nor the manifested things; there was neither space nor the particles; there was no differentiation; there was no cosmic vitality or the *prāṇa*; only Brahman existed with its *Svadhā* (*Māyā*, *Prakṛti* or *Śakti*) as a single, non-dual entity.[23]

The nondual, primary Being, without becoming, has been termed *asat* in both the Vedas and the Upaniṣads.[24] But it is not a nihilistic idea of "nothing" or non-existence. It is really *the* nondual existence that is unmanifested, unbroken (*akhaṇḍa*), undifferentiated (*avyākṛtam*[25]), homogeneous, attributeless, functionless and indescribable. Thus what is termed *asat* (non-existence) is really "sat" (existence).[26]

Māyā (*Svadhā, Mūlaprakṛti, Avyakta, Śakti*), the power of Brahman, is insentient (*jaḍa*) and hence cannot be the efficient cause (*nimitta kāraṇa*) of the Universe. The scriptures declare that *Prayatiḥ* or *Īśvara* is the efficient cause[27] of the Universe. Brahman, Being changeless (*avikāra*), cannot be the substantial cause. Being functionless and attributeless, It cannot become the efficient cause. Hence, the scriptural mention of Brahman being the source (*yoni*[28]) and the cause[29] of the origin, sustenance and dissolution of the Universe may be figuratively[30] understood. In the language of Śaṅkara, Brahman is not the cause, not the non-cause and not both, and Brahman is not the efficient cause, not the substantial cause and not both (*na kāraṇaṁ nāpyakāraṇaṁ na cobhayaṁ nāpyanubhayaṁ na ca nimittaṁ na copādānaṁ na cobhayam*[31]). *Māyā*, the power of Brahman, is the material cause and *Īśvara*, the reflection of Brahman in *Māyā*, is the efficient cause of the Universe.

The desire to create is a prerequisite to the activity of creation. Brahman does not desire. It is *Īśvara* who does not like loneliness[32] and desires to have companions. It was only One and that One wanted to be many.[33] Of course, He did not have any need to be fulfilled by the created Universe.[34] He did not like solitude and inactivity; He hated to be alone, and He wanted to play (*līlā*[35]). And so did *Īśvara* desire[36] to create the Universe.

The same *Īśvara* offered Himself to be functional in three ways

— as an architect and a builder,[37] as a sustainer, controller and administrator,[38] and as a destroyer and devourer.[39] Thus, the same *Īśvara* is known as Brahmā, Viṣṇu and Rudra as the functionary of the first, second and third type, respectively.

The first product of *Māyā* was the *apraketa-salilam* (the undifferentiated waters, variously termed as *āpaḥ*, *nāra*, *ka*, *arka*. The cosmic egg or embryo that was formed contained this primordial *āpaḥ*. *Īśvara* became *Svayambhū* or the self-caused (the same as Brahmā) and entered into the cosmic egg. He stayed inside the egg for a period of one *divine* year. Brahmā inside the cosmic egg is known as *Hiraṇyagarbha* or the golden embryo. The egg burst into two pieces and this resulted in a gigantic cosmic explosion.. The temperature of the early Universe was extremely high. In the hot cosmic soup, differentiation began. *Prāṇa* or the cosmic vitality differentiated from *āpaḥ*. This was the first cosmic event, that occurred. simultaneously with the explosion of the cosmic egg, to indicate the birth of time (t_0). The totality of the world-matter (energy) is known as *Virāṭ* (the Cosmic Mind, or the *Mahat* of the Sāṅkhya) which functioned by being reflected by the light of Consciousness, Brahmā or Prajāpati. What was *Hiraṇyagarbha* inside the cosmic egg became known as Prajāpati after the cosmic explosion. All the quanta, particles and forces that were created through differentiation of only one principle became known as Prajās, and Brahmā, the creative Divinity as the Lord of *Prajās* (Prajāpati). The second differentiated entity was *ākāśa*, *kha* or *aditi*, which was produced from *prāṇa*. *Ākāśa* or *aditi* represents the single unified field including space.

In the superheated cosmic soup or plasma (the Vedic term is *apāṁ napāt*) of the early Universe, particles were born from *ākāśa* or *aditi* and again reconverted into *ākāśa* or *aditi*. This was a two-way traffic in a dynamic state of flux. The Vedas express it as *dakṣa* born from *aditi* and *aditi* born from *dakṣa*.[40] The scriptures say that *devas*[41] were produced after *dakṣa*. In this context, *devas* may be regarded as shining particles (the Sanskrit root *div* means "to shine") rather than gods. The Vedas refer to the vigorous dancing of the *reṇus* (particles) in the superheated cosmic plasma (*atrā vo nṛtyatāmiva tīvro reṇurapāyata*[42]).

The Universe expanded and is still in expansion although the speed of expansion is decelerated. The post-explosion temperature had a gradual fall. A predominant element, viz., hydrogen, was formed in the early hot Universe. This was the gaseous matter or *vāyu*. Spherical balls of compressed hydrogen were formed in different locations of space. Without giving the details of the formation of galaxies, stars, planets and satellites, the Vedic scriptures briefly describe the sequences of the formation of the Earth. As a result of extreme compression of the gaseous ball, the *vāyu* liquefied and thus the Earth became a liquid ball (*āpaḥ*). The periphery of the liquid ball lost heat and was thus converted into a solid sphere. What has been described here has been expressed in the *Taittirīya Upaniṣad* as follows: "*Ākāśa* was produced from that or this; *vāyu* from *ākāśa*, heat from (compressed) *vāyu*, liquid from heat (heated *vāyu*), and solid from liquid were produced (sequentially)."[43] The sequence given in the *Taittirīya Upaniṣad* is the same as in the *Brahma-sūtra*.[44] Modifications in this sequence have been suggested elsewhere.[45] Whatever may be the details of the sequences, one salient feature of the Vedāntic cosmogony is its evolutionary nature.[46] As Śaṅkara says: "The whole Universe has not suddenly come at a time; it has been gradually evolved (*krameṇa, na yugapat*[47]).

The Vedas and the Upaniṣads do not favour a linear and eternal Universe without a beginning and an end. The cosmic processes are cyclic. In the evolutionary phase, the universe is undergoing expansion. It will be followed by an involutionary phase of contraction. In the phase of contraction, all products of the Universe will be sequentially converted back into its previous state[48]: solid → liquid → heat → gases → *ākāśa*. The *ākāśa* will merge into *prāṇa, prāṇa* will merge into *āpaḥ*, and finally *āpaḥ* will be dissolved in *Māyā*. The time of the beginning of the cosmogonic process may be termed as t_o (the birth of time) and the time of the dissolution as t_m (maximum time or the death of time). Since time is only a mental construct and there cannot be a concept of time in the absence of events, there is no time before the first step of the manifestation and the last step of the dissolution of the Universe.

A Universe does not come into existence only once. The processes of the creation and the dissolution of the Universe repeat in cycles[49] that had no beginning and will have no end. The Upaniṣadic name of this cosmology is the "spider's model"[50]. As the spider spreads forth its web and reabsorbs it again, so is the Universe that evolutes and involutes. The Vedas describe the oscillating Universe by the "shuttle model"[51]. The weaver operates his shuttles (*tasarāṇi*) alternately, the forward activity of the weaving (*pravaya*) being followed by the backward activity (*apavaya*). And so are the cosmic processes of evolution and involution. Another Vedic nomenclature of the pulsating Universe is the "bellows model"[52]. It simulates the alternate movements of the bellows (*bhastrikā*) of the blacksmith.

This is a summary presentation of the Vedic and the Vedāntic cosmology. According to the *Viṣṇu Purāṇa*, the time span from t_o (time of creation) to t_m (time of dissolution) is known as a *para*[53] which contains 311.04 trillion (1 trillion = 10^{12}) Earth years. According to another calculation,[54] the duration of one *para* is 369.95616 trillion Earth years. One-half of a *para* is one *parārdha*. The first *parārdha* in a cosmic cycle is the period of expansion and evolution. The second *parārdha* is the period of contraction and involution. A *kalpa*[55] is another cosmic time unit which extends for a period of 4.32 billion Earth years. How far these estimations are correct cannot be ascertained at the present level of our knowledge. Science has entered into the field of cosmology only in the twentieth century. Within a short period, a lot has been known about cosmology and cosmogony. It would be appropriate to present the rapid development of modern cosmology in the remaining pages of this chapter.

We have so far discussed the Vedic and the Vedāntic cosmology. We do not know whether all of this knowledge was speculative or intuitional or empirical. But it is interesting to know that this ancient cosmology has parallelism with that of modern science. It does not stop there. It provides sufficient materials to penetrate the barrier wall and open an outlet for the thoroughfare of modern cosmology which begins from nowhere and ends in a blind alley.

Most astronomers of the nineteenth century and those of the early twentieth century believed in a static Universe. The study of the Universe was based on the laws of motion and the law of gravitation, as given by Newton. Hence it is not a fact that these astronomers accepted absolute non-motion of all the entities of the Universe. They assumed that there is no systematic large-scale motion of the major constituents of the Universe and that the Universe as a whole is static.

The Newtonian and the post-Newtonian age, extending to the earlier part of the twentieth century, had a concept of an eternal

Universe, with no beginning and no end, existing in a background of infinite and absolute time and space. No satisfactory model of the Universe was developed by centring around this static picture. This concept of a static Universe had a problem also. Assuming that all the constituents of the Universe are held at rest at any static moment, one has to consider the gravitational pull, due to which these constituents tend to move towards one another. This would violate the static concept and result in a Big Crunch. Alternatively, it may be assumed that the constituents of the Universe fly away from each other at some starting moment. They may continue to move away from one another for all time to come. The moving constituents may come to momentary rest and then start contracting under the gravitational influence. Finally, they may be squeezed to a point and we do not know what would happen after that. With the use of the cosmological principle and the Weyl postulate, E.A. Milne and W.H. McCrea developed a model of the Universe in 1934. This was the simplest model in Newtonian cosmology.

Albert Einstein proposed his general theory of relativity in 1915. He tried to construct a static model of the Universe in line with the attempts of the earlier cosmologists. This, however, failed to yield a satisfactory static model since Einstein's general theory of relativity or his theory of gravity, like Newton's, opposed a static Universe. Einstein conceived of a force of repulsion between two masses and this force increased in proportion to the distance between them. This repulsive force was described by the "λ-term" which he introduced in his equations of the general theory of relativity. He intended to produce a model of the static Universe. In order to do this, the force of gravitation must be counteracted by a force of repulsion. Thus the Universe could be held static between these two forces. Einstein proposed this model in 1917 and it is known as the "Einstein's Universe" Einstein's Universe is finite in volume but unbounded.

At the beginning of the twentieth century astronomers had a limited view of the Universe. They had a belief that the entire Universe consisted only of our Galaxy (the Milky Way). Soon this idea had to be abandoned. A vast number of galaxies of various types were detected in the observable Universe. It was further discovered that the galaxies move away from one another. This gave birth to the concept of an expanding Universe which replaced the older concept of the static Universe.

This discovery of the expanding Universe was done in 1929 when the American astronomer and cosmologist Edwin Powell Hubble (1889-1953) observed the "red-shift". He was working on the 250-cm telescope at Mount Wilson Observatory in Southern California. He observed a displacement towards the red of the spectral lines of distant galaxies. It was interpreted as a Doppler effect. Christian Johann Doppler (1803-53), an Austrian physicist, discovered this effect in 1842. The frequency of waves from a source moving towards an observer is increased above that from a stationary source; and waves from a source moving away from an observer are decreased in frequency. Doppler recognized that the effect applies not only to sound but also to light. In 1843, A.H.L. Fizeau (1819-96) applied Doppler's results and showed that the spectral lines of stars should be shifted towards the red end of the spectrum according to the speed at which they are receding from the observer (the Doppler shift). In 1929, Hubble measured the recessional velocities of eighteen galaxies and discovered that these velocities increased in proportion to their distance from Earth. This work gave the first direct evidence in support of the concept of an expanding Universe.

Newtonian Universe and Einstein's static Universe have already been discussed. After the discovery of the expanding Universe, the concept of a static Universe had to be abandoned. Cosmologists made attempts to construct mathematical models of the Universe. They went in for special types of model rather than very general models. They based their model on a couple of symplifying assumptions, viz., the "Weyl postulate" and the "cosmological principle"

Hermann Weyl (1885-1955) was the famous German mathematician who contributed to the study of symmetry, topological spaces and Riemannian geometry. The Weyl postulate gives a precise mathematical definition of the regularity of the Universe. According to it, a cosmic time serves as a reference coordinate for the Universe as a whole. It considerably helps to simplify the large-scale structure of the Universe. The various astronomical objects may be visualized to be moving in the Universe in a jumbled kind of way, intersecting each other at random points in space. Alternatively, they may be visualized to stream along regular tracts without intersecting each other. This second alternative, depicted in Figure 9.1, corresponds to the Weyl postulate.

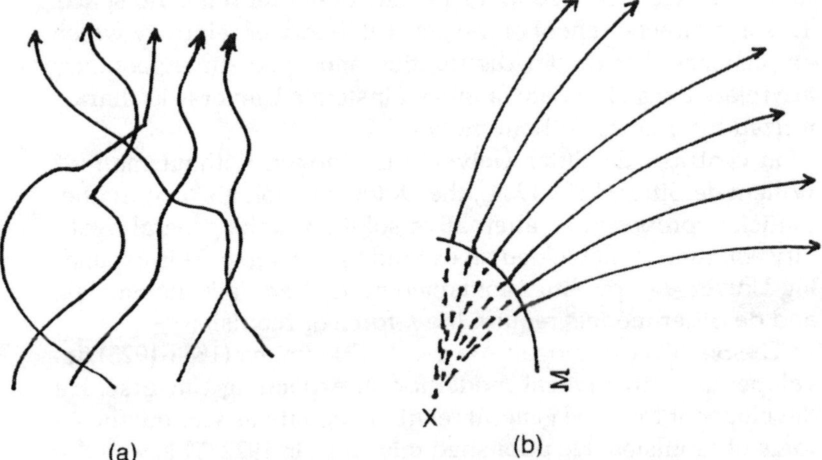

Fig. 9.1. Illustrations of jumbled motion versus motion according to Weyl's postulate.

The cosmological principle is a basic assumption that the Earth is not located at any special position in the Universe. The position of the Earth is typical. The large-scale features of the Universe which we observe would also be observed by any other suitably chosen observer in other locations of the Universe at the present-day. It is assumed that our position in the Universe is nothing special to enable us to observe the large-scale features the way we are doing.

With the help of these two assumptions (the Weyl postulate and the cosmological principle), cosmologists described the structure of the universe in terms of two physical quantities, viz., the "sign of curvature" of the Σ-spaces and the "expansion factor". The Σ-spaces may be imagined as spaces of positive, negative or zero curvature. The expansion factor may be denoted by a function S (t) of the cosmic time t. An increase of S (t) with t indicates an expanding Universe; a decrease of S (t) with t indicates a contracting Universe; whereas if S (t) stays unchanged, the Universe remains static. Cosmologists resort to Einstein's equations to decide the actual behaviour of S (t) and to determine if the Σ-surfaces have positive, negative, or zero curvature.

Einstein found a solution to the general relativity equations that yielded a static Universe. In the Einstein Universe, the "curvature" of space is related to the density of matter filling up space. This is a direct offshoot of the general theory of relativity which emphasizes that matter distribution and space-time geometry are related in an intimate fashion. Einstein's Universe is characterized by "matter without motion".

In contrast, de Sitter Universe is "motion without matter". Willem de Sitter (1872-1934), the Dutch cosmologist and mathematician, proposed an alternative solution to the general relativity equations that yielded an expanding Universe. This expanding Universe of de Sitter contained no matter. Both the Einstein and de Sitter models require the λ-force of repulsion.

The Soviet cosmologist Alexander Friedmann (1888-1925) developed a mathematical model for an expanding Universe. He developed it from the general relativity equations without the λ-force of repulsion. He published this work in 1922. This was the first realistic model of an expanding Universe that was consistent with Einstein's general theory of relativity and Hubble's observations of red-shifts. The Friedmann solution laid the foundations for the Big-Bang theory of modern cosmology.

In 1927, the Belgian astronomer and cosmologist Georges Edouard Lemaître (1894-1966) found a solution to Einstein's equations of general relativity that resulted in an expanding Universe. Friedmann had already come to this conclusion earlier. What Lemaître said by his mathematical calculation in 1927 was observationally shown by Hubble in 1929. Lemaître further suggested that the Universe must have begun from a small and highly compressed state, which he referred to as the "cosmic egg" or "primeval atom". He got this idea by backward extrapolation. He conjectured that radioactive decay had resulted in an explosion of the "primal atom". Although the findings of Lemaître were not fully appreciated at the time, he was the originator of the modern Big-Bang theory for the origin of the Universe.

Sir Arther Eddington pursued his cosmological investigations in the same line as that of Lemaître. Eddington and Lemaître took the λ-term of Einstein seriously. In the Eddington-Lemaître model the Universe spends a considerable time in the near-static Einstein state, and then expands to infinity. They believed that galaxy formation took place in the static phase.

Plots of S (t) *versus* t for three different Friedmann models of the Universe may be considered here. In Figure 9.2 the cosmic time t has been plotted on the X-axis and the expansion factor, S (t), on the Y-axis. Three curves corresponding to positive, zero, or negative curvature of the Σ-surfaces have been shown. All the three curves start from the point S = 0, t = 0. The function S (t)

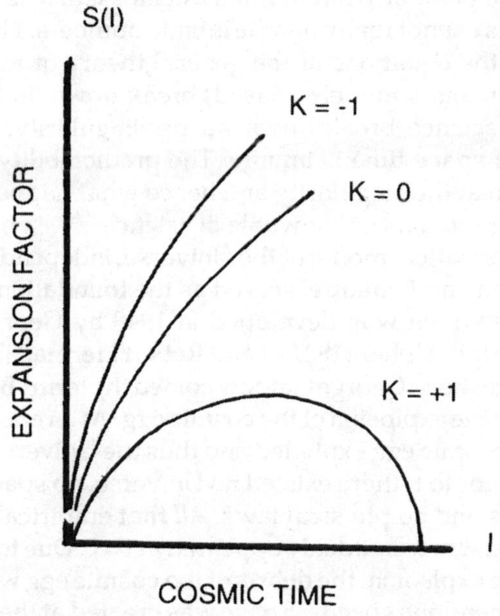

Fig. 9.2. Three different Friedmann models of the Universe.

continually increases with t when the curvature is zero (k=0) or negative (k = –1). In both the cases, we have an ever expanding Universe. When the curvature is positve (k = 1), S increases up to a certain maximum value, and then starts decreasing. This positive curve represents a Universe that expands up to a certain stage and then contracts until S = 0 is reached. It is not possible to deduce from Einstein's general relativity that a contracting Universe, on reaching the stage of S = 0, will re-expand. Thus contraction follows expansion but not *vice versa*. This is unlike a pulsating model in which the expansion and contraction phases alternate.

Mathematically speaking, S = 0 corresponds to a "singularity". At S = 0, the mathematical equations cannot be given precise meanings since certain quantities become zero or infinite. The density of matter and energy or, in other words, the density of the Universe, the curvature of space-time and the velocities of matter particles are infinite at S = 0. The tracks of all galaxies in the Weyl postulate meet at one point when S becomes zero.

This is the point of what mathematicians call a "singularity". Mathematics cannot really handle infinite numbers. Hence, at the singularity, the equations of the general theory of relativity (on which Friedmann's model is based) break down. In fact, all the theories of science break down at the singularity, where the curvature of space-time is infinite. The predictability of science breaks down at the singularity and hence what happened before the Big-Bang remains unknowable in science.

The mathematical model of the Universe, independently given by Friedmann and Lemaître, served as the foundation of the Big-Bang theory which was developed in 1948 by George Gamow (1904-68), Ralph Alpher (1921 -) and Robert Herman. The Soviet-American physicist George Gamow coined the term "Big-Bang" to characterize the explosion of the cosmic egg. At an epoch denoted by t = 0, the cosmic egg exploded and thus the Universe came into existence. Prior to t_0 there existed no Universe, no space, no time, no observers and no physical laws. *All* that empirically exists is the Universe, which suddenly appeared at t = 0. Due to the kinetic energy of the explosion, the debris of the cosmic egg were thrown apart at tremendous speeds. Space was created at the time of the explosion and it expanded along with the cosmic expansion. The gravitational pull between the different constituents of the Universe counteracted the outward force and thus retarded the speed of expansion. In case the Σ-surfaces have positive curvature (k = + 1), the expansion would sometime be completely stopped and then the Universe would start contracting. In case of a negative or zero curvature, the expansion of the Universe would be slowed down, but it would never come to a complete stop. In that case, the expanding Universe would never undergo a phase of contraction. The present age of the Universe has been estimated at around 10 to 20 billion (1 billion = 10^9) years (somewhere between 15 to 18 billion years).

Three possible geometries of the Universe, classified as close, open and flat, arise from the standard Big-Bang model. We will use a ratio designated by the capital Greek letter Ω (omega) which decides the nature of the geometry. The critical energy density of the Universe is that energy density which is just sufficient to eventually halt the expansion of the Universe. The ratio of the energy density of the Universe to its critical density is designated by Ω. If $\Omega > 1$, the Universe is closed with a spatial geometry of a positive curvature (spherical) and a finite volume. In this case, the gravitational self-attraction is sufficient to eventually halt the expansion and cause the Universe to recollapse. If $\Omega \leq 1$, the Universe is open with a spatial geometry of negative curvature (hyperbolic) and an infinite volume. In this case, the expansion of the Universe will continue forever. If $\Omega = 1$, the Universe is flat with zero curvature (Euclidean) and an infinite volume. In this case, the Universe expands forever; but the expansion rate approaches zero. The three types of the Universe, viz., open, flat and closed, correspond to the curve (a), (b) and (c) of Figure 9.2, respectively.

Cosmologists are still not sure whether the Universe is open, closed or flat. If Ω was ever exactly equal to 1, its value would remain unchanged forever. But if Ω differed slightly from 1 an instant after the Big-Bang, the deviation from 1 would grow rapidly with time. The value of Ω today lies between 0.1 and 2. A second after the Big-Bang, its value was equal to 1 to within 1 part in 10^{15}. The standard Big-Bang model merely assumes the fact of the beginning of Ω so close to 1 as an initial condition, without offering any explanation. This failure to explain this fact is the flatness problem, which was first pointed out in 1979 by Robert H. Dicke and P.J.E. Peebles of Princeton University.

In the late 1940s and the early 1950s, George Gamow and his colleagues Ralph Alpher and Robert Herman discussed the evolution of the Universe from about one second to three minutes after the "hot Big-Bang". Gamow conjectured the early Universe to have mainly consisted of high-intensity radiation rather than matter. The present Universe is matter-dominated as a result of its expansion that reduced the intensity of radiation much more rapidly than the density of matter. In the mid-1940s George Gamow suggested that high density and high temperature were prerequisites for the synthesis of elements which existed in the few moments immediately after the Big-Bang. In 1948, Ralph Alpher, H.A. Bethe (1906 -) and George Gamow suggested the first explanation of the abundances of the chemical elements that originated due to the thermonuclear processes in the early hot Universe. This work has been known as αβλ theory. In a number of subsequent papers, jointly published by Alpher and Herman, and Alpher, Herman and Follin (J.W. Follin, Jr.), the synthesis of elements in the early hot Universe could be established as an integral part of the standard Big-Bang model. Their work particularly explained the universal abundance of helium.

In 1939, Bethe proposed the carbon cycle. This was the first elaborate theory for the formation of stellar energy through a series of nuclear reactions, culminating in the fusion of four hydrogen nuclei to form a helium nucleus and the generation of excess energy that is radiated. In 1956, Gamow showed that the heavier elements could only have been formed in the hot interiors of stars.

Alpher and Herman had another suggestion in 1948. Their line of argument was like this: If the Universe began with a "hot Big-Bang", it must have been dominated, in the early epoch, by intense electromagnetic radiation, which would gradually have cooled or red-shifted as the Universe expanded. Basing on the then-current astronomical data, they calculated the present residual background radiation observed as having a spectral distribution characteristic of a black body at a temperature of about 5 K. In 1949, Alpher and Herman proposed the present-day temperature of the microwave background radiation as 5 K whereas Gamow's prediction was 7 K in 1953. Such a weak radiation was not experimentally detected until 1964 when Arno Allan Penzias and R.W. Wilson observed it. The current observed value of this background radiation is 2.73 K.

The hot Big-Bang cosmogony, as described by Gamow, has undergone profound modifications in the light of newer knowledge obtained from cosmological research during the later half of the twentieth century. Some of Gamow's predictions and speculations have become obsolete. Nonetheless, it would be interesting to state some of his ideas that were very important in the mid-twentieth century and that would never be irrelevant historically in the future.

The Universe, immediately after the Big-Bang, was radiation-dominated. The radiation consisted of photons (light quanta). Gamow supposed the Universe to be made initially of photons and neutrons. The one-second-old Universe had a temperature of 10^{10} K. Gamow predicted that the 700-second-old Universe had a temperature of about 0.5 billion K and that at this time it had roughly equal number of neutrons and protons. In Gamow's scheme there was no proton in the beginning and it was generated as a result of the neutron decay. The neutron is not a stable particle. It decays into an electron, a proton and an antineutrino in about 700 seconds. To express it more precisely, of a given population of neutrons only a half remains intact after 700 seconds. Before the Universe was three minutes old, *all* its matter existed in the form of a few particles like electrons and neutrinos with their antiparticles and protons and neutrons with their antiparticles. All these different particles were in thermodynamic equilibrium at the high temperature prevalent at this early time.

The hypothesis of Gamow, Alpher and Herman regarding the production of proton from neutron in the early Universe was greatly modified in 1950 by the suggestion of the Japanese astrophysicist C. Hayashi. According to Hayashi, electron-positron pairs were produced at the expense of photons when the initial electromagnetic radiation was powerful. The positrons that were produced combined with neutrons to form protons according to the following reaction:

$$n + e^{+} \rightarrow p + \upsilon$$

At the very high temperature prevalent at the beginning of the Universe, all particles such as neutrons, protons, electrons, positrons, neutrinos and antineutrinos were in thermal equilibrium. In that extremely heated condition, the particles were constantly in vigorous movement and it was not possible for any two or more particles to coalesce together to form nuclei of elements.

As the Universe expanded its temperature fell. At a stage three minutes after the Big-Bang, conditions were conducive to induce nuclear fusion of neutrons and protons into light nuclei like deuterium, helium, lithium, and so on.

The primordial nucleosynthesis took place when the temperature of the early Universe was in the range of 10^9 to 10^8 K. The main synthesis of nuclei occurred in the temperature range of $10^9 - 5 \times 10^8$ K when the age of the Universe was about 180 to about 700 seconds. According to Gamow, Alpher and Herman, the neutron and the proton were fused together to form deuterium (heavy hydrogen) in the presence of sufficiently high density of matter. Two deuterium atoms then combined to form helium, and, in this case also, the quantitative formation of helium depended upon the density of matter.

The primordial nucleosynthesis could not continue beyond the helium ($^4_2$He) stage in any significant way. It was a fact that some more light nuclei like deuteron ($^2_1$H), triton ($^3_1$H), helium ($^3_2$He), lithium ($^7_3$Li) and beryllium ($^{11}_4$Be) were formed; but these were formed in much smaller fractions. The nuclei of the elements mentioned here beyond the helium ($^4_2$He) stage are unstable and hence they reverted to helium soon after they were formed.

By the process of addition of neutrons and protons, the synthesis of stabler nuclei like carbon, oxygen and so forth cannot occur. Hence carbon ($^{12}_6$C) and elements with more than six protons could not be synthesized in the hot soup of the Universe immediately after the Big-Bang. It was pointed out by Fred Hoyle in 1954 that it is in principle possible to produce carbon from three helium nuclei. Such a process of carbon production, however, did not materialize in the early period since the Universe had a temperature below the one adequate for such a reaction after the first three minutes immediately following the Big-Bang. Hoyle showed that this process of carbon production occurred inside stars at a much later period. It may be generalized here that further nucleosynthesis of heavier nuclei took place in the interior of stars. Sometimes much later some of the stars exploded, resulting in the wide dispersal of their core-contents in vast space. Thus the carbon and other heavier elements that are present on the Earth and elsewhere were originally cooked in the interior of some stars and eventually dispersed due to supernova explosions.

During the cooling period from 10^{10} to 10^9 K, electrons (e^-) and positrons (e^+) had a tendency to annihilate each other and thereby to produce pairs of photons (γ). The reverse reaction did also take place, i.e., electrons and positrons were also produced from photons in the presence of a sufficiently large number of energetic photons. When the temperature exceeded five billion (5×10^9) degrees, both reactions were taking place in a thermodynamic equilibrium. As a result of this reversible reaction, the population of electrons and positrons was maintained. As the temperature dropped below five billion degrees, there was a sharp decline in the number of photons with enough energy to create electron-positron pairs. At this stage, electron-positron annihilation began to dominate. The annihilation process continued further and the pairs had been effectively eliminated from the cosmic brew by the time the Universe had cooled to about a billion (1×10^9) degrees. The annihilation of the pairs of electron-positron resulted in an increase in the number of photons.

Our Universe has an excess of matter over antimatter. It is problematic to explain this if the initial creation of equal numbers of electrons and positrons is accepted as a fact. It is assumed that there was an excess of electrons over positrons prior to the annihilation process. Due to this fact of the initial unequal numbers, free electron's could be present after the annihilation process was completed. When the Universe cooled to the temperature range of 3,000 to 4,000 K, free electrons combined with free protons to form electrically neutral hydrogen atoms. This is how free electrons were removed from the cosmic brew and the most predominant element of the Universe, viz., hydrogen was formed.

The main features of cosmogenesis, as have been outlined here, were in accordance with the hot Big-Bang model of Gamow. At this stage we may take a trip backward in time and make a rough estimate of the evolutionary stages of the standard hot Big-Bang model. We do not know exactly what happened during the first 10^{-43} second after the Big-Bang. This is known as the Planck era. During this time, the Universe had a temperature of 10^{32} K and a density of 10^{94} g per cubic centimetre. From the point of view of classical physics, 10^{-43} s is the beginning of the Universe. In such extreme conditions of high temperature and high density, quantum gravity effects might have been important at time 10^{-43} s after the Big-Bang. The present space-time structure might have broken down at this time into a sort of space-time "foam".

The Big-Bang that brought the Universe into existence produced energies as great as 10^{19} GeV. Supergrand unification of all the four fundamental forces took place in the Planck era with this energy. The diameter of the Universe at time 10^{-43} s was 10^{-33} cm. With the continuous expansion of the Universe since the Big-Bang, the size of the Universe has been increasing. At any particular time, the size of the observable Universe is the distance travelled by light since the Big-Bang. Since the Universe's present age is about 15 to 20 billion years (1 billion = 10^9), its present diameter is about 15 to 20 billion light-years.

At around 10^{-35} second after the Big-Bang, the temperature of the Universe was about 10^{28} K. During the time-interval between 10^{-43} s and 10^{-35} s, the strong force, the weak force and the electromagnetic force were unified into a single one. This period is known as the GUT (Grand Unified Theories) era. As the messenger particle of the electromagnetic force is the photon, likewise the grand unified force is transmitted by one kind of particle. These particles are superheavy, some 10^{15} times as heavy as the proton. The Grand Unified Theories predict the existence of these particles. These particles might have modified the matter particles in the generation of a tiny asymmetry between the amount of matter and antimatter during the early period of cosmogenesis. This could explain the excess of matter over antimatter needed at 10^{-5} s.

The point just mentioned here needs some elaboration. The Universe in which we live today is made of matter. When particle antiparticle pairs were formed in the early Universe, the number of particles was expected to be equal to that of antiparticles. When they annihilated one another, the Universe would have been left with zero matter and antimatter. But, contrary to this expectation, the pesent Universe is made of matter. Where did the antimatter go? This was the question which puzzled physicists for a long time.

In 1964, Val L. Fitch and James W. Cronin at the Brookhaven National Laboratory showed that CP (C for "charge conjugation" which turned matter into antimatter and P for "parity reversal" which interchanged left and right) was violated.

The GUT and the superstring theories make use of the CP violation in accounting for the fact that we do not see an equal amount of matter and antimatter in the Universe, which is matter-dominated. As a result of CP violation, there was a slight imbalance of matter over antimatter (roughly one in every 10^8). This asymmetry occurred at 10^{-32} s or so. When matter and antimatter annihilated each other in the lepton era with the creation of radiation, the tiny fraction of the original matter which was in excess of the antimatter was left over. This left over matter constitutes our physical Universe. Thus the present matter is like a fossil, left over from the original annihilation of matter and antimatter. Had there been no CP violation, the present Universe with matter could not be thought of.

The time corresponding to an energy of about 10^{15} GeV was about 10^{-37} s. For GUTs to be operational, an energy above 10^{15} GeV (1 GeV = 1.16×10^{13} K) was necessary. The present temperature of the Universe, i.e., 2.7 K (or about 2.5×10^{-13} GeV), may be compared with GUTs temperature of 10^{15} GeV. This involves a factor of 4×10^{27}, by which the linear scale of the Universe has expanded since the GUTs epoch. The horizon size at the GUTs epoch was about 10^{-26} cm. Magnetic monopoles with a characteristic energy of 10^{16} GeV existed in this epoch. According to the prediction of GUTs, some points in space were excited, or, in other words, "false" vacuum was created. As suggested by Alan Guth,the Universe found itself in the false vacuum at around the GUTs era (10^{-35} s). The false vacuum possessed a negative pressure (a tension) which effected a *repulsive* gravitational force. As a result of this powerful repulsive effect, the Universe embarked on a period of exponentially accelerating expansion, the so-called inflationary scenario of Alan Guth. At around 10^{-32} s, the false vacuum decayed into the "true" vacuum and all the vacuum energy was released in the form of particles and heat.

As the Universe passed through the GUTs era at 10^{-35} s and entered the hadron era (10^{-35} s to 10^{-6} s), the strong force and the electroweak force were separated. The electroweak unification continued till about 10^{-12} s when the energy was about 10^{2} GeV. With further cooling, the physical condition of the Universe reached a stage where the electromagnetic force was separated from the weak force. After this, the cosmological materials consisted of a soup of all the fundamental particles such as quarks, leptons, etc.

During the hadron era (10^{-35} s to 10^{-6} s), strong interaction physics influenced the state of the Universe. At some point during this era, the Universe was a sort of "quark soup" due to the dissociation of the nucleons into their constituent quarks. Protons and antiprotons did not exist in this phase. Still the asymmetry between matter and antimatter was maintained in the form of an asymmetry between the number of quarks and antiquarks.

The period from 10^{-6}s to 1 s is the lepton era. At the time 10^{-5} s, the temperature of the Universe was above 10^{13} K. At this temperature, the background photons were energetic enough to produce pairs of hadrons. Only after 10^{-5} s do all the matter and antimatter pairs annihilate, leaving just those matter particles without partners. This is a crucial event in the history of cosmogenesis. All the matter of the Universe today is derived from these left over matter particles. Had there been no asymmetry, all the matter and antimatter would have annihilated at 10^{-5} s to produce a Universe of pure light.

At 1 s the temperature of the Universe was 10^{10} K, hot enough for pairs of electrons and positrons to be created. Before 1 s the number of electrons and positrons was roughly equal to that of photons. At around 10^{-3} s, the quarks congealed into protons and neutrons. In the lepton era (one microsecond to one second after the Big-Bang), the primeval cosmological material consisted of only the lighter particles, viz., protons, neutrons, electrons, muons, pions, the antiparticles of all the particles mentioned, neutrinos, photons and gravitons. Before this time, heavy particles containing strange and charmed quarks had already disappeared. During this lepton era, annihilation of particles took place. After about 10^{-6} s, the temperature was not high enough to sustain the antiprotons and antineutrons. The annihilation of muons took place at around 10^{-3} s. Finally, around 1 s, the positrons were annihilated. Thus, the Universe was left with neutrons, protons, electrons, neutrinos, photons and gravitons.

The lepton era was succeeded by the plasma era which extended from 1 s to 10^{13} s. Nucleosynthesis in the hot Big-Bang took place during the period from 1 s to 10^3 s. When the Universe was 700 seconds old, it had a temperature of about 500 million K. At this stage the numbers of neutrons and protons were roughly equal. Since at this temperature the thermal energy dropped below the binding energy of compound nuclei, neutrons and protons could fuse together in the presence of sufficiently high matter density. The primeval nucleosynthesis during the period from 1 s to 10^3 s produced about 25 per cent by weight of helium. The remaining matter was almost entirely free protons (hydrogen ions). Nucleosynthesis could not proceed further in the hot Big-Bang since, after a few minutes, the temperature fell to a level at which further fusion reactions were not possible. In the short time available, very little of the nuclear material managed to assemble into nuclei heavier than helium.

The matter of the Universe consisted of ionized gases (25 per cent helium and about 75 per cent hydrogen) during a long period of the plasma era, i.e., from 10^3 s to 10^{13} s. The Universe continued to cool. But the rate of cooling diminished with time. It took about 10^5 years before the temperature fell to around 10^4 K. Since kT dropped below the ionization energy of hydrogen at this temperature, the free protons and electrons combined to form atomic hydrogen. This was the stage at which the cosmological material became transparent to light. Hereafter the matter and radiation were largely decoupled.

The outlines of the standard Big-Bang model seemed satisfactory. Most cosmologists have accepted it especially after Arno Penzias and Robert Wilson discovered the relict background radiation in 1965. Nevertheless, some problems of this model remained to bother many cosmologists during the 1970s. The most important of these problems were the singularity, the flatness, the homogeneity, the isotropy and the dimensionality of spacetime.

One way of understanding the singularity is to conceive of a state of infinite density and zero volume at time t = 0. What was there before the singularity? Where did the singularity come from? What was the precursor material of the Universe? What made the cosmic egg explode? These questions were not answered by the standard Big-Bang model.

According to Einstein's general theory of relativity, we have a finite and a closed Universe, the geometry of which is different from the Euclidean geometry of flat space. In an open Universe, parallel lines diverge from one another. In contrast, parallel lines in a closed Universe cross one another like the meridian lines on the globe of the Earth. Our observational evidences indicate that our Universe is very close to being flat. Why is our Universe flat? The standard Big-Bang model does not answer this question.

The Universe expanded as a result of the initial Big-Bang explosion. It is still expanding, although at a much slower rate, since the remaining outward explosive force is still greater than the implosive gravitational force. But, why is the expansion rate so fine-tuned? Had the rate of expansion been otherwise, either faster or slower, we would not have been here. If the Universe would have expanded at a slower rate, it would have recollapsed before life had time to arise. Galaxies could not have been formed if the rate of expansion would have been faster. What agent is responsible for the precise force of the Big-Bang explosion and the exact fine-tuning of the rate of expansion of the Universe? The standard Big-Bang model does not answer such a question.

If the explosion was chaotic, the Universe could have expanded at different rates in different directions. But that has not been the case. The rate of expansion is the same in all directions. That means the so-called chaotic explosion was not really a chaos. It was somehow precisely designed and accurately controlled. Through which agency and what mechanism this phenomenon was brought about cannot be answered by the standard Big-Bang model.

The Universe looks the same in all directions, if viewed on the large scale. To express it technically, it is isotropic. We have indirect evidences to indicate that the cosmological expansion was isotropic even one second after the Big-Bang.

The Universe also looks the same everywhere when considered on scales larger than clusters of galaxies. Matter is distributed evenly through the Universe. The size of the observable Universe is about 10^{28} cm. In this vast Universe, the density of matter deviates from a perfectly smooth distribution by an amount not more than one part in 10,000. Thus, for all pratical purposes, the Universe is homogeneous. The standard Big-Bang model cannot account for this large-scale isotropy and homogeneity.

We may postulate that everything in the starting of the Universe was smooth. This postulate may solve the problems of the isotropy and the homogeneity. But, on what basis do we make such a postulate? The Big-Bang explosion was supposed to be chaotic. Wherefrom did we get the order amid an utter disorder? This itself remains as an enigma.

Even though the Universe is homogeneous on larger scales, it is not homogeneous on smaller scales since it contains clusters of galaxies and galaxies made of stars, planets of stars and satellites of planets. Some small disturbances in the early history of the Universe could have produced these minor inhomogeneities in an otherwise homogeneous Universe. What these disturbances were could not be ascertained by the standard Big-Bang model.

The standard Big-Bang model is based on Einstein's general theory of relativity. According to this theory, the presently expanding Universe would stop its expansion and start its contraction provided it has enough mass for recollapsing. Only 10 per cent of all the mass is visible to us. If the rest of the mass is invisible but is present, the Universe will recollapse and eventually have a Big Crunch. The invisible matter may be in the form of dark matter. It may be present in black holes. The neutrinos may contribute to the missing mass. These are relic particles produced in the Big-Bang. There should be 10^9 relic neutrinos for each proton or electron in the Universe. Thus the cosmos may be regarded as a sea of neutrinos punctuated only rarely by atoms and subatomic particles. These neutrinos had been considered to be massless until the Russian group headed by V.A. Lyubimov claimed in 1980 that neutrinos have masses (in the range of about 16 – 40 eV for υ_e, with an average of 30 eV). Whether neutrinos are massless particles or they are with mass is still controversial. But, if not neutrinos, there may be some undiscovered particle(s) to provide the missing mass. Various theories have predicted particles such as magnetic monopoles, photinos, axions, gravitinos and winos, many of which are grouped together as WIMPS (weakly interacting massive particles). These particles may provide the required mass but because of their weak interactions may be hardly detected. The cosmic string idea of 1988 may also solve the problem of the missing mass. The cosmic strings are thin, massive, thread-like objects that are predicted to exist by some GUTs (not by all). They have a thickness of about 10^{-29} cm and a mass of about 10^{22} g cm^{-1}, or 10^7 solar masses per light-year. These strings were perhaps produced copiously in a random arrangement in the early Universe. Although the cosmic string is not a particle, it is an incredibly long skinny bit of left over energy from the Big-Bang. The cosmic string may fill up the missing mass in the universe that would eventually recollapse. In consideration of all these points it may be safely presumed that the Universe will recollapse. The imploding Universe will finally reach the singularity with zero volume and infinite mass. The field equations of Einstein do not predict in favour of a subsequent Big-Bang and a re-expansion. Is that the end of the Universe? Would the Universe vanish forever? Would it stay in the singularity stage for eternity? Can we use the term "eternity" after the death of time? These questions remain unanswered in the standard Big-Bang model.

The problem of the dimensionality of space-time is another enigma in the standard Big-Bang model. Many mathematicians now believe that space may have more than three dimensions.[56]

In the most interesting of these models, space has ten dimensions, the eleventh dimension being time. All but three dimensions of space have been "compactified" (they have shrunk into thin tubes). Why did only seven dimensions shrink? Why not six or eight? The standard Big-Bang model has no explanation for the effective three dimensions of space.

In spite of these and some more enigmas of the standard Big-Bang model, many cosmologists are not prepared to give it up. It is still the most favoured model in modern cosmology. Its potent rival is the steady state model that directly antagonizes it. Many modifications have also been suggested to the standard Big-Bang model. We will leave this standard model here and discuss some of its rival and associate models.

It is a historical coincidence that in the same year both the Big-Bang theory and steady-state theory were born. In 1948 three British astronomers, Hermann Bondi, Thomas Gold and Fred Hoyle, put forward the steady-state theory[57], which became a rival of the Big-Bang model. In many ways both these theories are opposites of each other. In the Big-Bang model, we have an evolving Universe with an explosive origin and a finite age having a beginning and an end. In contrast, the steady-state model is characterized by a Universe without a beginning or an end, without any large-scale change, and with a continual creation of matter and energy in relation to its steadily expanding volume. Although the modern steady-state theory was first postulated in 1948, this concept was in vogue in ancient India. The ancient school of Mīmāṁsā philosophy developed this steady-state concept in contradistinction to the Vedāntic cyclic and evolving models with beginnings and ends.

Bondi and Gold modified one of the cosmological assumptions to formulate their model. According to the cosmological principle, the Universe is homogeneous and isotropic at a given cosmic time. This requirement does not preclude any change at all. The Universe may vary from one Σ-surface to another; in other words, it may change with time. Bondi and Gold postulated that the Universe looks the same at all cosmic times. This new principle was called the "perfect cosmological principle" (PCP) by its authors. According to the PCP, the Universe is uniform in structure not only in space but also in time. The Universe of Bondi and Gold does not change with time as well as in space and its physical laws are unchanging. Such an unchanging Universe is called the "steady-state Universe".

The theory of Bondi and Gold had to answer the critics' question. The concept of the expanding Universe has already been established in science. The Universe will have a thinning out of the material as it continues its expansion. But the PCP requires the material density of the Universe to remain the same. In order that the Universe expands and simultaneously maintains its material density unchanged, matter is to be steadily or continuously created to make up for the depletion produced by the expansion. But where does the new matter come from? If it is assumed that the new matter comes from nowhere, it violates the law of conservation of matter and energy. Bondi and Gold did not have any satisfactory answer to their critics' objection. If one sustains the steady-state theory, one must explain the synthesis of light nuclei and the background microwave radiation without recourse to the superheated condition of the Universe.

Hoyle tried to answer the questions posed by the critics of Bondi and Gold. He proposed a modification of the right hand side of Einstein's field equations by adding an extra scalar field. He called it the "Creation field" or the "C-field".

The C-field may be considered as an energy reservoir. New matter is assumed to be created out of this reservoir. This concept of an energy reservoir appears at the first sight to avoid the violation of the law of conservation of matter and energy. Deeper scrutiny, however, reveals that this idea runs into difficulty. If we continue to subtract positive numbers from one positive number which may be even too large, we must finally come to a stage where nothing will eventually be left. The same thing will happen to the positive reservoir of the C-field.

To get round this difficulty, Hoyle made use of a simple mathematical concept of the subtraction of positive quantities from a negative quantity. In such a case, any number of subtractions would never reach a state of zero remainder. Thus Hoyle imagined a reservoir of negative energy and provided a conceptual foundation on which the overall energy is conserved.

In 1960, Maurice Pryce worked out an elegant mathematical formulation for the C-field. The C-field comes into effect only when particles are created. The C-field radiation originates at the time of the creation of a particle. The carrier of the C-field radiation is a particle that has energy and momentum equal and opposite to that of the created particle. The carriers of this radiation are particles of zero spin, no charge and zero rest mass. They travel with the speed of light. The C-field determines the energy and momentum of the created particle, but it does affect the motion of any existing particles. It has a repulsive gravitational effect. A region of space-time containing C-field radiation repels matter.

The C-field differs from a standard positive energy field by virtue of the unusual feature that the former has negative stresses and negative energy. In 1951, W.H. McCrea developed his ideas on the mechanism of the expansion of the Universe. He conjectured negative stresses to arise from what goes on in the vacuum and because of these negative stresses does the Universe expand and is mattter continually created.

At this stage, an analysis is necessary for the justification or refutation of the concept of Hoyle's C-field. The mathematics of Hoyle is apparently justifiable. But, mathematics, being a deductive science, is not necessarily true in the sense of conforming to facts if the major premise is factually untrue. In such cases, the mathematical deduction is logically valid, but the conclusion is factually untrue. Hoyle's speculation of a negative reservoir of energy is factually fallacious. Conceptually speaking, all reservoirs are positive. The word "reservoir" has always a positive meaning as far as the storing of something is concerned. A nihilistic reservoir is a logical absurdity. The minus (–) symbol in mathematics has an in-built meaning of relativity. A certain X_1 is negative in relation to a certain X_2; but the negative X_1 is not nothing. From the relativistic theory Paul Dirac proposed in 1930 the negative energy states for electrons. But it may not be misconstrued that the negative energy states are absolute void, empty or vacuum. If something is produced from nothing, we mathematically express it as "something = nothing" or "X = not – X". Such self-contradictory statements are nonsensical and are certainly false on the basis of linguistic and conceptual analysis. Hoyle's concepts of C-field as a negative reservoir and *cretio ex nihilo* are not different. From the logical point of view, it becomes impossible to recognize the validity of the C-field theory of Hoyle.

Of course, all the models of the Universe in modern cosmology are silent on the question of the source of the matter and energy of the Universe. The Big-Bang model has no answer to the question: "Wherefrom does the matter (including energy) of the Universe originate at t = 0?" The law of conservation of matter and energy becomes sacrosanct in science after the creation; but it is intentionally ignored in connection with the source of all the matter and energy of the Universe as a whole. Advaita Vedānta does not recognize anything like void, vacuum, empty, nothing or *śūnya*. It does recognize the full (*pūrṇa*). Its law of conservation does not concern matter and energy. In its cosmology, the Universe has a beginning (*sṛṣṭi*) and an end (*pralaya*). The cosmic processes of manifestation and dissolution are repetitive *ad infinitum*. In such a cosmology, the law of conservation of matter and energy is relevant to the manifestation phase only from t_o to t_m. This law has no meaning to the processes antecedent to the creation and subsequent to the dissolution. The conservation law of Advaita Vedānta, as given in the *Bhagavadgītā*, speaks of the conservation of Being (*nāsato vidyate bhāvo nābhāvo vidyate sataḥ*[58]). The literal meaning of this Sanskrit text is this: "Becoming from something that does not exist is not a fact. To become nothing out of something that exists is not a fact." It is categorically said here that nothing cannot be something and that something cannot be nothing. This principle is otherwise known as *satkāryavāda* (the doctrine of origination from something existent) in Vedānta and Sāṅkhya. Regarding the Sanskrit text of the *Bhagavadgītā* referred to here, the meanings of the two words *sataḥ* and *bhāva* need special mentions here. The word *sataḥ* means "from that which exists" (the Sanskrit verb root *as* means "to exist"; *as + satṛ = sat*; *sataḥ* in the fifth case, singular). The word *bhāvaḥ* (*bhū + ghañ*) means "to become", or origination, or to become a product. When Advaita Vedānta says, "*Māyā* is the substantial cause of the Universe", it does uphold the law of conservation. But *Māyā* is neither matter nor energy, and hence the law of conservation of matter and energy is not maintained at the time of creation (the Universe manifests from *Māyā*) and dissolution (the Universe is dissolved in *Māyā*).

The opinion of most physicists swung to the side of the Big-Bang model in 1965. This was due to the observational result of Arno Allan Penzias (1933-) and Robert Woodrow Wilson (1936-) two scientists at the Bell Telephone Laboratories at Halmdale, New Jersey. They published a paper with the title "A Measurement of Excess Antenna Temperature at 4080 Mc/s" in 1965 in the *Astrophysical Journal*. They were looking for sources of contamination while trying to refine the radio equipment. Working at the high microwave frequency of 4,080 megahertz (wavelength 7.35 cm.), they found more radio noise than they had expected. They were surprised to know that their antenna started picking up radio noise uniformly from all directions. This accidentally happened in the spring of 1964. They precluded any particular source of the radiation due to the lack of directionality. But they could not pin point the cause of the background radiation. Two cosmologists of Princeton, Robert Dicke and Jim Peebles, suggested eventually that the microwave background radiation was a relic of the Big-Bang. This Penzias-Wilson discovery was anticipated by Gamow, Alpher and Herman in the late 1940s. After getting the observational evidence for the expanding Universe, most cosmologists were almost ready to abandon the steady-state theory. They were convinced that the Big-Bang theory is correct. Penzias and Wilson were awarded the Nobel Prize for physics in 1978.

Whatever may be the mathematical model, it is an observational fact that the Universe is expanding. The discovery of Penzias-Wilson lent strong support in favour of a Big-Bang explosion which coincided with the beginning of time and space. It is not a fact that the Universe is expanding into empty space that is eternal and infinite. Space is a component of the Universe. The galaxies fly away as space itself expands. An important problem with which cosmologists grapple is still not conclusively settled. Is the Universe open? Will it continue to expand forever? Is the Universe closed? Will space-time meet an edge in future? To discuss this problem, we may restate the three kinds of generalized Friedmann models which have already been depicted in another form in Figure 9.2. Figure 9.3 presents the three possibilities of the Friedmann model. In curve (a) the Universe has low density and escapes its own gravity. The galaxies move apart so fast that gravity cannot stop them. In this case the Universe has to expand forever. The rate of expansion approaches a uniform value. In curve (b) the galaxies move apart at just the critical rate to avoid recollapse. The Universe continues to expand forever, but at a diminishing rate. Curve (c) corresponds to a high-density Universe in which the galaxies move sufficiently slowly so that the gravitational attraction between them stops the expansion.

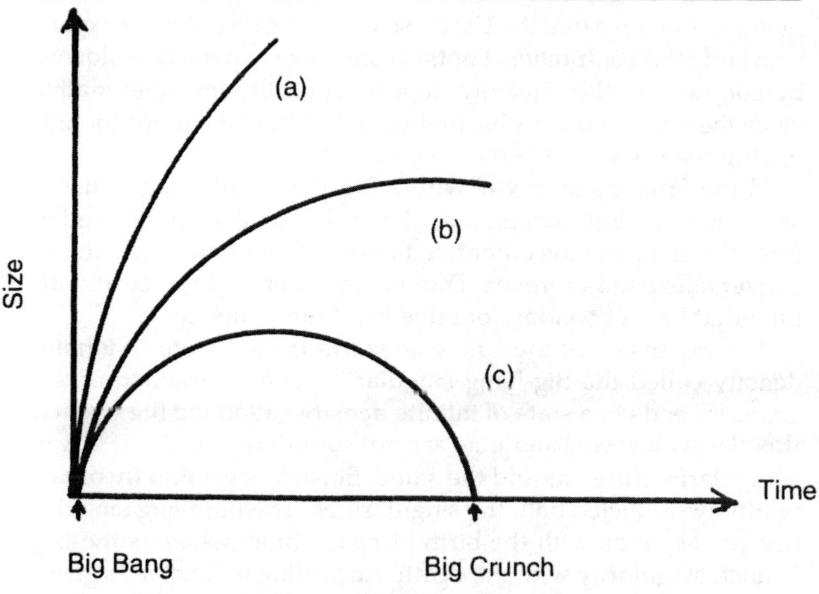

Fig. 9.3. Three fates of the Universe as predicted by the Friedmann model.

Then the Universe recontracts, finally obliterating itself at a Big Crunch. Curve (c) starts with a Big-Bang and ends in a Big Crunch. Both the Big-Bang and the Big Crunch are singularities.

Cosmologists compare the present rate of expansion of the Universe with its present average mass density (ρ) and thereby determine the model that corresponds to our Universe. The closure density of the Universe has been estimated; it is $\rho_c \cong 10^{-29}$ g cm^{-3}. If the visible component, which is mainly in the form of galaxies, is considered, the matter density of the Universe is estimated around 3×10^{-31} g cm^{-3}. This falls short of the closure density. There is also some amount of energy density. The bulk of the radiant energy in the Universe resides in the microwaves. More matter density is required for the recontraction of the Universe. Cosmologists have been thinking of the invisible matter density. Dark matter is a probable source of the invisible density. Black holes may be another source. If the neutrino has a positive mass even though it is infinitesimally small, the large number of neutrinos of the Universe contribute a significant amount of mass that may account for the recollapse of the Universe. Most cosmologists believe that the Universe will some day stop its expansion and start contraction. For this concept of expansion followed by contraction, they heavily depend upon the invisible matter since the mass of the visible matter in the Universe is not enough to stop the expansion.

In the Friedmann model with a Big-Bang and a Big Crunch, space is finite but unbounded, like in the Einstein static model. Space is infinite in the other two Friedmann models in which the Universe expands forever. This is, however, not the case with time that has a boundary or edge in all three models.

The expansion of the Universe starts from a state of infinite density called the Big-Bang singularity. The contraction of the Universe ends in a state of infinite density called the Big Crunch singularity. If events and time are not considered at all, these two signgularities are one and the same. Einstein's general theory of relativity predicted both the singularities. The Big-Bang singularity corresponds with the birth of space-time, whereas the Big Crunch singularity with the death. According to Einstein's general theory of relativity, the volume of the Universe is zero at the singularities. Some others hold that all the matter (energy) of the Universe is overcompacted into a dimensionless point (monoblock) at both the singularities.

What is this singularity? How do we define it? Singularity is a point in space-time at which the space-time curvature becomes infinite. In such a state, physical variables such as density, tidal forces, pressure etc., become infinite, and the gravitational field is infinitely strong. All the physical laws would break down at the space-time singularities. The concept of singularity has a mathematical connotation. At the start of the expansion or the end of the contraction of the Universe, the differential equations that are fitted into the model become infinite. When this happens in mathematics, not only in cosmological problems, but in all general cases, the differential equation is said to contain a mathematical singularity. This is a stage that gives an indication of the breakdown of the theory.

With all the evidences at our hand, we may accept the Big-Bang and the Big Crunch model as an *ad hoc* theory. The next questions that pop up are: What would happen to the Universe after the Big Crunch? Would it be zero without any further chance of reappearing? Would it bounce back and expand again? Would the alternate phases of expansion and contraction continue *ad infinitum*? Or, in other words, is there anything like the oscillating or the pulsating Universe?

We may assume that the cosmic egg suddenly appeared and subsequently underwent the Big-Bang explosion. Further, we may assume that the contracting Universe would be reconverted into the cosmic egg that would finally disappear. These two assumptions violate the law of conservation of matter and energy. They imply that cosmic egg was created out of nothing and it would finally be converted into nothing. This concept of nothing→ something→ nothing encouraged some Christian believers to reascertain the *creatio ex nihilo* hypothesis of the Bible and the concept of Divine Creatorship.

To obviate these difficulties, W.B. Bonnor[59] has put forward the view that the Universe has unlimited past and future. As the singular state in the contraction phase is approached, some mechanism starts to operate which slows down the contraction and ultimately reverses it. The Universe thus bounces back and starts its expanding phase again. This gives a picture of an unending series of oscillations.

Bonnor's oscillating or pulsating Universe is speculative. It can never be observational since there would be nobody to observe the last part of the contracting phase and the bouncing back from the Big Crunch singularity. There is also no theoretical ground or mathematical foundation to support Bonnor's hypothesis. As the contracting phase approaches the Big Crunch singularity, the gravitational field would tend to be infinitely large and the speed of contraction of the squeezing Universe would be tremendously accelerated. There is no mathematical explanation for the slowing down of the contraction of the Universe as it approaches the singularity.

There is a second objection to Bonnor's concept of the oscillating or the pulsating Universe. It violates the Second Law of Thermodynamics. According to this law, the Universe is gradually using up its mechanical energy and converting it irrevocably into heat. This would amount to a sort of running down of the Universe. In violation of the Second Law of Thermodynamics, Bonnor's oscillating Universe is a perpetual one. But it cannot be a perpetual machine when some day its utilizable energy is bound to be zero.

The spider model[60] of the Universe, as described in the Vedānta, and the shuttle model[61] or the bellow model,[62] as described in the Ṛg-Veda, are often confused to be identical to the oscillating model of Bonnor. Whereas Bonnor's Universe is eternal without a beginning and an end, the Vedic or the Vedāntic Universe is finite and repetitive. It manifests from *Akṣara* or *Māyā*. The beginning of manifestation corresponds with t_0 or the birth of time. It expands and evolves. Then it contracts and undergoes the processes of involution which is the reverse of evolution. Finally is the dissolution, the complete reabsorption of the entire Universe into *Akṣara* or *Māyā*, the power (*śakti*) of Brahman. This is in conformity with the field equations of Einstein. According to these equations of the general theory of relativity, the volume of the contractive Universe would ultimately be zero. A Universe with zero radius is to be accepted in science as its final disappearance, something being converted into nothing and eternal nothing. This is the reason for the silence of the hot Big-Bang theory about the fate of the Universe after the Big Crunch. But the silence is not an answer; it is the agnostic confession of reaching a blind alley, a cul-de-sac with no outlet ahead and with a one-way valve behind for no possibility of return. But it is also a fact that science has become unscientific by accepting an impossible concept of the final disappearance of the entire Universe as nihil. The concept of the monoblock or the singularity as the starting and the ending point of the repeated oscillations is also not scientific. Some objections to this concept have already been stated. Furthermore, the concept of the entire Universe contained in a dimensionless point (if such a point is taken as the singularity) does not seem to be plausible. If singularity is considered in the mathematical sense, the infinities obtained in the differential equations give a clear indication that something is wrong in this approach which is to be abandoned or modified. This sort of impasse in cosmology is due to the non-acceptance of the Vedāntic concept of Brahman and *Māyā*. The whole cosmic processes may be compared with the functioning of a fridge. The only difference lies in the dissipation of heat of the fridge to the outside environment and the reconversion of the entropy of the Universe into utilizable energy through the dissolution process. The Universe is a monoblock-body without an outside environment into which the question of the transfer of energy does not arise. Its unutilizable heat energy is not transferred; it is dissolved in *Māyā* to be reconverted into utilizable energy in the next cosmic cycle. The Vedic seers do not subscribe to a Universe that is static or linearly moving with the *ad infinitum* extension of the line into the past and the future. Neither does their Universe appear only once from nothing and disappear only once into nothing. Their Universe is not eternal, oscillating between a point of singularity and an edge of maximum expansion. The Vedic[63] Universe is cyclic, the processes of manifestation and dissolution being repeated in each cycle.

The Big-Bang theory has a number of versions, of which Bonnor's oscillating Universe is one only. Another specific Big-Bang was proposed by Edward P. Tryon who visualized the Universe as a fluctuation of the vacuum.[64] He did not get a satisfactory answer to two of his questions pertaining to Bonnor's oscillating Universe. First, what is the mechanism by which the Universe bounces back from the point of singularity? Second, how do we account for the particular values for energy, electric charge, baryon number, lepton number, etc.? In Tryon's model, he assumed that the Universe appeared from nowhere, with a zero net value for all conserved quantities. His concept of vacuum fluctuation is to be understood in the sense of quantum field theory.

The quantities of two categories of substances are conserved in physics. They are discrete and continuous. In the first category come the elementary particles whose characteristics such as electric charge, baryon number, lepton number, strangeness, etc. are conserved. All these quantities of particles and antiparticles are equal in magnitude and opposite in sign so that the net is zero. The conservation of the continuous substance (as a fact, everything is both continuous and discrete) mainly concerns energy, which includes matter also ($E = mc^2$). In addition to the enormous amount of mass energy of the Universe, there is another form of energy which is gravitational potential energy. Like other binding energies in physics, gravitational binding energy is negative. According to Tryon's calculation, the negative gravitational energy of any piece of matter can cancel the positive mass energy of mc^2. Thus the net energy of our Universe is zero.

It has been commonly accepted that the density of matter that has so far been observed is less than the critical value required for the Universe to be closed. The determination of the cosmic deceleration parameter by Sandage[65] indicates that our Universe is probably closed. From this, it is to be inferred that ρ exceeds ρ_C.

If this is not wholly due to visible matter, it may be combinedly due to the visible and the invisible matter. Tryon believes that our Universe is closed. P. Bergmann[66] has put forward strong arguments to prove that any closed Universe has zero energy. From such consideration, Tryon holds that our Universe may have zero net values for all conserved quantities and that it could have appeared from nowhere without violating any conservation laws. He describes universes of different sizes springing into existence from empty space. These are mere cases of quantum fluctuations. The occurrences of such events are without any cause, but are random ones as permitted by the statistical laws of quantum theory.

Tryon's speculative model of vacuum fluctuation is based on quantum field theory. The spontaneous, temporary emergence of particles from a vacuum is known as vacuum fluctuation. This phenomenon is quite commonplace in quantum field theory. A common example is the emergence of an electron, a positron and a photon from a perfect vacuum, as revealed by quantum electrodynamics. These three particles suddenly appear from nowhere, exist for a brief while, and then annihilate each other to disappear without leaving any trace behind. Such a phenomenon does involve violation of energy conservation; but it happens only for the brief particle lifetime Δt permitted by Heisenberg's uncertainty relation $\Delta E \Delta t \sim h$. The more energy tied up in the particles, the faster do they vanish. The vast quantity of mass energy of the Universe is cancelled by the gravitational binding energy which is negative. Thus, our Universe, being a fluctuation of zero total energy, is able to live for many billions of years. Basing on the assumption that our Universe has a zero net value for all conserved quantities, Tryon believes that it may simply be a fluctuation of the vacuum, the vacuum of some larger space in which this Universe is embedded. He refutes Bonnor's oscillating concept. His assumptions may be summarized as follows: The Universe appeared as a fluctuation of the vacuum. It is undergoing its initial expansion. It has quantum numbers of the vacuum, including zero energy. It is homogeneous, isotropic and closed. It consists equally of matter and antimatter.

Tryon's concept of vacuum fluctuation is another version of *śūnyavāda* (the doctrine of void or nothing). He accepts *creatio ex nihilo*, which is a logical impossibility. His concept of vacuum as absolute void or nothing is unacceptable in the light of the quantum field theory on which his assumptions have been based. His statement "the vacuum of some larger space in which the Universe is embedded" has the implication of a many-worlds theory. His concept of space-time seems to be eternal, without a beginning and an end.

Tryon conceives of a very large space-time in which universes pop into being like bubbles in champagne. He proposes that our Universe is simply one of those things which happen from time to time. His bubble Universe is a random event. It has no intelligent planner, designer and executor. The appearance, existence and disappearance of the bubble is causeless and purposeless. Tryon's model does not answer the question "Why does an insentient space-time obey quantum theory's laws?"

Amounts of matter and antimatter are equal in the fluctuation Universe of Tryon. Physicists' searches so far make this unlikely. This is another lacuna in conceiving the Universe as a vacuum fluctuation.

That our Universe has a zero net value for all conserved quantities can be explained by the Vedāntic theory. The Universe manifested from *Māyā*. *Asat* (a potential entity without exhibition of properties) became *sat* (entity that manifests properties). The manifested entities appeared in pairs the members of which were equal in magnitude but opposite in sign. Let us take the example of the charge of an electron and a positron. Before the manifestation of this particle-pair, the net charge of the potential entity was zero. After the manifestation, an electron and a positron carried – 1 and + 1 charge, respectively. Thus the net value of charge before and after the manifestation remains the same zero. What holds true for the charge is true for all the conserved quantities. The same concept is also applicable to the total energy of the Universe. Before manifestation it was zero and after manifestation it is zero. The Unmanifested (*asat*) = the Manifested (*sat*), since the later consists of equal and opposite entities with net value of zero. But, from this premise we cannot infer that everything of the Universe appeared from nothing. As it has been discussed earlier, the concept of nothing → something → nothing (the so-called vacuum fluctuation) is not logically valid and hence rejected in the Vedānta. The source of the manifested Universe, according to Vedānta, is *Māyā*, the power of Brahman which is pure Consciousness. The foundation of the whole cosmic process is not nihil. The cosmos which is an apparent chaos for some purposes has been intelligently designed, harmoniously coordinated and efficiently executed by *Īśvara*, the reflection of the Universal Consciousness (Brahman) in its power (*Māyā*).

Tryon's concept of nothing as the source of the Universe did not gain scientific credibility. Nonetheless, it was not rejected by many physicists and cosmologists. It caught the imagination of a number of researchers in cosmology and opened a new vista in cosmogenesis. It triggered the pace of cosmological research on a new line which is now known as the "Inflationary Universe". Alan H. Guth [67,68,69] was the founder of this new concept of the inflationary Universe. Guth's work developed to theorize about the instant or so immediately following creation. Physicists had been trying to search for a "unified field theory" before Guth developed his idea of inflation. The total unification of the four basic fields/forces might have been a fact during the incredibly brief interval of 10^{-30} seconds after the creation. What happened during this brief interval was the central focus of Guth's research that eventually produced the new concept of the inflationary Universe.

Before we discuss Guth's inflationary scenario, we may give the background of the evolution of the ideas that led to the evolution of the concept of negative pressure. Back in the history of science, Newton was very much puzzled with the non-implosion of the Universe in the presence of the pulling force of gravitation. He was somewhat satisfied by the idea that the Universe is acentric, that space is infinite and that the pulling force in the vast Universe acts on every side. Einstein was seized with the same problem. He conceived of a static Universe by adding an optional term to his gravitational field equations. He speculated a cosmic force to counteract the gravitational force in order to prevent the Universe from imploding under its own gravity. This new force was thought to be repulsive rather than attractive, pushing rather than pulling. It could be named "antigravity" or, more accurately, "cosmic repulsion force". It was further assumed that it did not act conspicuously at close range but accumulated in strength at astronomical distances. After Hubble's discovery of the expanding Universe, Einstein's concept of a static Universe could not be accepted and the need for a cosmic replusive force did not exist. He abandoned the cosmic repulsion force in disgust by saying that it was the biggest blunder in his life. By accepting Einstein's cosmic repulsion force as really existent, the Dutch astronomer Wilhelm de Sitter, in 1916, mooted the idea of a Universe caught by runaway expansion. If the Universe were devoid of ordinary matter, argued de Sitter, the usual pulling force of gravity would be absent. In that case, the Universe would expand to run away forever, since it would come under the sole influence of the cosmic repulsion force.

The history of science repeated. The cosmic repulsion force or antigravity that Einstein threw out of the door re-entered through the window. The inflationary scenario that was presented by Alan Guth in 1980 took help of the concept of the huge cosmic repulsion superforce that momentarily dominated gravity causing the new-born Universe to explode, before fading into insignificance.

We have to grasp the concepts of the true vacuum, the quantum vacuum and the false vacuum in order to understand the inflationary scenario. Previously the vacuum, void or empty space was considered as a passive receptacle which was an absolute nothing without activity. This concept of the vacuum has been drastically changed. According to the quantum theory, "emptiness" means "the absence of all particles"; but it does not mean "space which contains nothing" or "space which is nothing". Even a perfect vacuum is filled with forces and fields. Neither is a vacuum associated with inactivity. The vacuum is now regarded as a ferment of quantum activity. What we call matter particles and radiation quanta are only minor disturbances bubbling up over the background of the vacuum sea. According to Heisenberg's uncertainty principle ($\Delta E \Delta t \sim h$), it is permissible to "borrow" an amount of energy, ΔE, for a duration of Δt. If Δt is short enough, ΔE is used to produce virtual particles which disappear immediately after their appearance in order to repay the loan. Virtual particles are of two types, viz., (1) "messenger" particles that move to and fro between two source particles in order to transmit any of the four fundamental forces, and (2) particles that suddenly appear from the vacuum-sea as a result of vaccum fluctuation, even in the absence of source particles. The vacuum state contains limitless quantities of short-lived particles. These particles suddenly appear as if from nowhere, exist only fleetingly and then suddenly disappear, apparently being converted to nothing. When they momentarily exist, they are able to interact and engage in complex processes.

According to the inflationary scenario of Alan Guth, the initial state was the true vacuum state. This state featured empty space with zero pressure and "energy fluctuation", although it was said to be devoid of matter and energy proper. It is conventional to define the energy density of the true vacuum state to be zero. But there does not seem to be any reason to expect the vacuum energy density value to be zero. The vacuum energy can arrange itself in more than one way. The vacuum can become excited and adopt a number of energy states. These several energy states of the vacuum would look identical in certain physical conditions. This was appreciated in the late 1970s in connection with the unification of the four fundamental forces.

The four fundamental forces/fields may be regarded as four vacuum states involving energy leaps by huge amounts from one state to another. Alongside these energy differences among the vacuum states, there are equally enormous changes in their pressures which are all negative.

The initial true vacuum state does not last. There is a transition from it to the false vacuum, which contains energy without matter. The true vacuum is subject to energy fluctuation. The field to provide the energy to the false vacuum is absent in the true vacuum, although not completely. Energy fluctuations took place in the field of the true vacuum, resulting in the development of a false vacuum in a small region somewhere in space at one moment. The false vacuum had a large, positive energy density and a large negative pressure. It served as the driving force behind the runaway expansion in the inflationary scenario.

When did the inflation begin? The period may be estimated by considering the relevant energy scales. The energy scales of most inflationary models are much less than the Planck scale and hence inflation is discussed in the context of the Grand Unified Theories. The GUTs predict a phase transition at a critical temperature of about 10^{27} K. The phase transition from the low temperature broken symmetry phase to the high temperature symmetric phase occurred at this temperature.

In the excited vacuum state or the false vacuum state, the cosmic repulsion force was too strong to cause the expansion of the Universe at a huge rate. On the basis of Einstein's general theory of relativity, it has been known that a false vacuum would be bound to expand suddenly and explosively filling more and more space with false vacuum. Here we may refer to the cosmological constant which was introduced in 1917 by Einstein to his equations of general relativity. He did this in order to allow a static model of the Universe. This cosmological constant is proportional to the energy density of the vacuum. Its value is very small or perhaps zero at the present epoch. But, during the high temperature primeval phase of the GUTs era, the vacuum energy temporarily gave an enormous value. This led to a repulsive force which opposed gravity and grew in strength with distance. According to the model of the inflationary Universe, this repulsive force was the cause of this inflation. This started functioning when the Universe was 10^{-35} s old. The strength of the repulsive force was 10^{120} times greater than what Einstein needed to maintain a static Universe. As a result of the negative pressure of the false vacuum, a typical region of space doubled in size every 10^{-34} second or so. This hyper-expansion proceeded exponentially. Every 10^{-34} second, every excited region of space doubled its size and then went on doubling again and again in a progression. This type of expansion was named "inflation" by Alan Guth in 1980.

The inflationary era continued for 10^{-32} s or longer. During this period of exponential expansion, the Universe increased by a tremendous factor, not less than 10^{25}. During this incredibly brief phase of the inflationary scenario, the Universe grew from one-billionth of the size of a proton to several centimetres.

An excited state tends to be unstable. So was the false vacuum. It is a general feature that a system seeks out the state of lowest energy. This is true of the false vacuum. Thus the inflationary phase of the Universe could not be infinite. Like all excited quantum systems that are unstable, the excited vacuum or the false vacuum had to terminate. The false vacuum decayed abruptly into the true vacuum, the lowest energy vacuum state, which is empty space today. This change was analogous to a phase transition such as from a gas to a liquid. When this happened, the repulsion force disappeared.

After the colossal expansion of the Universe in the inflationary phase, the transition to the broken symmetry phase finally took place. The phenomena of spontaneous symmetry breaking have already been discussed in connection with the separation of the unified forces. The roles of Higgs fields and Higgs particles in spontaneous symmetry breaking may be briefly mentioned here. A set of fundamental fields, named after Peter W. Higgs of the University of Edinburg as Higgs fields, induce spontaneous symmetry breaking. The Higgs fields are scalar, i.e., they do not point in any direction unlike the electric and magnetic fields. The unified symmetry is spontaneously broken if one or more of the Higgs fields acquire a nonzero value. When this happens, the state attains the lowest possible energy density and is called the true vaccum state. The Higgs fields oscillate about their true vacuum values through the mediation of Higgs particles. The Higgs mechanism for the unified electroweak theory uses a set of Higgs fields which are distinct from those that are hypothesized to break the grand unified symmetry. Like any field that has an associated messenger particle, a Higgs particle is associated with a Higgs field. This is analogous to the photon that transmits the electromagnetic force. A neutral Higgs particle, with a mass energy in the vicinity of 100 GeV, predictably functions in the Glashow-Weinberg-Salam model. The Grand Unified Theories predict Higgs particles that have mass energies of the order of 10^{14} GeV. The false vacuum in the inflationary phase had a number of Higgs fields associated with it. All these fields would be continually fluctuating. When the inflationary Universe in the rapid phase of expansion was not compared with the critical temperature of the phase transition, the Higgs fields would each have a value of zero. The system cooled to well below 10^{27} K with the values of the Higgs fields remaining at zero. This was the supercooling of the Universe in the same analogy of water being supercooled to more than 20 K below its freezing point. A zero value of the Higgs field implies a large density of the false vacuum. When the temperature fell due to expansion, the condition became thermodynamically favourable for one or more of the Higgs fields to develop a nonzero value. This brought the system to its broken symmetry phase.

The false vacuum decayed into the true vacuum and the inflation stopped. At the end of inflation, the Universe was empty and cold. But, immediately after the inflation ceased, the Universe became intensely hot, its temperature rising to about 10^{27} K. Like the release of the latent heat of steam condensing to water, the energy density of the false vacuum was set free to reheat the

Universe and fill it with light as well as particles and antiparticles. From this point on, the Universe continued to expand and cool at a much reduced rate as described by the standard Big-Bang model.

A temperature of roughly 10^{27} K was hot enough for the GUT processes to occur. Thereafter the evolution of the Universe took place according to the standard Big-Bang theory.

The concept of quantum "tunnelling" may be briefly discussed here. This was first described by Sidney Coleman of Harvard University. The phase transition in the inflationary model occurred by tunnelling, which allowed change-over from the false to the true vacuum. Tunnelling occurred in small regions of space, which at the completion of the tunnelling, found themselves in a state of true vacuum with lower energy than the surrounding false vacuum. The false vacuum had negative pressure while the true vacuum had zero pressure. In Guth's model, the false vacuum may be symbolically envisioned to have laid in a high valley surrounded by a barrier of mountains which descended to the much lower level of the true vacuum on the other side. Hence quantum tunnelling was necessary to penetrate the barrier. Bubbles formed with the occurrence of tunnelling.

Near the end of 1981, the concept of quantum tunnelling was modified by a new approach by A.D. Linde of the P.N. Lebdev Physical Institute in Moscow. What Linde proposed was known as the "new inflationary model" to be distinguished from the original model proposed by Alan Guth in July, 1980. The same ideas were also put forward independently by two American physicists Andreas Albrecht and Paul Steinhardt of the University of Pennsylvania.

The new inflationary scenario begins just as it does in the original inflationary model. It also has the same assumption that the early Universe had regions of space that were hotter than about 10^{27} K and were expanding. In these regions thermal fluctuations would drive the equilibrium value of the Higgs fields to zero. As a result the symmetry would be unbroken. With further expansion, the temperature fell and it was thermodynamically favourable for the system to undergo a phase transition. In this transition, at least one of the Higgs fields acquired a nonzero value and this resulted in a broken symmetry phase. In the new scenario[70] the false vacuum lies on a tall plateau which slopes down extremely gently for a while and thereafter descends very rapidly down a canyon to where the true vacuum lies.

Now we may place the inflationary scenario on the anvil and get a critical view of it. The standard Big-Bang model could not say anything about the source of the cosmic egg. Whence did the cosmic egg come and why did it explode were the thorny questions in the standard model. These problems have been apparently solved by the inflationary theory which says that empty space itself was excited and then exploded under the repulsive power of the quantum vacuum. We are yet to solve another problem regarding the source of the colossal energy of the primeval explosion. The mass of the observable Universe is $\not\equiv 10^{21}$ $M_\odot$ ($1\,M_\odot = 2 \times 10^{33}$ g = 1 solar mass). There is also radiation energy. For the outward rush of the galaxies and swirling activities of all celestial bodies, energy is continuously expended. There are about 10^{68} joules of energy in the observable Universe. Wherefrom did this vast amount of energy come?

The energy came out of empty space, out of the quantum vacuum, says the inflationary scenario. The Universe started out with essentially zero energy. But all the energy the Universe gained during the first 10^{-32} second. The question still persists: What was the source of this energy? What do we mean by saying that the source was empty space or quantum vacuum? In the final analysis, we have to admit that empty space is not really empty and that it is the immediate source of the energy.

The cosmic repulsion behaved like a fluid with negative pressure. The energy of a negative pressure fluid goes up rather than down when it expands. This is exactly what happened in the inflationary period. The total energy of the vacuum kept on rising from the beginning to the cessation of the inflationary era. When the quantum decay of the false vacuum put a stop to the inflation, all the accumulated energy was released in a single great burst. Thus was all the heat generated in the Big-Bang. This heat energy was the source of all the matter and energy of the total Universe. After the inflationary phase, the negative-pressure expansion was taken over by the conventional positive-pressure expansion, and the temperature of the Universe began to decline again.

The vacuum which was regarded as absolutely empty is nature's magic jar of energy in the inflationary scenario. In principle, there is no limit to how much energy can be self-generated by negative-pressure (inflationary) expansion. This novel concept accepts the principle of *ex nihilo* creation and rejects the traditional belief that "nothing can come out of nothing". The inflationary theory has tried to establish that all the cosmic matter and energy appeared spontaneously from nothing. It further holds that, in spite of the evolution of the enormous quantity of energy of the Universe, the net energy of the Universe is zero due to the equality of the positive and the negative mass-energy and gravitational energy, respectively.

Guth's inflationary scenario apparently solved some problems faced by the standard hot Big-Bang model. The "fine-tuning" of the Universe is explained by the nature of the exponential expansion that automatically adjusted to yield exactly the right values. The large-scale uniformity of the Universe is another major puzzle for which inflation provides an explanation. Of course, the Universe is not completely uniform or homogeneous. There is a small degree of clumping here and there, as evidenced by the present existence of galaxies and galactic clusters. This sort of small-scale inhomogeneity can be explained by the inflationary scenario. Inflation occurred while the quantum state of the Universe was in the unstable "false" vacuum state. Eventually the false vacuum decayed into the true vacuum. The cosmic repulsion disappeared and inflation ceased. The latent energy of the false vacuum became the heat and matter of the Universe. In all quantum processes there are fluctuations in the rate of the decay of the false vacuum. That was what exactly happened when the decay of the false vacuum did not occur simultaneously throughout space. Inflation ended sooner in those regions which decayed slightly faster than others. This is the cause of the irregularities that appeared in the final state.

According to one prediction of the standard Big-Bang model, a superabundance of magnetic monopoles (each of which corresponds to an isolated north or south magnetic pole) was created in the primeval phase. But, contrary to this prediction, magnetic monopoles are absent today. Alan Guth wanted to solve this cosmological problem by his invention of the inflationary scenario. Inflation involved the enormous swelling of space and thus it effectively diluted the magnetic monopoles to practically zero density.

The inflationary scenario appears to have achieved a great success in explaining the origin of the Universe. We have a self-creating Universe, coming into existence out of nothing. A number of celebrated physicists are extremely busy in manipulating mathematics in an attempt to establish the truth about creation *ex nihilo*. Among them are Alan Guth at MIT, Sidney Coleman of Harvard, Alex Vilenkin of Tufts University and Edward Tryon and Heinz Pagels in New York. They believe that "nothing is unstable" and that out of this nothing has the Universe blossomed forth spontaneously in obedience to the laws of physics.

One of the primary aims of science is to explain facts. One of the primary requisites of becoming a scientist is to be free from dogmas or preconceived ideas. Rational thinking is not the same as rationalizing one's own bias against sound evidences. It is unfortunate that *sometimes* we try to explain away facts, stick to our dogmas and make vain attempts at rationalizing our bias against the strength of clear evidences. It is claimed that the inflation theory has explained everything about the origin of the Universe. It is gratifying that some enigmas of the standard Big-Bang model have been dissolved. But how far all the problems have been convincingly solved is still a moot point. Let us analyze some points to test this claim.

These questions puzzled the cosmologists in the standard Big-Bang model: What happened before the Big-Bang? Whence did the cosmic egg come? Similar problems also persist in the inflationary scenario. Do we understand the properties of the true vacuum? Is it nothing or something? Is it the reservoir of energy? Is it uncreated and eternal? Has it a beginning and an end? How did the Universe arrive in the false vacuum state in the beginning? What happened before inflation? The mystery remains as a mystery.

The inflationary scenario takes it for granted that space is uncreated and eternal. It has no idea at all regarding the existence of time before the inflation. Was there activity before the inflation? Can we conceive of time without activity? Is time eternal? Has time a beginning and an end? Is time reborn if cosmic processes are regarded as cyclic? If space is eternal, time has to be eternal in the modern concept of space-time. Space is very much part of the physical Universe. The inflation theory has to explain where space itself came from. Einstein's field equations indicate the birth and death of space and time. The original Big-Bang model incorporates this concept. Advaita Vedānta holds that space is created and that the created space would some day be dissovled.

When the Universe is now expanding, it is doing so into a continual swelling of space which is finite and curved. The region of the Universe accessible to our telescopes daily swells up by 10^{18} cubic light-years. Space is not eternal. It was created in the beginning. That being so, the inflationary scenario stands on a base which apparently exists like a phantom but really does not exist.

The concept of vacuum and space needs clarification in the inflationary scenario, whose foundation is the false vacuum. Guth's inflation theory leans heavily on the quantum theory, which regards space as a beehive of activity. Hence, in the modern sense, space is not empty and nothing. The concept of "nothing" has been classical in Western religion, philosophy and Newtonian science. It has enjoyed an ontological status in the Western philosophy. Emptiness or absolute void was implied in the concept of vacuum; space was inseparably tied with this vacuum. Although *śūnya* was an important concept in Buddhist philosophy, it was a meaningless term in the Vedānta which recognized *pūrṇa* (full) rather than *śūnya*. It is paradoxical that quantum mechanics that no longer regards space as void or empty tenaciously retains the concept of nothingness. In the light of newer knowledge of the twentieth-century physics, it is impossible to separate space from vacuum, both being full and not empty. Then, where is the nothingness in the initial true vacuum of the inflation theory? If it existed, whence did it appear? If it is beginningless and something, how can we call it "nothing"? Whenever we say "X exists", X is something, provided X really exists. Anything that exists is something. It may be matter, energy, field, force, space, vacuum or anything else. "Nothing exists" is a nihilistic statement and is meaningless too. When we say "X is stable" or "X is unstable", we mean thereby that X corresponds to something. The statement "Nothing is unstable" is a nonsensical statement when we use the word "nothing" in the sense of a positive substance. If it is a substance, it cannot be nothing; it is necessarily something.

The modern cosmologist who develops the inflation theory may not believe in theology; but he has not been free from the influence of the concept of creation *ex nihilo* given in the Bible. Of course, the Bible says that God created the Universe from nothing. Science, being materialistic, rejected the Creator; but it did not abandon the concept of creation out of nothing.

The truth or falsity of a statement like "something is created out of nothing" cannot be verified by experimentation. Neither can it be settled by mathematics. It can be decided by logical analysis only. If nothing becomes something, we may mathematically express it as "nothing = something", which is the same as "not-A = A". This is self-contradictory and hence is necessarily false. Anything that is not self-contradictory has the likelihood of its occurrence. On the contrary, anything that is self-contradictory can never occur. Hence, the claim of the inflation theory that the Universe has been self-created out of nothing cannot be true.

There is no Brahman, no God and no *Māyā* in the inflation theory. It does accept the existence of the Universe that has been self-generated out of nothing. The basic constituent of the Universe is energy, which is zero if we compute its net value from the equal amounts of the positive mass-energy and the negative gravitational energy. Thus, in essence, the theory is wholly nihilistic.

Advaita Vedānta has some features common with those of the inflation theory. Śaṅkara also asserts that the Universe is essentially nothing and that all the cosmic phenomena are illusory. But he abhors nihilism and posits Brahman as the Reality. The Universe exists only as dependent on Brahman. *Māyā* (the power of Brahman), which is not existent and existent and non-existent, is the substantial cause of the Universe. Advaita Vedānta does talk of the inflation (*tapasā cīyate Brahma*[71]). But it does not talk in nihilistic term. The illusory world which is an empirical reality (*vyāvahārika satya*) has a substratum (*adhiṣṭhāna*) that is the absolute Reality (*pāramārthika satya*). Śaṅkara recognizes that substratum only as the Reality. That substratum is Brahman.

With this much discussion on the inflationary Universe, we switch over to the Multi-World Theory (MWT). The basic idea is that several bubbles rather than one appeared and inflated like baloons in the void. At the very beginning there were vacuum fluctuations at several excited spots, each one hotter than a trillion quadrillion degrees. Each bubble inflated exponentially and supercooled at the termination of the inflation. Each inflated baloon regained heat as described earlier. The inflationary expansion was followed by a relatively slower expansion which is continuing till today, although at a much decelerated rate. Each bubble eventually became a world. Thus we have multiple worlds in the Universe.

The well-known quantum theoretical dictum may be quoted here: "Whatever can happen, will". Many bubbles rather than one can appear in the excited vacuum, or as the Harvard physicist Sidney Coleman calls a "false vacuum". And so appeared several bubbles at different spots. E.P. Tryon noted in 1973 that vacuum fluctuations were utterly commonplace. From this he derived the implication of the probable existence of many worlds. He stated: "Every phenomenon that could happen in principle actually does happen occasionally in practice". And he further said: "Our Universe is simply one of those things which happen from time to time".

In 1974, Carter[72] proposed the idea of a World Ensemble which consists of an infinite number of different co-existing worlds. He did this in order to fulfill a useful cosmological function by logically grounding the "Anthropic Coincidences".

Tryon's concept of quantum fluctuation and Guth's concept of the inflationary scenario provided the ground on which MWT was erected. The 1979 article[73] of G.F.R. Ellis and G.B. Brundrit suggests that we live in a low-density, homogeneous, open and infinite Universe. There do they indicate: "It is highly probable that there exist infinitely many worlds on which there are 'duplicate' populations to that on our own worlds."

Alan Guth gave the first version of the inflationary Universe in July, 1980. This concept was born from the long-standing search for a unified field theory. It focused on the first 10^{-30} seconds of the Universe's existence during which the total unification of the four basic fields/forces occurred. The inflationary model had a feature which turned out to be of relevance for MWT, although such a possibility was not noted by Guth.

In 1982, J. Richard Gott[74] of Princeton made a synthesis of cosmology, cosmogony and MWT. He has proposed an infinite number of universes created like bubbles in a hot liquid of great but finite density. Each of these universes is itself "open" or infinite and will continue to expand forever.

Gott's bubbles formed out of de Sitter space. Willem de Sitter first studied this type of space in 1917. To Einstein's field equations of general relativity de Sitter added a cosmological constant which was a sort of negative gravity, similar to Einstein's universal repulsive force. According to de Sitter's concept, any individual point in the Universe tends to move away from another point at a constantly increasing rate. Gott visualizes the smooth formation of the initial bubble out of the surrounding de Sitter space. This version eliminates the singularity at the beginning. It also explains the large-scale uniformity of the Universe. In both Gott's model and the inflationary scenario, there is a brief phase of constant density immediately after the creation of the bubble. In this early period of expansion, each part of the Universe was causally related to every other part. Thus the rough spots were smoothed out and a homogeneous cosmos was created. What has been said here of one bubble holds true for the genesis and development of infinite number of bubbles. Thus Gott's investigation of Guth's inflationary domains (bubbles) eventuates in a comprehensive Multi-World Theory.

If there are many worlds, we have to refer to the world in which we live as our world. We cannot see the other worlds by our telescopes. In the various inflationary scenarios, the entire observable Universe, some 10^{28} cm across, originated from a tiny region which was only 10^{-33}cm across (the Planck length). It was created by chance from a quantum fluctuation,[75] in accordance with the uncertainty principle of Heisenberg. If this idea of quantum fluctuation is accepted, it is also necessarily to be accepted that our Universe cannot be infinitely large, that at the moment of creation it must have contained a finite amount of energy, that it must have been closed, and that the newly appeared Universe must have been smaller than 10^{-33} cm across. The standard Big-Bang model tells us that the density of the Universe was 10^{94} g/cubic cm when its size was 10^{-4} cm, about 10^{29} times the Planck length (10^{-33} cm). What was the density of the Universe at the Planck length of its size cannot be conjectured at this level of our present knowledge The initial volume of our Universe must have been zero. Is that not the singularity? Cosmologists of the inflationary model have been trying to avoid the singularity which unavoidably appears and re-appears in one way or the other.

Nothing existed before the moment of creation. The Universe appeared from that "nothing". As a result of quantum fluctuation, false vacuum emerged in a sea of true vacuum. The false vacuum with a negative pressure appeared like a bubble. This bubble inflated like a baloon. The rate of inflation was too fast. It expanded exponentially doubling its diameter every 10^{-34} second.

This expansion (termed inflation) probably lasted for less than 10^{-30} second. It lasted till the transition to the broken symmetry phase was complete. The inflation or exponential expansion ended and thereafter the standard Big-Bang expansion commenced. This transition phase was very crucial for the creation of heat and particles. In the analogy of the release of the latent heat at the time of the condensation of supercooled steam to water, a phase-transition took place from false to true vacuum and the energy difference between the two states was released. This extra energy reheated the bubble to about 10^{14} GeV and created a large number of fast-moving particles. What happened next and how the Universe evolved have already been described.

The Big-Bang expansion would not last forever. Scientific evidences are accumulating to strongly indicate that the Universe would eventually stop its expansion and then enter into a phase of contraction. It would undergo a Big Crunch, the opposite of a Big-Bang. Finally it would come back to the stage of singularity. In the inflationary scenario, the final homecoming of the Universe would be true vacuum, the nothing. The Universe was nothing before the creation. All its energy and matter was created out of zero energy. The Universe became something out of nothing. Again that something would be nothing. In that "nothing", there would be no observer, no matter and energy, no physical laws and no God. This is the cosmological concept of the vacuum fluctuation and the inflationary scenario.

In this chapter an attempt has been made for a comparative presentation of the cosmology of the Vedānta and the modern cosmology of science. The nothing (*asat*) of the Vedānta is something positive, although it is sense-imperceptible (*dig-deśa-guṇa-gati-phalabheda-śūnyaṁ hi paramārthasad advayaṁ brahma mandabuddhīnām asad iva pratibhāti*—Śaṅkara[76]). On the contrary, the nothing of science is absolute void, a total vacuum. This concept of void in science is not at all comprehensible especially when vacuum in the twentieth century physics is a potential source of energy quanta and matter particles. The source of the illusory Universe, according to the Advaita Vedānta, is *Māyā*, the power (*śakti*) of Brahman. *Māyā* itself is not real. It is solely dependent on Brahman which is the nondual Reality. The Universe which is empirically existent but really non-existent is thus finally rooted not in *Māyā* but in Brahman. The Universe which has been compared with an inverted pipal tree is not rootless (*nirmūla*); it is rooted in Reality (*sanmūla*) which is Brahman, the One and nondual One. Thus the cosmology of the Vedānta is based on positive Existence (*sat*) whereas that of modern science is completely nihilistic.

"Nothing exists" is a nonsensical statement in the Advaita Vedānta. What exists is existent (*sat*) and that which exists is Brahman. This Brahman is Consciousness (*Cit*) : It is not insentient (*jaḍa*), not even partially sentient; it is absolute sentience and nothing else but sentience. According to the Advaita Vedānta, not only matter and energy, but also ideas and concepts have a source; and this source is Brahman. No vacuum fluctuation, no false vacuum, no singularity, no cosmic egg, no Big-Bang, no inflationary scenario and no Big Crunch are possible unless the World-Tree is rooted in Brahman which is absolute Consciousness. Brahman is also infinite (*ananta*) in the sense that it cannot be measured, perceived and ascertained by any means and cannot be described in any language. It is neither the substantial nor the efficient cause of the Universe. *Māyā*, the power of Brahman, is the substantial cause of the Universe. *Māyā* itself is not existent (*sat*), not non-existent (*asat*) and not existent and non-existent (*sadasat*). Such an indescribable (*anirvacanīyā*) entity is the precursor of the Universe. At the time of the dissolution, the Universe dissolves in *Māyā*. But, *Māyā*, being insentient, cannot become the Creator, the efficient cause of the Universe. Brahman, being non-functional (*akartā*), cannot be the Creator (*sraṣṭā*), the Preserver (*goptā*) and the Destroyer (*saṁhartā*). *Īśvara*, the reflection of Brahman in *Māyā*, is the efficient cause of the Universe. In another interpretation, *Īśvara* is Brahman with *Māyā* as the *upādhi* or limiting adjunct (*māyopahita*). No planning, designing, legislation, execution, coordination, control and administration are possible without the agency of consciousness. *Īśvara*, being the Universal Consciousness, operates through the substantiality and instrumentality of *Māyā* and thus becomes the efficient cause of the Universe.

A quiescent and non-functional state of Being is the state of perfect order (*ṛta*) and existence (*satya*[77]). This is the state of zero entropy. This state is also spaceless (*anākāśa*) and timeless (*akāla*). The Universe was born in the form of a cosmic egg from the womb of the imperishable (*akṣara*) and unreal (*asat*) *Māyā*. The cosmic egg exploded and the cosmic processes became operational. Space was born with the cosmic explosion. Time which is not a cosmic entity but a mental construct of sequential activity was born with the initiation of cosmic activities.

The world-machine cannot be perpetual. Its utilizable energy would be zero in synchronicity with the development of a maximum entropy. On the other hand, the world cannot sustain itself for even a single moment in the stage of the maximum entropy and zero utilizable energy since the sustenance of matter, energy, space and fields involves an expenditure of energy. This stage of cosmic impasse is, however, avoided by a built-in mechanism in the Universe. The Universe stops its expansion and starts a phase of contraction. The expansion phase is evolutionary and the contraction phase is involutionary, one being the opposite of the other. Finally, the Universe dissolves in *Māyā*. In this dissolution process, entropy also dissolves, and in the next cycle of creation a Universe re-appears with zero entropy. It cannot be said that the Universe re-appears with a definite quantity of energy. *Māyā* is not energy. At the beginning of the manifestation of the Universe, *Māyā* as such does not become the energy of the Universe. The Universe starts with zero energy, zero particles and zero properties. Energy quanta appear in positive and negative forms in equal quantities. Particle-pairs appear from energy with positive and negative characteristics. All the fundamental properties of energy quanta and matter particles appear oppositely to balance each other (*viruddhadharmavān*[78]). Thus, whatever manifests in the Universe has a net value of zero.

So does the Vedānta give a description of the world-tree. It is an inverted tree. Its branches, sub-branches, leaves and flowers are unreal in essence but real empirically. It appears due to the vibrations of the three *guṇas* (strings) of *Māyā*. It is antithetical to Brahman which is real and devoid of *guṇas* (*nirguṇa*). When considered in this sense, it is said that the world-tree is inverted. But this inverted tree is not self-dependent and self-subsistent. It does not hang in the inverted position in nothing. It is rooted in Brahman. This is the central theme of the Vedānta which is at variance with the modern cosmology. The other details of modern cosmology can be very well accommodated in the Vedāntic cosmology without any conflicts. The central question is: Can science satisfactorily explain cosmology and cosmogony on the basis of pure materialism and mechanistic interpretation?

NOTES

1. BG, XV.1.
2. BG, XV.2.
3. KTU, II. 3.1.
4. ṚV, X.81; 82; TBrā, II. 8.9.6.
5. CU, III.19.1.
6. BGŚB, Intr.
7. ŚBrā, VI.1.2.3.; MBh, XII. 299.3; MS, I. 9; BPu, I.1.39; GPu, I. 4.6-11; HV, I.1.36-38; KPu, I.4.40-41; PPu, III.3.31; VPu, I.2.54-60; BDPu, I.1.3. 24-27; VāPu, IV.76b-79; Bhā, II. 6.21; III.6.6.
8. CU, III.19.1.
9. PU, I.4.
10. P.C.W. Davies, and J. Brown, (ed.), *Superstrings*, Cambridge University Press, Cambridge, 1988, pp. 100, 162, 187.
11. M. Kaku, and J. Trainer, *Beyond Einstein*, Bantam Books, New York, 1987, pp. 14-15.
12. PU, I.5.
13. ṚV, X.129.3; BU, I.2.6; PU, I.4.
14. ṚV, X.129.5; CU, III.19.1.
15. ṚV, X.129. 3 & 5.
16. MUU, I.1.8.
17. ṚV, II.35; X.30.
18. ṚV, I. 89.10.
19. ṚV, I.89.10; I.164.33; X.72.4.
20. BU, I.2.5.
21. ṚV, X.72.6.
22. ṚV, X.129.2; 3; 5; BGŚB, Intr., BG, VII.6; VIII.18; IX.7; XIV.3-5.
23. ṚV, X.129.1-2.
24. ṚV, X.72.2-3; X.129.1; BU, I.2.1; CU, III.19.1; VI.2.1; TU, II.7.1.
25. BU, I.4.7; CUŚB, III.19.1.
26. BU, I.4.1; I.4.10; I.4.11; I.4.17; V.4.1; CU, III.19.1; VI.2.1; TU, II. 7.1; KTU, II.2.13.
27. ṚV, X.129.5; BU, IV.3.10; BG, IX.7; XIV.3-5.
28. BS, I.1.2; I.4.26; I.4.27; MAU, 6; MUU, I.1.6; III.1.3; TU, II.7.1; III.1.1.
29. BS, I.1.2; I.1.4.I.4.23-28; BSŚB. I.1.2.; I.1.4; I.1.5; I.1.10; I.1.11; I.2.2; I.2.9; I.4.23; I.4.24; I.4.25; I.4.26; I.4.27; I.4.28; II.1.14; II.2.1; BU, II.5.19; ŚU, VI.9; MAU, 6; TU, III.1.1; BGŚB, VII.6; XIII.19.
30. BS, II.1.26; II.1.27; BSŚB, II.1.26; II.1.27.
31. ŚUŚB, I.3.
32. BU, I.4.3.

33. CU, VI.2.3.
34. BS, II.1.32.
35. BS. II.1.33.
36. ṚV, X.129.4; BS, I.4.24; II.3.13; BSŚB, II.3.13; CU, VI.2. 3 & 4; TU, II.6.1.
37. ṚV, X.81, 82, 121; YV, XXXI.19; BSŚB, I.1.2; I.1.4; I.1.5; I.1.11; I.2.2; I.2.9; I.3.30; ŚBrā, I.9.3.10; TBrā, III.12.3.1; BU, II.6.3; IV.6.3; VI.5.4; KTU, II.1.1; MUU, I.1.9; III.1.3; ŚU, III.4; VI.18; ŚUŚB, I.3; TU, III.1.1; BG, XIV.3-4; MBh, XII.160.11-12; HV, I.1.25-33.
38. BSŚB, I.1.2; I.1.4; I.1.5; I.1.11; I.2.2; I.2.9; ŚU, III.2; ŚUŚB, I.3; TU, II.6.1; III.1.1; BG, IX.5; XIII.22; BS, I.2.18; I.3.10; I.3.11; I.3.43; BSŚB, I.2.18; I.3.11; II.3.23; BU, III.7.3-23; III.8.7-9; IV.4.22; BUŚB, III.8.9; MAU, 6; ŚU, II.17; III.1; III.2; III.4.
39. AV, XI.7.1; BS, I.2.9; BSŚB, I.1.2; I.1.4; I.1.5; I.1.11; I.2.2; I.2.9; BU, I.2.5; KTU, I.2.25; MAU, 6; TU, III.1.1; Bhā, IV.7.42; VPu, VI.4.39.
40. ṚV, X.72.4.
41. ṚV, X.72.5.
42. ṚV, X.72.6.
43. TU, II.1.1.
44. BS, II.3.7; II.3.8; II.3.9; II.3.10; II.3.11; II.3.12.
45. MUU, I.1.8; II.1.3.
46. TU, II.1.1; III.2.1; III. 3.1; III.4.1; III.5.1; III.6.1.
47. MUŚB. I.1.8.
48. BS, II.3.14.
49. ṚV, X.190.3; ŚU, VI.1.
50. MUU, I.1.7.
51. ṚV, X.130.
52. ṚV, X.72.2.
53. VPu, I.3.5.
54. VPu, I.3.20-22.
55. VPu, III.2.50; VI.3.11-12; BDPu, XXXII.86; BG, VIII.17.
56. P.C.W. Davies, "The Eleven Dimensions of Reality", *New Scientist*, 9th Feb., 1984, p. 31.
57. *Rival Theories of Cosmology*, by H. Bondi, W.B. Bonnor, R.A. Lyttleton, and G.J. Whitrow, (1960), pp. 12-21, Oxford University Press, Oxford.
58. BG, II. 16.
59. As in ref. 57, pp. 1-11.
60. MUU, I.1.7.
61. ṚV, X. 130.
62. ṚV, X.72.2.
63. ṚV, X.190.3; SU, VI.1.
64. E.P. Tryon, Is the Universe a Vacuum Fluctuation?, *Nature*, Vol. 246, No. 5433, Dec. 14, 1973, pp. 396-97.
65. A.R. Sandage, Phys. Today, 23, 34 (1970).

66. P. Bergmann, Quoted by E.P. Tryon, In : *Physical Cosmology and Philosophy*, ed. J. Leslie, Macmillan Publishing Co., New York, 1990, p. 218.
67. A.H. Guth, The Inflationary Universe : a possible solution to the horizon and flatness problems, *Physical Review*, D 23: 347, 1981.
68. A.H. Guth, *10^{-35} seconds after the Big-Bang*, MIT preprint CTP 991, 1982.
69. A.H. Guth, and P.J. Steinhardt, The Inflationary Universe, *Scientific American*, ***250***, 116, 1984.
70. A.H. Guth, and P.J. Steinhardt, *Scientific American*, Vol. 250, No. 5, p. 90, 1984.
71. MUU, I.1.8.
72. B. Carter, Large number coincidences and the anthropic principle in cosmology, In : M.S. *Longair, Confrontation of Cosmological Theories with Observational Data*, Reidel, Boston, 1974, p. 291 ff.
73. G.F.R. Ellis, and G.B. Brundrit, *Quarterly Journal of the Royal Astronomical Society*, ***20***: 37-39, 1979.
74. J.R. Gott, Creation of open Universes from de Sitter space, *Nature*, ***205***: 304, 1982.
75. E. Tryon, *New Scientist*, March, 1984, p. 14.
76. CUŚB, VIII.1.1.
77. ṚV, X.190.1.
78. KTUŚB, I.2.21.

X

SYMPHONY AND SILENCE

THE UNI-WORLD or multi-world is likened to a symphony. The string(s) of the *vīṇā* or the violin is vibrating. As a result of the vibrations, different musical tones are created. The world is the sum total of the musical tones; it is a grand orchestra. The music is different from the musical instrument. The music is not the same as the strings of the musical instrument. The music is not real, but is apparent. It is an empirical reality. The musical instrument is neither real nor unreal. Its nature is indescribable. Through its instrumentation only, the world-orchestration of manifold melodies is produced. The musical instrument does not exist independently. It dependently exists as a vibration-instrument in the hands of the Great Musician. The Musician is the only Reality, the nondual Absolute Reality. Who plays the *vīṇā*? Who is the musician? Is the music being played without a musician? For whose enjoyment is the music meant? Is it for man? Is the world-orchestra anthropocentric? We will discuss the structures of the musical instruments, the functions of the instrumental strings, the music, the Musician, the audience and the purpose of the musical orchestra.

The Universe has been well designed. Both its macrostructure and microstructure have been *intelligently* planned. What has been appreciated by the seer of the *Brahmasūtra* about the world-design (*racanā*) has also been echoed in the following statement of Paul Davies:

> Nature displays a hierarchy of structure. From the smallest known constituents of the atom to the large scale arrangement of the galaxies, we observe systems with characteristic organization and size, each level of structure interlocking

with the others in a highly ordered way. What determines the scale of these structures and their relation to one another?[1]

The Universe is too large, but finite in size (radius $\simeq 10^{26}$m). Its horizon distance is the maximum distance, at any given time, that a light signal could have travelled since the beginning of the Universe. It has a mass of 10^{53} kg. Its age is 10^{18} seconds. A planetary system (a star with planets) may have a size of 10^{11} m. Stars are located in star clusters, each cluster having a typical size of 10^{18} m. Star clusters are within a galaxy with a typical size of 10^{21} m (10^{5} light-years in diameter). Our galaxy, the Milky Way, contains around 10^{11} stars of mass comparable to that of the Sun, $M_{\odot}$. Galaxies cluster together into agglomerations. A cluster of galaxies may have a total mass of around of 10^{14} $M_{\odot}$ and sizes of about 10^{23}m.

The microstructures of the Universe are too small. During the first 10^{-43} seconds (Planck time) of the Universe's existence, the smallest structures predicted by known physics occur at the Planck length (10^{-35} m). During this Planck era, Newton's law and Einstein's general theory of relativity cannot describe gravity. According to the general theory of relativity, gravity is a distortion or curvature of spacetime. Einstein's concept does not exactly conform to Planck era spacetime which resembles more a sponge-like, or foamy structure, on the Planck length and Planck time scales. The spacetime foam is characterized by the quantum theory of gravity, which has not yet taken a solid stand in physics. As usual with the quantum theory according to which particles and fields can undergo spontaneous fluctuations of a random nature, violent fluctuations can occur in the curvature of spacetime in the regime of quantum gravity on Planck length and time scales. The quantized gravity has a size of 10^{-35} m and a mass of 10^{-8} kg.

The component parts of protons and neutrons are quarks. The elementary, structureless particles are quarks and leptons that are less than 10^{-18} m in size. The nuclei of atoms are constituted by protons and neutrons, combinedly called nucleons, that are bound together by the strong nuclear force. The proton and the neutron Have similar masses, the latter being heavier by less than 0.1 per cent only. A proton has a mass of 10^{-27} kg with a size of about 10^{-15} m. The three constants viz., m_p (the mass of a proton), h (Planck's constant) and c (speed of light) can be combined into a quantity to give the Compton wavelength of the proton:

$$h/m_p c \sim 10^{-15} \text{ m}$$

The atomic nucleus consisting of nucleons has a size of 10^{-14} m. On the other hand, an atom which is made of nucleons and electrons has a size of 10^{-10} m.

The macrostructures of the Universe are too large whereas its microstructures are too small. The seer of the Upaniṣads had a realization of the vastness and the smallness of these structures and thereby exclaimed, "Smaller than the smallest, larger than the largest" (*aṇoraṇīyān, mahatomahīyān*[2]).

It is not enough to say that the structures of the Universe are too large and too small. It is more thought-provoking to note that all structures and sub-structures have been intelligently designed to serve specific purposes. In other words, the anatomy and the histology of the Universe are strictly teleological. Had the Universe been chance-structured, gratuitously, randomly and chaotically shaped, it would have been far from being a cosmos.

In addition to the structures of the Universe, the functions of the Universe are well designed. At the outset, we may ponder over some universal constants, furnished in Table 10.1.

Table 10.1. *Some fundamental constants*

Name	Symbol	Numerical Value (SI units)
Planck's constant	h	6.63×10^{-34}
Speed of light	c	3.00×10^{8}
Newton's gravitational constant	G	6.67×10^{-11}
Cosmological constant	$\wedge$	$< 10^{-53}$
Boltzmann's constant	k	1.38×10^{-23}
Hubble constant	H	2×10^{-18}
Rest mass of proton	m_p	1.67×10^{-27}
Charge on proton	e	1.60×10^{-19}
Rest mass of electron	m_e	9.11×10^{-31}
Weak force constant	g_W	1.43×10^{-62}
Strong force constant	g_S	15
Cosmic photon/proton ratio	S	10^{9}
Permittivity of free space	ξ	8.85×10^{-12}

The fundamental constants of nature largely determine the essential features of most physical structures. However, there is no rigid constancy of a few of the constants listed in the table. As for example, the Hubble constant (H) and the cosmological cosntant ($\wedge$) vary over cosmological time scales. We know that H is not intended to be constant; H^{-1} is roughly the age of the Universe. The cosmological term $\wedge$ varies exceedingly weakly with time at the present epoch. However, its variations were quite spectacular during the early epochs of the Universe. The cosmic photon to proton ratio (S) is also not strictly constant. Photons are continually being created and absorbed. Nevertheless, variations in S over cosmological times are small.

The fine structure constant which is a dimensionless ratio (a pure number) is denoted by alpha (α). It is derived from some constants, as given below:

$$(\alpha) = e^2/4\pi\, \xi\, \hbar\, c = 1/137.036$$

Here c is the speed of photons, $\hbar$ is Planck's constant divided by 2π, ξ is the electric constant and e is the electric charge. The fine structure constant enters into all processes involving the interaction of matter and radiation.

The constants mentioned in the foregoing paragraphs and many derived mumerical relations, not mentioned here, are cosmic coincidences. Are these coincidences accidental? Are they predetermined and precisely planned? In this connection, the words of Paul Davies may be quoted here:

> .... the nature of the physical world depends delicately on seemingly fortuitous cooperation between distinct branches of physics. In particular, accidental numerical relations between quantities as unconnected as the fine structure constants for gravity and electromagnetism, or between the strengths of nuclear forces and the thermodynamic condition of the primeval universe, suggest that many of the familiar systems that populate the universe are the result of exceedingly improbable coincidences.[3]

Here we mention a famous numerological case that provides a glaring instance of cosmic coincidences. This is the well-known large number 10^{40}.

The gravitational fine structure constant, $Gm_n^2/\hbar\, c$, which is denoted by α_G, is 5.90 x 10^{-39}. Thus α_G^{-1} is roughly equal to 10^{40}.

The Hubble radius (r_H), which is the Hubble time (t_H= 5.00 x 10^{17})

multiplied by the velocity of light (c), or in other words $c\ H^{-1}$, is 1.5×10^{26}. This ct_H is the distance travelled by light in Hubble time and is the maximum size of the Universe. The number of protons (N) located inside the Hubble radius is roughly equal to 10^{80} which is the square of the ubiquitous number 10^{40}.

The number of particles contained in a typical star is given by the following simple formula :

$$N_* \sim \alpha_G^{-3/2} \sim 10^{60}$$

This number (10^{60}) is $(10^{40})^{3/2}$, which is again an astonishing coincidence.

This Hubble time (t_H=5.00 x 10^{17}) has already been mentioned. The proton Compton time (t_N) is 4.41 x 10^{-24}. The Hubble time divided by the proton Compton time (t_H/t_N) is roughly equal to 10^{40}.

Planck time (t_P), derived from the relation, $(G\hbar/c^5)^{1/2}$ is 5.39 x 10^{-44}. The Hubble time divided by the Planck time, (t_H/t_P) is roughly equal to 10^{60} which is the same as $(10^{40})^{3/2}$.

This curious number, i.e., 10^{40} also appears in the following relations:

$$\alpha_W \equiv g_W\, m_e^2\, c\hbar^3 \sim (10^{40})^{1/4}$$
$$S \sim (10^{40})^{1/4}$$
$$N_{*g} \sim N_g \sim (10^{40})^{1/4}$$

Here α_W is the weak fine structure constant (equivalent to $g_w m_e^2\ c/\hbar^3$=3.05x10^{-12}); g_w is the weak force constant (1.43 x 10^{-62}); m_e is the rest mass of electron (9.11 x 10^{-31}); c is the speed of light; $\hbar$ is Planck's constant divided by 2π; S is the cosmic photon to proton ratio; N_{*g} is the number of stars in a galaxy; and N_g is the number of galaxies in the Universe.

The messenger virtual particle (m_X) in the grand unified field is exceedingly massive ($\ngtr 10^{15}\ m_P$), where m_P is the mass of a proton. The proton lifetime (t_P) has been predicted from the GUTs as $\ngtr 10^{30}$ years. Most GUTs predict m_x in the range of 10^{15} to $10^{16}\ m_P$. The average lifetime of a proton is also predicted to be about 10^{31} years. This proton lifetime (t_p) divided by Planck's time (t_p) is roughly equal to 10^{80}, which is the square of the magic number 10^{40}. The value of m_X comes close to the Planck mass m_P, which is derived from $(\hbar c/G)^{1/2}$ and is equal to 2.18 x 10^{-8}. The Planck mass has been calculated entirely from the fundamental constants of gravity and quantum theory. If a theory of quantum gravity is established in the future, the Planck mass is predicted to be the mass of the superheavy mediating particle of the supergrand unified theory. The apparent coincidence of $m_X \sim m_P$ would perhaps explain the superunification of all the four fundamental forces of nature.

The Universe would have been a different one had any one of the universal constants been different from what it is. There could not be a Universe at all if something like gravity would have been missing. There could be no galaxies, no stars, no planets and no human body without gravity. Without a force to oppose the gravity everything in the Universe would have imploded to meet a crunch death before the Universe evolved. There could have been no atomic nuclei without the nuclear force. No chemical reactions would have been possible without the electromagnetic force. If the proton would not have been stable unlike the present one, no element formation could have taken place. The Big-Bang explosion which was apparently chaotic was precisely tuned to explode with the right amount of force. An explosive force of lower strength could have brought about the cosmic implosion before the evolution of the Universe. A higher rate of the initial expansion might have dispersed the matter and radiation to rarefied dilution without the formation of galaxies. The cosmic expansion could have taken place at different rates in different directions. The expansion could have involved anisotropy and inhomogeneity. Nothing of that sort has happened. On the contrary, the expansion was precisely tuned to produce a Universe which is uniformly expanding to a high degree at any single time and which is isotropic and homogeneous. On a large scale (greater than the size of a cluster of galaxies, that is $\gtrsim 10^{23}$m), the cosmic material is distributed remarkably uniformly. There was some mechanism to produce inhomogeneity on a small scale and so were galaxies formed.

A very few physical examples have been cited here to serve as a representative sample as evidences of the cosmic design. Anything we study in science, whether physical or biological, is a revelation of the overt or covert design of the Universe. A design has been translated into the structures of the Universe. The well-structured Universe functions in a purposeful way. The Vedāntic seer lays emphasis on this orderly design (*racanā*[4]) and the harmonious functioning. He infers a divine designer-cum-executor or ruler[5] from the cosmic design. Śaṅkara says that ruling or execution (*praśāsanam*) is not possible on the part of insentient nature (*praśāsanaṁ ca pārameśvaraṁ karma nācetanasya pradhānasya praśāsanaṁ sambhavati. na hyacetanānāṁ ghaṭādikāraṇānāṁ mṛdādīnāṁ ghaṭādiviṣayaṁ praśāsanamasti*) and that this is done only by God (*Parameśvara*).[6] There is, however, a difference in the God concept of many religions and that of the Advaita Vedānta. In many religions, God is the potter and the world is the pot which is made from nothing by the Almighty God. In this concept, there is no necessity of any clay to serve as the material cause. The Almighty God who is unborn and eternal functions in shaping the world and controlling it. The Advaita Vedānta does not subscribe to the idea that a functional Being can be without a beginning and an end. The nonfunctional, attributeless, formless, nondual Brahman is the only Being, without becoming, to be timeless and to have no beginning and end. There is nothing else, not the world and not even God, to be called the Absolute Reality (*pāramārthika satya*). The world is an empirical reality (*vyāvahārika satya*) only. It is created; the created world is sustained; finally the world is dissolved. *Māyā*, the power of Brahman, which is unmanifested (*avyakta*), becomes manifested (*vyakta*) and this process is the creation. The manifested world, after the great world period (*para*) is dissolved in *Māyā*. This process is the dissolution. The processes of creation, sustenance and dissolution are cyclic *ad infinitum*. Who is the doer of these cosmic activities? This is the central question in the Advaita Vedānta. Insentient nature cannot be the doer. It is also not eternal to execute and coordinate the job. *Māyā* is also insentient and cannot be the doer. The cosmic designer, executor and ruler is Consciousness and One only.[7] But it is self-contradictory to say that Brahman is functionless and attributeless and at the same time the doer and the ruler. Śaṅkara says that the same Brahman, on account of the differences in limiting adjuncts (*upādhibhedena*), is called differently. Whereas Brahman is unconditioned, the same Brahman is the individual ego (*jīva*) and the supreme, controlling Lord (*Īśvara*), depending upon the limiting adjunct (*tasmān nirupādhikasyātmano nirupākhyatvān nirviśeṣatvād ekatvācca neti netīti vyapadeśo bhavati; avidyākāmakarmaviśiṣṭakāryakaraṇopādhirātmā saṁsārī jīva ucyate; nityaniratiśayajñānaśaktyupādhirātmāntaryāmīśvara ucyate; sa eva nirupādhiḥ kevalaḥ śuddhaḥ svenasvabhāvenākṣaraṁ param ucyate*[8]). According to the Advaita Vedānta, *Īśvara* (God) is the executor and ruler of the world. Brahman with *Māyā* as the limiting adjunct (*upādhi*) is *Īśvara*. Alternatively, the reflection of Brahman in *Māyā* may be regarded as *Īśvara*. In no case, *Īśvara* is a Being which is second to Brahman. This *Īśvara* is otherwise known as Brahman with attributes. He has all attributes and powers to create, sustain and dissolve the Universe.[9] He functions as the efficient cause of the world, the material cause of which is *Māyā*. But, since *Māyā* is not an independent entity, it is said that the world is selfmade or God manifests Himself as the Universe (*ātmakṛteḥ pariṇāmāt*[10]). Before He created the Universe, He had desired[11] to have it. Some questions are asked here: Why did God desire to create the world? Did He have any want to be fulfilled? Did He have any insatiable propensity to create a world? Was He not fully satisfied? Was He fully saturated or was He unsaturated with patches of void and spots of vacancy? Was He full of unmixed bliss (*ānanda*) or had He admixture of agony and ecstasy? All these questions have been answered negatively. There was no need of a world for God (*na prayojanavattvāt*[12]). It was created just as sports or a play (*lokavattu līlā kaivalyam*[13]).

The unequivocal assertion of the Advaita Vedānta on the divine designer and ruler of the cosmos is not similarly reflected in science, which is empirical and objective. Science abhors speculation and hence is antimetaphysical. Only whatever is known through sense-perception and controlled experimentation is reported by the scientist. And hence the British philosopher A.J. Ayer[14] prescribes to speak of that much only that is verified or verifiable. Ludwig Wittgenstein,[15] the famous philosopher of the twentieth century, also leans heavily on the principle of verifiability in his *Tractatus*. Whatever has been said on the principle of verification or verifiability is *generally* true in the philosophy of science. It may, however, be appreciated that all that is empirically known may not be the whole truth, that all empirical knowledge may not be true at all with reference to the exact correspondence of the empirical knowledge to the object it refers to, and that the whole truth which lies beyond our empirical world may ever remain unrevealed to us. Many postulates of quantum physics and the twentieth-century cosmology are intrapolative or extrapolative and sometimes speculative. Inference is not forbidden in science-activity. If evidences, based on sense-perception, strongly indicate some conclusion which is not directly testable, it is prudent on the part of the seeker to accept the *ad hoc* inference unless and until some contrary evidences are forthcoming. If a harmony is established between the experiential evidences and the derived speculations to synthesize an integral view without a self-contradiction or an external contradiction, rational thought processes conducive to intellectually germane speculation should not be discouraged. The following opinion of Einstein on speculation may be of immense value for such a discussion:

> It has often been maintained that Galileo became the father of modern science by replacing the speculative, deductive method with the empirical, experimental method. I believe, however, that this interpretation would not stand close scrutiny. There is no empirical method without speculative concepts and systems; and there is no speculative thinking whose concepts do not reveal, on closer investigation, the empirical material from which they stem. To put into sharp contrast the empirical and the deductive attitude is misleading, and was entirely foreign to Galileo.[16]

Speculation should be permissible in both science and philosophy on some conditions. First, it should have a strong foundation of empirical evidences. Second, it should be rationally justifiable. Third, it should not be validly contradicted either internally or externally. Fourth, it should present a comprehensive view of the whole issue and provide a satisfactory, integral explanation of the phenomena in question in a perspective of totality. Such a conditional speculation is likely to be free from the contaminants of wishful thinking, mad imaginations and wild confusions. In the transitional domain of science, in the emerging twilight zone of our knowledge and in the area of phase transition between knowledge and ignorance, wisdom should serve as the rudder to sail towards our goal. The wisdom of the Vedāntic seers should not be whisked away by saying that what they said is purely speculative.

Figure 10.1 depicts some cases of wild speculation. The observed points do not show any specific trend to warrant an intrapolation or extrapolation. On the contrary, Fig. 10.2 provides a strong case for valid intrapolation and extrapolation. Even if these intrapolative and extrapolative activities may be termed "speculative" in philosophy, such actions are not unjustifiable. Intrapolation and extrapolation are permissible in science

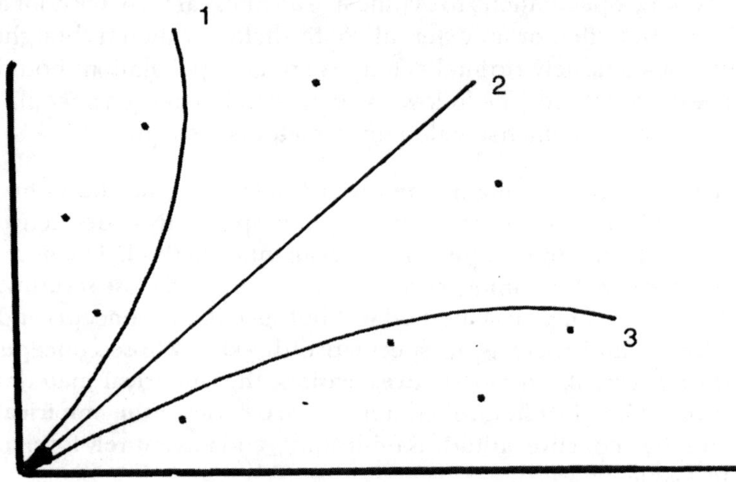

Fig. 10.1. Three wild speculations without any specific relation to the observations.

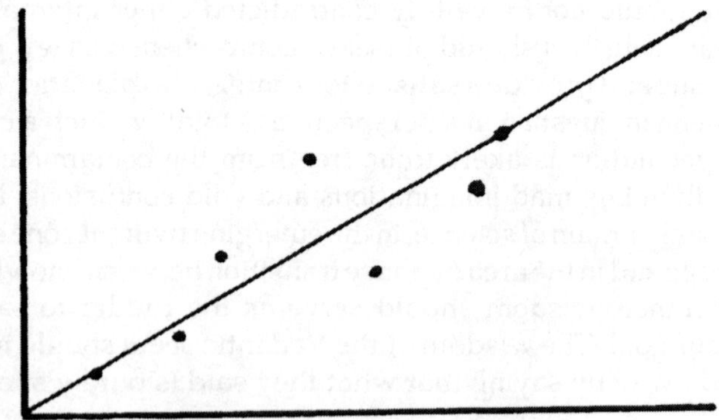

Fig. 10.2. Empirically observed points supporting intrapolation and extrapolation.

without the loss of rationality. Such supportive speculation should also be acceptable in philosophy. It is to be admitted that any extrapolative and/or intrapolative thought cannot be accepted as certainly true. After all, synthetic propositions, if true, are probably true whereas analytic propositions are certainly true.

Whether one is a Vedāntic seer or a modern physicist, there does not seem to be any difference between the inner realization of the former and that of the latter. The modern scientist says that the Universe is "fine-tuned". The totality of the Universe, or else the observable spatiotemporal region is fine-tuned to life's needs. Had there been even tiny changes in the basic properties of the Universe, life forms of any plausible kind would have been excluded.

The early twentieth-century physicists like Eddington[17] and Dirac[18] pondered over the dimensionless physical constants in relation to the large number (10^{40}) which might characterize the structure of the Universe. Dirac considered unlikely the accidental correspondence of the apparently unrelated, enormous numbers, and suggested some unknown causal connection. Rough approximations led Eddington and Dirac to believe that some very large numbers were intimately related. It was the assumption of Dirac that various elegant ratios of natural phenomena were products not of chance but of necessity. R.H. Dicke[19] is critical of Dirac's interpretation of nature's numerology and thinks that the latter has mistaken an observational necessity for a cosmic necessity that dictates the ratios at every epoch. Dicke further adds: The ratios hold necessarily true in any epoch when physicists can be there to observe them. The thinking of Dicke is in line with many twentieth-century philosophers who regard laws of nature as uniformities only.

The British physicist Brandon Carter[20] described a group of ideas associating the structure of the Universe, its constants and the laws of nature with the conditions that are necessary for the evolution and existence of life. Carter states: "What we can expect to observe must be restricted by the conditions necessary for our presence as observers." The principle of relating basic world features to our own existence as observers has its origins with great physicists such as Ludwig Eduard Boltzmann (1844-1906). But it was Carter who introduced the term "anthropic principle". Some other physicists who are proponents of the anthropic principle are Robert Dicke, Freeman Dyson,[21] Stephen Hawking,[22] Martin Rees[23,24] and John Wheeler.[25] Some of these scientists go so far as to claim that man's existence as an observer exerts a biological selection effect on the Universe, by which the otherwise mysterious numerical values of the fundamental physical constants may be explained.

In a chapter with the heading "The Anthropic Principle", Paul Davies writes:

> Normally 'the observer' is discounted in consideration of physical science. We are here, it is usually assumed, just 'for the ride'. Some scientists have challenged this traditional assumption, declaring that the structure of the physical world is inseparable from the inhabitants that observe it, in a very fundamental sense. They argue that there does indeed exist a guiding principle which works to fine-tune the cosmos to incredible accuracy. It is not a physical principle, however, but an anthropic principle.[26]

It has already been emphasized that our own existence as conscious organism is delicately dependent upon the structure of the Universe. Had any of the finely-tuned conditions failed, life would have been impossible and the Universe as we perceive would have also been impossible. In this connection Carter remarks· "The existence of any organism describable as an observer will only be possible for certain restricted combinations of the parameters." Carter's idea has been known as the "strong" anthropic principle which may be summarized by the sentence— "Any Universe with observers in it must be observer-permitting". The "weak" anthropic principle which is a version of Bayes' theorem of statistical sampling has been well stated by J.D. Barrow and F.J. Tipler.[27] Their argument was introduced in 1961 by Robert Dicke in a particular form to explain the existence of coincidences between the values of cosmological quantities of very large magnitude.

Some scientists have committed logical fallacy by putting the cart before the horse. John Barrow writes: "Our existence imposes a stringent selection effect upon the type of Universe we could expect to observe." He further states: "Many observations of the natural world, although remarkable *a priori*, are seen in this light as inevitable consequences of our own existence." While writing on the significance of the ratio of photons to protons in the Universe, D.V. Nanopoulos shares the sentiments of Barrow by saying "Our existence puts strong limits on the ratio". John

Wheeler says: "Here is man, so what must the Universe be?" Barrow, Nanopoulos and Wheeler are positive in their assertion that the structure of the Universe is *constrained* and is rather *selected* by our existence. Carter's notion is somewhat different when he says that we would not be here to observe the Universe as we are doing it had the frundamental parameters assumed appreciably different numerical values. It cannot be definitely ascertained which one of the two alternative views has been supported by Bryce DeWitt who expresses an analytical statement, "The world we live in is the world we live in". Any analytical statement like "A is A" is a redundant expression and so does DeWitt express his view perhaps in a deliberately ambiguous phase.

It would be correct to say that life would have been impossible had not the world parameters been finely-tuned. But it does not seem to be logical by asserting that the world we perceive would not have existed as such in our absence. The opinion of Paul Davies, as given below, bears a similarity to what has been said here:

> From the strictly physical point of view it seems mysterious, to say the least, that the existence of conscious beings can actually bring about the celebrated coincidences. Clearly any direct causal connection is impossible. Special physical conditions may produce man, but man can hardly be attributed the credit for establishing his own environmental requirements.[28]

A logical analysis cannot lend support to the strong anthropic principle. Hence there is no philosophical justification for this principle to gain validity. Quantum measurement theory can, however, provide a plausible physical justification for the strong anthropic principle. The process of measurement in quantum physics appears to demand the participation of a conscious observer at a fundamental level. Niels Bohr's Copenhagen interpretation of quantum mechanics categorically asserts that no phenomenon can be said to exist unless it is an "observed" phenomenon. In order that quantum wave functions are collapsed to bring phenomena into being, observers are unavoidably necessary. Whether the electron is a wave or a particle is decided by the measurement of the participator. The passage of a photon through slit A or B is decided by the observation of a conscious observer. The participation of the participator plays a central role in quantum physics in 'creating' reality. This concept of the quantum theory has stimulated John A. Wheeler[29] to suggest a participatory anthropic principle, which indicates that observers must exist in order to bring the Universe into being. It may be useful to add here the version of Eugene Wigner who argues that consciousness may be necessary to collapse wave functions.

Some scientists advance a theological interpretation of the anthropic principle. Being impressed by the apparent fine-tuning of the Universe, B.J. Carr[30] indicates that God might have chosen to create just the kind of cosmos in which living beings could evolve. Richard Swinburne[31] agrees with Carr and thinks that God very tidily explains this Universe's life-generating character.

Some scientists in favour of the anthropic principle are either atheistic or agnostic in approach. In contrast, some others like Carr and Swinburne infer the existence of God from the fine-tuning of the Universe. But, not everyone is happy with such theistic implication. Heinz R. Pagels[32] claims that the anthropic principle is not testable. Stephen Jay Gould[33] is of the opinion that there is no evidence to support any belief in the existence of God from the premise of the anthropic principle.

Anyone who observes the design of the Universe, its laws and harmonious functioning has to infer the existence of a designer and executor. If he doesn't, it may be considered that he refuses to accept the truth due to his strong dogmas, prejudices and biases. Science has this antitheistic dogma and any amount of convincing, inferential evidences in favour of a theistic interpretation is bound to be rejected. A man convinced against his will is of the same opinion still. Wherever the concept of God becomes inevitable to explain facts, there does the scientist make a vain attempt to explain away. Whether it is the anthropic principle to explain the fine-tuning of the Universe, or the hidden variable theory to explain the indeterminism in quantum mechanics, many scientists have attempted to explain away facts instead of providing rational explanations.

Most of the scientists who endorse the anthropic principle do also explain away facts and put the cart before the horse. They interpret the fine-tuning without any reference to God. They hold that the whole Universe is fine-tuned from the beginning because *Homo sapiens* is to be evolved and the ultimate end of the Universe is to serve man. The notion of the final cause and teleology is implied in such an idea. Such a concept of anthropocentrism springs from the Bible which declares that God created man and that He created everything else for the pleasure of man. The pre-Copernican idea of geocentrism has also been revived in the anthropic principle. Thus, those scientists who are even staunch proponents of atheism have also fallen a prey to the anthropocentric and geocentric influences of the Bible in their interpretation of the anthropic principle.

Humanism has various flavours. Secular humanism, from the time of F.M.A. Voltaire (1694-1778) and David Hume (1711-76), rejected the dogmatic claims of orthodox Christianity and became man-rather than God-centred. This was strongly reinforced by the advancement of science at the expense of revealed religion in the nineteenth century. Scientific humanism accepted the scientific method as the sole source of knowledge and was wedded to the doctrine that the natural and social sciences alone can provide a comprehensive, rational explanation of the Universe and human life. Whatever may be the flavour of humanism, a central theme common to all flavours is the proposition that man is the highest end. Human beings have a potential value in themselves and all other things in the Universe are subordinate to this value. This particular aspect of humanism which gives an apex position to man in the whole Universe is implied in the anthropic principle.

The Universe has been created fifteen to eighteen billion years ago. The Earth has existed during the last 4.5 billion years. Man has been here 32,000 years. It took a hundred million years to prepare a conducive environment on the Earth for him. Man is one of the products of evolution. He is one of the effects of a chain of causes. There is no rational basis to presuppose the fine-tuning directed towards the goal of the evolutionary emergence of man and his cozy living. Simply on the basis of statistical probability, we cannot rule out the evolution of intelligent beings in our galaxy and other galaxies. We also cannot assure that man is the best evolved biological specimen in the whole Universe. In consideration of all these facts and arguments, we conclude that the anthropic principle does not seem to be a rational principle to explain the fine-tuning of the Universe.

Science does not pollute and vulgarize itself by inferring the existence of God from premises of the design, the fine-tuning, the co-ordination and harmony and the intelligent functioning of the Universe. There is no need for it to enter into the domain of religion in order to accept the existence of God. It can still remain away from myths and superstitions and vague metaphysical speculations even though it accepts the divine principle just like any other scientific principle. Science must disentangle itself from its age-old theophobia to recognize the hidden constant rather than the hidden variable and the divine principle rather than the anthropic principle.

The testability of cosmology is a moot point in science. Adolf Grünbaum[34] has written on the pseudo-problem of creation in physical cosmology. It is an established principle in science that anything which is not experimentally verified is not acceptable. Many ideas of modern cosmology have not yet been experimentally verified. Some of these like the singularity, the cosmic egg, the explosion of the cosmic egg, the processes that took place especially in the Planck era are likely to be ever unverifiable. Some scientists point out the irrationality of the acceptance of an untestable concept in science.

The principle of empirical verification or verifiability exerted tremendous impact on philosophy. The emergence of positivism took place in the last quarter of the nineteenth century. This was mainly scientific positivism developed by some scientist-philosophers. G.R. Kirchhoff, in 1874, propounded his positivism by denying that science explains "why" things happen as they do. In his opinion, every "why" is a "how" for the scientist who discovers new connections between phenomena without passing beyond phenomena to "underlying reasons".

Ernst Mach (1838-1916), the Austrian physicist and philosopher, made up his ideas on positivism as early as 1872 and published them first in 1883. No statement was acceptable to him unless it was empirically verifiable. He defended a phenomenalistic position by maintaining that all empirical statements can and must be reduced to sensations. The philosophical theory of phenomenalism, as propounded by John Stuart Mill (1806-73), holds that material things are "permanent possibilities of sensation". This concept was further developed more elaborately in the twentieth century by analytic philosophers. They hold that statements about material things are equivalent in meaning to statements about actual and possible sense-data.

A school of logical positivism was developed in the 1920s by the Vienna Circle under the leadership of Moritz Schlick (1882-1936) and Rudolph Carnap. In the same Vienna, Ernst Mach taught physics and "inductive philosophy" during the period from 1895 to 1901. Schlick was appointed as a Professor of the philosophy of inductive science in 1922, succeeding great philosopher-scientists like Ludwig Boltzmann (1844-1906) and Earnst Mach. He gathered around him a group of philosophers, among whom were Rudolf Carnap, Otto Neurath, Friedrich Waismann. and mathematicians and physicists, including Kurt Gödel, Phillip Frank, Karl Menger and Hans Hahn. This group, known as the Vienna Circle, had an antimetaphysical attitude, a firm faith in radical empiricism and the methods of modern logic, which they considered to be the logic of science. It was deeply influenced by the ideas of Bertrand Russell and the earlier thought of Ludwig Wittgenstein, especially by the latter's *Tractatus Logico-Philosophicus,* first published in 1921. The British philosopher A.J. Ayer was a strong supporter of the Vienna Circle. It asserted the meaninglessness of all propositions that are neither verifiable by empirical observations nor demonstrable as tautological or analytic. According to logical positivism, it is not logical and scientific to make statements on those that are untestable.

The earlier thoughts of Ludwig Wittgenstein (1889-1951) have been presented in his book *Tractatus Logico-Philosophicus.* He holds that "all philosophy is a critique of language".[35] "Philosophy aims at the logical clarification of thoughts. Philosophy is not a body of doctrine but an activity. A philosophical work consists essentially of elucidations."[36] "The correct method in philosophy would really be the following: to say nothing except what can be said, i.e., propositions of natural science—i.e., something that has nothing to do with philosophy—and then, wherever someone else wanted to say something metaphysical, to demonstrate to him that he had failed to give a meaning to certain signs in his propositions."[37] The logical positivists have made use of the following famous statement of Wittgenstein: "What can be said at all can be said clearly; and whereof one cannot speak, thereof one must be silent." In this connection, Frank Ramsey (1903 - 30), who was a staunch follower of Wittgenstein, commented: "But what we can't say we can't say, and we can't whistle it either." The expressions "cannot speak" and "can't say", used here, do not mean the inability of the vocal organs and the mouth to utter statements. Any statement, unless it is tautological, must not be made, say Wittgenstein and Ramsey, if such a statement is not empirically verified or verifiable. Thus, according to the condition imposed by Wittgenstein's *Tractatus*, most of the cosmological and cosmogonical statements and those made on God, Brahman, *Māyā*, etc., are meaningless.

In spite of the empirical attitude presented in the Tractatus by Wittgenstein, he has written some mystical statements that do not conform to the standards of empiricism. He says: "What can be shown *cannot* be said."[38] "There are, indeed, things that cannot be put into words. They *make themselves manifest*. They are what is mystical."[39] "What we cannot speak about we must pass over in silence."[40] These mystical statements of Wittgenstein may be compared with that of Śaṅkara who says: "That (Brahman) can be indicated but cannot be spoken of (*tallkakṣyate, na tūcyate*[41]).

The later Wittgenstein changed his earlier view on philosophy given in the *Tractatus*. His *Philosophical Investigations*[42] contained ordinary language of philosophy. In this book he gave emphasis on the meaning in use. But, it seems, even his later philosophy of ordinary language, dealing with meaning in use, does not help the philosophy of science which may relate to the concepts pertaining to cosmology and cosmogony.

The Vienna Circle dissolved as a school at the end of the 1930s. Its ideas could not be upheld either in philosophy or in science. It is not maintained here that the verifiability principle is totally wrong. It is still the best acceptable test of science. But everything of the Universe cannot be known through science. It, being empirical, can tell that much which has been known through sense-perception. And sense-perception does not reveal the totality of the Universe. It is to be further recognized that we cannot be sure of the correctness of our knowledge gained through our senses. The limitations of empirical verification are to be realized and the areas of human knowledge where the verification tool is totally unusable are to be recognized. We can draw valid inferences from verifiable propositions although our inferences may not be verifiable. Analysis may not be the sole activity of philosophy. We can have both analysis and synthesis to integrate our knowledge and vision. Basing on our verifiable knowledge, we can frame hypothesis by intrapolation and extrapolation. As long as our integral theory explains the Universe without self-contradiction and external counter-evidences, we can incorporate our unverifiable inferences (based on verifiable data) in our total theory. This approach has not yet been appreciated by the twentieth-century philosophy. Long back in the seventh or eighth century A.D., Śaṅkara gave stress on the inferential evidence from the orderliness of the world for the recognition of the existence and functioning of an intelligent Being (*anumānaṁ pramāṇam upanyasyati; cetanāvantaṁ praśāsitāram asaṁsāriṇam antareṇa naitad uktam*[43]). He sees the proof of God in the laws of the Universe. The cosmic regularity expresses a hidden intelligence that acts as the guiding principle.[44]

The concept of philosophy has undergone a tremendous change in the twentieth century. In the eighteenth century and before, philosophy embraced all human knowledge including science. In the nineteenth and the twentieth centuries, science expanded in breadth and depth and became too technical and mathematical. The scientists became over-busy in investigating into the *what* of the Universe. Philosophers who were asking the why of the Universe became disinterested in the solution of synthetic problems. They could not comprehend the complexities of advanced science, did not ask the question "why", and tried to dissolve the problem. They left their territories one by one and finally decided to restrict philosophy to language analysis only. In this connection, Stephen W. Hawking remarks: "Philosophers reduced the scope of their inquiries so much that Wittgenstein, the most famous philosopher of this century, said: 'The sole remaining task for philosophy is the analysis of language.' What a comedown from the great tradition of philosophy from Aristotle to Kant."[45]

It is an admitted fact that language analysis is an important tool in all activities of philosophizing. Concept analysis goes together with language analysis in order that philosophy can throw more light to remove the darkness of our ignorance, clarify the fogginess and muddiness of our thought and render our vision clear. However, many linguistic philosophers err in dogmatizing language analysis as the *only* philosophical activity. They declare all other philosophy as metaphysical nonsense. But, how can they be correct? We can make synthetic propositions about a thing that we perceive through our senses. "The steel-chair in the room is broken." This is a proposition whose truth or falsity can be verified. Such a verification is empirical only. All empirical verifications provide us knowledge that is useful for our living. That is what the Vedānta declares as "truth in use" (*vyāvahārika satya*). How can we be sure of the reality of the empirical truth? There is no way to be sure of the absolute truth of our empirical knowledge. The world we perceive is certainly something. It is not nothing . We perceive it as X, Y or Z. But what it really is may not be what is perceived by us. There is no way to be sure of the exact correspondence of our perception of an object to the object itself.

The science of physiology of our sense-organs and our peripheral-cum-central nervous system has already thrown much light on the mechanism of our perceptions. A summary presentation of this mechanism has been given in chapter II of this book. But science is still now incapable of ascertaining the exact action of concept-forming in the cerebral centres. Whether the brain and the mind are identical or they are different entities is still a controversial issue. For many scientists, they are one and the same. Vedānta does not agree to this view that the brain and the mind are identical. Functioning of the newly formed zygote and the early embryo in the mother's womb is purpose- and intelligence-guided. It may be mentioned here that the nervous system appears in the embryo at a stage later than this and the brain develops at a still later stage. The brain cells are not materially different from the other body cells with regard to the development of consciousness. The elemental composition of the brain, its inorganic and organic composition are regarded by the Vedānta as insentient (*jaḍa*). Hence the explanation provided by the physiological sciences regarding the nature and the origination of consciousness and the agency of the cerebral centres in concept-formation is rejected by the Advaita Vedānta.

When we see, hear, smell, taste and touch and thereby get some knowledge about something, the concept about that something is made in one of the different cerebral centres in the brain. It may be worth mentioning here that the concepts are made *in* the cerebral centres and that these are not made *by* these centres. According to the Vedānta, the cerebral centres are themselves insentient and hence cannot be the source of sentience or consciousness. In the opinion of the Vedāntic seers, the concepts are made in the mind (*manas*) that uses the cerebral centres as instrument for the generation of the concepts. Again, the Vedāntic seers regard the mind as a *material* subtle entity that forms the principal part of the subtle body (*antaḥkaraṇa* or *liṅga śarīra*). By the reflection of the consciousness of the *jīva* (soul) on the insentient mind (*manas*), the latter is rendered conscious and subsequently uses the cerebral centres that generate the concepts. And again the *jīva* is not different from the Universal Consciousness or Brahman except the former being conditioned by the limiting adjunct (*upādhi*) of the body and the organs, the products of ignorance, desire and work, and the latter being unconditioned.[46] Thus the self (*jīvātmā*) or the soul is the passive agent or *kartā*[47] (doer) of the generation of concepts in the cerebral centres. This agency of the self is qualified by Śaṅkara who attributes it to the self as an inducer (*pravartaka*[48]) in a figurative sense only. According to him, the light[49] of the self, which is pure consciousness,[50] illumines the body and the organs through the *antaḥkaraṇa* (internal organ) and thus they perform their functions, being illumined by it.[51] Śaṅkara compares the nature of the light of Consciousness with glittering gold.[52] A number of scriptures endorse the view that the self (*jīva*) is a reflection of Brahman (*ābhāsa eva ca*[53]) on the gross and the subtle body. Devoid of the reflection of the light of Consciousness, the sense-organs and the brain are insentient like clods of clay or pieces of stones or logs.[54] Everything of the Universe is lighted by the reflection of Brahman alone.[55]

Advaita Vedānta, while accepting the empirical existence of the world, rejects its reality. It is an illusion of B appearing as non-B, its substratum being Brahman which ever remains as B without any modifications whatsoever. The discovery of quantum mechanics in the twentieth century endorses the Vedāntic view of the unreality of the world. In such a context, we have to revise the verification principle of the logical positivists. A proposition is accepted as true if and only if it is verified by our senses, or, at least, it is verifiable. This principle is immensely valuable in scientific investigations and ordinary life conditions where truth is restricted to empirical use. Such a truth is a relative one and its acceptance is *ad hoc* only. The principle of verification or verifiability is totally useless in areas lying beyond the circle of empiricism. To such areas beyond the scope of sense-perceptibility, language is inapplicable and hence language-analysis is useless.

Concept-analysis is applicable to fields of concept-generation.

That which is sense-imperceptible is unthinkable (*acintya*) in any concretized form. Hence concept-analysis is inapplicable to the area which is beyond that of sense-perceptibility.

Language-analysis uses a second-type of proposition which is analytic. Identity statements such as "A is A" are analytic. The statement "A is A" is certainly true. The statement "A is not-A" is certainly false. Sense-perception or empirical verification is not necessary to determine the truth or the falsity of such statements. But, an analytical statement is redundant. The subject and the predicate are identical or equivalent in meaning. In the statement "A triangle has three angles", the subject and the predicate carry the same meaning. All analytical statements do not reveal any new truth. The verification of the truth of such statements does not need sense-perception. For affairs pertaining to the world or the objects (*vastu*) of the world, language analysis of analytical propositions is less important, although we very often do use this technique to clarify our thoughts and remove confusion. This technique, however, is the only one for establishing the reality of Brahman.

Both quantum mechanics and Advaita Vedānta deny the reality of the world. Matter and energy (matter is nothing but energy packet) cannot be accepted as reality in quantum physics. Space, field or force also cannot be accepted as reality. All these have beginnings and ends. The evolutionary Universe as a whole, with a beginning and an end, and with uncertainties of everything, cannot be the reality. Whether we like it or not, the world has to be negated. Can we say that this apparent, empirical world came out of nothing, that it phenomenally became something and that finally it would be converted into nothing? Some quantum physicists accept this notion of nothing → something → nothing. But such a notion is outright rejected by Advaita Vedānta on the basis of logical analysis, that has already been discussed. This notion of nothing is the other name of nihilism. When the world is negated, something else is to be posited, unless we opt for nihilism (*śūnyavāda*).[56] Śaṅkara says that we cannot accept nihilism for reasons purely rooted in logic. He further contends that "I am" or "I exist" (*ahamasmi*) is the realization of everybody and "I am n't" or "I do not exist" (*nāhamasmi*) cannot be said by anyone. This "I" is the self (*ātmā*) which is not different from Brahman in Śaṅkara's analysis. The solipsistic idea that I alone exist and that nothing else exists is both empirically and logically unacceptable. We cannot reject everything else by accepting the individual ego only since such acceptance cannot integrally explain the totality of the cosmos and existence as a whole. Any "I" as the individual ego cannot be the sole, timeless existence and the source and Lord of all. On the basis of this logic, Advaita Vedānta[57] says that Brahman has to be accepted as *the* Reality. Whatever exists, and permanently, unchangeably exists, without any commitment or qualification to the nature of existence, is Brahman. And this Brahman, in no circumstances, can be verified. It is illogical to apply the verifiability perinciple to Brahman.

Here one may question: "Why is it illogical to apply the verification principle to Brahman?" A synthetic proposition is verified. Verification is always empirical. Through our sense-perceptions we are able to know if some synthetic statement is true or false. Through our eyes we see; through our ears we hear; through our olfactory organ we smell, through our taste-buds in the mouth we taste; and through our skin-receptors we feel the touching sensation. Our empirical verification may be performed directly through our sense-organs; it also may be mediated through some instrumentation and through our sense-organs. Brahman is not an object (*avastu*, *aviṣaya*),[58] and, being devoid of form, attributes and functions, it cannot be the source of sense-data to be transmitted by our sense-organs to our brain. Hence Brahman is sense-imperceptible[59] and also unthinkable (*acintya*[60]) in terms of any definite, concrete conceptual framework. No language can be used for It since It has nothing to be described. Śaṅkara[61] elaborates this point very convincingly in the following way: All words used in propositions are meant to convey sense by means of their link with notions of class (*jāti*), acts (*kriyā*), attributes (*guṇa*) and relations (*sambandha*). Brahman has no genus, no actions, no attributes and no relations. Such a nondual, non-objective, non-relational, formless, attributeless and functionless Being is indescribable. No language can be used for It. Thus the question of framing any synthetic, linguistic proposition on Brahman does not carry any meaning.

The use of logic is relevant only to a situation where language is applicable. No language can be used for Brahman and hence no logic can be applied to It. Thus the Vedānta says that Brahman is unarguable (*atarkya*[62]).

We accept Brahman through language analysis (*śabdapramāṇa*[63]) only. In this type of analysis, we make use of analytic or identity statements. It has already been said that nihilism is unacceptable. We cannot say that no world and nothing including "I" exist. At the same time we cannot precisely determine what exists in its own state. We can say only this much that "Whatever exists is existent (*yadasti tat satyam*)". This is one analytical statement, with its subject and predicate being equivalent. Such a statement is certainly true. Next, we want to give a name to whatever exists and that name is "Brahman" (*yat satyaṁ tad brahma*). And thus Advaita Vedānta says: Whatever exists is Brahman (*sanmātraṁ hi brahma*[64]).

Whatever exists (in the absolute sense, *pāramārthikena*[65]) is Consciousness (*caitanya, vijñāna, jñāna, bodha*). Advaita Vedānta does not find any difference between Existence (*satya*) and Consciousness (*bodha*). It is not a relation between something or somebody and some attribute possessed by the former. Brahman is devoid of discriminatory marks (*alinga*[66]); It has no attributes (*nirguṇa*); It is unattached (*asaṅga*[67]) and non-relational (*asambandhī*[68]). Hence *Advaita Vedānta* rejects the relation between Consciousness (*cetanā*) and possessor of Consciousness (*cetanāvān*) with regard to Brahman and establishes the identity of Existence and Consciousness.[69] When the *Taittirīya Upaniṣad* says: "Brahman is Existence, Consciousness and Indeterminate (*satyaṁ jñānamanantaṁ brahma*)", it does not intend to define Brahman (which is *anirukta*[70] or indefinable) or to use some attributes for It (which is *nirguṇa*[71] or attributeless). The first two words are used in a referential way to point to the same ontological Being. The third word (*ananta*) is often translated as infinity. In this context, however, it has a different meaning. Brahman is *amātram*[72] (dimensionless); It is *anākāśam*[73] (spaceless) and *akālam*[74] (timeless); It is without a preceding state (*apūrvam*[75]) and without a succeeding state (*anaparam*[76]); It is without an interior (*anantaram*[77]) and without an exterior (*abāhyam*[78]). It is *susūkṣmam*[79] (subtle). Such an ontological entity is bound to be *aprameya*[80] (immeasurable). It has no beginning and no end (*anādyanantam*[81]). It has to be indeterminate.

Thus the concept of existence with its relation to verification has two tiers in Advaita Vedānta. The worldly objects, which are products of *Māyā*, are to be verified through sense-perceptions in order that one may claim that they exist. It may be mentioned here that existence is not to be predicable of anything. "The rose is red" and "The rose exists" are not comparable propositions. We define a rose. When somebody says, "This flower is rose", we examine it according to our definition. If what we perceive conforms to our definition, we accept it as a rose; if it doesn't, we reject the claim. Whether something exists or not cannot be decided without our sense-perceptions. Brahman does not belong to the category of the worldly products. Hence the existence of Brahman cannot be decided by empirical verification through sense-perceptions. According to Śaṅkara,[82] the use of language such as "Brahman exists" or "Brahman does not exist" is nonsensical. Either of these claims cannot be decided by human intellection.

It is meaningless to raise the question of the verification of the existence or the non-existence of Brahman through sense-perception, if the epistemology of Advaita Vedānta is properly understood. Our sense-perceptions and concept-formations are dependent upon Brahman. Our sense-organs are insentient; our brain-centres are insentient; our mind (*manas, antaḥkaraṇa*) is also insentient. Without the reflection of Consciousness (Brahman) in our sense-organs, cerebral centres and mind, we cannot gain even a trace of consciousness. The *Kena Upaniṣad*[83] says that Brahman is the ear of the ear, the mind of the mind, the speech of the speech, the *prāṇa* (vitalizing principle or viton) of the *prāṇa* and the eye of the eye. It is impossible for our sense-organs to grasp Brahman. "There the eye goes not, speech goes not, nor the mind. How can one teach It when we do not know and understand It?"[84] "Our speech cannot express Brahman; our mind cannot think of It; our eyes cannot see It; our ears cannot hear It; our *prāṇa* cannot vitalize It. But, by It alone, our speech is expressed, mind thinks, eyes see, ears hear and *prāṇa* vitalizes."[85] The seer of the *Bṛhadāraṇyaka Upaniṣad* says that the real perceiver is Brahman that cannot be perceived by our sense-organs. "One cannot see the seer of seeing, cannot hear the hearer of hearing, cannot think of the thinker of thinking, and cannot understand the understander of understanding."[86] The *Paramātman* (Great Self) is not perceived through our sense-organs; but He is the perceiver of whatever we perceive. "He is unseen but is the seer, unheard but is the hearer, unknown but is the knower, unthought of but is the thinker. Except Him alone, there is no other seer, no other hearer, no other perceiver, no other thinker."[87] This very idea has been expressed in a slightly different form bythe same *Bṛhadāraṇyaka Upaniṣad.*[88] The *Kaṭhopaniṣad*[89] also confirms this idea that by Brahman alone one perceives form, taste, smell, sounds, touches and coital pleasure. The Supreme is Pure Consciousness (*śuddhacaitanyam*) and is the source of all knowledge, which is symbolically expressed by the Upaniṣadic seers[90] as light. The worldly light cannot illuminate the Supreme. Whatever light any worldly object possesses is due to the reflection of the light of Brahman.

Thus Brahman which is ever sense-imperceptible has to be admitted as *the* Reality due to reasons put forward earlier in this chapter. The verification principle of the Logical Positivists is totally inapplicable in this case. The noumenon is ever silent (*upaśānta*[91]). It is beyond the distinction of subject and object. What has been called Silence in this chapter is Brahman, the *Turīya* (fourth) state of existence. The *Māṇḍūkyopaniṣad* describes this state of absolute quietude in the following way: "*Turīya* is not that which cognizes the internal, not that which cognizes the external; not what cognizes both of them, not a mass of cognition. It is neither cognitive nor non-cognitive. It is unseen, empirically uncognizable and ungraspable. It has no distinctive marks. It is unthinkable and unnameable. It is the essence of the concept of one Self. It is the single Being with the becoming worlds completely dissolved (*prapañcopaśamam*). It is serene, benign, nondual."[92]

The nondual Brahman alone exists and there is no diversity whatsoever (*neha nānāsti kiñcana*[93]). This is the central question of *Advaita* philosophy that has been exhaustively discussed in various chapters of this book. Is monism correct? Is pluralism correct? Can we accept realism or idealism? Are all the things we perceive in our practical life real? These pertinent subjects have been discussed, and it has been concluded that reality is two-tiered—absolute (*pāramārthika*) and empirical (*vyāvahārika*). The noumenon is the absolute reality. It exists timelessly without modifications, without actions and without exhibiting properties. It exists non-relationally without depending on anything else. The world also exists; but it empirically exists with full dependence on Brahman for its existence. It has a beginning and an end, although its phenomenal existence is cyclic and repetitive. While it exists, it is ever in motion, ever changeable or modifiable and none of its conjugate variables can be determined simultaneously with exactitude. If the noumenon and the phenomena are considered in this context, both the nonduality and the diversity can be simultaneously accepted (*ata ekatvaṁ nānātvaṁ cobhayamapi satyameva*[94]).

It is contradictory to say that the Silence generates sounds. And so is the case with Brahman, being actionless and motionless, to be associated with the cosmic music. It does not play the *vīṇā*. It does not produce the vibrations of the string of the *vīṇā*. Brahman cannot be called the Great Musician. It is unconcerned with the *vīṇā* and the cosmic music.

Īśvara (God) is the Great Musician. His musical instrument or the *vīṇā* is *Māyā* with three strings—*sattva*, *rajas* and *tamas*. These strings vibrate (*kampana* or *spandana*[95]), and, as a result, innumerable musical tones are generated. The strings of the *vīṇā* vibrate and such vibrations produce air-waves that propagate. The vitalizing principle or *prāṇa* which is a product of *Māyā* propagates in the form of pulsating waves, with crests and troughs and with varying wavelengths.[96] As musical tones appear as a result of the vibrations of the string, so does appear the Universe of diversity consequent upon the pulsations of *prāṇa*. Gauḍapāda strongly advocates this vibration theory by saying that the world is produced as a result of the vibration of the *prāṇa*.[97]

We enjoy the musical tones. They appear real to us. We are passionately reluctant to accept any claim of the unreality of the enchanting melody, the amusing orchestra. But, when we scientifically analyze, we have to accept the unreality of the symphony. And so says Śaṅkara: "The world which issues out of Nescience or *Māyā* is not real."[98] The musical tones that we perceive and enjoy are not real although those are not nothing. Similarly the becoming entity (*bhūta*) is unreal (*mithyā*) although it, being experienced, is not nothing (*nābhāva upalabdheḥ*[99]). Advaita Vedānta uses the two words *satya* (real) and *mithyā* (unreal) in a highly technical sense, and unless their concepts are properly comprehended, one is likely to miss the very essence of this philosophy. The Being (*sattā*) which is the noumenon is different from the becomings that are the phenomena. The nondual Brahman or the noumenon is the *bhūmā* (Infinite) whereas the phenomenal world is *alpa* (finite). "Where one sees nothing else, hears nothing else, understands nothing else, that is the Infinite. But where one sees something else, hears something else, understands something else, that is the finite. The infinite is Brahman; the finite is the

Universe."[100] Śaṅkara says that the empirical dualities are absent in the experience of the Infinite.[101] When one gets the immediate experience (*aparokṣānubhūti*[102]) of Brahman, one does not perceive the manifold world in that state; the cosmic symphony, the sweet melody of the cosmic music, the miraculous world-orchestra disappear in that *Turīya* (fourth) state.

In the Śāṅkhya philosophy the three constituents (*guṇas*) of *prakṛti* (the primeval nature), viz., *sattva*, *rajas* and *tamas*, gain much importance in the genesis of the world. When these three *guṇas* are equipoised, *prakṛti* remains in a dormant or quiescent state.[103] The manifested world does not exist in this state of equilibrium. The equilibrium of the three *guṇas* must be disturbed in order that cosmogenesis would start. The Śāṅkhya, being a school of realism, does not subscribe to the vibration theory. The Advaita Vedānta has adopted the concept of the three *guṇas* belonging to *Māyā*,[104] and framed the vibration hypothesis to explain the genesis of the world. The three *guṇas* vibrate and consequently the vibrations of the *prāṇa* generate the motion of waves that propagate and present the multiplicity of the world. Gauḍapāda was very much influenced by the Vijñānavādins, idealistic philosophers of one of the Buddhistic schools. He refers to the vibration of the *citta*, *manas* or *vijñāna* (mind), brought about through the agency of *Māyā*.[105] He holds that the world is the empirical expression of such vibrations. A world that does not depend upon itself for its existence but depends upon the absolute Being (*paramārtha*) can be said to exist empirically (*asti kalpitasamvṛtyā*), but not absolutely (*paramārthena*).[106]

A comparative presentation of the vibrating Universe, as propounded in Advaita Vedānta, Kashmirī Śaiva Philosophy and modern science has been done in different chapters of this book. The superstring theory of physics has come to be known in the 1980s and afterwards. As is expected, science does not say anything about the agency that causes the superstring to vibrate. But that is not the case with the Advaita Vedānta and the Śaiva philosophy. It is *Īśvara* who plays the *vīṇā*. The string of the *vīṇā* cannot vibrate without *Īśvara* Who is the Musician of the cosmic orchestra. Everyone of us perceives the world which is nothing else other than the vibrations of some superstring. We listen to the music; we enjoy it. But we do not know the Musician who plays the music.[107]

The music is not an assemblage of some disordered sounds. It is well-orchestrated; it is finely tuned; it is precisely controlled and regulated. The fine-tuning of the Universe has already been discussed in this chapter with reference to cosmology and the structuring and functioning of the physical world. What has been told about the fine-tuning of the physical world also holds good, in principle, for the biological world. Both the macro- and the micro-structures of the living organisms from the stage of the virus, bacteria, amoeba, plants, animals to that of man have been designed accurately for specific purposes. The functioning of the organs, tissues, cells and sub-cellular constituents is finely regulated to meet specific needs. All the organs of an organism function with perfect coordination. What happens in the body is not regulated by the individual who even does not know the events that happen. Even if somebody knows something about the anatomy, the physiology and the biochemistry of the system, he himself does have no control over the structuring and functioning of his own body. The DNA and the RNA that are important materials inside the cell control the protein synthesis of the body. But these materials are made of some purine and pyrimidine bases, pentose sugars and phosphoric acid. The purine or pyrimidine bases are composed of common elements like carbon, hydrogen, oxygen and nitrogen that are all insentient. The human brain cells are made of such common elements that are devoid of consciousness. We cannot ascribe the intelligent structuring and functioning of the biological organism to insentient elements like carbon, hydrogen, nitrogen and oxygen. One may argue that the organic compounds that have evolved are capable of functioning in particular ways and that some special organs that have evolved are capable of functioning to meet special ends. According to this concept, what we call consciousness appears at a certain stage of evolutionary development. Many scientists have been satisfied with the Darwinian theory of evolution. The genes generate themselves in conformity with their own identity. They duplicate themselves. But they also mutate. The changed genes survive if they adapt to the environment. Otherwise they perish. It is a question of the struggle for existence and the survival of the fittest. The preservation or the extinction of a gene is solely dependent on its ability in adapting to the environment. The mutation of a gene is wholly random; it is purely a chance-phenomenon. This Darwinian theory, as has been presented here in a nutshell, is correct in its limited perspective. Evolution is an experimental finding. It has been practicable for the scientist to successfully manipulate the genes to serve specific purposes. Artificial mutation and evolution of new strains in the same species have been achieved by the scientist in the laboratory. Hence the process of evolution is not disputed here. Advaita Vedānta does hold the view that the world evolves.[108] But the Vedāntic evolution is not materialistic, mechanical and chance-oriented. The world evolves under the presiding (*adhyakṣīya*) influence of God.[109] The Darwinian evolution is only species evolution. It is merely a narrow portion of a wider phenomenon. Evolution begins with the Big-Bang explosion. Microparticles and particles evolve. Nuclear formation and element formation take place. Inorganic evolution is followed by organic evolution. Special genetic compounds such as DNA and RNA are subsequently formed. This leads to the appearance of viruses followed by the appearance of unicellular organisms. What Darwin describes is the subsequent stage of species evolution. The Vedāntic seers believe that *Īśvara* (God) enters into every created thing including microparticles, particles, elements, compounds, DNA, RNA, viruses, bacteria, protozoa, plants, animals and human beings and His presiding presence is enough to induce Nature to evolve according to plans, designs and objectives with perfect co-ordination.[110]

Science investigates into the 'what' and 'how' of phenomena. It does answer the *empirical* question of 'why'. But it remains silent on the *transcendental* 'why'. We may take a small sample of biological examples of the fine-tuning. The human species (*Homo sapiens*) has twenty-three pairs of chromosomes in each of its somatic cells. Sperms and ova are formed in the testes and ovary, respectively. Each sperm and each ovum contains only twenty-three chromosomes. This halving process is brought about through a reduction division, otherwise known as meiosis. In the somatic cells, however, cellular multiplication takes place with the duplication of each chromosome pair and without the meiotic process. The chromosome duplication in the somatic cell is known as mitosis. Now the question is; Why does meiosis take place inside the ovary and the testis in the processes of ovogenesis and spermatogenesis? Had there been no meiosis, reproduction of the species would be impossible. A zygote with 46 + 46 chromosomes would be something else other than the human one.

The chromosome number of the species (46 in *Homo sapiens*) must be maintained in order that the reproduction of the species would be perpetuated. Ordinarily one ovum is ovulated either from the right or the left ovary sometime during the mid-menstrual period of the woman. On the other hand, many millions of sperms are present in the semen of one ejaculation. All the sperms run a race in the female genital tract. They swim up through the vagina and the uterus and try to reach the ovum. The first sperm enters into the ovum. Immediately after this, a wall is formed around the freshly fertilized ovum. This wall is impenetrable to any other sperm. The red flag is hoisted by the referee. The race terminates. If there were a scope for a second or a third sperm to enter into the ovum, the chromosome number of the zygote would be 69 or 92, respectively. There cannot be a human species with more than 46 human chromosomes. What is required is accurately preplanned, intelligently designed and efficiently executed. The mother and the father are ignorant of these processes. Even if they know, they are as helpless as the ignorant person in consciously manipulating these processes. The idiotic ovum or sperm does not play this intelligent game. Who is the referee or the umpire of the game is not a valid question for the scientist. He satisfies himself by explaining away. The whole event automatically happens. Nature does it. Nature has provided ways and means to do it. Who or what is this Nature? A vague word is used in defence of materialism to fight out the entrance of God into the domain of science. This is nothing else other than a sheer dogma of science which claims to be rational. It should be realized that this dogma of science is not the answer to fight out the dogma of religion.

Embryogenesis is a wonderful phenomenon. The zygote multiplies. One cell becomes two, four, eight, sixteen and more. The multicellular embryo differentiates into ectoderm, mesoderm and endoderm. Different organs are formed. Specialized tissues and organs are differentiated. The brain, the spinal cord and the peripheral nerves are formed from the ectoderm. The skin is also formed from the ectoderm. But, in spite of the common source, the skin cannot play the role of the nerve-fibre or the nerve-cell, and the nerve-cells in the spinal cord cannot do the functions of the cerebral nuclei. The liver, the kidneys, the heart, the eyes, the ears, etc. are wonderful special organs, made of fine-tuned macro and micro-constituents. Their source material is the same zygote.

Why do they differentiate to become specialized tissues and organs? We do not know the answer. How do they differentiate to serve specific ends? We do not know the answer. The engineering of these organs is beyond the comprehension of the highly educated and intelligent specialist. In addition to the fine-tuned micro- and macro-anatomy, the functioning or the physiology of each system of the body is too wornderful for us.

The study of various sciences provides ample evidence of the existence of a Provident Who, in advance, provides what is to be needed in future. We may take a few common biological examples to illustrate this point. The foetus inside the mother's womb collects sufficient quantity of iron from the mother's blood and stores it in the foetal liver and spleen. This is done to manage the first four months of the post-natal life during which mother's milk is the sole food which is deficient in iron. Does the foetus do it consciously? Certainly not. Does the mother make the foetus do it? The answer is also 'no'. Both the mother and the foetus do not do it. Still provision is made in the foetal life for a useful purpose in the future.

Subsequent to the fertilization of the ovum and the formation of the zygote, the opening of the uterus (*os uteri*) is completely sealed by a mucus-plug. Micro-organisms through the *os uteri* from the vagina cannot enter the uterus in which the foetus develops. Immediately before the parturition, on the onset of labour pains, the mucus-seal is dissolved and consequently the *os* is opened. Who provides this mechanism for creating a non-infective environment in the uterus? Does the foetus or the mother do it? Nobody can answer this question affirmatively.

During the gestation period, the mother's pelvic cavity is to be enlarged to accommodate the enlarging foetus. The corpus luteum of the ovary secretes a hormone known as relaxin that causes the relaxation of the pelvic ligaments. It is to be admitted that this is a provision, although there may be differences of opinion on the question of a Provident.

The gravid uterus is to vigorously contract in order to expel the foetus at the time of the delivery. This is achieved by the action of the hormone oxytocin on the muscle fibres of the uterine wall. This hormone is secreted by the posterior pituitary gland on the onset of labour pains. The 'how' question of the uterine contraction is thus answered. But, why is it so fine-tuned? Who has provided such a mechanism? This question is forbidden in science.

The new-born baby needs mother's milk. And so is milk provided in the mother's mammary glands. In the pre-puberty conditions, there is no difference in the micro and the macro-structures of these glands between boys and girls. The girl's glands become different on the onset of puberty. Under the influence of the pituitary, the ovarian and the thyroid hormones, the ducts and the alveoli of the mammary glands develop and fat is deposited in the bosoms. The anterior pituitary hormone, prolactin, is secreted in the post-parturient stage for the initiation and the maintenance of milk secretion. How are these physiological and biochemical mechanisms fine-tuned? Who is the Provident of these mechanisms? Such questions are beyond the scope of science.

The baby is born and is exposed to a variety of infections. His own immune system may not be immediately ready to fight the bacterial and viral invaders through the formation of enough antibodies. To compensate this deficiency, a mechanism has already been provided. The baby has already collected some immune bodies from the mother's system. Secondly, the colostrum milk (milk secreted during the first few days after the child's birth) is rich in gamma-globulin that can antagonize any infection. How is this protective mechanism provided and who provides it? Such a question is transcendental to science.

Volumes can be written on the fine-tuning of the Provident's provision. Only a few examples are cited here to pinpoint the issue. But, it is a pity that this issue is not an issue in science.

We may forget the macrocosm and concentrate on our own body, the microcosm. We cannot explain this microscosm without a reference to God. Evidences for the existence and the functioning of God are ubiquitously available with us. But we consciously and artificially make vain attempts to explain away those evidences. We try to be rational by our recourse to irrationalism. We should give up any dogma of theophobia. If science unavoidably needs 'God' to explain the scientific phenomena, it should shun its theophobia and antitheistic dogma. Whether it is the developed human organism or the primitive micro-organism, each biological system is fine-tuned. We are to recognize it, appreciate it and rationalize it. The protheistic rationalization in science would effectively counteract the religious dogmas that stifle the progress of mankind and the quality of humanity. Moreover, the theistic rationalization would purge out the superstitions of religions, purify the religious theories and practices and rationalize religions that would be able to humanize man.

What the Vedānta says on the Silence and the Symphony is not exactly identical to the view of the non-dualistic Kashmiri Śaiva philosophy. In the latter system, the Absolute Consciousness or *Paramaśiva* is both *Prakāśa* (knowledge) and *Vimarśa* (activity). This *Vimarśa* is *Śakti*. Whatever changes are brought about in the Universe are done through the agency of *Vimarśa* or *Citi*. *Paramaśiva* vibrates, and as a result of this vibration (*spanda* or *spandana*), the manifestation, maintenance and dissolution of the Universe are possible.

Paramaśiva is bipolar. The male pole is *Śiva* and the female pole is *Śakti*. The *Śakti* or *Vimarśa* aspect of the same Being is dynamic. The vibration or pulsation (throbbing) of *Śakti* is *spandana*. Thus, *Parameśvara*, being motionless, is ever in a state of pulsation.

Whatever may be the details of the two systems (Advaita Vedānta and Advaita Śaivism) and the subtle differences between them, as described in Chapter III, they are essentially similar. Brahman is motionless and functionless. So also is the *Prakāśa* aspect of *Paramaśiva*. *Śakti* or the *Vimarśa* aspect of *Paramaśiva* is dynamic like the *Māyā* of Brahman. The three strings of *Śakti* vibrate in various combinations and permutations. As a result, the *prāṇa*, a product of *Śakti* or *Māyā* (a cosmic vitalizing principle) pulsates. These pulsations produce varieties of musical tones. These tones are the leptons, quarks, atoms, molecules, stars, planets, satellites, galaxies, galaxy-clusters and galaxy super-clusters. These musical tones are the four fundamental forces and their messenger particles. The fields and the field-particles are all the manifestations of the vibrations of the strings of *Māyā* or *Śakti* or *Māyāśakti* and the consequent pulsation of *prāṇa*. Here lies the ontological importance of *Māyā* for cosmogenesis. *Māyā* is not independent and is under the control of *Parameśvara* Who does not have propensity (*pravṛtti*) to create without the former. Thus *Māyā* is quite meaningful (*arthavatī*).[111]

Images are necessary for an easy grasping. We may form an

image of the goddess Sarasvatī with a *vīṇā* in hands. We may form an image of Lord Śiva as *Naṭarāja* with a drum (*ḍamaru*) in one of his hands and engaged in a vigorous *tāṇḍava* dance. All these are myths. When these myths are taken in a literal sense, we end in religious dogmas. When the myths are interpreted symbolically with emphasis on the spirit rather than the letter, we get the true meaning.

Fig.10.3: The vibrations of the superstring.

The Universe may be a uniworld or a multiworld. Both its vastness and smallness may be unfathomable. Its wonderful macro-and micro-structures may not be determinable with any degree of exactitude. Its physical laws and constants, its order and chaos, its reality and unreality may vigorously shake our thinking faculty. Its hidden variable, its anthropic principle, its teleology may arouse a deep sense of mystification in us. Our

Fig.10.4: Naṭarāja in tāṇḍava dance—the vibrations of the drum.

wonder and awe, our rapture and silence may induce a profound state of hypnotic trance in us. But, does it hurt us when we analyze the whole thing and come to the conclusion that the Universe we live in and so passionately love is immaterial and apparent? Is it believable for us to accept the fact that the total Universe is only the product of the vibrations of some string which we do not perceive and perhaps cannot ever perceive?

There is no reason for us to despair. The whole world-tree which is apparent is rooted in reality. The inverted pipal tree does hang from an unchanging, imperishable and timelessly existent reality. The world is rooted in *sat* (*sanmūla*[112]) rather than nihil. As a fact, the hidden variable is a misnomer. It, indeed, is the hidden constant (*dhruva*[113]).

Can we cognize the hidden constant? Can we directly have an experience (*aparokṣānubhūti*) of the hidden constant?. If and when we do that, we indeed become that hidden constant. It no longer becomes hidden to us. There are no "It" and "We", no "that" and "I", no "you" and "I", no subject and object. "That (nondual One) indeed is below and above. It is behind and in front. It is to the south and to the north. It is indeed all this (world) .... I, indeed, am below; I am above. I am behind; I am in front; I am to the south; I am to the north. I, indeed, am all this (world)."[114] I am Brahman (*ahaṁ brahmāsmi*[115]). That thou art (*tattvamasi*[116]). That is silent. That can be directly or immediately experienced (*patyagātman*,[117] *sākṣāt, aparokṣāt*[118]). But, even after It is realized or experienced, it cannot be expressed in language and it has to be passed on in silence (*tallakṣyate, na tūcyate*[119]).

The empirical (*vyāvahārika*) world of plurality is the phenomenal existence which is quite meaningful for us. Its substratum is Brahman on which it depends for its existence and functioning. When we do recognize the plurality for empirical purposes, reality is both one and many. And so do the Upaniṣadic seers say that it is He who makes the one seed many (*ekaṁ bījaṁ bahudhā yaḥ karoti*[120]). The ever quiescent Brahman is absolutely silent; It is motionless, actionless and changeless. But Its power (*māyāśakti*) vibrates and creates a musical melody, a wonderful symphony, a magical orchestra. This orchestra of multiple tones is the world of plurality. You and I, the Earth and the Moon, the Sun and the Milky Way are mere components of the grand symphony. The pulsating waves of *prāṇa* present the cosmic symphony which we experience as the Universe. The musical instrument is *Māyā* with its three vibrating strings. The noumenal Existence simply exists. It is the fundamental Consciousness, indefinable, indeterminable, immeasurable Existence. It does not vibrate. Neither does It play the music. The symphony with its apparent existence is masterminded by the Great Magician and Musician, otherwise known as *Īśvara* Who is the same Brahman, but with attributes, with *Māyā* as His limiting adjunct (*māyopahita*). His music composition is wonderful. His orchestra is enjoyable, although hardly intelligible.

NOTES

1. P.C.W. Davies, The *Accidental Universe*, Cambridge University Press, Cambridge, 1982, p. 1.
2. KTU, I.2.20.
3. P.C.W. Davies, The *Accidental Universe*, Cambridge University Press, Cambridge, 1982, p. 77.
4. BS, II.2.1.
5. BS, I.2.18; I.3.10; I.3.11; I.3.43; II.1.28; II.1.30; BSŚB, I.2.18; I.3.11; II.1.28; II.1.30; II.2.2; II.2.3; II.2.4; II.3.23; BU, III.7. 3-23; III.8.9; IV.3.10; IV.4.22; BUŚB, III.7.23; III.8.9; ŚU, III.1; III.2; III.4; VI.11; VI.12; KTU, II.2.12; II.3.2; II.3.3; TU, II.6.1; II.8.1; BG, IV.6; VIII.9; X.3; XIII.22; BGŚB, IV.6.
6. BSŚB, I.3.11; BUŚB, III.8.9.
7. BSŚB, II.2.9.
8. BUŚB, III.8.12.
9. BS, II.1.30.
10. BS, I.4.26.
11. BS, I.4.24.
12. BS, II.1.32.
13. BS, II.1.33.
14. A.J. Ayer, *The Foundations of Empirical Knowledge*, Macmillan, London,1969.
15. L. Wittgenstein, *Tractatus Logico-Philosophicus*, Routledge & Kegan Paul, London, 1961 (1st German edn., 1921; 1st English edn., 1922).
16. A. Einstein, and L. Infeld, *The Evolution of Physics*, Cambridge University Press, Cambridge, 1938, Foreward, p. XVII.
17. A.S. Eddington, *Theory of Protons and Electrons*, Cambridge University Press, Cambridge, 1936.
18. P.A.M. Dirac, *Proc. Roy. Soc.*, A, **165**, 199 (1938).
19. R.H. Dicke, Dirac's Cosmology and Mach's Principle, In : *Physical Cosmology and Philosophy*, ed. John Leslie, Macmillan Publishing Company, New York, 1990, pp. 121-24.
20. B. Carter, Large Number Coincidences and the Anthropic Principle in Cos-

mology, In : *Confrontation of Cosmological Theories with Observational Data*, ed., M.S. Longair, International Astronomical Union, 1974, pp. 291-98.

21. F. Dyson, The Argument from Design, In : *Disturbing the Universe*, Harper & Row, New York, 1979, pp. 245-53.
22. S. Hawking, *Stephen Hawking's Universe*, Avon's Books, New York, 1989, pp. 109-17.
23. W.H. McCrea, and M.J. Rees, eds., *The Constants of Nature*, London, 1983.
24. B.J. Carr, and M.J. Rees, The Anthropic Principle and the Structure of the Physical World, *Nature*, 278 : 12 April, 605-12, 1979.
25. J.A. Wheeler, Beyond the End of Time, In : *Physical Cosmology and Philosophy*, ed., John Leslie, Macmillan Publishing Company, New York, 1990, pp. 207-15.
26. P.C.W. Davies, *The Accidental Universe*, Cambridge University Press, Cambridge, 1982, pp. 110-11.
27. J.D. Barrow, and F.J. Tipler, *The Anthropic Cosmological Principle*, Oxford University Press, Oxford, 1986.
28. P.C.W. Davies, *The Accidental Universe*, Cambridge University Press, Cambridge, 1982, p. 122.
29. J.A. Wheeler, and W.H. Zurek, *Quantum Theory and Measurement*, Princeton, New Jersey, 1982.
30. B.J. Carr, On the Origin, Evolution and Purpose of the Physical Universe, In: *Physical Cosmology and Philosophy*, Macmillan Publishing Company, New York, 1990, pp. 134-53.
31. R. Swinburne, Argument from the Fine-Tuning of the Universe, *Idem.*, pp.154-73.
32. H.R. Pagels, A Cosy Cosmology, *Idem.*, pp. 174-80.
33. S.J. Gould, Mind and Supermind, *Idem.*, pp. 181-88.
34. A. Grunbaum, The Pseudo-Problem of Creation in Physical Cosmology, *Idem.*, pp. 92-112.
35. L. Wittgenstein, *Tractatus Logico-Philosophicus*, Routledge and Kegan Paul, London, 1961, 4.0031 (1st German edn., 1921; 1st English edn., 1922).
36. *Ibid.*, 4.112.
37. *Ibid.*, 6.53.
38. *Ibid.*, 4.1212.
39. *Ibid.*, 6.522.
40. *Ibid.*, 7.
41. TUŚB, II.6.1.
42. L. Wittgenstein, Philosophical Investigations, Basil Blackwell, Oxford, 1963 (1st published, 1953).
43. BUŚB, III.8.9.
44. TUŚB, II.8.1.
45. S.W. Hawking, *A Brief History of Time*, Bantam Books, New York, 1989, p. 185.
46. BS, I.1.16; I.1.17; I.2.20; II.1.21; BSŚB, I.1.16-17; I.2.20; I.3.19; II.1.21; II.3.17;

BUŚB, III.8.12; VC, 243-4.

47. BS, II.1.30; BSŚB, II.1.30; BU, IV.3.10; CU, III.14.4; VIII.7.1.
48. BS, II.2.2; BSŚB, II.2.2-4.
49. BSŚB, I.1.4; III.2.18; VC, 211.
50. BSŚB, I.1.4; I.3.19; III.2.16; III.2.18; BU, II.4.12; III.9.28; IV.5.13; BUŚB, IV.4.18; IV.4.20; TU. II.1.1; AU, III.3; MAU, 5; ŚU, VI.11; VI.13; KLU, 18; ŚS, I.1; ŚSŪV, I.1
51. BUŚB, IV.3.10.
52. BUŚB, IV.3.11.
53. BS, II.3.50; BSŚB, II.3.50; ABSS, Ch. IV, p.198; SPS, II.35; *Śakti and Śākta*, by Sir John Woodroffe, Ganesh & Company, Madras, 8th ed., 1975; p. 198 (1st published, 1918).
54. BUŚB, IV.4.18.
55. ŚU, VI.14; KTU, II.2.15; MUU, II.2.11; BG, XV.6.
56. BSŚB, II.3.7; II.3.9; III.2.22; TUŚB, II.6.1.
57. BSŚB, I.1.1.; II.1.14; TU, II.6.1; KTU, II.3.12-13.
58. BSŚB, I.1.2; I.1.4; BGŚB, XIII.12.
59. BSŚB, I.1.2; II.1.27; BGŚB, II.25; BU, IV.5.15; MUU, III.1.8.
60. MTU, V.1; VI.17; VI.19; VII.1; MAU, 7; MTNU, VI.17; GMK, IV.41; IV.52; BG, II.25; XII.3; BGŚB, II.25.
61. BGŚB, XIII.12.4.
62. KNUŚB, I.4; KTU, I.2.9; MTNU, VI.17.
63. BS, II.1.27; BSŚB, II.1.27.
64. BSŚB,II.3.9; BU,V.4.1; V.5.1; CU, VI.8. 3-7; VI.9.4; VI.10.3; VI.11.3; VI.12.3; VI.13.3; VI.14.3; VI.15.3; VI.16.3; VIII.3.4.; MTU, VI.3; VI.7-8; TU, II.1.1.
65. BSŚB, I.1.4; I.3.19; II.1.27; GMK, I.17.
66. ŚU, VI.9; KTU, II.3.8; MTU, VI.31;VI.35; VII.2.
67. BU, III.8.8; III.9.26; IV.2.4; IV.3.15-16, IV.4.22; IV.5.15; GMK, IV.96.
68. BSŚB, I.1.2; BGŚB, XIII.12.4; GMK, IV.16.
69. BSŚB, III.2.21.
70. TUŚB, II.6.1.
71. ŚU, VI.11; MTU, VI.10; VII.1; BG, XIII.14; XIII.31; BGŚB, II.20, XIII.12; XIII.31.
72. BU, III.8.8.
73. BU, III.8.8; IV.4.20.
74. MTU, VI.14.
75. BU, II.5.19; GMK, I.26.
76. Ibid.
77. BU, II.5.19; III.8.8; IV.5.13; GMK, I.26.
78. Ibid.
79. MUU, I.1.6; III.1.7; BG, XIII.15; BGSB, XIII.15; KTU, I.3.12, SU, IV.14; V.12; VI.3; MTU, II.5; KLU, 16.

80. BU, IV.4.20; BGŚB, II.18.2.
81. KTU, I.3.15.
82. BSŚB, I.1.2; BGŚB, XIII.12.
83. KNU, I.2.
84. KNU, I.3.
85. KNU, I.5-9.
86. BU, III.4.2.
87. BU, III.7.23.
88. BU, III.8.11.
89. KTU, II.1.3.
90. KTU, II.2.15; MUU, II.2.11; ŚU, VI.14.
91. BSŚB, III.2.17.
92. MAU, 7.
93. KTU, II.1.11; BU, IV.4.19.
94. BSŚB ,II.1.14.
95. BS, I.3.39.
96. KTU, II.3.2; KTUŚB, II.3.2.
97. GMK, I.6; II.20.
98. MUUŚB, II.1.3.
99. BS, II.2.28.
100. CU, VII.24.1.
101. CUŚB, VII.24.1.
102. BU, III.4.1-2; III.5.1.
103. SK,I.61.
104. ŚU, IV.5.
105. GMK, III.29; IV.47; IV.51; IV.72.
106. GMK, IV.73.
107. BU, IV.3.14.
108. BSŚB, II.3.6; MUUŚB, 1.1.8 (*krameṇa, na yugapat*); TU, II.1.1; II.2.1; II.3.1; II.4.1; II.5.1; III.2.1; III.3.1; III.4.1; III.5.1; III.6.1.
109. ṚV, X.129.7; BU, I.4.7; CU, VI.3.2; ŚU, VI.11; BG, IX.10.
110. TU, II.6.1; ŚU, II.17; BU, I.4.7; II.5.18; III.7.3-23; CU, VI.3.2; CUŚB, VI.3.2; BSŚB, II.3.13; III.2.21.
111. BS, I.4.3; BSŚB, I.4.3.
112. CU, VI.8.3-6; IUŚB, 4; BSŚB, II.3.9.
113. BU, IV.4.20; KTU, I.3.15; MTU, VI.38; VII.3; BG, XII.3.
114. CU, VII.25.1.
115. BU, I.4.10.
116. CU, VI.8.7; VI.9.4; VI.10.3; VI.11.3; VI.12.3; VI.13.3; VI.14.3; VI.15.3; VI.16.3.
117. BSŚB, Intr.; I.1.4.

118. BSŚB, Intr.; BGŚB, II.18; BU, III.4.1-2; III.5.1.

119. TUŚB, II.6.1.

120. KTU, II.2.12; ŚU, VI.12.

AUTHOR INDEX

SUBJECT INDEX

GREEK LETTERS

Page	Chapter	Greek Letter small	Greek Letter capital	Name of Greek Lettr	Number used
63	II	δ		delta	1
182	VI	υ		nu	2
183	VI	υ		nu	2
201	VI	π		pi	2
202	VI	π		pi	1
205-06	VI	π		pi	3
208	VI		T	upsilon	1
208	VI	ψ		psi	1
209	VI		Λ	lambda	2
			Σ	sigma	7
			Ξ	xi	5
			Ω	omega	3
			K	kappa	1
210	VI		Δ	delta	1
210, 211	VI	π		pi	3
217	VII	υ		nu	1
218	VII	υ		nu	1
		λ		lambda	6
222	VII	ψ		psi	3
226	VII		Δ	delta	5
		π		pi	1
233	VII	ψ		psi	1
233	VII	ψ		psi	2
239	VII	γ		gamma	4

page	Chapter	Greek Letter small	Greek Letter capital	Name of Greek Lettr	Number used
240	VII	γ		gamma	4
267	VIII	α		alpha	2
268	VIII		Δ	delta	2
		υ		nu	1
284	VIII	π		pi	1
307	IX	λ		lambda	1
310	IX	λ		lambda	2
310	IX	λ		lambda	1
312	IX		Σ	sigma	1
			Ω	omega	1
313	IX		Ω	omega	7
314	IX	α		alpha	1
		β		beta	1
		γ		gamma	1
315	IX	υ		nu	1
316	IX	γ		gamma	1
324	IX		Σ	sigma	1
329	IX	ρ		rho	1
333	IX	ρ		rho	2
			Δ	delta	3
334	IX		Δ	delta	6
337	IX		Λ	lambda	3
357	X		ξ	epsilon	1
358	X	α		alpha	2
			ξ	epsilon	2
		π		pi	1
358	X	α		alpha	2
359	X	α		alpha	2
		π		pi	1
660	Index	Λ		lambda	2

665	Index	ψ		psi	1
668	Index		Σ	sigma	2
671	Index	,	Τ	upsilon	1

SYMBOLS

(Mathematical and others)

Page	Chapter	Symbol	Number	Remarks
64	II	$\propto$	1	infinity
185	VI	$\surd$	1	square root
202	VI	$\hbar$	4	
221	VII	$\hbar$	2	
226	VII	$\hbar$	1	
226	VII	$\hbar$	1	
	VII	$\gtrsim$	1	greater than or equal to
249	VII		1	infinity
267	VIII		1	
285	VIII	$\sim$	1	aproximate equality
313	IX	$\leq$	1	Less than or equal to
334	IX	$\sim$	1	
337	IX	$\sim$	1	
342	IX	$\geq$	1	greater than about
356	X	$\odot$	2	used as $M_{\odot}$
357	X	$\sim$	1	
357	X	$<$	1	less than
358	X	$\hbar$	2	
359	X	$\hbar$	1	

	X	~	2	approximate equality
	X	*	1	asterisk
	X	ħ	3	
	X	*	2	asterisk
	X	~	4	approximate equality
	X	≥	2	greater than about
360	X	≥	1	greater than about